SALTGRASS PRAIRIE SAGA

A GERMAN AMERICAN FAMILY IN TEXAS

Jim Burnett

TEXAS A&M UNIVERSITY PRESS
COLLEGE STATION

Copyright © 2025 by Jim Burnett
All rights reserved
First edition

∞ This paper meets the requirements of ANSI/NISO Z39.48-1992 (Permanence of Paper).

Binding materials have been chosen for durability.

Library of Congress Cataloging-in-Publication Data

Names: Burnett, Jim, author.
Title: Saltgrass prairie saga : a German American family in Texas / Jim Burnett.
Other titles: Sam Rayburn series on rural life.
Description: First edition. | College Station : Texas A&M University Press, [2025] | Series: Sam Rayburn series on rural life | Includes bibliographical references and index.
Identifiers: LCCN 2024056584 | ISBN 9781648432736 (cloth) | ISBN 9781648432743 (ebook)
Subjects: LCSH: German American families—Texas—Biography. | German Americans—Texas—Social life and customs—19th century. | Women Immigrants—Texas—Social conditions—19th century. | Frontier and pioneer life—Texas. | Texas—History—Civil War, 1861–1865. | LCGFT: Biographies.
Classification: LCC F395.G3 S87 2025 | DDC 929.20973—dc23/eng/20250210
LC record available at https://lccn.loc.gov/2024056584

Cover images: Battle of Bayou Bourbeau (Louisiana, 1863) courtesy of Florida Center for Instructional Technology. Several key characters in this book fought in this Civil War battle; John and Johanette Stengler courtesy of Chambers County Museum at Wallisville; Texas cattle drive courtesy of Cushing Memorial Library and Archives, Texas A&M University.

CONTENTS

Series Editor's Foreword,
by M. Hunter Hayes vii

Preface ix

Acknowledgments xi

Introduction 1

1 • The Old Country 5

2 • To the Rhine and Beyond 11

3 • A City Built of Boards 17

4 • A County Called "Liberty" 25

5 • The Family Adds a Texan 31

6 • Plenty of Beeves 37

7 • Prairie Harvest 45

8 • Rivers, Roads, and Railroads 52

9 • Upheaval 60

10 • Mustered 66

11 • Sabine Pass 72

12 • The Unseen Enemy 78

13 • Doctor Stengler 84

14 • Disbanded 90

15 • Regrouping 94

Contents

16 • Under Fire 99

17 • Adapting 104

18 • Year's End 113

19 • "The Heavy Roll of Artillery" 123

20 • From Saddles to Steamers 137

21 • An Expensive Solution 143

22 • Eagle Grove 151

23 • "A Country Laid in Waste" 160

24 • Pickets, Pastures, and Postmen 166

25 • Raising the Flag in Texas 173

26 • A "Most Extraordinary Feat" 179

27 • Fire and Ice 188

28 • Soldiers Young and Old 200

29 • Uncertainty 213

30 • Finale 220

31 • Home Again 232

32 • Legacy 247

Appendix 1: List of Key Characters 255

Appendix 2: Abbreviations 257

Notes 259

Bibliography 285

Index 297

SERIES EDITOR'S FOREWORD

Schoolchildren across Texas learn early that the Lone Star State's history is one marked by struggle and triumph. From the formation of the Texas Republic to its entry into the Union as the twenty-eighth state, followed in turn by the Civil War and then booms and busts in a host of agricultural and industrial enterprises, Texas has curated a reputation of proud resilience. Texas has been home to generations of native Texans and others who migrated to the state in hopes of forging a better life. Less commonly known, perhaps, is that by the mid-nineteenth century, German immigrants accounted for the highest concentration of Europeans in the new state.

Their influence on Texas culture has created an enduring legacy, encompassing barbecue and breweries, classical and polka music, dance halls and biergartens, becoming inseparable from parts of Texas' unique character even as some aspects of German heritage, notably the Texas German dialect, have largely faded into history. On the western edge of the so-called German Belt, stretching from Galveston and the Coastal Plains to the Hill Country, the names of cities such as Boerne, New Braunfels, and Fredericksburg provide reminders of how German pioneers have shaped Texas. Here, in *Saltgrass Prairie Saga*, Jim Burnett personalizes this important component of Texas' history by introducing readers to one family of immigrants who uprooted their lives in what is now Germany's Rhineland-Palatinate state to sail to an unknown future in Texas.

Burnett writes with a descriptive empathy of the many tribulations and tragedies that Johanette and Johann (John) Stengler and their children—products of Johanette's three marriages—faced before they could leave their homeland to undertake a two-month voyage in late 1845 to Texas. The Stenglers' arrival coincided with Texas' annexation into statehood. Burnett's keen sense of detail imparts a poignant vividness to the family's own history, which mirrored in many respects that of their new home. "The Saltgrass Prairie," Burnett writes at the end of chapter six, "had exceeded the Stenglers' dreams for a brighter future in Texas, and their success was due in large part to their willingness to blend their German traditions and work ethic with the pioneer skills needed to survive and prosper on the frontier."

Burnett includes excerpts from the family members' own narratives through letters and journals, and even John Stengler's memoir, published originally in a local newspaper, all eliciting a sense of the family's tenacity to adapt and thrive despite the difficulties they faced. As their family expanded through marriage and the acquisition of farmland in Southeast Texas, the family tree grew new branches as its roots expanded into the fertile soil.

Burnett's title, *Saltgrass Prairie Saga*, is apt, and the image of an expansive saltgrass plain provides a rich metaphor for a tale of immigrants building a home in an unfamiliar land. Notable in part for its hardiness, saltgrass (*Distichlis spicata*) has roots that bind the soil, forming sod, nourishing and sustaining a diverse ecosystem. It thrives in environments that could otherwise seem hostile. Burnett marries this image with one that suggests familial stability and legacy, deftly conveying a sense of the family he brings to life in these pages. For more than twenty-five years, the Sam Rayburn Series on Rural Life has published books that combine scholarly inquiry with well-honed narratives that present an array of perspectives on rural Texas history and life, and it is with both admiration and pleasure that I welcome Jim Burnett and his *Saltgrass Prairie Saga* to the series.

—**M. Hunter Hayes**
General Editor
Sam Rayburn Series on Rural Life

PREFACE

In today's world, handwritten letters are becoming increasingly rare, so it's easy for us to forget how important pen, ink, and paper were in the daily lives of previous generations. Correspondence from centuries past is a potential treasure trove for historians, and while old letters may convey factual information, they can also offer valuable insights into the writer's thoughts, emotions, and views of the world around them. All those elements are found in a sizeable collection of letters written by members of a family who came to Texas from a small German village in 1845. Here's a brief explanation of how the information found in those documents intersected with my own experience to inspire this book.

In the early 1980s my wife, Velma, received a phone call from a distant relative named Berta Mary Wilborn Dawson (1915–1986). Velma had minored in German at Rice University, and she had long been curious about a vague family story concerning an unidentified ancestor who had come to Texas from Germany. Berta Mary had learned about Velma's interest and invited us for a visit.

Berta Mary lived for most of her adult life on a successful Southeast Texas ranch first settled in 1876 by her late husband's grandparents Charles and Mina Wilborn, whose names appeared frequently in 175 family letters written between 1855 and 1877. The letters offered no details about this couple's lives before their marriage in Texas in 1850, but they included one intriguing hint: many of them had originally been written in German.

In the 1960s, the letters in German were translated into English by Oscar Haas (1885–1981) and his wife, Clara, who were researchers and prolific writers focusing on nineteenth-century German immigration to Texas. Berta Mary's collection included copies of their translations and photocopies of an additional sixty-nine family letters handwritten in English. At the end of our visit, Berta Mary graciously gave us a complete set of those documents. Some years later, when the idea for this book began to take shape, the Haas family graciously provided permission for me to use their parents' translations in the development of this project.

As I gradually read through all this material, it became apparent that it had considerable historical value for its glimpses into rural life in nineteenth-century Texas from a rarely told perspective: a German American family who had settled somewhere in Texas *other* than the Hill Country.

My education and work experiences include historical research, supervision of a living history farm that depicts pioneer life in the nineteenth century, and natural resource management in an area in Southeast Texas that shares many similarities with the setting for this book. As a result, these letters sparked my interest and led to a decades long search for additional details about these individuals and the times and places in which they lived. That research, along with the contents of the letters themselves, provided the material for this book. I have left the word choices, spelling, punctuation, and capitalization in the letters largely intact to reflect the usages of the time, with some minor editing when necessary for the sake of readability.

I decided early in this project that I would not simply compile an annotated collection of the letters, useful as that might be for historians. I have instead combined excerpts from the letters with pertinent details from other period sources, weaving them into a narrative that puts this information into the broader context of the surrounding people, places, and events. All of the content on the following pages is based on extensive research and is thoroughly documented in the bibliography and endnotes. I hope you will find the result to be both engaging and informative.

ACKNOWLEDGMENTS

The author gratefully acknowledges the assistance provided by the following individuals and organizations during his research for this book and for their permission to use material quoted or cited in the text: The Anahuac (Texas) *Progress,* for permission to reprint an autobiography of John Stengler, originally published in the *Progress* on February 10, 1910; the *Baylor Business Review,* for permission to quote a short passage from the article "Sharing the Wealth," which appeared in the Spring 2008 issue of that publication; Ms. Vicki Betts, retired librarian at the University of Texas at Tyler, for her transcriptions from Civil War-era newspapers available online at UT Tyler Scholar Works; Mr. Bill Block, for permission to quote referenced material from the work of his father, the late W. H. Block; Mr. David Bright, editor of the website Confederate Railroads (www.csa-railroads.com), for permission to use cited material on early Texas railroads; The Dolph Briscoe Center for American History, the University of Texas at Austin; the Chambers County Clerk's Office, Anahuac, Texas; the Chambers County Museum at Wallisville, Wallisville, Texas, for permission to reproduce photographs of Stengler and Hankamer family members and for permission to quote material from their Stengler, Wilborn, and Hankamer family files, including the diary of John W. Hankamer; the Cushing Memorial Library and Archives, Texas A&M University; Ms. Cassie Dickson, for permission to publish the photograph of a cane reed from a historical loom; the Galveston and Texas History Center, Rosenberg Library, Galveston, Texas; Mr. Mike Haas, for permission to quote from translations and transcriptions of Stengler, Hankamer, and Wilborn family letters prepared by his grandparents, the late Oscar and Clara Haas; Mr. Ray Hankamer Jr., of Houston, for access to his collection of Hankamer family documents and for permission to publish the photograph of Mr. Charles Hankamer; the Houston History Research Center, Houston Public Library; Ms. Susan Morgan Leveille, for her explanations about eighteenth-century weaving; the Liberty County Clerk's Office, Liberty, Texas; The Portal to Texas History website at the University of North Texas Libraries, for access to nineteenth-century newspapers; the Sam Houston Regional Library and Research Center, Texas State Library and Archives Commission, for use of cited materials from the Julia Duncan Welder Collection; San Jacinto Museum and Battlefield Association, La Porte, Texas, for permission to quote from a 1940 transcription of the eighteenth-century diary of William B. Duncan (the transcribed copy is now archived at the Sam Houston Regional Library and Research Center); the Sophienburg Museum and Archives, New Braunfels, Texas, for permission to quote from cited material in their collection; Texas State Library and Archives, Austin, Texas; the Louis Round Wilson Special Collections Library, University of North Carolina at Chapel Hill. Special thanks are due to the staff at Texas A&M University Press, including Thom Lemmons, Abagail Chartier, and Matt Joyce, for their expert help in the production of this book; to M. Hunter Hayes, general editor of the Sam Rayburn Series on Rural Life; and to Robyn Dadig, Marbert Moore, and Sue Richardson, who made valuable suggestions early in the project about the organization of the material. Finally, this project would not have been possible without the unfailing encouragement and support of my research partner and life companion, Velma Burnett.

SALTGRASS PRAIRIE SAGA

INTRODUCTION

Sometimes a good place to look for an intriguing new story is in the dusty corners of an oft-told old one.

The colorful history of Texas is filled with an abundance of memorable characters and events, but some important details have been largely overlooked or are now fading from memory. Among them are true tales involving classic Texas themes: cowboys and frontier ranches, rustic prairie homesteads and tidy German farms, and the Civil War in Texas.

Few topics say "Texas" more than cowboys and ranching, but we usually associate those subjects with the sweeping plains in the central and western sections of the state. Some readers may be surprised to learn that the state's fabled cattle business had many of its earliest roots east of Houston, not west of Waco, and by the 1830s large ranches were operating on an immense expanse of coastal prairie only a few miles from Galveston Bay. The herds of "beeves" in the earliest Texas cattle drives went east to places like New Orleans, decades before longhorns plodded up more famous routes such as the Chisholm Trail to Wichita and Abilene, Kansas.

"Howdy!" has long been a common greeting in Texas, but why did some of those early cattlemen in Southeast Texas have a distinctly German accent? By the mid-1840s, Texas was still a wild and largely unsettled land, rich in potential but short of people. The just-formed state's need for more citizens coincided with a wave of European immigrants who were abandoning deep family roots and crossing the Atlantic in search of a brighter future. Many of them reached America through large cities like New York or Boston, but for others, their Promised Land was a strange and distant place called "Texas."

Thousands of these new arrivals came from German-speaking states, and their intended destination, via the young but thriving seaport of Galveston, was the Hill Country of Central Texas. They were enticed by offers of free land in fledgling colonies of fellow Germans, and the state is justly proud of a European heritage that is still evident in towns like New Braunfels and Fredericksburg. Largely forgotten today, however, is another side of the story: many of those eager pioneers failed to reach their destinations, victims of a series of calamities in 1846. In the wake of those disasters, some of these new Texans decided to end their journeys in places like Houston and Galveston.

Among these newcomers were John and Johanette Stengler, who left the picturesque village of Dietz in what is now central Germany in October 1845. Their destination was the independent Republic of Texas, and they made the trip with their seven children, ranging in age from seventeen months to fourteen years. Even as they were surviving a harrowing two-month crossing of the Atlantic, crowded onto the sailing ship *Harriet* with some 176 other German emigrants, momentous changes were underway in their future home.

The Stenglers finally stepped ashore in Galveston on New Year's Eve 1845 and soon learned they were to be both Texans *and* Americans. The US Congress and president had approved the annexation of Texas as the newest member of the United States of America on December 29, 1845, and that news reached the state in early January 1846.

This family came to Texas in search of promising opportunities and their own land, but after hearing about concerns with the new German settlements in Central Texas they decided to consider other options. In mid-1846 they headed to Southeast Texas, where a vast coastal grassland, sometimes called the Saltgrass Prairie, is broken by dark forests lining the banks of murky bayous. This was, by any definition, the frontier, and John Stengler later described their new destination as "full of all manner of game and wild beasts, where people lived far apart."

It was, literally, a world away from their previous life in a centuries-old German village, and these new arrivals faced daunting challenges. There were few other Germans in the area, and the family spoke almost no English, possessed limited finances, and had little or no experience with agriculture and rural living. They were, however, determined, adaptable, and educated, and over the next fifteen years, they firmly established themselves as both livestock raisers and farmers. I have used the word "homestead" at times on the following pages to describe the results of their efforts, because, in a time and place when much of what they needed was homegrown and handmade, these new Texans quickly blended American pioneer skills with their European traditions to become largely self-sufficient, moving well beyond a typical frontier "beef and beans" lifestyle to produce a surprisingly varied cornucopia harvested from their own fields and gardens.

The Stenglers' arrival occurred amid perhaps the most significant quarter-century in the history of the Lone Star State. During the span of twenty-five years ending in 1861, Texas underwent a series of tumultuous changes, from control by a distant and sometimes difficult government in Mexico, to independence as a republic (1836), to statehood in the United States (1845), and finally, to secession from the United States to become part of the Confederate States of America (1861).

By 1861 two of the family's six sons and their only daughter were married and had children and homesteads of their own. Life was far from easy, but the future was promising until, in their sixteenth year in their new homeland, they found themselves on the brink of a most unwelcome crisis: the Civil War. Like every other family in both the North and South, they faced a critical decision with immense consequences. Would their loyalty be to the Union . . . or the Confederacy?

The extended Stengler family did not own any slaves, and there is no surviving written confirmation about their position on secession, but voters in their area overwhelmingly supported the idea. Even so, many residents of Southeast Texas were in no rush to take up arms and head for distant battlefields. It's clear from letters and diaries that their primary concern was the defense of their families and homes from a feared military invasion.

A year into the conflict, and faced with an impending military draft, a little band of four German American brothers enlisted together in a Confederate cavalry unit being raised in their home county. Before the war ended, the three remaining male members of the extended Stengler family (father, son-in-law, and teenage son) would also see military service.

Although several of these men experienced months of hardship and occasional fighting outside the state, most of their time was spent within a hundred miles of home. Their assignment was to protect key points along the Texas coast from attacks by larger and better-armed Union forces. They became, ready or not, "saltgrass soldiers."

Some of these men traveled and occasionally fought on horseback, on foot, and even briefly on a cottonclad gunboat. They experienced days of brutal winter travel across frozen swamps and icy rivers, and at times their most feared foes were not Union troops but yellow fever, malaria, and other deadly diseases.

Southeast Texas was the target of several attempted Union invasions, but compared to major battles like Gettysburg and Antietam, these clashes were brief and involved relatively small numbers of troops. As a result, they are now largely relegated to brief footnotes in the state's history, and therein lie some intriguing but seldom-told stories. How, for example, did fewer than fifty Texans quickly defeat a federal armada of more than two dozen ships, five artillery batteries, and several thousand troops at Sabine Pass in 1863?

The answer is found in a series of truly improbable events, and although this brief battle is now all but forgotten, its impact was significant. The Union's failure to gain a firm foothold along the Texas coast spared the state from the widespread devastation experienced by many other locations in the country where farms and towns became battlefields.

The war years were also a challenging time of survival for wives, children, and older parents left to tend family farms in a sparsely populated countryside. The young men rode off to war, but livestock still needed attention, and crops required planting, tilling, and harvesting in a time when that work was all done by hand, horse, mule, or oxen. Many staples of daily living were in short supply, but these determined families persevered with a combination of hard work, ingenuity, and time-tested frontier skills.

All of these key elements from nineteenth-century Texas—settlement and life on the frontier, the early years of cattle ranching, the valuable contributions of German immigrants to the new state's development, and the impact of the Civil War on the state and individual Texans—converged in the lives of this extended family.

Copies or translations of 175 family letters written before, during, and after the Civil War have survived. Many of them were originally written in German, and some of those communications have not been previously published. Together with diaries and numerous other firsthand accounts, the letters offer detailed personal insights into the thoughts and daily lives of these early Texans. Through their eyes, we'll take a fresh look at some little-known aspects of the state's history, from the frontier years to the twentieth century.

Here, often in their own words, is their story.

— 1 —

THE OLD COUNTRY

I humbly request that the Certificate for Admission for Emigration, together with all other required papers for the voyage be furnished as soon as possibly convenient.

—JOHANN STENGLER, October 3, 1845

If she'd had even a moment to spare, Johanette Stengler might have paused for one final look at the valley that had been her only home for all of her forty years—but she had trunks to pack and a ship to catch. There's no question the view was a lovely one in the fall of 1845; a guidebook to Europe for wealthy travelers described it as "picturesque." The Lahn River wound a lazy path through verdant hills and under a weathered stone bridge that had already served the villagers of Dietz for at least six hundred years.[1] An imposing castle, towering over the town from its perch on a rocky promontory, was even older.[2]

The scene may have been idyllic, but for the Stengler family, the future here held little promise. From the largest cities to the smallest hamlets, times were hard for many Germans in 1845, but Johanette Stengler was a survivor—and she had a dream. Her family of nine was soon headed to a far-away place called Texas, and the possibilities there were altogether different![3]

For more than a decade, books, newspaper articles, and letters from German emigrants to Texas had touted the virtues of that fledgling nation: free land, fertile soil, lovely landscapes, and a low cost of living. Some writers compared the area's favorable climate to Mediterranean locales, and wild game and fish were said to be abundant. The Republic of Texas had won its independence from Mexico in 1836, and it welcomed new settlers from Europe. What more could an ambitious young family want?[4]

FIGURE 1. The village of Dietz in 1655. This sketch shows the walled town and its castle. From "Extract from the *Topographia Hassiae* by Matthäus Merian 1655," http://commons.wikimedia.org/wiki/File:Diez_De_Merian_Hassiae.jpg.

Johanette's household was one of those families, thanks to her marriage four years earlier to Johann Stengler. With those vows, her new husband suddenly gained not only a wife but responsibilities far beyond those of most men in their early twenties. His bride had been previously widowed, not once, but twice, and she had buried one child and been left with five others under the age of ten.[5]

The new Mrs. Stengler must have been a compelling catch, a determined woman, or both. At the time of their marriage, Johann Stengler was almost twenty-three; she had just turned thirty-six. Given her experiences thus far, perhaps she felt it would be wise to marry a younger man, but Johann certainly didn't marry for her money.

By all accounts, Johanette's finances were modest at the time of her third marriage in 1841. Her father and grandfather had both been tailors in Dietz, and she had been orphaned at the age of fourteen. Her first husband, Gottfried Krantz, had been an "Inspector of Springs," likely associated with the natural mineral water that was sold from the nearby village of Fachingen. That marriage left her with one surviving child, a daughter.[6]

Her second husband, Johannes Hankamer, had been a waggoner (a teamster) in Dietz. Their six years of marriage left her with four young sons and a heavily mortgaged house in the village. It provided a welcome roof over their heads, but it would likely bring little cash if sold. The first four years of her third marriage added two more sons to the Stengler family, and their house was becoming crowded. Johann's position as an official inspector of chimneys and fireplaces was an important one, but it held meager long-term prospects for a father with six young sons and a daughter entering her teens. Now, if a man could only acquire enough land of his own, a family like his had a chance to prosper![7]

The opportunity for that land seemed tantalizingly within reach in 1845, as promising news about Texas continued to spread across the central German states. The spark for this excitement was an organization called the Verein zum Schutze deutscher Einwanderer in Texas (The Society for the Protection of German Immigrants in Texas). It was often referred to as the Adelsverein, or simply the Verein; on the following pages, the terms Verein and society will be used interchangeably.[8]

This venture, organized by a group of German noblemen, had secured a grant of nearly four million acres from the fledgling Republic of Texas, which was rich in land but short on both funds and settlers. One solution for this new country was to give away—or sell at bargain prices—over 41 million acres of land to raise cash, pay its debts, and promote settlement.[9]

Groups like the Verein offered a supply of new residents for Texas, although historians differ on whether the underlying motives of the society were financial, philanthropical, philosophical, political, or some combination thereof. Whatever their purpose, the organizers were not hesitant about promoting the virtues of their new colony. One publication offered this promising assessment of Texas: "In relation to climate, fertility of the soil and easiness of possession, it offers to the emigrant more advantages than any other land on earth."[10]

Those enticing descriptions were supplemented with illustrations that

FIGURE 2. This artist's depiction of Houston was published in 1844 in the frontispiece of Matilda C. Houstoun's *Texas and the Gulf of Mexico*, vol. 2. Courtesy of Louis Round Wilson Special Collections Library, University of North Carolina at Chapel Hill.

began appearing in publications in the 1840s. Romanticized views such as the one in figure 2 were more typical of the Rhine River Valley than Houston's Buffalo Bayou, but they probably helped reassure potential immigrants from Europe that perhaps Texas wasn't so different from home after all.[11]

The area certainly sounded appealing, and the society's offer was a tempting one. Under the terms of a written agreement, each head of a family was expected to deposit 600 florins, at that time the equivalent of about $240 in US currency. In return, the Verein promised to provide passage across the Atlantic on a "commodious" ship, wholesome food en route, and transportation inland to the society's land for the emigrant, his family, and their baggage.[12]

Each colonist would also receive a basic house, or the means to build one, and access at fair prices (or on credit) to the livestock, tools, and supplies he needed to become self-sufficient. After certain conditions had been met, each family would receive title to 320 acres of land; single men over the age of seventeen would be allotted 160 acres.[13]

If Texas under those conditions wasn't paradise, it was close enough for thousands of Germans like Johann and Johanette Stengler. On October 3, 1845, the young father submitted his request to the society, stating his intention to emigrate to Texas with his wife, "six children, and an infant." He "humbly request[ed] that the Certificate for Admission for Emigration, together with all other required papers for the voyage be furnished as soon as possibly convenient."[14]

Johann Stengler received a prompt and encouraging response. He "immediately proceeded with the auctioning of our houses, furniture, and properties, because we were told we would have to hurry in order to be in Antwerp on October 25, 1845, on which date our ship would depart." Carl Bingel, a friend and neighbor, planned to join the Stenglers with his own family on the move to Texas, but suddenly, both households were stunned by a potentially disastrous setback. They were not the only ones leaving town in these difficult times, and those often-hasty departures, combined with an already depressed economy, apparently created a buyer's market for both real estate and household goods.

The young father's next letter to the society contained an urgent request, and his distress is clearly evident in his words.

> The auctioneering however did not turn out like we had anticipated. So now after all we probably will not be able to make it, for I am short 180 florins required for the voyage from Antwerp to the colony, and Carl Bingel is short 216 florins.
>
> We therefore humbly ask the Society, whether it were possible, to advance us the above amounts. We would willingly work it off when we arrive at the colony. Otherwise it will be impossible for us to emigrate.
>
> I do not know what to do. My profession was chimney and fireplace inspector which I already have transferred to another party. I have a big family, 7 children, and Carl Bingel has a family of 5 heads.
>
> We do not know which way to turn. We believe that in Texas, Bingel and I could quickly work it off. My intentions are to follow

masonry or the shoe making trade. . . . We therefore beg an early reply so we can send the pledge money.

In anticipation, we remain the petitioners.
Respectfully,
Johannes Stengler and Carl Bingel
Dietz, Nassau[15]

Either the society was receptive to this plea or the two men found other solutions to their financial difficulties because they quickly received word to head promptly to Antwerp to board their assigned ship. The Verein was, if nothing else, very efficient in signing up emigrants and getting them across the Atlantic, because less than three weeks after Johann Stengler's initial letter requesting the "necessary papers for my journey," the family was approved for the trip.

That journey proved to be long, difficult, and at times dangerous, but Johanette Stengler had already demonstrated both determination and resilience through three marriages and the birth of eight children during her four decades of life. That "survivor's attitude" would be seriously tested in the weeks and years ahead, on both the open sea and the vast prairie of the Texas frontier. First, however, the family needed to get to Antwerp, Belgium, in time to catch their ship, and they would soon learn that even a moment's inattention while traveling with seven children could have frightening consequences.[16]

2

TO THE RHINE AND BEYOND

*We came to the high sea and saw
nothing anymore but water.*

—JOHANN STENGLER, November 4, 1845

The scene in Dietz on a late October morning was one repeated thousands of times across Europe in 1845 and 1846. A cluster of friends and relatives gathered around a wagon amid the excited chatter of youngsters, while quiet goodbyes were shared by the older children and adults. There were brave smiles, at least a few tears, and promises to send letters. The hard decisions about which treasured items to take and which to leave behind had been made, and the trunks, which now seemed so few in number, were carefully hoisted into the wagon. The trunks held all the worldly goods the family would have when they arrived in Texas—and for their two-month crossing of the Atlantic.

Finally, the last farewells were completed, everyone was settled in the wagon, and with a jolt and a rattle of wheels, the Stengler family's journey was underway. Johann recorded the date of their departure, October 21, 1845, in a journal he kept for the trip. Their immediate destination was the town of Koblenz, about thirty miles distant, on the Rhine River. It's unlikely any of the family had ever traveled more than a few miles from their home, so we can only imagine their wide-eyed wonder when they caught their first glimpse of one of Europe's great rivers. At Koblenz, they boarded a river steamer that would carry them past the cities of Cologne and Rotterdam to the port city of Antwerp, Belgium, about fifty miles inland from the North Sea.[1]

Due to Johanette's trio of marriages, this family of future Texans included a mix of surnames and ages. The four Hankamer boys were Johann Wilhelm (age eleven), Karl Christian (nine), Frederick Adolph (eight), and Karl Ludwig (six). They were followed by her two sons with Johann Stengler, Karl George (three) and Rudolph, who was only fifteen months old. At age fourteen, the only daughter in the household was Wilhelmina Krantz, the sole surviving child from Johanette Stengler's first marriage. Early in their journey, Wilhelmina penciled her name and the date inside the front cover of a small Bible printed in the old German Fraktur typeface.

Her handwritten inscription also cited two Bible verses, offering an insight into her upbringing and her optimism about the future. Her chosen passages were appropriate for the occasion. Translated into English, they were Hebrews 13:14: "We have here no continuing city, but the future one we seek;" and I John 2:17: "And the world passes away, with its desires; the one, however, who does the will of God abides in eternity." Beneath those verses, she added the notation, "On the Rhine, 23 Oct. 1845."[2]

An entry in Johann Stengler's journal for October 27 recorded the first major incident of their journey. It was their seventh day since leaving Dietz, and Johanette—who probably enlisted some help from her teenage daughter—undoubtedly had her hands literally full with fifteen-month-old Rudolph. That left Johann with the unenviable task of keeping the other five boys occupied and out of trouble amid the distractions of travel on a river steamer. He doesn't offer any details, but somewhere near Rotterdam, Johann noted: "Wilhelm nearly had an accident. He came very near falling into the sea, but the good Lord saved him." It was a sobering reminder that this trip was not without serious risks.

On October 29, the ninth day of their trip, the family arrived at Antwerp, the port that served as the point of departure for many Germans headed to America. Before they boarded their ship for Texas, there was some final paperwork to be signed, including a standard "Immigration Agreement" completed between the head of each household and the society.

Under this contract the Verein would provide to each married head of a household 320 acres of land in Texas, but only after several requirements had been met. The immigrant must live on the land granted to him for three consecutive years, counted from the day he took possession; fence and keep in cultivation fifteen acres of land during those three years;

build a dwelling on the land; and submit to the colonization plan of the society and the laws of the land.

For Germans with little hope of ever owning a farm in Europe, it seemed a reasonable—even enticing—offer, but there was one other important condition: if any of these requirements were not fulfilled, the land and any improvements made by the immigrant would revert to the Verein. A copy of the contract was signed at Antwerp on October 30, 1845, by three individuals: Johann Stengler; Gustav Elley, the society's agent; and the "Texian Consul, Consulate of the Republic of Texas for the port of Antwerp."[3]

Those officials were busy men during the mid-1840s. An article on the front page of *The Civilian and Galveston Gazette* on February 21, 1846, addressed the situation.

> The tide of emigration from Germany has induced the King of Prussia to issue a sort of mandate to his subjects, disapproving of their going to America; but so great is the discontent of his subjects, that the wishes of the King have been answered only by a constant rush to the ports of Bremen, Hamburg, and Antwerp, for the purpose of getting away as fast as possible. Thirteen vessels sailed in one week with emigrants for Texas, whose departure, says a writer from Brussels, is assisted by a society of German Princes. The number of German Emigrants to the United States and Texas during the past year was 45,000 from Bremen alone.[4]

Included in those thousands were some 185 men, women, and children who boarded the sailing ship *Harriet* in Antwerp on October 31, 1845. The Stenglers' fellow travelers crowded aboard the *Harriet* included thirty-eight single men, two married couples without children, and twenty-four families with children. A widow with one child and a man with two children were the only single parents on the passenger list. While most of the heads of household were in their twenties or thirties, three of the men, all single farmers, were over fifty. There was no age given for many of those listed, but the oldest known passenger making the voyage was seventy-two-year-old George Gottshuz. Dreams of a better life in Texas were not limited by age.[5]

Antwerp is about fifty miles inland from the coast, and the ship finally left mainland Europe behind and reached the North Sea on November 4,

1845. Johann Stengler recorded that important milestone in his journal: "We came to the high-sea and saw nothing anymore but water." England was not far away, but it was out of sight, and the impression that their ship was now sailing on a vast ocean must have loomed large in their thoughts in the hours ahead. Johann Stengler's journal records several terrifying nights that surely caused at least some of the passengers to wish they had never left their former homes.

> In the night of the 5th to 6th a severe storm tossed the ship [so] that we all thought we were lost, but by the help of God we were saved. . . . On the evening of the 8th, we had another storm, more violent than the one of the 5th to the 6th. The night of the 8th to the 9th was the most horrible night through which I have ever lived. The wind was so tempestuous that all on the ship thought we would sink to the bottom of the sea. The waves broke over the ship and sent the water down into the hold of the ship with great force so that we could not stay in our rooms. . . . The next morning the storm had not yet abated, however was not as turbulent as during the night. The storm continued until the 12th of the month, thereafter it was calm.

It's possible that none of the passengers had ever been on an ocean voyage, so their terror during such a storm was understandable. Their first two weeks on the sea were also a time of both tragedy and rejoicing on board the *Harriet*. Johann recorded in his journal that two children died, and one was born aboard the ship during the early part of the voyage.

After their harrowing experiences with the violent storms, the weather proved to be fickle. Johann noted that from November 19–23, "there was a calm so that we hardly moved 3 hours a day. Thank God the calm did not last long." Finally, the travelers were blessed with "a good wind," which lasted through December 7. On that day they had their first sight of land in over a month. "This was the first chance we again got to see God's earth, though we were still 5 hours distant we were highly elated to once again see dry land," he wrote. From December 8 "to the morning of the 14th we sailed on the Gulf of Mexico . . . which at first was not too rough, but by the 18th most of us got sea-sick."[6]

On December 23, fellow passenger Christian Vogel noted their best news in nearly two months as they spotted "at once on a foggy morning the City of Galveston and the mainland where we also saw many ships. What a joy for us to see our long-awaited goal."[7]

FIGURE 3. Galveston in 1844, image from the frontispiece in Matilda C. Houstoun's *Texas and the Gulf of Mexico*, vol. 1. Courtesy of Louis Round Wilson Special Collections Library, University of North Carolina at Chapel Hill.

With their destination finally in sight, the weary travelers rejoiced at the thought of celebrating Christmas on dry land, away from the confines of the ship. Alas, with Galveston tantalizingly in view, they were faced with a frustrating delay and remained on the *Harriet* for eight more days. Sandbars at the entrance to Galveston Bay were a notorious hazard for mariners, and the problem was aggravated after a cold front passed through the area. Strong northerly winds could blow enough water out of the shallow bay that "crossing the bar" was impossible except for ships with a very shallow draft.[8]

That was the case for the *Harriet*, and an explanation of the delay was noted in a letter from fellow passenger Christian Vogel to his family back in Germany.

> We could not enter the harbor because the water was too shallow and full of sandbanks, therefore we had to remain at anchor over Christmas until the last of December, when a steamship met us so that we could land on God's ground still in the old year. So, we were from the 31st of October until the last of December on the water; we journeyed however not longer than 49 days on the open sea.[9]

Vogel's comment recognized the symbolism of beginning and completing their trip within the same calendar year, and that setting foot on Texas soil on the final day of 1845 was cause for both relief and celebration. Along with the other new arrivals from Europe, the Stenglers did not plan to be in Galveston very long. It was, after all, only a temporary way station, a place to have their arrival officially noted, after which they would be provided transportation on the next leg of their journey to the society's new colony in Central Texas.

It was certainly fitting that the first sunrise the family experienced on Texas soil also ushered in a new year. Another account says the day began with beautiful sunny skies and spring-like temperatures, and despite the strangeness of this place, it must have seemed an auspicious introduction to their adopted homeland.[10]

January of 1846 also brought major changes for everyone living in Texas, long-term residents and newcomers alike. After years of uncertainty and debate, the annexation of Texas to the United States was finalized on December 29, 1845, two days before the Stenglers' arrival, and confirmation of that event reached Texas in early January. The family left Europe bound for the independent Republic of Texas but arrived in the newest state in the United States of America. They would now be both Texans *and* Americans.[11]

The Stenglers heard about those changes during their first month or so in Galveston, but that news paled in importance to other reports spreading through the island city. There was trouble brewing in the Verein's new colonies, and the Stenglers' plans for a new home on their own land in Texas suddenly seemed as unsettled as the stormy seas they had experienced during their just-completed voyage across the Atlantic.

3

A CITY BUILT OF BOARDS

The cattle run free in the city and in the field round about . . . but nobody minds.
—CHRISTIAN VOGEL, February 18, 1846

Galveston was unlike any city the Stenglers had ever seen—and probably beyond their wildest imaginations. One would expect the sights, sounds, and even the smells of any town on another continent to be different for newcomers, and Galveston was certainly all that, and more. Christian Vogel traveled with the Stenglers on the *Harriet* and wrote to relatives after their arrival in Galveston. His letter provides one impression of Texas' largest city in early 1846:

> The examination of Galveston was to us a strange one which we had never before seen. The city numbers about 2500 inhabitants, most of the houses are built of boards and wood and stand on posts, so that under the houses everything is hollow where the pigs and the dogs run under it . . . and their children play there. We often saw that from six to eight oxen would travel from one place to another which delayed us. The cattle run free in the city and in the field round about without being brought to a stall even once in a year, but nobody minds.[1]

Another German who arrived in town that same year also noted there was only one brick house in the whole city; everything else was built of wood. Johann Stengler was a brickmason, and when he pleaded with the society for a loan to help with his travel costs to Texas, he believed he could use his skills to "quickly work it off." We don't know if he viewed the scarcity of bricks in Galveston as a disappointment or an opportunity.

One of the more colorful descriptions of the town was provided by Mrs. M. C. Houstoun, a wealthy Englishwoman who visited Galveston twice, in

FIGURE 4. Galveston cotton docks in 1845 by an unknown German artist. Courtesy of Rosenberg Library, Galveston, Texas.

1843 and 1844. She wrote that the "houses and religious edifices at Galveston . . . are all raised a foot or two from the ground. . . . This is ingenious; it raises the house out of the road, and in the summer keeps out the snakes . . . to say nothing of the pigs." It was quickly apparent to recent arrivals that this New World was still very rough around the edges![2]

The family's first impressions about the weather, however, should have been encouraging. A visitor to Galveston on the day the Stenglers arrived wrote about the balmy temperatures, noting that he enjoyed a stroll on the beach and saw roses blooming in town. This introduction to a seemingly tropical Texas was, alas, short-lived, and that same evening brought a reality check concerning the Texas climate. A strong cold front, or "norther" as it was known locally, blew into the area, bringing an abrupt change in the weather. A drop of forty degrees during a single day was not uncommon with these northers, and such unpredictable and sudden changes could be a shock to newcomers.[3]

The January weather may have been fickle, and this small city "built of boards" may have lacked the sense of permanence found in European towns, but Galveston was probably a pleasant surprise for newcomers in terms of its ability to supply both necessities and luxuries. Few items other than raw agricultural products were being produced in Texas in 1846, so Galveston's role as the point of import for almost everything else gave it particular importance in daily life for the entire state. A few days before the Stenglers arrived in town, *The Civilian and Galveston Gazette* newspaper advertised a wide variety of goods and services available in town.

The Galveston Drug Store offered, "a choice assortment of Genuine Drugs and Medicines, Chemicals, Paints, and Dyestuff . . . [and] prescriptions carefully prepared at all hours." For the ladies, the store also offered luxury items such as powder puffs, fancy soaps, lavender water, and Persian scent bags. Other establishments promoted items "just received" from Boston or New York, including several types of sugar, pepper, raisins, rice, coffee, assorted teas, grapes, lemons, fresh almonds, cheese, dried apples, and lamp oil. Brandy, rum, and gin were offered by the keg, and whiskey was available by the barrel.

Elsewhere in town, more practical items, such as cut nails, rope, and pumps, vied for space with hand tools, axes, and wood saws. Other advertisements offered a reminder that this new city was perched on the edge of a vast frontier. "Powder, shot, and lead" were also readily available for purchase. Finally, the December 17, 1845, edition of that same Galveston newspaper announced the arrival of "D. H. Pallais, Clock and Watch Maker and Jeweler." Perhaps his choice of location for his new business, "next door to the Sheriff's Office," was a coincidence—or maybe it was merely prudent recognition that Galveston could still have a rough-and-tumble side.[4]

The merchants of Galveston may have been prepared to provide all the items the Stenglers required, but Galveston was intended to be only a temporary stop en route to the Verein's new settlements in Central Texas. After their arrival was recorded by an agent for the society, the family expected to travel by boat another hundred-plus miles down the coast to Matagorda Bay. There they would disembark at the rudimentary port of Indianola, near present-day Port O'Connor, and then head inland to their new home.[5]

The Stenglers and many of their fellow new arrivals soon learned that the Verein was reasonably efficient at getting immigrants across thousands of miles of ocean from Europe to North America, but the much shorter trip from Galveston to their final destination posed a much bigger challenge. Due to the sudden influx of immigrants and a shortage of transportation from Galveston to Indianola, the society unexpectedly found itself in the temporary lodging business. About 700 of the 3,600 immigrants who arrived in Galveston in the final months of 1845 were still in town at the end of the year, waiting for boats to carry them down the coast. These temporary residents were housed in buildings rented by the Verein, yet another unplanned expense that strained the organization's already inadequate finances.[6]

In retrospect, the delay proved to be a blessing for the Stenglers—and may have saved their lives. In early 1846, rumors about troubles in the Verein's new colony swirled through the immigrant community, and Johann and Johanette began to have second thoughts about their intended destination. With the benefit of hindsight, we now know there was ample reason for concern about the new arrivals' plans for Texas.[7]

The transatlantic voyage they had just experienced had been difficult, but it paled in comparison to the rigors of the upcoming trip from Indianola to New Braunfels. That 150-mile journey was over rough terrain that alternated, with the unpredictable weather, between choking dust and impassable mud. There were few if any bridges or even established roads between Indianola and the new settlements, food and safe drinking water for people and their animals were often lacking, and there was even talk about the possibility of hostile "Indians."[8]

The physical challenges posed by the countryside were compounded by poor management by the Verein. Organizers had seriously underestimated both the financing and the logistics required for the venture, but the society had finally succeeded in hiring teamsters to transport settlers from the coast to the interior settlements. In early 1846, a major blow to the group's plan was delivered by the growing threat of hostilities between the US and Mexico. Teamsters discovered it was more profitable to work for the army and the drivers abandoned their plans to work for the society.[9]

As a result, the Verein's expected overland transportation simply disappeared, and hundreds, perhaps thousands, of immigrants were stranded on a primitive section of coast more than one hundred miles south of Galveston. They were left without any means of moving their personal belongings—or themselves—across 150 miles of very unforgiving terrain to their destination.[10]

All of those factors—inadequate funds, poor planning, harsh conditions, and a lack of transportation—combined to create a disaster for the Verein and its immigrants. With hundreds or perhaps even thousands of new arrivals marooned on the coast near Indianola, there were outbreaks of scurvy, cholera, and other diseases, and food and other necessities were in short supply. Some of those who did manage to struggle their way inland carried the sickness to the fledgling German settlements, which experienced their own serious epidemics.

During 1845 and 1846, over seven thousand Germans came to Texas from Europe, and many of them failed to survive their first year in the state. The precise number of deaths will never be known. Estimates by both contemporary writers and more recent histories vary widely, but credible sources place the number lost somewhere between one thousand and three thousand adults and children. Modern Texas is justly proud of its German heritage in what is today called the Hill Country, but the tragedy that befell some of these early arrivals has been largely forgotten today.[11]

The Stenglers arrived just as this crisis was beginning to unfold, and whatever sources warned them to rethink their plans certainly proved to be accurate. Many of the recent arrivals who changed their plans remained in Galveston or nearby Houston, and they found the island city to be surprisingly welcoming. By the mid-1850s, between one-third and one-half of the population of Galveston had German roots. That percentage may have been smaller in 1846, but the Stengler family found a surprisingly strong sense of community during their first few months in Galveston. Some businesses had German-speaking owners, so the newcomers didn't immediately face the language barrier they expected.[12]

Despite that sense of community and the availability of those "Genuine Drugs and Medicines," the Stengler family's first month in Texas was marred by tragedy. The youngest child in the family, Rudolph Stengler, was barely eighteen months old in January 1846, and although no details are known, an entry in a family Bible noted his death on the twenty-third day of their first month in the United States.

One other important change in the family occurred after they arrived in Texas. At some point, like many of his fellow immigrants, Johann

Stengler switched his name to the anglicized form "John," and most of the other family members followed suit. The household included three sons from Johanette's second marriage to Johannes Hankamer, and in the years to come Johann Wilhelm Hankamer was referred to as John William, J. W., or simply William. To reduce confusion with other family members named John, I'll refer to him as John W. Hankamer from this point forward in this narrative.

In similar fashion, Karl Christian Hankamer became known as Charles, and Frederick Adolph Hankamer's name appears in written records as both Frederick and Fred. Nicknames were in use then as now, and to the family, he was simply known as "Fritz." That shorter form will be used from this point forward. The two youngest sons in the family were the result of Johanette's marriage to John Stengler. Karl Georg Stengler was shortened to George, and John Henry Stengler's name was Americanized from birth. His arrival in the world on May 27, 1847, marked another milestone for the household: he was the first in the family to be born in the United States.

The one daughter in the family, Wilhelmina Krantz, came from Johanette's first marriage, to Gottfried Krantz, and she also saw some adjustments in her name in their new home. In the years to come, in both family correspondence and some official documents, she was usually referred to simply as "Mina."

There seems to have been only one holdout to Old World traditions in terms of chosen names: Johanette continued to be known by her original name throughout her life, although variations in spelling are found in a few documents. Her tombstone honors the memory of "Johanette Stengler," and that version will be used throughout this account.

As the months passed in their first year in Texas, this family faced a critical decision. Turmoil in the Verein's new colony caused them to seek another location for their new home—but where might that be? Galveston's thriving German community was bustling with newly arrived immigrants, but many of them were in similar circumstances and looking for long-term work. For a brickmason, this town built of wood probably seemed distinctly unpromising, and the flat, treeless island did not look very appealing for a homestead.

There was certainly no shortage of land in other parts of Texas, as illustrated by an advertisement in *The Civilian and Galveston Gazette* on

December 17, 1845, which described "a healthy, fertile region watered by excellent and never-failing springs—good stock range & etc."

The owner of "two large tracts of land in Robertson County" was offering to give two hundred acres to each of "two or three respectable families . . . of good moral character, to help protect the owner's interest in the property."[13]

Such offers may have sounded promising, but there were, of course, some details to consider. That land was located about 175 miles northwest of Galveston, and as the Verein's difficulties with the disappearing teamsters had shown, the logistics of simply getting there posed a serious challenge for many prospective settlers. Such a trip would be difficult for even a robust single man; it was definitely a risky undertaking for a family that included six children.

Several writers who traveled extensively in Texas during the 1830s and 1840s described an area where developed roads were virtually nonexistent and navigation was very difficult. During wet weather, the path taken by previous travelers could be obliterated. Most routes headed inland from the coast passed through vast expanses of open prairie that at times extended to the horizon. In such areas, there were no landmarks, and on cloudy days when the sun wasn't visible to help determine one's direction, even experienced travelers could become lost for days.[14]

The Stenglers' decision about where to settle in Texas was not an easy one, and there was one more major complication—the threat of a war with Mexico and concerns about a possible invasion by an army that still chafed from the loss of this same territory barely ten years earlier. After Texas' successful fight for independence from Mexico in 1836, a 125-mile-wide swath of land between the Nueces and Rio Grande rivers in southern Texas remained in dispute. The annexation of Texas by the United States in late December 1845 pushed the two nations to the brink of war, and on February 21, 1846, an article in *The Civilian and Galveston Gazette* reported Mexico was raising a large army "for the invasion of Texas." Hostilities between the United States and Mexico began with a skirmish in April 1846 in the far southern tip of Texas, near the Rio Grande. The first full-scale battle occurred near Brownsville the following month.

Would the conflict spread to the rest of the state? No one knew, of course, but the situation made a lasting impression on one member of the

Stengler household. Charles Hankamer was a boy of ten that spring and related in later years that "the memory remained a vivid one throughout his life," after he saw soldiers leave Galveston to participate in the war.[15]

The Stengler family certainly faced a dilemma. Getting to their intended destination in the Verein's colony sounded very risky, the security of most of southern or Central Texas was suspect due to the developing war with Mexico, and their prospects in Galveston seemed limited. Finances were also a problem; the Stenglers had already paid to the Verein most of the money raised by the sale of their house and personal belongings in Germany. In addition to their passage to Texas, that fee was supposed to guarantee both 320 acres of land and at least basic housing in the new colony in Central Texas. If they decided to go elsewhere, the family would lose both their money and those opportunities.

Decades later, a local newspaper published a short autobiography of John Stengler. In that account, he explained the family's decision, and the reason for their change of plans after arriving in Galveston: "In 1845 I immigrated to Texas for Fisher and Millers Colony [in Central Texas], arrived in Galveston December 31, 1845. We heard of the suffering of the people who had gone to said colony and I stayed in Galveston 'till June 1846, when I moved to Anahuac."[16]

Anahuac was a small settlement about thirty miles northeast of Galveston, and given the absence of roads, that short journey would have been made by boat across Galveston Bay and then Trinity Bay. While that trip must have seemed easy compared to their harrowing two-month voyage across the Atlantic, it was no less significant for their future. After months of uncertainty in temporary quarters in Galveston, the Stengler family was finally beginning the search for their home in Texas.

We don't know if the name of their new location influenced their decision, but it was both symbolic and appropriate for these new Americans. They were headed for Liberty County, Texas.

— 4 —

A COUNTY CALLED "LIBERTY"

This entire country was full of all manner of game, and wild beasts. People lived far apart in those days.
—JOHN STENGLER, 1910, describing Liberty County of 1846

If the Stengler family was surprised by Galveston and its "houses built of boards," we can only imagine their initial reaction to rural Liberty County. Unlike their former home, Southeast Texas had no imposing castles, rocky hilltops, arched bridges, or walled cities. This new land had no rocks or hills at all, towns were tiny settlements, and houses built of *any* materials whatsoever were few and far between.[1]

Nineteenth-century American naturalist Frederick Law Olmsted visited Liberty County in 1854, described its principal characteristics as "lowness, flatness, and wetness," and noted, "The country is sparsely settled, containing less than one inhabitant to the square mile." At first glimpse, the Stenglers' new home may not have been what they expected, but it was not lacking in potential.

Between the Gulf of Mexico beaches and the dense inland forests lay a vast coastal grassland now sometimes called the Saltgrass Prairie. Olmsted described the area as "beautiful, perhaps, as an uncultivated flat can be, the prairies being pleasantly broken by islands and large masses of wood; pine and oak predominating, but cypresses, gums, and magnolias appearing in the bayou bottoms, as the banks of the sluggish brooks are here called."[2]

Another traveler was enthusiastic about the area's potential for new settlers. "No country in the world can be compared to this, in the ease and facility of raising stock," he wrote. "All the herdsman has to do, is look after them, so they may not stray away, and some portion of the year, yard them to prevent their growing wild. . . . Hogs keep in good flesh all the year; and in autumn, when the nuts fall from the trees, grow fat. Horses, cattle, and hogs can, therefore, be kept in this country without any more trouble than merely looking after them to prevent their straying away."[3]

Yet other writers touted the area's potential for farming. In 1834 one claimed that despite "poor soil . . . it is capable of producing considerable crops, even with the least possible labor. Indian corn, if merely dropped into holes made with a stick, will grow and yield pretty well even without hoeing." Claims that a corn crop could succeed without *any* hoeing were certainly optimistic, but this land also offered other potential sources of food. Wildfowl were said to be "abundant hereabouts at this season, particularly geese . . . which form vast flocks whose noise may be heard for several miles." There were also ducks and wild turkeys, and deer were numerous, sometimes appearing in large herds.

Not all that wildlife was harmless, however, and only some of it was widely deemed desirable for the dinner table. The woods also contained "wolves, bears, panthers, wild cats, wild hogs, foxes, rackoons [sic], and squirrels. Wild cats and panthers are rather scarce, and never attack men unless very hungry or hard-pressed at bay. The wild hog is very fierce, and, it is said, will generally attack a man even unprovoked."[4]

This untamed landscape and natural bounty barely fifty miles from present-day downtown Houston may be difficult for us to visualize today, but in 1846 this area could still be accurately described as the frontier. When the Stenglers arrived, Liberty County encompassed considerably more territory than it does today; its boundaries extended from Galveston Bay eastward for about thirty-five miles, and from near the Gulf of Mexico inland for some ninety miles. That's an area roughly the size of Delaware, and the 1850 US census tallied only 2,522 people in the entire county.[5]

The Stenglers' destination in June 1846, the small settlement of Anahuac, was about thirty miles northeast of Galveston by boat. It was one of the few named towns in the region shown on maps at the time, but a modern historian notes that early Texas travelers had to be skeptical about "believing that all names and lines on maps meant towns and roads. Often a name written large designated only one or two houses, and lines indicated *routes* as distinguished from *roads*."[6]

Both roads *and* towns were in short supply in Liberty County in 1846,

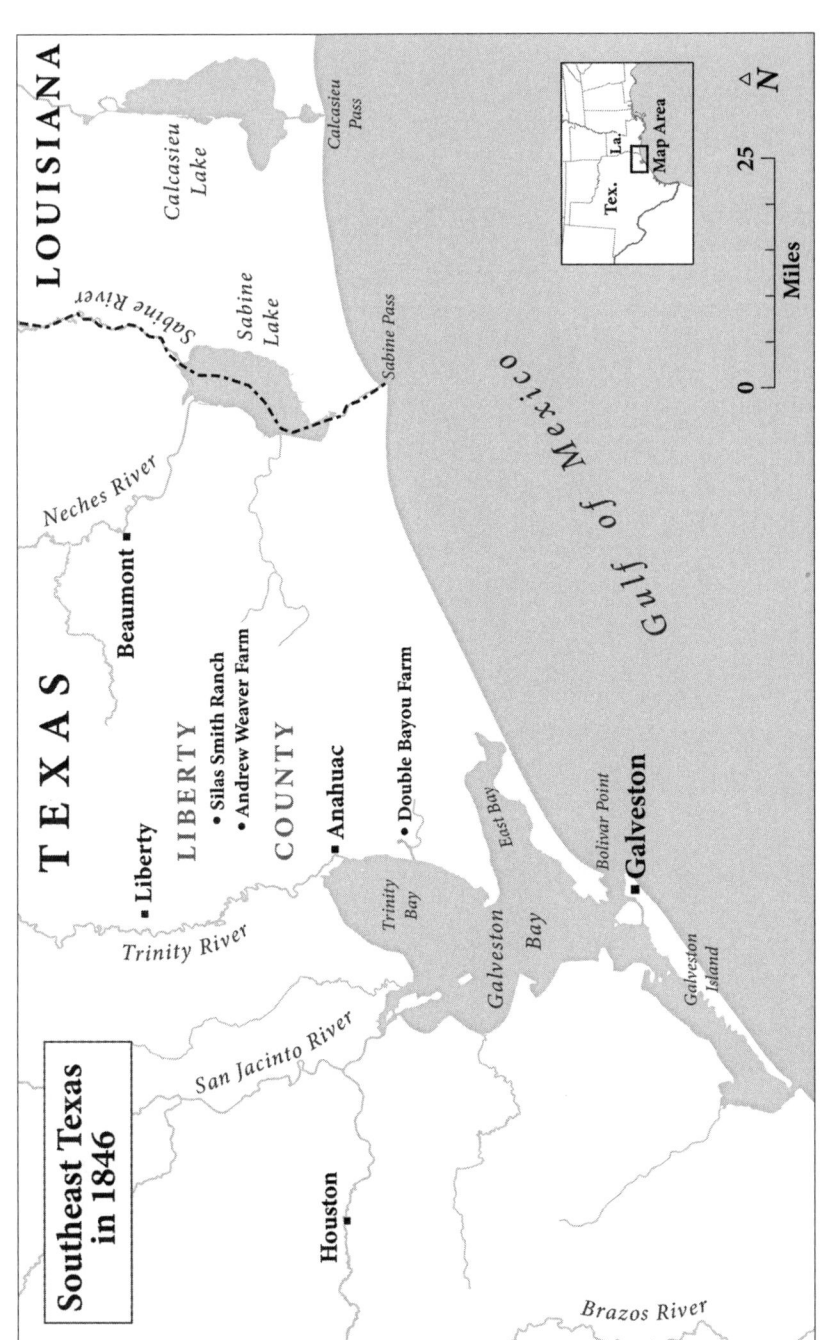

FIGURE 5. Southeast Texas in 1846.

and years later, John Stengler wrote a brief autobiography that summed up the character of their new location. "This entire country was full of all manner of game, and wild beasts," John noted. "People lived far apart in those days. There were so few settlers in the country and none of my family understanding English, we were rather in a bad condition to get information, as there were but few Germans in these parts at that time."[7]

John Stengler was correct about there being "few Germans" in the vicinity. According to the 1850 census, only ten of the 312 households in Liberty County were headed by an adult who had been born in Germany. The total number of German-born residents in all of those families—including seven members of the Stengler household—was only forty-four men, women, and children.[8]

Rural Liberty County was certainly a big change from life in Galveston, with its thousands of residents and large German population. From the standpoint of a familiar language and culture, it would have been easier for the family to simply remain in that city, but doing so would negate a key reason for their move, which was to acquire enough land of their own to support their large family.

That explanation for their move to Liberty County is supported by a 1926 newspaper article that summarized the life of Charles Hankamer. It notes that in 1846, at the age of ten, "he was needed to help work the small farm." Within a few months, the family moved again to what Charles later described as "a larger and better farm." This move came in the autumn of 1846 to a farm near what is now the town of Hankamer.[9]

This second farm may have been larger and better, but it also came with a bonus—a German-speaking landlord. Andrew Weaver was one of the earliest German immigrants to the area, arriving in 1831 and settling about a dozen miles north of Anahuac. His wife, son, and three daughters were all born in Germany, and two of the daughters still lived in Liberty County when the Stenglers arrived. After Andrew's death in August 1846, his widow went to live nearby with one of those daughters, Mrs. Elizabeth Barrow. That put the family in the market for a reliable tenant to live on the now-vacant home place, provide watchful eyes over the rural property, and keep the land in production.[10]

The local grapevine connected these two households with shared German roots, and while living at the Weaver place these new Texans celebrated an important milestone. On May 27, 1847, John Henry Stengler became the first member of the family to be born in the United States. He was the ninth child born to Johanette with one of her three husbands over a span of eighteen years. At the time of John Henry's birth, Johanette was forty-one years old; her husband was twenty-eight.[11]

Finding fellow Germans in the Weaver family was helpful for the Stenglers, but the limited number of other German-speaking neighbors was an added incentive for the family to develop their English skills. Acquiring this new language may have been helped by the family's background, which placed a high value on education. Their oldest daughter, Wilhelmina, had finished the standard eight years of school before they left Germany, and the three oldest sons had spent some time in the classroom before the family emigrated. A newspaper story published late in the life of Charles Hankamer noted, "At the age of six, he was in a strict Prussian school learning to read and write in Latin."[12]

Family letters confirm that all of the adults except Johanette Stengler were reading and writing in their new language by the early 1860s. After the Civil War, John Stengler and two of his sons were elected to various county offices, including tax assessor, justice of the peace, and county commissioner, a clear indication of both their communication skills and the respect they had earned in the community.

The Stenglers remained on the Weaver property for only about two years, but during that time, John and his family established a reputation as hard workers. "While living at the Andrew Weaver place," John later wrote, "one Dr. Whiteman, living at Goose Creek, came over to see if I would not move over to his place and cultivate his farm, but not knowing the man or place, I wouldn't go. . . . [Instead I] moved to Double Bayou [about sixteen miles to the south] in 1848, where I lived for about two years." One advantage of that area was its much easier access by water to Galveston.[13]

Real estate and tax records indicate John Stengler did not acquire any land during his first four years in Texas, but that wasn't surprising. The family was starting from scratch with little capital, and it took time to get established in their new country. As they were doing so, the nature of the county also continued to change, albeit rather slowly. Despite the small population and wild nature of the land, civilization was beginning to make gradual inroads in the area, and it wasn't always necessary for the Stenglers and their neighbors to make the trip by water to Galveston to obtain even basic goods and services.

By 1850 the county was home to three blacksmiths, four wheelwrights, a cooper, and a saddler—all essential tradesmen in a rural economy. Clothing needs were often met within each household, but if desired, more experienced help could be obtained from a shoemaker born in England and two tailors, one from France and one from Germany. Despite these varied backgrounds, most of the residents of the area were solidly connected to the land. Like John Stengler, the occupations of nearly two-thirds of the heads of household shown in the 1850 census of Liberty County were listed as either farmers, stock raisers, or in a few cases, planters.[14]

The county had also attracted a druggist and five physicians, although most of these doctors were just getting established in their professions—four of the five were under the age of thirty. If they were looking for some on-the-job training, these physicians had no shortage of potential patients. Due in large measure to the region's semitropical climate and flat, poorly drained terrain, diseases such as "intermittent, bilious, and malarial fevers" were common, especially in the summer months. One writer from that period noted, "In all the low country, and on the streams of water, the inhabitants are more or less afflicted with the fever and ague."[15]

The precise cause wasn't recorded, but perhaps one of those maladies was the culprit in a sad event during the family's stay in the Double Bayou area. On August 14, 1849, Karl Ludwig Hankamer died at the age of ten and became the second of Johanette's children to be buried in Texas. Once again, her survivor's mentality was put to the test.[16]

A new decade began less than five months after that loss, and the 1850s finally provided some of the opportunities that had prompted the Stenglers to cross the Atlantic. One of the primary motivations for their move to Texas was the chance to acquire their own land, but the first member of the family to do so might come as a surprise—it was their teenage daughter, Wilhelmina.

5

THE FAMILY ADDS A TEXAN

I moved up to what was then known as Cracker's Neck,
near my daughter, and son-in-law Charles Wilborn,
and lived there during the civil war.
—JOHN STENGLER, 1910, describing 1850

The ideal site for a homestead in the early days of Texas statehood included a reliable source of water for people and their animals, a nearby source of timber for buildings and fuel, and land suitable for raising both livestock and crops. Good neighbors anywhere in the vicinity and reasonable access to a town would be bonuses, and sometimes those neighbors influenced a family for generations.

When John Stengler moved his family to Liberty County in 1846, he observed that "people lived far apart," so the arrival of his family to occupy the recently vacated Andrew Weaver place must have been a welcome development in the area. The term "neighbors" was relative in this sparsely settled countryside, where households were often well out of both sight and sound of each other, and that was probably the case with the Stenglers' new home.

Although the precise location of both houses isn't known today, the Stenglers and the Silas Smith family lived within two or three miles of each other, and that distance may well have been even less. The Stenglers and their six children, ages fifteen down to four, had plenty in common with the Smiths, whose household in 1846 included an eleven-year-old daughter, two teenage sons, and an unmarried twenty-four-year-old stepson, Charles Wilborn.[1]

Silas Smith moved to Texas from Louisiana in about 1830 with his wife and family and settled in the southern portion of present-day Liberty County. One of the earliest Anglo landowners in the area, his arrival in those years made him eligible for a generous grant of a "headright and a labor" of land, totaling 4,605 acres. In 1842 he received an additional grant of 3,485 acres "on the headwaters of Turtle Bayou" from the Republic of Texas.[2]

He was a good fit for the area, and by 1850 Silas Smith had developed a substantial livestock operation. His listing on the US census and county tax rolls for that year included thirty horses, seventy "milch" [milk] cows, four working oxen, 350 other cattle, and twenty-five swine. There were almost certainly additional cattle with his brand roaming the surrounding open range.[3]

The Stenglers, still newcomers to the area, were not nearly so prosperous. In 1848, two years after becoming neighbors to the Smiths, the Stenglers moved about sixteen miles farther south, to the Double Bayou area. By then, however, a significant friendship had developed between the oldest son and daughter in the two families—Charles Wilborn and Mina Krantz.

During her first two years in Texas, Mina was still developing her English language skills, and it seems unlikely that Louisiana-born Charles Wilborn spoke much, if any, German. Even so, young ladies of marriageable age were in short supply in Liberty County, and language barriers could be overcome, especially when matters of the heart were involved. The 1850 census for the county showed only seventy-nine unmarried women between the ages of sixteen and fifty, compared to 231 single men between sixteen and sixty. It probably didn't take long for the single daughter in the Stengler household to catch the attention of her bachelor neighbor.[4]

Acquaintance eventually led to matrimony, and on April 4, 1850, the Stengler-Hankamer-Krantz blended family expanded once again with Mina's marriage to Charles Wilborn. She was nineteen years old, he was twenty-seven, and she became the first child from the Stengler household to establish her independence from her parents and put down separate roots in Texas.[5]

As was often the case in those years, the newlyweds initially moved in with the groom's parents, but it didn't take them long to get their own place. Early land records for both Liberty and Chambers counties are somewhat incomplete due to courthouse fires in the 1870s, but by 1851 Charles Wilborn is shown on the county tax rolls with six hundred acres near Turtle Bayou, not far from the Silas Smith ranch.

It was a good location, described in later deeds as the "homestead known as the Charles Wilborn Place." Turtle Bayou provided a convenient source of water, timber along the waterway was available for both buildings and firewood, and the surrounding prairie offered grazing for livestock and ample space for crops. Charles's personal property by 1852 included five horses and 325 head of cattle, so it was a very promising start for the new couple. Seven years after she left Germany as a teenager, Mina and her husband were already firmly established in the growing Texas livestock business.[6]

This marriage also prompted yet another move by the rest of Mina's family. John Stengler later wrote that in the same year as the wedding, he moved his family back from the Double Bayou area to a place not far from their previous home on the Weaver property. He described their new location as "what was then known as Cracker's Neck, near my daughter, and son-in-law Charles Wilborn."[7]

The name "Crackersneck" frequently appeared in family correspondence during the mid-nineteenth century, spelled as a single word, although more recent local references also use the two-word version. The "Crackersneck" form will be used in the following narrative, to remain true to the original letters. Regardless of the spelling, you won't find it on modern maps. When a post office was established there in 1904, the name of the small community was changed to Hankamer, after I. A. Hankamer, the first postmaster and a grandson of John Stengler.[8]

Located roughly halfway between Houston and Beaumont and about two miles north of present-day Interstate 10, Hankamer is on the northern edge of what is now Chambers County. In 1858, the southern part of Liberty County and a small sliver of western Jefferson County were combined to form a new county named "Chambers." When that division occurred, the Wilborn and Stengler homes, located about two miles northwest of Crackersneck, were very close to the new county line but remained within the far southern edge of Liberty County.

Mina's marriage to Charles Wilborn also helped solidify her family's decision about a place to settle down. In February 1855, John Stengler purchased forty acres in southern Liberty County from his son-in-law, and the two families became neighbors in the truest sense, living within easy walking distance of each other. Nine years after he and his family left Dietz, John Stengler was finally a landowner in Texas. Compared to neighbors like Silas Smith, forty acres may seem a small piece of property, but it was far more than the Stenglers ever hoped to own in Europe.⁹

If better opportunities for their large family were a key motivation for John and Johanette's move to Texas, their hopes continued to bear fruit during the 1850s. Once again, the family of their early neighbor Silas Smith played a key role. In September 1857, the only daughter in Silas Smith's household, twenty-two-year-old Lurenda Smith, became the bride of the oldest son in the Stengler family, John W. Hankamer, age twenty-six. The following April, they purchased 319 partially wooded acres on the east bank of Turtle Bayou, adding yet another household from the extended family to this area.¹⁰

The close ties between the two families didn't end there but continued for yet another generation. In 1872, a granddaughter of Silas Smith, also named Lurenda Smith, married John Henry Stengler, the American-born youngest son of John and Johanette Stengler. It may be true that good fences make good neighbors, but in frontier areas, good neighbors can also be excellent sources for sons- and daughters-in-law.

One more son from the Stengler household took a wife during the 1850s. Sometime after his twenty-third birthday in January 1859, Charles Hankamer married a girl from the local area, eighteen-year-old Joanah Higginbotham, and they, too, soon settled in the same vicinity. In September 1860, Charles purchased fifty-two acres "with improvements" fronting on Turtle Bayou, but his property was located just south of the new county line, and thus in Chambers County.¹¹

Not all of John and Johanette's children were ready for matrimony in the 1850s, and the year before Charles Hankamer's marriage, his younger brother Fritz decided to try his fortunes in Texas' largest city at the time. Galveston was within a day's boat ride from home, and an exchange of letters in 1858 between the two brothers offers not only a glimpse into their daily lives but also a reminder that young men in almost any time and place share some universal interests.

Charles was twenty-two and his brother Fritz was twenty when Charles wrote in March 1858 to pass along news from home. He noted progress on getting the corn crop planted, and reported, "Grass is coming fine and the cattle begins to look well, and there is a yearling now and then." Both brothers had been living with their parents as they entered adulthood, and John Stengler wisely allowed his sons to begin building their individual herds on the family property. In his letter, Charles promised his brother, "I'll brand or tend to having your calf branded for you."

News of home duly dispensed, Charles got down to more pressing matters in a young man's life: "I have been mighty busy since you left. I have hardly been in town, but I will go there before long, and see all the girls, for this is rank nonsense, to be always working and not even go to see the girls once in a while, don't you think so, too?"

Charles was apparently content to remain at home, but that didn't dampen his interest in news about the "big city" of Galveston. "You must answer this right off," Charles continued. "Tell me how you like your new home and what you have learned and about the girls, stores, ships, tides, in fact anything which is interesting."[12]

The following month on April 15, 1858, Charles sent a second letter to Fritz, and it included a reminder of the potential perils of the livestock business: "Since I wrote you the last letter we had bad luck up here. I and George was out on the prairie on the 4th of April, and Bets [a horse] fell with George and broke his leg; it is not broken clear in two, but [he] has been bound to stay in bed ever since, it is getting better, but he is not able to set up yet."

The brothers' married sister, Mina Wilborn, also wrote to Fritz during his time in Galveston. "I hope you have a good position where you can earn something," she said. "If you can earn something, I wish you would stay, if not, I wish you would return home." Mina's letter also included some insights about her life on their prairie homestead. Mina was by then twenty-seven years old, had three children (ages five, three, and thirteen months), and was three months pregnant with her fourth. Her role as a mother certainly gave her plenty to do, but she stayed busy on the family farm as well.

Like most rural wives of the time, Mina was in charge of the family's flock of chickens. Either the growing family ate a lot of chicken and eggs, or she was busy selling or bartering those items, because she had quite a flock. "I have 142 chickens," she wrote. "Our corn looks fine but a black bug eats some and some had to be replanted. We have planted about 800 hills of sweet potatoes, look real nice. Charles [Wilborn] sold the 2 young yoke oxen. We have also 18 sheep." It's clear the young couple was off to a very promising beginning.[13]

The final letter in this series was from Charles Hankamer to Fritz on June 2, 1858. In addition to news about the local economy and challenges with their crops, it also confirmed that some of the abundant wildlife reported by earlier accounts was still found in the area.

> I have killed 2 big bucks lately and one turkey; George killed 2 deer last Sunday but they were small. . . . His leg is getting well. . . . In fact, he is able to do most any kind of work. I have to help him a good deal though, his corn is not very good, the bucks [deer] and worms troubled it a good deal. It is all laid by now except a small piece which he had to plant over, and he has a good many potatoes planted. . . . [He] is at work for John White, he is building a house for two hundred dollars, he has got the frame up now and he would like for you to help him there. . . . I have been at work for Charles [probably Wilborn] for $15 a month and had all my sewing and washing done also, and can get more at other places, and there is more work than I can possibly do.

Fritz Hankamer apparently didn't find his time in Galveston to be productive, because he soon returned home, and his brief attempt at city life was the exception for the family. By the end of their first full decade in Liberty County, the members of the Stengler family had become well established as both stock raisers and farmers in this rural area. The hopes and dreams of the family members were coming to fruition, and at least part of their success was tied to what was already becoming a Texas institution: the livestock business.

Large-scale cattle operations were uncommon around the Stenglers' former home in Europe, so their expectations for Texas were probably focused more on raising crops than cows. Their decision to settle on the cattle-rich coastal prairie rather than in the budding German colonies in Central Texas opened new and unexpected opportunities for the family, and those prospects were strengthened by Mina's marriage to the son of a successful rancher. Charles Wilborn brought knowledge and experience to the family, which was invaluable to John Stengler and his sons as they acquired and built their farms and herds.

Movies and Western novels have created a stereotype of the Texas cowboy, but that image overlooks an interesting bit of local color in Southeast Texas. There, in the early days of ranching on the Saltgrass Prairie, a small group of young cattlemen said "Howdy!" with a German accent![14]

6

PLENTY OF BEEVES

I expect to get to ride the prairie now. . . . [T]he Smith heirs are agoing to begin to gather their cattle next week.

—CHARLES HANKAMER, June 2, 1858

Cowboys and ranching are such integral parts of Texas lore that it's easy to forget that 350 years before the Stenglers arrived in Liberty County, there was nary a longhorn—nor any similar cattle—to be found in all of North America. The ancestors of our present-day domestic cattle shared something in common with the Stengler family and thousands of other German Americans—they were all immigrants from Europe.[1]

The New World has long been home to bison (often called "buffalo"), but the animals we usually consider cattle didn't arrive until the Spanish brought the first of their kind to the Caribbean islands in the 1490s and to Mexico in the 1520s. A herd of more than one thousand of the animals reached the vicinity of present-day El Paso in 1598, and over the next hundred years, cattle were often included with expeditions to establish Spanish missions across Texas.[2]

By 1714 cattle were reported to be roaming "in great abundance" in eastern Texas near the Neches River, and by the time colonists from the United States and Europe began arriving in the area in the 1820s, there were countless thousands of wild cattle roaming the grasslands between Louisiana and the Rio Grande.[3]

The stage was thus set for future empires and legends, and one of the first to seize the opportunity was James Taylor White. He arrived in Southeast Texas from Louisiana by 1828 with his wife and a small herd of high-quality cattle, numbered by some accounts at no more than a dozen head. The Whites settled northeast of Galveston in what later became Chambers County and grazed their cattle on the surrounding grassland.[4]

In a strategy that later became widely practiced in the American West, White and his riders took ownership of some of the wild cattle found throughout the prairie and river bottoms. Those animals, combined with the growth of the small herd he brought from Louisiana, quickly produced numbers that would gladden the heart of any modern CEO.

James Taylor White has been described as the first cattle king in Texas, and his "Crossed W" brand, still in use by his descendants, is said by some sources to be the oldest active Texas cattle brand. A visitor to the area in 1831 reported that "although he [White] had been in the country but three or four years, he had between three and four thousand head of cattle." Another contemporary account stated that in 1842, the rancher owned "about 40,000 acres of land and about thirty thousand head of cattle."[5]

Other sources are more reserved concerning White's wealth, but whatever numbers you choose to accept, the growth from his initial small herd was very impressive. Estimates of the number of cattle throughout Texas in the mid-1800s vary widely—which is not surprising. These animals were at least semi-wild, they roamed vast areas of unfenced range at will, and they could easily hide from humans in the dense cover found in "tree islands" and in the river and bayou bottoms.[6]

Despite those challenges, one group had an incentive for confirming how many cattle, horses, hogs, and other livestock were claimed by each landowner, and their records provide perhaps the best estimate of the number of cattle in the state. Those determined individuals were the tax assessors.

The governments of both Mexico and later Texas recognized the potential revenue from livestock and tried with mixed success to tax the animals that were multiplying rapidly on the prairie. Those assets were literally "moving targets" due to the difficulties cited above, so the assessors may have relied at least partially upon the tally books kept by most individual stock raisers.

Tax rolls counted only the animals branded or otherwise marked by stockmen, so their totals did not include the unclaimed wild cattle that had thus far eluded the periodic roundups. As a result, the assessors' numbers undercounted the total number of livestock populating the

Texas countryside, a reality that makes the figures they did record even more impressive.

One history of the Texas range says taxes were paid on 382,873 cattle in the state in 1846, the year the Stenglers arrived in Liberty County. The animals continued to multiply, ranchers continued to brand as many as they could catch, assessors continued to tally them, and just fourteen years later, in 1860, the state's tax rolls listed more than 3.5 million head![7]

There may have been plenty of cattle roaming the countryside that were free for the taking, but weren't most of these animals simply too wild to be of any value to early ranchers? Opinions vary, and some historical accounts say many of these bovines were simply hunted like any other wild animal for their meat and hides. However, it is clear from those tax records that at least some of those cattle were captured, branded, and then released to roam the prairie, where they continued to reproduce at an impressive rate.[8]

This cycle of catch and release on the open range was a successful formula for building a herd at minimal cost, and it continued to be practiced in Southeast Texas for most of the nineteenth century. During Frederick Law Olmsted's 1854 trip through the area, he spent a night near the Trinity River at "one of the largest stock farms of the district," and later shared his observations in a book published in 1857.

Olmsted's visit occurred during what he called the "annual gathering and branding of the calves," and his firsthand account offers a good summary of the early cattle business in Texas. "They rode through the range, driving in the cattle that were ranging wide," Olmsted wrote. "In spite of rogues and accidents of all sorts, the increase was very rapid. Cows are never sold, except as part of a 'stock,' so that the herd enlarges in compound ratio." According to Olmsted, this single early ranching operation enjoyed an annual increase to their herd of five hundred head. He also noted the importance of periodic roundups and branding of new calves: "The law allows no property [rights] in a weaned calf unbranded, and anyone finding such places his own brand upon them, or slaughters them for his personal use."[9]

With so much livestock—and relatively few people—one might wonder if a market existed for all that beef. The answer was definitely "yes," and that brings us to another often-overlooked part of the story of Texas.

Thanks to Hollywood and books about the American West, when we hear the term "cattle drive" we tend to picture long and dusty treks from southern and Central Texas to places like Dodge City or Abilene, Kansas. Those drives are an important part of our history, but routes such as the Chisholm Trail were developed many decades after the lesser-known Opelousas Trail, which ran from southern Texas and across Louisiana to the Mississippi River.[10]

Some of the first eastbound cattle were probably moved from the vicinity of San Antonio to southern Louisiana along the Opelousas Trail in 1779, but the route saw its heyday from the 1820s until 1881, with interruptions during the Civil War. In 1860, New Orleans was the sixth-largest city in the United States, with a population of 168,675. That was a lot of mouths to feed, Texas beef was readily available, and the port of New Orleans was one of the most important in the country before the Civil War. In 1856, more than 1.1 million pounds of beef from Western sources, primarily Texas, were shipped from New Orleans to other locations around the world.[11]

During a span of sixty years, cattlemen like James Taylor White and William Duncan moved large herds along this route from Texas to Louisiana, with annual totals reaching perhaps fifty thousand head in the mid-1850s. A visitor from the East who visited the area in 1838 later wrote that White might be the "richest man in Texas," based on the combination of his large herds and the considerable fortune he had accumulated. Some sources claim that at the time of his death in 1851, James Taylor White had at least $150,000 on deposit with New Orleans banks. The colorful history of Texas includes many storied cattle ranches, including the King Ranch and the XIT, but these were all developed well after the cattlemen of Southeast Texas laid the foundation for the state's cattle empires.[12]

When the Stengler family arrived in Liberty County in 1846, White and several other large ranchers were already well established, but land and unclaimed cattle were still available for newcomers. A decade later, free-roaming cattle also caught the attention of the US Bureau of Topographic Engineers when it prepared its *Map of Texas and Part of New Mexico, Compiled Chiefly for Military Purposes*. In the area northeast of Galveston, the map includes the notations "Beef plenty" and "Prairie." Those cattle represented a valuable meat supply for military planners. When a Confederate officer made another reconnaissance of this same area in

January 1862, he confirmed that the Anahuac vicinity had "good water, good grass, and beef abundant in the neighborhood."[13]

Today we'd probably describe people like James Taylor White as ranchers, but that wasn't the label always used in the mid-1800s. The line between "farmer" and "rancher" is sometimes blurred even today, although one term or the other can be a point of pride for some individuals. During the federal census in 1850 and 1860, the occupations for adults in each household were recorded, and the results from Southeast Texas might be surprising to us today.

The 1850 census of Liberty County listed occupations for 410 individuals; 216 of them, including John Stengler, were identified as a "farmer," while only thirty-one people called themselves either a "stock raiser" or "stockman." The size of the operation was not a factor, since the two landowners shown with the largest number of cattle, James Taylor White and Solomon Barrow, were listed as "farmers."[14]

Ten years later, the 1860 census for both Liberty and Chambers counties listed *no* "stock raisers or stockmen" at all; at least for census purposes, these individuals had all become "farmers." Since tax collectors were anxious to count and include as much livestock as possible, perhaps these rural businessmen saw no reason to call attention to the fact they were primarily raising and selling cattle.[15]

The term "rancher" doesn't appear in either census, although it will be used at times in this narrative since the word is widely accepted today to describe someone whose primary occupation is the raising and sale of livestock. In contrast, the term "farmer" will be used in the following text to refer to those whose primary livelihood comes from crops (or products of livestock such as milk). The members of the extended Stengler family represented a combination of both activities, especially in their earlier years in Texas when they were gradually building up their herds.

The 1860 census does reflect the growing number of cattle being moved to markets outside the county. That census included eight men who described themselves as either a "beef driver, stock driver," or "cow driver," and the vast majority of these animals were still headed east to Louisiana and beyond. Beeves—the plural term for cattle that was in common usage at the time—had become valuable assets in this area during the years leading up to the Civil War. The Stenglers and their relatives never approached the level of success enjoyed by the White family, but this

FIGURE 6. This sketch of a Texas cattle drive is from *Harper's Weekly*, October 19, 1867. Courtesy of Kelsey Illustrator's Prints Collection, Cushing Memorial Library and Archives, Texas A&M University.

extended family was beginning to find promising opportunities in their new homeland.[16]

Cattle and hogs were not the only cash crops for the family in their early years in Texas, but those animals were certainly an important part of their livelihoods. Three marriages—Mina Krantz to Charles Wilborn, John W. Hankamer to Lurenda Smith, and Charles Hankamer to Joanah Higginbotham—added "in-laws" from families with close ties to the Texas cattle business. Their experience was invaluable for the Stengler family members as the former Germans learned the ins and outs of life in rural Texas and developed the day-to-day skills needed to run a livestock operation.

Charles Wilborn grew up on his stepfather Silas Smith's ranch, and in addition to learning to be a cattleman, he probably inherited some of his parents' livestock. By 1856, both Silas Smith and his wife—Charles Wilborn's mother—had died, and in June 1858, Wilborn's brother-in-law Charles Hankamer wrote, "I expect to get to ride the prairie now. . . . [T]he Smith heirs [including Charles Wilborn] are agoing to begin to gather their cattle next week." Those periodic roundups (or "gathers") of cattle were an essential part of life in the cattle business, and another example is found in a June 22, 1862, letter from Mina Wilborn to two of her brothers. "Charles [her husband] is in the prairie toward Beaumont," she wrote. "They are rounding up oxen and calves for branding."[17]

By the time the Civil War began, the extended Stengler family had already begun accumulating both herds and real estate. In 1861 John and Johanette Stengler owned sixty-six acres, four horses, eight milch (milk) cows, and one hundred "other cattle," along with two working oxen and thirty swine. They also had valuable help in the form of sons Fritz Hankamer (age twenty-one), George Stengler (seventeen), and John Henry Stengler (twelve).

Fritz had returned home after moving to Galveston three years earlier to test his prospects in the city, and one of the letters between Fritz and his brother Charles Hankamer on June 2, 1858, offered some firm information about the state of the cattle business for smaller stock raisers such as this family. "Mr. Frank [a distant relative in Galveston] wants to know about the price of beeves and if he could drive them from Elm Bayou to Bolivar Point in a day," Charles wrote. "Tell him he can get beeves for $12 and cows for $10, yearlings for $5.50, calves for $4.50, but it will take very near two days to drive to Bolivar Point from Elm Bayou. Tell him that beeves are very fat."[18]

This letter points to another potential market for livestock from Liberty and Chambers counties: Galveston. It was the largest city in Texas in 1850, and second only to San Antonio in 1860, with its population growing from 4,117 to 7,307 during that span of ten years. Bolivar Point, in the southwest corner of Chambers County, is on the tip of a narrow peninsula that separates Galveston Bay from the Gulf of Mexico. That point was less than three miles by water from the eastern end of Galveston Island, so the city offered solid possibilities for cattle sales.[19]

Charles Hankamer's letter also helps us understand the opportunities afforded by the livestock business for families like the Stenglers, Wilborns, and Hankamers. Undeveloped land in central Liberty County suitable for farming and grazing was selling for between fifty cents and $1.25 an acre in the late 1850s, so if beeves were selling for twelve dollars each, just ten head could provide the cash to purchase about one hundred acres of such land. With seemingly endless acres of open range also available for free grazing, it was possible to develop sizeable herds with a minimal investment in real estate.[20]

By 1861, the extended family included the four separate farms of John and Johanette Stengler, Charles and Mina Wilborn, John W. and Lurenda Hankamer, and Charles and Joanah Hankamer. In the aggregate, those related households owned 1,382 acres and their herds—according to the county tax rolls and the 1860 US census—included seventeen horses, nine working oxen, twenty-nine milk cows, 195 hogs, and nine hundred "other cattle."[21]

The ownership of that much land and livestock would have amazed their friends and family members in Europe. During this same period in Germany, many farms were not large enough to fully support the families living on them, and other sources of income were often necessary. Although some of those European farmers owned an ox, the family milk cow often did double duty when it was time to plow, and ownership of a horse to use as a draft animal was unusual. European farmland was usually passed down within a family for generations, and the possibility of acquiring land measured in hundreds of acres was beyond comprehension for the vast majority of Germans.[22]

On the final day of 1845, a family of two adults and seven children arrived in Galveston from Germany with limited funds and few personal belongings. None of them spoke English, and they had little or no background in farming and ranching. Fifteen years later they owned considerable land and livestock and had become largely self-sufficient. The Saltgrass Prairie had exceeded the Stenglers' dreams for a brighter future in Texas, and their success was due in large part to their willingness to blend their German traditions and work ethic with the pioneer skills needed to survive and prosper on the frontier. One measure of their progress was found on their dining tables, which often offered a surprising variety of items harvested from their own fields and gardens.

7

PRAIRIE HARVEST

We are sending you for New Year potato bread, eggs, sausage, beef for hash, and a piece of pork.
—JOHANETTE STENGLER, December 30, 1864

When the Stengler family arrived in Galveston in late 1845, Texas was a land of contradictions in terms of the local cuisine. The area had been touted as a place with a mild climate that allowed many kinds of crops to be grown and livestock numbers to multiply rapidly. In addition to locally grown food, merchants in Galveston were reportedly well-supplied with goods from near and far. A magazine article in 1847 observed, "The stock of merchandise on hand seems to be very large for the market, consisting of every article demanded by the necessities and luxuries of man."[1]

One might reasonably assume, then, that Texans would enjoy a variety of foods at mealtime. Unfortunately, the price of those store-bought goods limited their use by many residents, and the majority of Texans had diets that were much more mundane. Several accounts from the 1840s through the 1860s described the standard fare on most Texas tables as beef, pork, and cornbread, items that were readily available with minimal expense and effort.

A traveler in East Texas in 1854 wryly noted that meals in rural inns consisted of "pork, fresh and salt, cold corn-bread, and boiled sweet potatoes," and that they were "absolutely invariable, save that the fresh pork and sweet potatoes were frequently wanting." A wealthy traveler who stayed in a hotel in Houston in 1844 didn't fare much better. Her breakfast "consisted of tough beefsteaks . . . eggs hardly warmed through and emptied over the meat, and squirrels."[2]

Many of the new Texans transplanted from Europe were accustomed to more variety at mealtime, although not all their American-born neighbors embraced these new ideas. Frederick Law Olmsted traveled widely in Texas in 1853 and 1854 and spent a night on a ranch not far from the Stenglers' home, near the small town of Liberty. He wrote that some Texans were not impressed with the dining habits of the area's German newcomers, who were said to be "living without bacon, and eating trash, such as fresh fish and *ripe cucumbers!*"[3]

German tastes, and the extra effort required to satisfy them, may have seemed unusual to some of their Texas neighbors, but upon their arrival in Liberty County, the Stengler family quickly got to work developing their land—and improving their menus. The impressive variety of items they raised, harvested from the prairie and forest, or made themselves allowed them to become largely self-sufficient. As a result, I often describe their new home in this narrative as a "homestead" rather than a "farm" or a "ranch."

Within a few years, their meals included not only the local staples of beef, bacon, and cornbread, but also sausage and smoked meat from their hogs, cheese and butter from their milk cows, and fresh eggs from large flocks of chickens. In addition to a large quantity of corn, they also raised peaches, watermelons, figs, grapes, and both sweet and Irish potatoes. On special occasions, the family enjoyed "cake from fine flour" and potato bread, and honey from their beehives was available for use as a sweetener.[4]

Over time, they even had the chance to enjoy some snacks that would have been considered luxuries for many Texans, especially during the Civil War. On May 15, 1864, Johanette Stengler wrote to two of her sons, who were then stationed not far from home. "[Since] I have such a good opportunity, I will send you a bottle of honey, also butter and popcorn."

In addition to their homegrown provisions, the family quickly learned to take advantage of the area's abundant fish and wild game. Several family letters mentioned successful hunts for deer and wild turkey, and during an assignment at Galveston during the war, at least one of the brothers spent much of his free time fishing. In a May 1863 letter to his sister, Mina Wilborn, Fritz Hankamer reported on that activity and confirmed that these German-born Texans did have some unusual tastes that occasionally went well beyond "fresh fish and ripe cucumbers."[5]

Dear sister, you wrote to me that if I catch any eels to save [them]. I will if I can catch any, but I don't know whether they will bite here or not, but I have catched 3 or 4 here at the wharf and there is a chance to catch more, I will try and do the best I can. If it was fish I would be able to send more than you would know what to do with, for I catch as many as I can carry every time I go fishing, and that is every day.[6]

While serving in the army, the young men were doing their own cooking, and it didn't take them long to ask for some advice from their older sister, Mina. She responded with some tips for upgrading their biscuits, using the limited ingredients they had in camp. "Scald a little cornmeal, add salt, and then finish it with cold water," Mina suggested. "Let it stand for 1½ or 2 days, stir it good. Then make your biscuits with the cornmeal mixture, add a little baking soda, then they will turn out much lighter and more digestible. Then you take a little of that dough and save it to start your next bread dough."[7]

At times during the war, the young men were able to make some short visits home. In addition to the welcome meals, these trips often provided a chance to take some prized items back to camp. In August 1862, Mina Wilborn encouraged her brother Fritz Hankamer to request leave with the comment, "I wish you were here. Our peaches are ripe." That was reason enough for Fritz to ask for some time off, and his brothers also benefitted from his trip. Fritz wrote back to Mina after he returned to camp and assured her, "I arrived here at about sundown last Thursday, the boys were all glad to see me, and the peaches for them went like hotcakes."[8]

The ability to grow much of their food was a major advantage for these new Texans, but family letters also remind us that agriculture is an activity fraught with many perils. "We had a little rain but not enough. Everything is dry including my garden," Mina Wilborn wrote in June 1862. "The corn was so nice but if it does not rain soon, we will not get any. . . . Our Irish potatoes did not turn out so well this spring."[9]

Johanette Stengler echoed similar comments in July 1862, noting the peaches "have not grown much . . . and the figs do not ripen at all. A few of the blue ones were ripe but that has been quite a while. The white ones fall off and are not ripe." Rain at the proper time was key, and at least one crop was doing better later in 1862. "The watermelons are beginning to ripen. They can grow better now because it rains," Johanette noted.[10]

Extremes in the weather have always been a threat to farmers everywhere. An unusual cold snap in March 1865 prompted Johanette to tell Fritz, "We had ice last week. I am afraid we will not get any fruit because the trees were in bloom already." The spring of 1865 was shaping up to be a tough year in the fields as well. John Stengler reported in April that his corn had been planted but failed to come up due to a prolonged period of heavy rain, and the crop would have to be replanted.[11]

Problems with the weather were certainly no respecters of persons. The wife of a prosperous plantation owner in Liberty County grew a large garden to help cope with shortages during the war—but to no avail. On May 19, 1863, she noted, "3 weeks ago last Saturday a hailstorm passed through a portion of this county, the hail was nearly as large as an egg. I had a very pretty garden, but it destroyed every vegetable in it, and now I am without any vegetables at all."[12]

Honey from their own hives was a source of pleasure as well as nutrition for the Stengler household, but even that crop was never assured. In September 1864, Johanette Stengler sadly told Fritz, "We have only 4 hives left. The others all died. John made room at the shed and put them there. We can pour water there and maybe keep them alive."[13]

Despite those challenges, good years outnumbered the bad for these families. Johanette Stengler sent a promising report to her son Fritz on September 15, 1863, noting, "We got 10 loads of corn and it is very nice corn, and our potatoes are very nice. We cook some every day. . . . Come home soon and I will gladly mash potatoes and I also have butter and cheese and honey. I have also put honey in cans for you."

The Civil War years brought added challenges for all Texans, but the Stengler family's ability to continue to grow virtually all of their food put them in a much better position than many others across the South. Even when their sons were away in the army, the Stenglers occasionally sent food from home to benefit the young soldiers. A letter from Johanette Stengler on December 30, 1864, had Fritz Hankamer eagerly awaiting the arrival of a package.

"Dear son, I will send you something for New Year," Johanette wrote. "We are sending you for New Year potato bread, eggs, sausage, beef for hash, and a piece of pork. When you come you may have more." Another letter from John Stengler to one of his sons in February 1865 anticipated an upcoming visit, and he undoubtedly whetted Fritz's appetite when he wrote, "Your mother is making biscuits for you."[14]

All in all, written accounts tell us the family ate pretty well on their farms, and they also learned to produce other items that greatly improved daily life. In a letter written in late December 1862, Mina Wilborn mentioned her pleasure that she had "a new ash pile." Her comment offers a good illustration of the mindset—and the frontier skills—that allowed households to be largely self-sufficient. Mina's renewed supply of wood ashes allowed her to "make as much soap as I want to when I have enough fat and ashes." So-called "lye soap" was made using two ingredients that were readily available on most farms: wood ashes and animal fat.

Johanette Stengler mentioned one source of that fat in a September 1863 letter: "We also slaughtered an ox. I got much tallow. He was very fat."[15] Having an abundance of both ashes and fat was a blessing but turning it into soap was a labor-intensive task. Ashes from fireplaces were cooled and collected in a wooden hopper or a barrel with small holes cut in the bottom. The barrel or hopper was raised high enough off the ground to allow a large pan to be placed underneath, and water was poured through the ashes. The water leached the lye from the ashes as it seeped out the bottom of the barrel and into the pan.

After additional steps, this lye solution was heated and mixed in a large pot with the fat until it began to thicken. Finally, this substance was poured into an open-top container to cool and harden. The resulting soap was used for cleaning everything from people to clothing.

In addition to its use in soap, tallow was prized as the key component in candles, which were important sources of lighting in a time when lamp oil or beeswax candles were expensive or hard to find. These candles were made by repeatedly dipping a string (to serve as a wick) into a container of melted tallow, or by pouring the melted tallow into a mold that already contained the wick.[16]

Although the majority of the countryside in coastal Southeast Texas was either open grassland or marshes, the Saltgrass Prairie was crisscrossed by a network of creeks, bayous, and several major rivers. The banks of those waterways, along with scattered tree "islands" that dotted the prairie, included dense stands of timber and shrubs, and those wooded areas provided other useful items for industrious settlers.

The Stenglers watched, listened, and learned skills that had been passed down through generations of American pioneers, and then they put them to good use. Letters from Johanette Stengler and her daughter,

Mina Wilborn, mentioned tree bark as a source of natural dyes for cloth, and a later chapter will discuss a variety of home remedies for everything from toothaches and stomach disorders to chills and fevers. Woodlands also provided some supplements to cultivated crops, and a diary kept for several years by John W. Hankamer refers to a trip into the forest to "gather Chincapins." The Chinkapin (or Chinquapin) Oak is also known as Swamp Chestnut Oak, and its acorns can be roasted and eaten.[17]

The low-lying marshes and stream banks also supported dense thickets of cane and low-growing plants called palmettos. Fibers from the fan-shaped leaves of the palmetto could be used for weaving a variety of items, including baskets and fans, and thin strips cut from younger fronds were used for lashings or cords. "Straw" hats made from palmetto fronds were practical for the hot, humid coastal climate, and activities such as "plaited on my hat" are listed several dozen times in John W. Hankamer's diary. Both John W. and Fritz Hankamer used their free time to become very skilled at making this headgear for themselves and family members, and for sale to others.[18]

During one three-month period in 1864, John W. completed at least seventeen such hats, and the enterprise was occasionally a good source of extra income. He sold one of his handwoven hats to Cpl. Jacob Beaumont of Company E for seventy-five dollars in paper currency and swapped another to H. V. Barrow for five pounds of tobacco. His brother Fritz topped that when a woman bought one of his hats, and "paid 2½ dollars in gold coin for it."[19]

Uses of palmetto and cane weren't limited to hats and baskets, and John W. Hankamer's diary also includes several dozen entries about making another surprising item: "sleighs." Those diary notations raise obvious questions for modern readers since snow was rare in coastal Texas. In this case, the term referred to a key component in looms that were used to weave cloth, and the word was spelled variously as "slay, sley, or sleigh."[20]

Also known as a "weaver's reed," this variety of sleigh included hundreds of thin slats held in place by a wooden frame. Individual threads were passed between these small slats in the sleigh as they were fed into the loom. Commercially made weaver's reeds normally used metal slats, materials that were expensive or simply unavailable in rural Texas, especially in the early 1860s.

FIGURE 7. A handmade weaver's reed, or "sleigh." Courtesy of Cassie Dickson.

In the case of John W. Hankamer's sleighs, all the components were made of hand-shaved pieces of river cane and lashed into place with "cords," which may have been woven from the fibers of palmetto fronds. During the Civil War, virtually the only cloth available for civilian use in Texas was woven on looms that were made locally, and the several dozen sleighs John W. crafted from natural materials were invaluable for both his family and neighbors. Figure 7 shows a handmade sleigh from this general period.

Whether relying on homemade candles and cloth, butter and honey, or homegrown fruit and vegetables, this extended family became largely self-sufficient through a combination of frugality, ingenuity, and hard work. Their ability to provide for many of their own needs was important for both financial and practical reasons. It was a long—and sometimes difficult—trip to the nearest store.

8

RIVERS, ROADS, AND RAILROADS

We have had plenty of rain so . . . it is hard to get anywhere, I had to swim almost today to get down here to Anahuac. . . . [T]he roads are very bad.

—CHARLES HANKAMER, May 14, 1858

A trip to town in the mid-1800s to collect mail and supplies was an experience that could range from an adventure to an ordeal for residents of Southeast Texas. Roads in those years were often little more than poorly defined paths, bridges were scarce, and periods of wet weather turned primitive routes into quagmires. Despite those difficulties, travel was necessary at times to obtain mail and items that could not be grown or made at home.

Travel near the Texas coast was often complicated during wet weather by the low-lying, poorly drained terrain. A letter from Charles Hankamer in May 1858 described the sixteen-mile round trip between the Stengler home and the village of Anahuac, where boats delivered mail and supplies from Galveston. "We have had plenty of rain so . . . it is hard to get anywhere," Charles wrote. "I had to swim almost today to get down here to Anahuac. . . . [T]he roads are very bad."[1]

Several published accounts mention the challenges for travelers in Southeast Texas in the 1800s. When Frederick Law Olmsted journeyed from Houston to Louisiana in 1854, he passed through the town of Liberty, not far from the Stenglers' home. Olmsted wrote:

> No wheeled vehicles traverse the region. In two weeks' ride we met with but one specimen, the "mud-cart" of a grocery peddler, whose wheels were broad blocks sawn from a log. No other road is known than the one by which cattle are driven to the New Orleans market,

and this one so imperfectly, that we added probably fifty stray miles to our distance, by following indistinct paths and erroneous information.[2]

One solution for travel in this coastal region was to use water transportation whenever possible. For the Stenglers and their neighbors, it was about forty miles by boat from Anahuac across Trinity Bay and Galveston Bay to Galveston's well-stocked stores. Local officials, businessmen, and residents in Liberty County also had dreams of regular steamboat service to and from Galveston via the bays and the Trinity River. In theory, the Trinity offered a water route deep into Texas, since the river runs inland for hundreds of miles to the then-young town of Dallas and even beyond.

There were many attempts to establish steamboat service on the Trinity River during the mid-1800s, with mixed success. The combination of sandbars, logjams, and unpredictable water levels made travel on all Texas rivers a chancy business, and maintaining reliable schedules was a challenge. Due to the Trinity's serpentine course, it was sixty-six miles by water from the town of Liberty to the river's mouth, more than twice the straight-line distance, and the cost of work on the channel to make it a viable year-round route into the state's interior was a major hurdle.[3]

Given those circumstances, it was understandable that some Texans looked to railroads as a better solution to their transportation needs. The flat to gently rolling terrain in much of the state posed relatively few physical barriers to rail construction, and government officials had large tracts of undeveloped public land to offer as incentives to potential developers.

Despite those lures, the Lone Star State was late to join this technological revolution. By 1850, there were about nine thousand miles of completed track in the US, but only a tiny fraction of them were located west of the Mississippi River—and none were in Texas. A decade later, the nation had over thirty thousand miles of rail lines, but the Lone Star State could claim only about 470 miles of track in a fragmented system operated by competing companies.

One of the reasons for the slow start was the lack of a critical resource—money. Despite the incentive of loans and free public land, the state's relatively small population and distance from potential investors in the eastern US and abroad were barriers to financing. Furthermore, not all

Texans were enthusiastic about the presence of these noisy contraptions that belched smoke and sparks as they chugged across the countryside.[4]

Texas finally saw its first operating railroad in 1853, when the Buffalo Bayou, Brazos, and Colorado Railway began offering service over a modest twenty miles of track between Harrisburg (on the Buffalo Bayou southeast of Houston) and Stafford (southwest of Houston). By December 1855 the line had reached the east bank of the Brazos River, and within eight years Houston had become the hub of Texas rail activity, with five companies operating in or near the city.[5]

Those modest entries into the railroad era were at least a start, although they received mixed reviews from passengers. In 1859, the young wife of a US Army officer was traveling from Austin to Houston, and her trip included a short leg on the Buffalo Bayou, Brazos, and Colorado Railway. Lydia Lane's journey required several grueling days of riding in either stagecoaches or open wagons in bitterly cold weather. Based on her terse comment, she was not overly impressed by the part of her trip spent on the train. "We had a ride on the only railroad at that time in Texas," she wrote. "The best thing I can say of it was, it was very short."[6]

Another written account of the period suggests train travel may have been more comfortable than the rough ride in a stagecoach, but even those advantages were sometimes questionable. Arthur Fremantle, an Englishman who wrote about his travels in Texas in the spring of 1863, offered his description of a short train trip west of Houston. He noted the seats in the two passenger cars "are comfortably stuffed, and seemed luxurious after the stage," but the start of the train ride left a lot to be desired.

> Before starting, the engine gives two preliminary snorts, which, with a yell from the official of "all aboard," warn the passengers to hold on; for they are closely followed by a tremendous jerk, which sets the cars in motion. Every passenger is allowed to use his own discretion about breaking his arm, neck, or leg, without interference by the railway officials.[7]

Schedules were rather flexible in the early days of Texas railroads, and train travel in those years was sometimes literally a "hands-on experience" for passengers. According to an 1862 report from a Houston newspaper, "The trains are punctual in leaving, but the time of their arrival varies occasionally, especially when the cars 'get off the track,' and there are not passengers enough to put them on again." That comment about passengers helping put a derailed train car back on the track makes more sense today if we know that some of the early passenger cars were based on designs for city streetcars, were relatively lightweight, and had only four wheels, which made them "difficult to keep on the tracks."[8]

The problem of cars "getting off the track" was often the result of two other factors common to early Texas railroads: poor roadbed construction and soggy soil, especially in areas near the coast. One example was reported by the Houston *Weekly Telegraph*, on February 12, 1861. Two cars of the Texas and New Orleans Railroad (T&NO) were filled with passengers when they ran off the track between Liberty and Houston, "completely upsetting in a deep water-hole. Fortunately, no damage was done," the paper reported, "except the frightening of the ladies and the complete drenching of the passengers."

Reliability notwithstanding, the fact that there was a railroad at all in this area in 1861 was still a source of some amazement in Southeast Texas. The story about this accident in the Houston newspaper concluded with the following observation: "Ten years ago, who would have imagined there would ever be a railroad accident in Liberty?"[9]

The railroad's route through the small town of Liberty wasn't by happenstance. In May 1858, as the new line's route between Houston and Beaumont was being determined, the town fathers began a vigorous courtship of officials with the Sabine and Galveston Bay Railroad and Lumber Company. Originally chartered in 1856 to connect the town of Orange with the Galveston Bay area by rail, this line changed its name in December 1859 to the Texas and New Orleans Railroad. Local leaders offered to donate to the railroad all the "unsold or unappropriated land" owned by the town on the west side of the Trinity River, which totaled more than nine thousand acres. Perhaps it helped their cause; within two years, trains were making stops at the depot in Liberty.[10]

The trains did offer at least the potential for speedier travel between key locations in Southeast Texas. On July 1, 1861, a railroad official proudly reported the T&NO had been extended to Orange, near the Texas-Louisiana border, and "is now in running order." As a result, "Galveston can readily be reached from Orange in ten hours." Despite its promising name and good intentions, such speedy travel was rarely if ever realized in the early years of this railroad. The Civil War ended any attempts to

FIGURE 8. This sketch of a train crossing Buffalo Bayou in Houston dates from shortly after the Civil War. It was included on a map of Houston published by W. E. Wood in 1869. Courtesy Houston Public Library, Houston History Research Center, image MSS430-0017.

extend its tracks into Louisiana, and the line was plagued by a host of challenges ranging from faulty construction and washed-out bridges to a lack of tools and skilled manpower to keep the equipment running.[11]

Some of those rails had been "laid temporarily for military transportation and need finishing," which was a polite way of saying the work had been rushed and the roadbed had been poorly built across ground that was often marshy. At times, the tracks were reported to be under the mud or water in multiple locations. Given these conditions, it's not surprising the line had problems with the cars getting off the tracks at frequent intervals.[12]

One Texan who traveled from Beaumont to Houston in March 1862 via the Texas and New Orleans Railroad was not impressed with his experience, which he later described in a letter to a Houston newspaper: "The trip to Beaumont hardly need be described to your readers. Everybody knows this is the roughest and most unpleasant Railroad in the world; it being not at all uncommon for the axles to be plowing through the water, if not occasionally slightly pressing the mud."[13]

A family traveling from Beaumont to Houston in January 1863 had a similar experience, with the wife offering this account: "After a long day's snail-like progress, the train stopping every few miles to take on a load of wet and soggy wood, and every few minutes to get up steam, slipping, sliding, and sometimes refusing point-blank to budge until all the men got out in the mud and slush to 'giv her a shove,' we reached Houston after midnight, tired, cold, hungry, and cross."[14]

Despite its shortcomings, the T&NO provided a valuable service for the residents of Southeast Texas, and Stengler family members used it at times for both travel and shipment of goods. A letter from Johanette Stengler to her son Fritz in October 1862 offers an example during her sons' first year away from home during the Civil War. Winter was approaching, and the train was the most convenient way to send winter clothes to the boys. "I think it best to put it all in a trunk and send it by railroad," Johanette Stengler wrote. "Your father wants to bring it by horse but it is too much for one horse."[15]

The trains also made it possible for the men to make occasional trips home from their various army camps in Southeast Texas during the Civil War. A stop on the T&NO known as Carter's Station was near the present town of Devers, Texas, about twelve miles from the family's homes near Crackersneck. An entry in John W. Hankamer's diary for July 18, 1864, offers an example of trips to catch the train: "Started about 9 o'clock from home, my wife went with me to Carter's Station, got there a little after eleven o'clock A.M. . . . [and] started on train about 12½ [12:30 p.m.], got to camp."[16]

That two-hour journey to the station with his wife was made by either horse or wagon, but most trips between the station and home were on foot—and took several hours longer. Soldiers returning from leave had to be sure they didn't miss their train, but the cars themselves were less dependable. At the end of another visit home, John W. Hankamer arrived at Carter's Station at 10:30 a.m., expecting the train to arrive around midday. His diary noted the "cars came at about 7 P.M., had blowed out a cylinder at Cedar Bayou."[17]

Such delays were common but not usually dangerous, although some incidents involved a catastrophe. The youngest soldier in the family, sixteen-year-old John Henry Stengler, served in a state militia unit later in the war and spent several weeks helping guard the telegraph line near Carter's Station. That assignment gave him good access to the local grapevine, and he shared an example of "breaking news" in a letter to his brothers on December 2, 1863. "I know some more news," he wrote. "A locomotive busted up two miles from here between here and Sour Lake Station." The engineer and another man were killed, "and there was a whole regiment of soldiers on the train, but none of them were hurt."

An army officer who was on the train, Capt. Julius von Bose, wrote an account of the incident that was published in the *New Braunfels Zeitung* on December 4, 1863. A summary of his story provides an example of the perils of Texas train travel in those years.

About twenty-five miles into their trip from Beaumont to Houston, the last car on the train ran off the rails. An explosion in the locomotive followed, killing the engineer and fireman. Hours later, a replacement locomotive arrived, and as the train continued toward Houston in the dark, word suddenly began spreading from car to car that there was a fire on the train. Captain von Bose wryly noted, "When it finally developed that the ammunition car was the victim [of the fire], there was a great exit from all cars."

That crisis was resolved, and the train eventually reached the San Jacinto River, where the locomotive lacked the power to climb a slight grade. After two failed attempts, half of the cars were uncoupled and the engine made two trips to pull all the cars "over the hump." The train was then reassembled, and the hundred-mile trip to Houston was finally completed about twenty-four hours after it began. By that time Captain von Bose had had his fill of train travel. He closed his account with the succinct comment, "Where we now go we do not know, but if only we could go afoot it would not matter."[18]

Two other early Texas railroads allowed residents of Liberty County to avoid "going afoot" for some trips. One was the Galveston, Houston, and Henderson Railroad Company, which was chartered in 1853 to build a line from Galveston through Houston and on to Henderson in Northeast Texas. It took six years to lay about forty miles of track to connect downtown Houston with Virginia Point, which was on the mainland just north of Galveston. A year later, in February 1860, a ten thousand-foot-long trestle was completed between Virginia Point and Galveston Island, giving Texas' most important port its first direct land connection with the rest of the state.[19]

A second Southeast Texas railroad that played a role in the Stenglers' story was the Eastern Texas Railroad, chartered in 1860 to run for nearly two hundred miles from the small port at Sabine Pass northward to Beaumont and then into Northeast Texas. By September 1861, only about two miles of track were needed to complete a link with the Texas and New Orleans Railroad at Beaumont. That connection would create a rail network joining Houston, Galveston, and other key locations in the state with the port at Sabine Pass, but several sources say it was not completed during the Civil War.

By October 1862, the rail connection from Sabine Pass to Beaumont was definitely out of service due to extensive damage in several locations. That was still the case in early 1863 when at least two of the Hankamer and Stengler boys spent several weeks helping make repairs to this railroad. Those losses were the direct result of long-simmering political disputes that finally boiled over in April 1861. It would take some time for the news to reach rural Southeast Texas, but the lives of the Stengler family—and those of every other American—would be forever changed by events that unfolded on a spring morning in the distant state of South Carolina.[20]

9

UPHEAVAL

The Moss Bluff Rebels . . . are now ready at a moment's notice to march in a body . . . to any point between their threatened homes & the coast.
— CAPT. ASHLEY SPAIGHT, March 10, 1862

In the predawn hours of April 12, 1861, a shot fired from a ten-inch mortar burst over Fort Sumter, located in Charleston Harbor. For the next thirty-four hours, Union and Confederate forces exchanged artillery fire until federal forces at Fort Sumter finally surrendered. The American Civil War was underway, and its effects would soon be felt across the country—including in far-away Liberty County, Texas.

Even before those shots were fired, Texas had already become the seventh state to withdraw from the Union. Chambers County residents voted 109 to 26 for secession; in Liberty County, the vote was even more decisive: 422 to 10. Those results aren't surprising, based on the background of area residents. The 1860 US census showed nearly nine out of ten inhabitants of the two counties were born in states that chose to join the Confederate States of America (CSA). The remaining minority without Southern roots were almost equally divided between newcomers who were natives of Union states and those, like the Stengler family, who had been born outside the United States.[1]

We don't have any specific written records of the family members' sentiments concerning secession, but those election results left little doubt about the views of their neighbors. Letters from later in the war do tell us the Stenglers' concerns were focused on protecting their homes and families. In April 1863, John W. Hankamer wrote to his sister, Mina, from his army camp near Galveston and told her if they could "drive the enemy off our soil there will be no more invasion. . . . [I]f our families can't be supported this war is bound to cease, for what else do we fight for if it is not them."[2]

Other than a naval blockade of Galveston, the direct impacts of secession on Texas were slow to develop. During the remainder of 1861 and early 1862, battles were fought in distant places with names like Manassas, Virginia; Fort Hatteras, North Carolina; and Fort Donelson, Tennessee. Given the ties by birth of most adult Texans to the Deep South, some men quickly volunteered for service in the Confederacy, anxious to defend their ancestral homes.

Other Texans bided their time, believing the war would be a short one. Much has been written about the motivation of those who eventually decided to fight for either the North or South, but for many who signed up from Southeast Texas, a key factor was a desire to protect their homes from a possible invasion by Union forces. The port city of Galveston was the state's primary connection for commerce with the rest of the world, making it a prime target for a Union attack.[3]

Less than two weeks after the start of hostilities at Fort Sumter, a group of Galveston men began keeping a round-the-clock watch for any threat from the Union Navy. For their observation post, they chose a cupola on the roof of the three-story Hendley Building, the tallest commercial structure on the pancake-flat island. Their perch offered a good view of both the Gulf of Mexico and Galveston Bay, and for nearly three months the lookouts' primary challenges were fighting boredom and mosquitos.

All was quiet until shortly before noon on July 2, 1861, when a steamer was sighted approaching Galveston from the southwest. The Union vessel, ironically named the USS *South Carolina*, dropped anchor just outside the sandbar at the entrance to the harbor at 1:10 p.m. It was joined by a second vessel, and a pilot boat was sent from the port to investigate. A notation in the lookout's log at 3:00 p.m. noted, "Both of these vessels are armed, and are a portion of the blockading squadron so long anticipated." The blockade of Galveston was underway.[4]

A second area of concern for Texans was located about one hundred miles up the coast from Galveston near the Texas-Louisiana border. Sabine Pass provided water access into the interior of both states via the Sabine and Neches rivers, and a local militia company called the Sabine Pass Guard was raised in the spring of 1861 to defend the area. A small dirt and timber fort was constructed near the coastal port that also bore the name "Sabine Pass." These troops patrolled the beaches along the Gulf of Mexico, drilled on foot and horseback, and practiced with their small collection of artillery pieces, but for the next year they saw no direct threats to their territory. Like those lookouts atop the Hendley Building in Galveston, their greatest challenges were bugs and boredom.[5]

About fifty miles north of Galveston, a lawyer from Alabama who had settled near the small community of Moss Bluff began efforts to raise a cavalry unit from Liberty and Chambers counties. It took Ashley Spaight about nine months, until the spring of 1862, but he eventually recruited a company of eighty-four men. They were dubbed the Moss Bluff Rebels.[6]

Spaight's recruiting efforts were likely aided by rumors—and the eventual passage—of a conscription law by the Confederate States Congress in April 1862. Under its provisions, most white males from eighteen to thirty-five years of age were subject to military service. In September 1862, this upper age limit was raised to forty-five, and in February 1864, the draft was extended to ages ranging from seventeen to fifty.[7]

The prospect of being drafted into a CSA unit that might be sent to fight in distant states provided a definite incentive for some men to volunteer, which allowed them to choose their outfit and type of service. Ashley Spaight's Moss Bluff Rebels offered an appealing option—it was formed as a cavalry unit. It's been said that most Texans in the 1800s would much rather ride a horse than walk, even if the trip was a very short one, so it's not surprising that many potential soldiers from the Lone Star State had a distinct preference for serving in the cavalry. Lt. Col. Arthur J. Fremantle was a British military officer who spent several months traveling in North America during the war, and he later commented, "At the outbreak of the war it was found very difficult to raise infantry in Texas, as no Texan walks a yard if he can help it."[8]

This attitude is clearly illustrated in a July 22, 1861, letter from Gen. N. P. West of the 2nd Brigade, Texas Militia, to Gen. William Byrd, adjutant general for the State of Texas. General West cited "some difficulties" in getting men enrolled in his units in Southeast Texas, noting, "As far as I can learn, the cause is the unwillingness of some of the people to serve as Infantry, deeming the Cavalry more honorable, and foolishly, less laborious."[9]

A year later, when CSA leaders were relying on both a call for volunteers and the impending draft to raise additional troops, Capt. Ashley Spaight of the Moss Bluff Rebels wrote to Col. J. Y. Dashiell, adjutant general for the State of Texas. Captain Spaight expressed his concerns about the possibility his men might be expected to serve as infantry rather than cavalry if his unit was incorporated into the CSA Army. His letter was written on March 10, 1862; the underlined text in the following excerpt also appears in Captain Spaight's handwritten original.

> On behalf of my company, the "Moss Bluff Rebels," I desire information in reference to the late Declaration of the Governor calling for 15,000 men.
>
> My company was organized in August last [1861] as Mounted Rifles under the Act of 1858 and reported to Gen. Hebert for coast defense in case of invasion. It has provided itself with sabers and shotguns, and has attained a considerable proficiency in <u>Cavalry Drill,</u> whilst the <u>Infantry Drill</u> has of course been neglected, except so far as it was necessary for mounted rifles.
>
> The question is does the call of the Governor embrace Infantry only, and if so, will this Cavalry company be required to give up its present organization to march <u>as Infantry,</u> or be disbanded? If both branches of this inquiry be answered in the affirmative, I respectfully submit that it will work a great hardship on the company by depriving it of eight months of diligent drill, to placing it in a service with which it is entirely unacquainted, to say nothing of the privilege of selecting the kind of service it prefers, which is expressly granted by the Act of 1858.

Captain Spaight's letter also offered confirmation that the men in his unit had signed up for the specific purpose of defending their homes and nearby coastal areas from invasion; they had no interest in more distant fights. He continued:

> I desire to propose one other question in this connection, which you will perceive by the following fact, is of immense importance to this particular community. My company embraces almost the entire male population of a large district of Liberty County, and a part of Chambers. We are within twelve or fifteen hours' march of any point of the coast between Sabine Pass & Galveston, & are on the tidewaters of the Trinity. . . .

Now the Governor under the late Militia Law has the authority to order us out <u>as a whole Company</u>. The question is whether the Governor under the circumstances detailed above would not consider that the public interest required that a portion of this company should be left behind as a home guard, but subject to be ordered out in case of emergency to limit the ravage of the enemy on the coast.

Nine-tenths of the company being men of family and a large proportion dependent on their individual exertion for the support of their families (hence the report to Gen. Hebert for coastal defense in case of invasion, and not for enlistment for the war) many of these men would leave with great reluctance & many misgivings, unless a sufficient protection be left behind.

I beg to be understood in a matter of much importance. The "Moss Bluff Rebels" were organized for use and not for show, & have always been and are now ready at a moment's notice to march in a body without leaving one behind to any point between their threatened homes & the coast.

Having full confidence that the Governor will take such action in the premises as the public interests, in his judgment may require, I must beg a prompt reply, as the final determination of the company is suspended upon it.

Your obt svt

A. W. Spaight

Captain of the "M.B.R."[10]

Captain Spaight and his men were apparently satisfied with the reply because on April 17, 1862, he sent another letter to the adjutant general of Texas. "I hereby tender for the Confederate Service for three years or the [duration of the] war the cavalry company known as the 'Moss Bluff Rebels,'" Spaight wrote. "Said company numbers eighty-four men, and is armed, equipped, and supplied with horses."[11]

With a military draft looming in the spring of 1862, service with Ashley Spaight's cavalry company looked increasingly appealing to the young men in the extended Stengler family. On March 26, 1862, Charles, John W., and Frederick ("Fritz") Hankamer and George Stengler signed up for Captain Spaight's cavalry company. Joining them in the unit were close family friend and fellow German immigrant Christian Bingle and Silas Smith Jr., Charles Wilborn's half-brother and thus Mina Wilborn's brother-in-law.[12]

They reported for duty on April 21, 1862, and in the months ahead, some of them would travel on foot, horseback, and briefly aboard a cottonclad gunboat. They would while away endless hours of boredom and loneliness, endure debilitating heat and swarms of mosquitoes, experience day after day of numbing winter travel across frozen swamps and icy rivers, and occasionally face hostile fire from their adversaries. Ready or not, these farmers and cattlemen from the Saltgrass Prairie were now cavalrymen.

10

MUSTERED

This muster roll exhibits truly the number and names of the men mustered into the Confederate States service.
—A. W. SPAIGHT, captain of the Moss Bluff Rebels,
April 21, 1862

The small community of Moss Bluff, located along the Trinity River in Liberty County, was not a place that normally attracted dozens of visitors at the same time. April 21, 1862, was not, however, an ordinary day. The area was home to Capt. Ashley W. Spaight, organizer of the Texas cavalry company known as the Moss Bluff Rebels, and it was time for the unit to be officially mustered into service for the Confederate States of America.[1]

The date also held special significance across the entire state. Twenty-six years earlier, on April 21, 1836, a makeshift army of Texans led by Sam Houston defeated a better-trained Mexican force under General Santa Anna. That victory, along the San Jacinto River just east of present-day Houston, secured Texas' independence from Mexico, and it occurred less than fifty miles from the muster ceremony at Moss Bluff.

Not unlike Sam Houston's volunteer army in that earlier conflict, Spaight's company and similar units being formed throughout the Confederacy were homegrown affairs. As members of a cavalry company, the men of Spaight's unit were expected to furnish their own horses and associated gear, for which they would receive payment of forty cents a day. Having men bring their own horses simplified life for CSA leaders, and they believed the men would take better care of their personal horses than animals issued by the government.[2]

The Confederacy was woefully short on weapons as well, as illustrated by a May 7, 1861, memorandum from William F. Austin, CSA adjutant and inspector in Galveston. He noted with understandable concern, "The available force embraced in the military command of Galveston amounts to twenty-five hundred men and upwards. Fully fifteen hundred of these men are without arms."[3]

Those dismal numbers in Galveston were actually much better than the situation across the entire Confederacy. CSA Gen. Joseph E. Johnston later wrote, "The Confederate States began the war with one hundred and twenty thousand arms of obsolete models and seven hundred of the recently adopted 'rifled muskets.'" These numbers would have been adequate to provide arms to between 10 and 15 percent of the men who eventually served in the CSA.[4]

Faced with this problem, leaders in the South tried a variety of methods to arm their troops. Citizens were urged to turn over their personal weapons to state ordnance officers, and in September 1861, CSA Gen. Albert Sidney Johnston urged men signing up for duty to "bring into the field every effective arm in their possession. Rifles and shotguns, double-barreled guns in particular, can be made effective weapons in the hands of your skilled horsemen."[5]

Military officials were soon given the authority to reimburse soldiers who provided their own firearms. According to CSA regulations, "Each man who may hereafter be mustered into service, and who shall arm himself with a musket, shot-gun, rifle, or carbine, accepted as an efficient weapon, shall be paid the value thereof, to be ascertained by the mustering officer." If the soldier didn't want to sell his weapon, he was entitled to retain ownership and receive a dollar a month from the army for its use.[6]

One obvious problem with asking individual soldiers to provide their own weapons was the lack of uniformity in the types of firearms carried in a unit. The roster of a company formed in January 1862 in Newton County, Texas, shows the men reported for duty with "33 rifles, 11 double-barrel shotguns, 4 single-shot guns, 1 musket, 2 revolvers, and 4 pistols." That made the task of keeping the troops supplied with the proper ammunition for their individual weapons very difficult.[7]

Supply problems or not, most soldiers had their preferences for the type of weapon they would carry, and because cavalry troops needed something that could be easily reloaded while mounted on a horse, there were valid reasons for some of those opinions. Firearms such as revolvers that could fire more than one time before reloading were in high demand, but they were not available in great numbers in the rural South at the start of the conflict.[8]

William Duncan served as the commanding officer for what would soon be designated Company F in Spaight's Battalion for almost all of the war, and on October 7, 1862, he wrote to his wife from the unit's camp south of Beaumont. He had asked relatives back home in Liberty to find a particular type of weapon for him, and he was pleased with the results. "I am very glad to hear your Uncle Edward has got me a Six Shooter," he said. "I would not take a thousand dollars for it if we were to get in a fight."[9]

It's unlikely any of the Hankamer or Stengler brothers owned—or could afford—any revolvers, but in accordance with CSA instructions, they did report for the mustering-in ceremony duly equipped with horses, tack, and weapons. Archival records for this particular CSA unit are unusually complete, and along with family documents, offer considerable information about all four young men at the time they reported for duty. Some of those details are included here to help readers form a mental picture of these key characters in this narrative.[10]

At age twenty-eight, John W. Hankamer was the oldest of the brothers and had recently become a father. He had been married to Lurenda (Smith) for about four years, and their son George William was born only ten days before his father reported for duty. John W. Hankamer was five feet, seven inches tall and had a fair complexion, hazel eyes, and brown hair.

Charles Hankamer, age twenty-six, married Joanah (Higginbotham) in 1859, and he was also a father. The couple had two small children at home when he reported for the army—a daughter, Ellen (twenty-one months old), and a new son, Frederick (four months old). Charles was five feet, eight inches tall, with a fair complexion and dark eyes and hair.

The other two brothers were both single and living on their parents' farm when they joined the army. Fritz Hankamer was twenty-four years old and was the tallest of the four brothers at five feet nine. He shared his siblings' fair complexion and had grey eyes and brown hair. George Stengler was the youngest of the group at age twenty; he was five feet, six and three-fourths inches tall, with a light complexion and dark eyes and hair.

The Descriptive Roll for the newly mustered company also recorded the names of nine men who were appointed as noncommissioned officers in the unit, with five designated as sergeants and four as corporals. Two of the Hankamer brothers had already made a positive impression on the company's leadership; Charles Hankamer was designated as the first corporal, and John W. Hankamer was listed as fifth corporal.[11]

Their fellow soldiers' backgrounds reflected Texas' history as a fairly new state, one which was attracting residents from around the world. The Descriptive Roll for the company completed near the end of the war lists information for 133 men who served in Company F at some point during the war. As one might expect, the majority were born in states that had joined the Confederacy, including thirty native Texans. Nearly one in seven, however, had no ancestral ties to the South. Nine of these volunteers were born in Union states, and another eleven, including the four Stengler and Hankamer boys, had been born outside of North America—seven in Germany, three in Switzerland, and one in England.

The majority of these men were in their twenties or early thirties, but twenty of them were old enough that they were not required by the new draft to serve at all. They included William Smith and W. R. Martin, who were both fifty-one years old when they enlisted. The youngest were two seventeen-year-olds, Joseph Andress, a native of Louisiana, and Henry Chapman, who had been born in Wisconsin.

Reflecting the rural nature of the area, most of these men listed their occupation as "farmer," although there was a smattering of other backgrounds. The unit included a lawyer, a teacher, four carpenters, a stock raiser, and a physician, although Dr. William Payne was discharged within six months. It's likely his skills were soon deemed much more valuable elsewhere than in a cavalry company.

Others had backgrounds that would be very useful in the unit's day-to-day activities. This cavalry outfit must have been delighted to have the skills of Lafayette Simmons, a thirty-two-year-old blacksmith. Christian Bingle, a close friend of the Stengler family, was a saddlemaker, and A. J. Criswell's experience as a wheelwright was very welcome since the unit usually traveled with wagons to help carry their gear.[12]

It took about two weeks to get the new troops organized and ready to travel, but by May 6, 1862, they were headed for the coast and the strategically important location known as Sabine Pass. Their route took them southeast across mostly open and often marshy country, made even wetter by rainy weather. On Sunday, May 11, the company reached its destination about three miles from the town of Sabine Pass, set up camp, and settled down to the task of learning to be soldiers. First Lt. William Duncan was very pleased with the men in the unit and in a letter to his wife noted, "I am certain that we have the best company that has gone into service from any part of Texas."[13]

Their first few weeks in camp included seemingly endless hours of instruction and "drill." Prior military experience among these new recruits was scarce at best, and understanding the meaning of specific commands, signals, and bugle calls would be essential during the confusion of battle. CSA receipts show that a drum and two bugles were purchased for Company F on two separate occasions during the war and the unit's roster included two "musicians." A recent arrival in another CSA unit later wrote that activities like drill, "roll calls by morning and night," and guard duty were used "to break the greenhorns in" and teach them "how it goes in war."[14]

By mid-May, it was already early summer on the Texas coast, and the repetitive drilling in the oppressive heat and humidity soon became tedious. Within two weeks of their arrival at Sabine Pass, however, the men of Company F received some news that added a sense of urgency to their otherwise dull routine.

Less than one hundred miles down the coast, but a world away from the isolation and tedium of Company F's makeshift camp, was Galveston. The most prosperous city in Texas, it included numerous shops and amenities, such as ice houses and gas service to homes and commercial buildings. It was also the most important port on the Texas Gulf Coast, and many items used by both individuals and businesses arrived in Texas via Galveston.

Texas still had little in the way of manufacturing, but it produced one valuable commodity in quantity: cotton. When Galveston was finally connected to the mainland by a railroad in 1860, its port assumed even greater importance, and in that same year, about two-thirds of all the cotton shipped from Texas passed through the island city. That factor alone made Galveston a key target for Union military planners.[15]

On May 17, 1862, the following message was sent under a flag of truce from Capt. Henry Eagle, commander of the US naval forces anchored off of Galveston. It was addressed to the commander of the Confederate forces in the city.

> Sir: In a few days the naval and land forces of the United States government will appear off the town of Galveston to enforce its surrender. To prevent the effusion of blood and destruction of property which would result from the bombardment of your town, I hereby demand the surrender of the place, with its fortifications and all batteries in its vicinity, with all arms and munitions of war.[16]

The city was poorly prepared to defend itself, and after a flurry of negotiations, the authorities in Galveston were given four days by Captain Eagle to "remove your families and property." Appearances were important to morale, and CSA Brig. Gen. Paul Hebert sent carefully worded instructions to his troops. "There is to be no surrender under any circumstances," Hebert wrote. "There may be, however, an abandonment, in the face of a superior force . . . when it would be folly to attempt resistance."[17]

There was, therefore, a vigorous "abandonment" of Galveston. Maj. J. C. Massie, the provost marshal, announced that "all the cattle, mules, horses, and surplus provisions must be removed from the island, and transportation would be furnished, on [train] cars and boats, to points on the mainland, for women, children, and other non-combatants. . . . I am moving heaven and earth to get everything away," Major Massie wrote in the *Houston Telegraph*. "After a few more days the enemy can have all that is left; and if they can make much use of it, they may have my head for a football."[18]

This military standoff proved to be more akin to a chess match than a ballgame. The Union threat of a bombardment of the town was averted, at least temporarily, but Captain Eagle had achieved a victory of sorts. A substantial portion of Galveston's population had left the island and did not return until after the war, reducing the once-thriving city to only a shadow of its recent glory. For the time being, the island remained in Confederate hands, but the Union Navy continued its blockade, and Galveston's usefulness as a port was greatly diminished.

Texans anxiously watched for further developments, and their wait was a short one.

11

SABINE PASS

We are here at the Pass, the most hateful place I've ever been at, a place where we will never hear from anywhere.
—CHARLES HANKAMER, January 11, 1863

At the point where the border between Texas and Louisiana drops southward into the Gulf of Mexico, there was little to suggest in 1862 that the area was of much interest to anyone other than an occasional fisherman. The unremarkable terrain was as flat as it was soggy, and with marshes, bayous, and rivers covering most of the coastal landscape, dry land was at a premium.

The one distinctive feature along this otherwise seemingly deserted stretch of coastline was a brick lighthouse, set well back from the beach on the Louisiana side of a sluggish waterway that flowed from the marsh into the Gulf of Mexico. The mouth of this outlet was guarded by a sandbar and mudflats, and mariners unfamiliar with the area might wonder why anyone bothered to erect a lighthouse at such an unpromising location. During the Civil War, it was almost a moot point; although the impressive tower did provide a landmark during daylight hours, the Confederates extinguished the light in August 1861, and it remained dark until the end of the war.[1]

The gap in the shoreline near the lighthouse was known as Sabine Pass, and it offered water access between the Gulf of Mexico and the interiors of both eastern Texas and western Louisiana through a shallow, winding, and difficult channel that led northward for a mile or so to the lower end of Sabine Lake. The lake, in turn, was formed by the joining of the outlets of two rivers, the Sabine and the Neches, which offered potential water access into eastern Texas and western Louisiana.

By 1847, a town known as Sabine City, on the Texas side of Sabine Lake, could boast of a newspaper, steam sawmill, and post office, and it had become a shipping point for not only cotton and cattle but also lumber from the vast inland forest known as the Big Thicket. The town's name was officially changed to "Sabine Pass" in 1861, although the "Sabine City" label lingered in some quarters for several years. From this point forward the name Sabine Pass will be used in this narrative for both the town and the geographic feature on the coast, unless the older title is part of a direct quote from a period document.[2]

With water access both to the Gulf of Mexico and inland locations, Sabine Pass was well-positioned for commerce. In early 1862 the Eastern Texas Railroad was nearly complete between Sabine Pass and Beaumont, and the Texas and New Orleans Railroad was operating between Beaumont and Houston. Despite its ambitious name, the T&NO had not yet crossed the border into Louisiana, but other rail lines radiated from Houston southeast to Galveston, southwest for about forty-five miles to the Brazos River, and west and northwest for about eighty miles. A long-established land route, the Atascosito/Opelousas Trail, also passed near Beaumont; this rudimentary road ran all the way from South Texas to New Orleans.[3]

Control of Sabine Pass was, therefore, of strategic value to both CSA and Union leaders. On July 8, 1861, CSA Navy Cmdr. William W. Hunter noted, "Sabine Pass is the military pathway from the sea to an important part of Louisiana and Texas, and controlling, to a great degree, the communication between those States." Sabine Pass may have been important to military leaders, but it was hardly a favorite with most of their troops. Company F was assigned here at intervals during the next two years, and in January 1863 Charles Hankamer offered his less-than-glowing opinion about the area. In a letter to his sister, Mina Wilborn, he wrote, "We are here at the Pass, the most hateful place I've ever been at, a place where we will never hear from anywhere."[4]

On June 6, 1862, less than a month after their initial arrival for duty on the coast, these men were glad to have a change of scenery. In their first of many moves during the war, the company shifted a few miles north to Grigsby's Bluff, one of the few pieces of high ground along the lower Neches River. Their new camp was located about eleven miles southeast of Beaumont, and today the site is occupied by the town of Port Neches.[5]

Shortly after their arrival at Grigsby's Bluff, the original organizer of

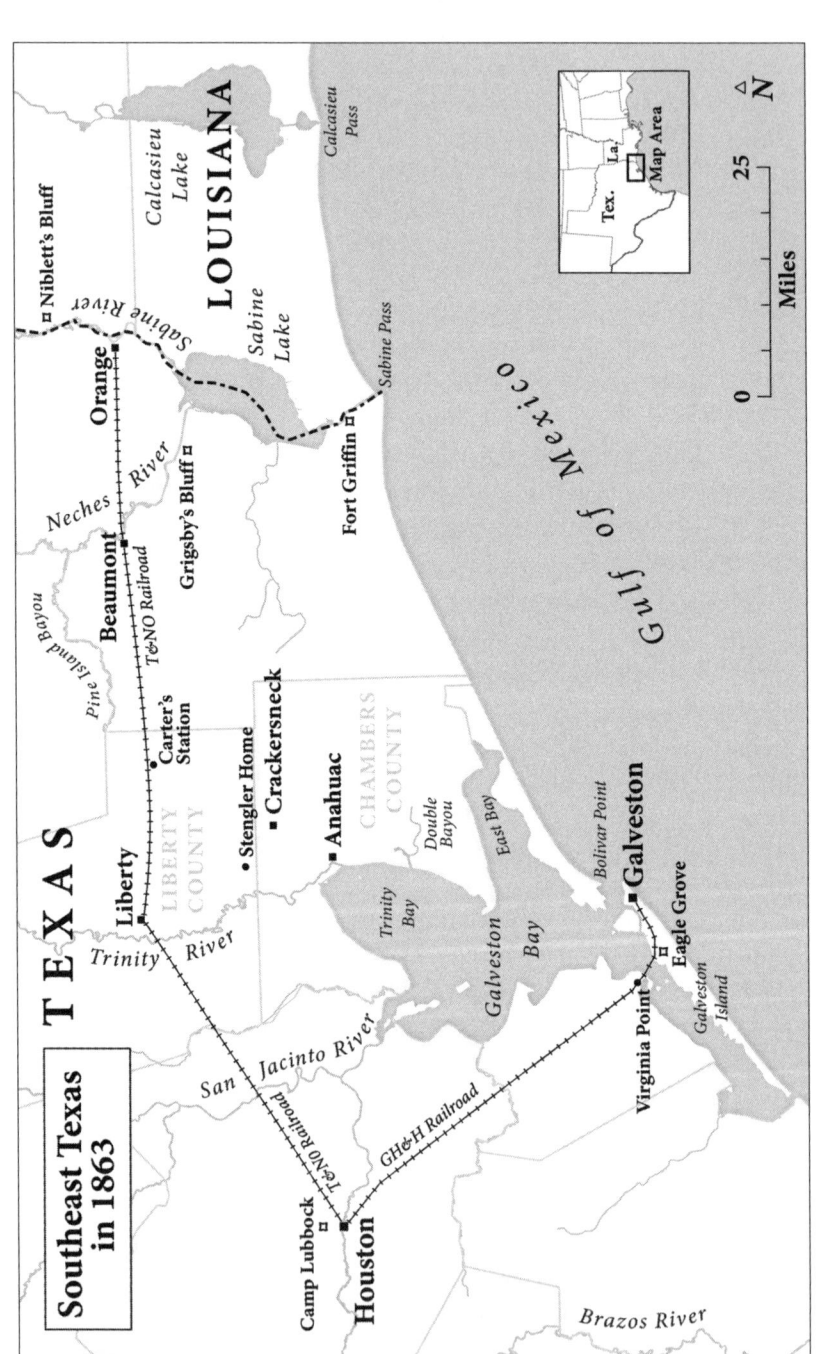

FIGURE 9. Southeast Texas in 1863.

their company, Capt. Ashley W. Spaight, was promoted to lieutenant colonel and given command of the battalion previously known as Liken's Battalion. This change on June 17, 1862, prompted a new designation for the organization—the "11th (Spaight's) Battalion, Texas Volunteers"—which would last for most of the war. The former Moss Bluff Rebels were now officially Company F (Cavalry) in the new battalion, which also included a second cavalry company, an artillery company, and three infantry companies.[6]

Spaight's promotion also created a vacancy for a new commander for Company F, and the selection of a new leader utilized a system that may be understandably viewed with some skepticism by anyone with military experience in more recent years. CSA company officers at that time were elected by the men in the unit; it was a populist approach that offered mixed results in terms of military success.

Charles Hankamer mentioned this process in a letter to Mina and Charles Wilborn, saying, "We will have to elect us a Captain . . . and I expect that it will be a close race between George Duncan and E. W. Brown. Either one I think will make us a good captain."

At the time of this vote, the company roster included two lieutenants with the surname "Duncan," although they were not related: 1st Lt. William B. Duncan and 2nd Lt. George C. Duncan. Charles Hankamer did not prove to be a successful political pollster, and the winner of the election was William B. Duncan, a successful planter, cattle trader, and local leader in Liberty County.[7]

For the past quarter century, William Duncan had been buying and selling cattle throughout the region and conducting drives of that livestock to markets in Louisiana. His detailed knowledge of both the people and terrain in a wide area across southern Texas and Louisiana would prove to be a valuable asset for the unit as the war unfolded.[8]

Even without an immediate threat from Union forces, Company F's new leader was faced with an abundance of challenges. Despite the hours of drill, the skills of his troops were still raw and untested, and a June 1862 letter from Charles Hankamer to Mina Wilborn confirmed that most of these recruits were still learning how to be soldiers. "We had an accident to happen here the night before last," Charles wrote. "A man by the name of Solomon Fisher while on guard at night alone at midnight shot himself accidentally. It is not dangerous although it was a narrow escape."[9]

Charles's news about the overall situation in their camp was mixed as well. "All of us boys are in good health but we have some sick men in our camp and I fear that this place is not very healthy," he wrote. His commanding officer shared similar concerns, noting in a letter to his wife on June 25, "I have had a good deal of bother . . . on account of the sickness that is in camp; there are several cases of fever now, and one man . . . from Wallisville is so low I think his recovery is very doubtful."[10]

The new officer's responsibilities also included not only the health and welfare of his unit but also the provision of adequate supplies for both men and horses. Charles Hankamer was concerned about their horses, noting the animals had received very little corn since they arrived on the coast. "We have to ride them every day and keep them tied and hobbled," he wrote, "and they are doing very bad."[11]

The shortage of corn for their horses was symptomatic of supply problems plaguing the CSA during the first year of the war and beyond. A list of rations for Company F in May 1862 showed the unit included eighty men, eighty-seven horses, and eight mules. For that entire month, they were allowed 37,758 pounds of hay and 24,273 pounds of corn. They received none of either.

The men fared only slightly better. For May 1862, the company was allowed 1,920 pounds of bacon (but received only 357); 3,200 pounds of beef (received 1,847); 2,880 pounds of flour (received 981); 3,200 pounds of cornmeal (received 1,131); and 240 pounds of beans and rice (received none).

If there's a universal item in demand for soldiers around the world, it's probably coffee, and that staple was undoubtedly high on the list of items bargained for and traded. In May 1862, Company F was allowed 144 pounds for the month (about 1.8 pounds per man) but received twenty-three pounds. What coffee they did have on hand could at least be sweetened, since the unit did receive 264 of its allowed 288 pounds of sugar.[12]

Other items on the rations list that were available in only limited quantities included vinegar, candles, soap, and salt. For May 1862, part of the problem may have been the fact Company F had just been mustered into service the previous month and had recently arrived at a new location, but similar supply problems were reported at intervals throughout the war.

Despite their difficulties, Charles Hankamer's attitude during his second month in the army was optimistic. "We have good news from the war, and . . . I expect that you know more about it than we do, I will only say that we have had 2 or 3 fights lately and we have been victorious every time. We begin to think that the war will soon come to a close, for Captain Spaight has said himself that he felt certain that it would come to a close in 6 months, he never says such things unless he had good information."[13]

That optimism would be tested during the summer of 1862. The men in Company F were about to face the unit's first life-and-death challenge, and although their enemy would arrive via the Gulf of Mexico, it was not the one they expected.

12

THE UNSEEN ENEMY

The greater portion of the inhabitants have fled.
—*GALVESTON WEEKLY NEWS*, September 17, 1862

During the second summer of the Civil War, the Texas coast proved to be a very dangerous place for soldiers and civilians alike. This threat, however—and the first casualties in Spaight's Battalion—did not result from shot and shell.

In July 1862 the Union naval blockade of Galveston was beginning its second year and was greatly reducing the flow of goods into the state. Federal ships also patrolled offshore waters from New Orleans to Galveston, but they had not yet stationed full-time watchers at the entrance to Sabine Pass. As a result, CSA Maj. Julius Kellersberg called "the pass at Sabine . . . a very important point, and in fact the only port from where we can receive our powder and other articles." Another officer referred to Sabine Pass as "our most important seaport."[1]

Those realities made some blockade runners willing to risk trips in and out of Sabine Pass, and one of them was the British steamer *Victoria*. In July 1862, the *Victoria* carried a shipment of much-needed munitions, and its arrival at Sabine Pass was welcomed by CSA officers. In retrospect, residents and military leaders alike wished the *Victoria* had been intercepted by the Union blockade, because the vessel also carried a dangerous stowaway.

Ports all along the Gulf Coast and throughout the Caribbean were notoriously unhealthy, especially during the warmer months, and sailors could easily pick up a variety of maladies while docked in places such as Havana, believed to be among the *Victoria's* previous ports of call. That fact of life in 1862 was noted by CSA Capt. K. D. Keith, who was stationed at Sabine Pass when the steamer arrived. He later wrote, "It was known there was sickness aboard the ship, but this excited no suspicion."[2]

Under those circumstances, this lack of concern was understandable, but it would soon prove to be very costly. Within a few days of the steamer's arrival, it became clear to some Sabine Pass residents that the sickness among this particular crew was cause for serious concern. Soon, both civilians and soldiers stationed in the area not only became sick, they also began dying at a frightfully increasing pace. Local doctors failed to recognize the disease and dismissed the concerns voiced by Captain Keith and a local civilian named Sarah Vosburg. They had both treated patients with the same symptoms in other locations, and their diagnosis, which would later be verified by more experienced physicians, was ominous.

Yellow jack had arrived in Sabine Pass.[3]

That seems an unusual name for a disease that killed as many as half its victims, but it was a logical one, derived from a common practice of the time. The sickness, more commonly known as yellow fever, was frequently associated with ships arriving from tropical locations, and during an outbreak, those vessels were often quarantined at a considerable distance from ports. Such ships were required by some jurisdictions to fly a yellow flag, or "jack," to indicate their "approach at your own peril" status.[4]

As the number of such reports grew, worry soon escalated into panic among area residents. According to CSA Captain Keith, "The fever spread rapidly and soon both civilians and soldiers dispersed." On September 3, 1862, the *Galveston Weekly News* published a letter from Sabine Pass dated August 22 with an ominous report: "There are about forty cases of yellow fever here in a mild form. Two are said to be dying this morning. There are from three to six new cases every 24 hours."[5]

Two weeks later, on September 17, the *Galveston Weekly News* reported that an experienced physician, Dr. George Holland, had visited Sabine Pass and confirmed there was "no doubt of the existence of yellow fever there." At the time of his visit, "there had been between fifty and sixty cases, twenty-five of which terminated fatally. . . . The greater portion of the inhabitants have fled."[6]

That reaction to a yellow fever outbreak was not uncommon. Residents who had the means to escape from the affected area did so, to the extent that businesses could be closed for months at a time. Towns outside the affected area were often unwelcoming to refugees trying to escape the threat of infection. In some cases, armed guards turned back trains or refused to let them stop and unload freight or passengers. There were even reports of frightened citizens burning railroad bridges or pulling up rails to keep trains from arriving from infected areas.[7]

Such fears were inspired by a combination of factors. They included the horrific symptoms for those who had a severe case of the disease and the high mortality rate, which ranged from about 10 percent to more than 50 percent. There were a host of theories—but no consensus—about the cause, transmission, and treatment of yellow fever, and that confusion added to the anxiety when outbreaks occurred.

An 1862 medical report described the questions of "contagiousness and communicability" as "much-vexed points," and definitive answers would remain a mystery for nearly another four decades. In the meantime, desperate remedies ranged from innocuous mustard plasters and hot baths to others, such as doses of lead, mercury, creosote, and carbolic acid, that could be even more dangerous than the disease itself.[8]

Recordkeeping was spotty, but statistics that do exist offer good reasons for the dread inspired by cases of yellow fever. Galveston endured at least eight epidemics of the disease during the nineteenth century; the first, in 1839, claimed a quarter of the town's population. Only four years before the 1862 outbreak at Sabine Pass, 4,845 people died from the disease in New Orleans, and the "Great Epidemic" of 1853 claimed nearly 8,000 lives in that city. One researcher estimated yellow fever killed between 100,000 and 150,000 people in the United States in the two centuries ending in 1900.[9]

Some of those victims succumbed during the Civil War. Ralph J. Smith was a soldier in Galveston, and he wrote about the irony of soldiers felled by sickness instead of bullets. "We were attacked during the summer of 1864 by a silent and insidious enemy against which our heaviest guns availed nothing," Smith said. "The Yellow fever invaded our camp and soon being epidemic, carrying off numbers who had courted death on numerous battlefields and endured the hardships of many campaigns, only to succumb at last to this dreaded scourge."[10]

As dangerous—and feared—as yellow jack was throughout the South in the 1800s, it was merely one of a host of maladies that afflicted the soldiers and sailors who left home to fight for both North and South. Other significant illnesses included malaria, dysentery, measles, mumps, typhoid fever, and pneumonia, and several researchers have concluded that as many as two-thirds of the men who died during the war were victims of disease rather than injuries incurred on the battlefield.[11]

Why the big surge in sickness among a population of primarily young—and presumably robust—men? There were a host of factors, including deplorable sanitation, poor nutrition, and contaminated drinking water in crowded military camps. Many of these men were from rural locales and had rarely been in contact with large concentrations of people before the war. As a result, they had not been exposed to many of the common childhood illnesses such as measles and mumps.[12]

Geography also played a major role in these situations. Survivors of yellow fever infections usually acquired at least partial immunity against the illness, so some soldiers from coastal areas were not affected by later outbreaks. They were said to be "acclimated" to yellow jack. However, soldiers and sailors from other parts of the country lacked this protection and were ready targets for the disease if their duties brought them to areas where the sickness was found.[13]

Yellow fever and malaria, another serious disease, share an important common denominator. Both are spread by mosquitoes, and family letters and other written accounts confirm the presence of those insects in abundance during the warmer months in much of the South. On March 6, 1863, George Stengler wrote to his sister, Mina Wilborn, from Sabine Pass, and he was not impressed with the area. "There is plenty of musketoes [sic] here and plenty of water all over the place," he said. "This is the ugliest mud hole I ever seen."[14]

CSA Lt. N. H. Smith was assigned to Sabine Pass in August 1863 to supervise work on fortifications there, and he sent several letters to his commanding officer in Houston. In them, he offered blunt descriptions of the problems caused by the biting insects.

"The musquetoes [sic] are so bad here that it is almost impossible for a man or horse to live," Lieutenant Smith wrote. A second letter that same day began with a wry name for his duty station: "Head Qr [Headquarters]

Army Musquetoes, Sabine Pass." He went on to warn, "Should it ever be your misfortune to be sent to this accursed of all places, bring with you a [mosquito] bar sufficiently large for you to lay with your feet stretched out, for I am just out of bed and my feet are so badly swollen that I can hardly wear a shoe."[15]

Although it didn't spark the same level of fear as yellow fever, malaria was a widespread, serious, and sometimes fatal disease, caused by a parasite that is transmitted from an infected person to its next victim via a mosquito bite. Victims suffer from high fevers and shaking chills, which can reoccur for years. Those symptoms gave rise to names such as intermittent fever, ague, malignant fever, bilious fever, congestive fever, and pernicious malaria.[16]

One or more varieties of such ailments were a problem for Stengler family members, and "fevers" of various kinds are mentioned in multiple family letters. On August 2, 1862, John Stengler recorded that his son George Stengler had "bin taken sick with the Bilious remittent fever," and on October 9, 1864, Charles Hankamer wrote from Camp Spindletop near Beaumont, noting, "I too have had another spell of fever since you left."

Unlike yellow fever, for which there was no effective treatment or cure, malaria sufferers could often find temporary relief with the use of quinine. The drug, derived from the bark of a tree native to South America, was heavily used by both Union and CSA military doctors, both as treatment and as a preventative for malaria. As the war progressed, the Union naval blockade made it increasingly difficult for the South to obtain quantities of quinine, and efforts to find a locally available substitute were unsuccessful.[17]

The drug's scarcity later in the war prompted John Stengler to write to his son Fritz in February 1865, while Fritz was stationed at Camp Lubbock on the outskirts of Houston. His father wrote, "I wish that you would inquire about the price of an ounce of quinine."[18]

While they were less likely to be life-threatening, other diseases also dogged troops of the North and the South, including the men of Company F. In early 1863, both Fritz Hankamer and George Stengler had the mumps, a malady that continued to crop up in camp for the next several months. The misery produced by the mumps in an adult could be severe, and it was no respecter of rank. Their commanding officer noted in his diary on March 8, 1863, that he was "very unwell with mumps."[19]

Whether the health woes were mumps or malaria, soldiers and civilians alike shared many of the same problems. Their solutions to those common challenges relied upon a combination of folklore and ingenuity, along with occasional help from what passed in that era for modern medicine. Some members of Company F also received occasional medical assistance from an unexpected source—a former brickmason and inspector of chimneys from the old country.

13

DOCTOR STENGLER

I hereby Certify that John Stengler has been Practicing Medicine in this neighborhood for four years.

—BENJAMIN ABSHIER, August 2, 1862

The 1860s were not a good time to need a doctor in Southeast Texas—or anywhere else for that matter. A veritable witch's brew of ailments posed a serious risk for civilians and soldiers alike, but defenses against those threats were often limited. Despite the dedicated efforts of physicians, the general state of medical care in the mid-1800s was rudimentary at best, and well-intentioned efforts could sometimes do more harm than good. One example is found in a January 1862 letter from an East Texas woman who mentioned a relative who had been sick and said, "Dr. Jack is giving her Strichnine [sic] pills and I think it will cure her."[1]

Techniques we take for granted today, including antibiotics, intravenous fluids, and blood transfusions were not yet in use during the Civil War. One of the few diagnostic tools available to physicians in 1862 was a stethoscope, and the quality of medical education was often questionable. There was, in fact, no mandatory process for examining or licensing physicians in Texas between 1848 and 1873.[2]

Dr. Claudius H. Mastin was a doctor in Alabama in the 1860s, and in 1874 he summed up some of the challenges facing the South during the war. "On the Confederate side," he noted, "cut off from the outer world by a rigid blockade, with the armies confined entirely to an agricultural region—with no manufactories, and with the scantiest supplies of medical resources, it was in many instances impossible to furnish adequate relief to sick or wounded, whether they were friends or foes."[3]

A Confederate surgeon interviewed after the war confirmed the lack of basic medications that were taken for granted only a few decades later:

"Of that large class of medicines, so useful in surgery and so much in demand in war times, called antiseptics, most of them . . . have been discovered and appropriated to surgical use since our war. In fact, I had but little else at my command except the cold-water dressing for wounds." The difficulty in obtaining medications during the war was also described by a Georgia pharmacist whose father served during the war.

> Druggists of the South had either to manufacture what they could from native barks and leaves and herbs and roots, or purchase at the Southern ports such supplies as the blockade runners brought in that were not intended for the government. . . . In the interior districts and small villages, the country doctors returned to the first principles and to the use of the plants of the fields and forests; and these agencies were about all they had to rely on, outside of whiskey and a little quinine, the latter frequently at $100 an ounce.[4]

Liberty and Chambers counties were home to a druggist, a dentist, and sixteen physicians in 1860, with most of them living in or near the town of Liberty. By 1862 some of those individuals had joined the military effort, and even though those who remained made house calls via horseback or buggy, medical care in rural areas was often a do-it-yourself proposition.[5]

Less than two months after heading off to the army, the Hankamer and Stengler men were writing home for medical advice, probably as a result of their less-than-healthy diet. On June 9, 1862, Mina Wilborn responded to one such request from her brother Charles Hankamer, whom she referred to by his German name of "Karl."

> I am sending you some medicinal grass, you know about it. Dear Karl, it is good for regulating the bowels but do not take too much of it. About 6 ounces of grass and about half a pint of water, let it boil a little, take it off the fire, cover it, and let it stand till cool. Take about half of it, if that does not help then increase the dose. You know it helped me. Lucinda said Johanne gave some to your dear children and it helped them.

In the absence of other options, such home remedies were relied upon for a wide variety of medical issues. One of Mina Wilborn's children suffered from a long-running problem with one of her eyes, and on December 26, 1862, she described an unusual attempt to correct it: "Martha's eye has not healed yet . . . [and] it seems as if something is over the eyeball. Charles has put some white sugar into the eye several times and it seems to do some good. The other day I held my hand over her good eye and she said she could not see. Now she says she can see a little."

Not all health concerns were life-threatening, but they could still create considerable discomfort, and time-tested remedies were often used for common aches and pains. On November 30, 1863, Mina Wilborn wrote to her brother Fritz, "Last week I had the toothache. I could find no relief until I made a mustard plaster. I am sending you some mustard. You have vinegar, you can mix it yourself."

Soldiers in military camps were also often called upon to help themselves and each other, a harsh reality the Hankamer and Stengler men discovered within their first few months in the army. On July 15, 1862, Charles Hankamer wrote to his sister, Mina, from Camp Spaight, between Beaumont and Sabine Pass: "I have not time to write much. . . . I am so worn out from tending on the sick that I cannot set up so late & it is getting late now, we are all well in our mess, but we have some eight or ten in our camp sick with the fever."

Family members could sometimes provide medications that might not be available in army camps, and Company F's assignments to locations in Southeast Texas during most of the war made it possible to send supplies via acquaintances traveling back and forth between home and camp. Such private couriers were the primary—and most reliable—means of sending letters and packages to the men serving in Spaight's Battalion.

Perhaps in response to Charles Hankamer's report of "fever" in their camp, his father wrote in July 1862 that he was enclosing some practical help with his letter, which would be delivered by an acquaintance. "Muller has two packages of pills for you, one for bilious fever, the other for chills and fever," John wrote. "Directions are in each package. For bilious fever take 5 for a dose and for chills and fever take 3 or 4 for a dose."[6]

As the above letter indicates, John Stengler's role in the area had expanded to include work as a medical practitioner. The Sam Houston Regional Library and Research Center in Liberty holds nearly a dozen documents signed by the elder Stengler to substantiate medical furloughs for members of Company F. His notes, which rely heavily upon phonetic spelling, also remind us that English was not John Stengler's native language. One such document reads:

Physical Reciet—George Stengler a Privot of Company (F) Lt. Col. Spaight's Battalion of Texas Volunteers has bin physically unable to perform Military duty for the following reason, he has bin taken sick on the 29th Day of July 1862 with the Bilious remittent fever. I think he will be able to be in Cervis [Service] in about 15 days from this date if no backset. This the 2nd Day of August 1862. John Stengler.

To lend further credence to this written excuse from duty, three local men added their "certification" at the bottom of the note about John Stengler's medical experience. The first reads: "I hereby certify that John Stengler has been Practicing Medicine in this neighborhood for two or three years. J. B. Beavis." The second addendum, signed by Benjamin Abshier, notes, "I hereby Certify that John Stengler has been Practicing Medicine in this neighborhood for four years," and a third certification was provided by Charles Wilborn.

Another medical "receipt" was written by John Stengler in August 1862 for C. Bingle, a private in Company F, "who is physically unable to perform Military Duty for the following reason—he has got the Liver Disease. I think he will be able to go in Cervis in a bout twenty days from this day if no backset. August 27th, 1862, John Stengler."

Private Bingle apparently suffered a "backset," and John Stengler provided a second note on September 26 for an additional ten days of leave. Perhaps he felt some additional authority for his opinion would be useful, so John added a suffix after his signature: "John Stengler Dr." By the following year, his signature had acquired an even more formal tone. On May 27, 1863, he submitted a note requesting a twenty-five day leave for Fritz Hankamer, who had "taken the hydrothorax" following an "attack of inflammation liver disease." This document was signed "John Stengler, M. D."

Given his useful role in this rural area, using that title was not inappropriate. As previously noted, there were no formal certification or education requirements in Texas at the time to become a "doctor," and some practitioners of this era were trained by a combination of self-education and hands-on experience.

Early in the war, John Stengler had already begun treating his medical practice as a business. On September 4, 1862, he wrote to his son Fritz, asking him to try to collect outstanding bills from some of the men in his unit: "I wish you would try and get my money from John A. Barrow and

H. Pruit. John A. Barrow's doctor bill is $12 and Pruit's doctor bill is $15. . . . [I]f you get . . . the above amount whenever they come into camp you would oblige me very [much] for doing so." The elder Stengler's attempt to charge for his services during difficult times shouldn't be viewed as unreasonable. Most of his treatments likely involved dispensing medications, and as already noted, many of those items were both expensive and in short supply.

When possible, John Stengler certainly provided medical help for his family. In a July 1862 letter, he noted that one of Mina Wilborn's sons was sick and explained, "Twice I have given Andrew his medicine." Mina Wilborn and her husband, Charles, had five children at home in August 1863, ages ten, eight, four, two, and a newborn son. Letters tell us that Mina and several of her children suffered from chronic health problems, and one daughter, Ellen, died at the age of four in November 1861.

That loss created understandable anxiety when another daughter, Martha, became seriously ill in the fall of 1862. Mina expressed her fears in a letter to her brothers Fritz and George on November 10: "We are all well except Martha. . . . I believe she has the illness my poor Ellen had. Last Tuesday she called her father and when he asked her what she wanted she said she had very bad pains in her left side. I can tell you she was very sick. She is a little better now but I am afraid. It is a year since my dear Ellen was sick and next Thursday it is a year since she died."

Little Martha recovered from that crisis, but the following year developed such a severe vision problem that she "had to be led around the house." In such situations, the family sometimes turned to local physicians for help. On October 29, 1863, Mina Wilborn wrote to Charles during one of his periods of military duty: "Martha's eyes are still mending slowly. I have got more medicine from the doctor."

Another letter to her husband on December 6, 1863, tells us this unnamed problem was not easily solved—and suggests that at least some medications were in short supply: "The doctor says he will not give Martha any more medicine, only a little quinine along, and put the drops in her eyes and bathe her all the time."[7]

Not all medical care, including some that was considered "newfangled," was readily embraced. On January 17, 1864, Mina wrote to her husband and expressed her concerns about a vaccination program, probably for smallpox, that was underway in his unit. "Dear Husband," she wrote. "I understood that some of the men in your company suffer right smart with their vaccination and we also understood that one man had died from it, and I have been a little uneasy about you, being it has served some of the balance so bad, I wish you would write as soon as possible and let me know how you are getting along."

Others were more open to the idea of smallpox vaccinations, although even wealthier individuals with considerable local influence could be reduced to "do-it-yourself" medical care. On March 7, 1863, Capt. William Duncan wrote to his wife, Celima, from Sabine Pass with instructions on how to vaccinate their children and the slaves on their plantation.

> I will also send a small scab of vaccine matter for you to vaccinate the children and everybody else, if you have not already done it, or had it done.... I will tell you how to use it. Take a small piece of the scab and put it on a piece of window glass—put a little water to it—half a drop, and rub the scab to pieces with the point of a knife, until it is perfectly dissolved and is the consistency of matter—then with the sharp point of a knife or a needle, prick or scratch the skin a little and put the matter in the place and let it dry. If the place is cut enough to bleed the matter is not apt to take, as it is washed away by the blood.... I do not think there is any danger in it.

Mrs. Duncan may have shared Mina Wilborn's concerns about the smallpox vaccination, or perhaps she was uneasy about having to administer it herself. Another letter from her husband eight months later, on November 4, 1863, suggests this had not yet been completed. The tone of this letter conveyed increased urgency, and it confirmed that his wife had limited professional medical help available: "I hope you will be able to keep the children from getting the whooping cough, but if they do catch it, you must do the best you can. I want you to try to procure some vaccine matter and vaccinate all the children, as I understand the smallpox is at Sabine Pass." William Duncan resumed his letter from Beaumont the following day on the same page, noting, "I got Dr. Robbins to promise to send you some good vaccine matter in a letter."

We don't know if the requested vaccinations against smallpox were carried out or if they were successful. Their potential value would be confirmed in the future, but for the moment, we'll turn our attention back to a more pressing crisis in the late summer of 1862—the yellow fever outbreak in Southeast Texas.[8]

14

DISBANDED

"I heard that the yellow fever was at Beaumont. I am very afraid you will get it in camp if you get not moved."
—JOHN STENGLER to Fritz Hankamer,
September 4, 1862

By August 1862 the men of Company F had been part of Spaight's Battalion for four months and felt they were ready to take on any military threat to their home territory. They had absolutely no interest, however, in a one-on-one fight against yellow fever.

Although part of Spaight's Battalion was stationed near Sabine Pass, Company F and Company E (infantry) were located about fifteen miles farther north. They were camped about a mile apart near Grigsby's Bluff, on the banks of the Neches River, and that location proved to be fortuitous. On August 26, a boat arrived from Sabine Pass with the disconcerting report that "yellow fever was there." John W. Hankamer shared this news in a letter to his sister, Mina, on August 30, and his comments summarized the prevailing knowledge about the disease in 1862. He recognized the seriousness of the yellow fever outbreak but tried to reassure his family that the men in Company F felt safe.[1]

> The yellow fever I hear is still as bad as ever at Sabine Pass, but it has not reached the camps of the soldiers down there yet who are stationed from one to two miles from town. If it is the yellow fever, which I expect it is, for it kills frequently, I think from what Col. Spaight says that he will move us somewhere, but where I don't know, but I don't think that we are in any danger from it, for we all know that you can't take the yellow fever from 30 miles distance, nor can you carry it in the country, but let that be as it may, we are all well, and as well satisfied as we could be away from home.

Family members back in Crackersneck weren't as confident as John W. Hankamer. On September 4, 1862, John Stengler wrote to his son Fritz: "I heard that the yellow fever was at Beaumont. I am very afraid you will get it in camp if you get not moved to the Pine Woods." Despite such fears, questions about whether the illness plaguing Sabine Pass was really yellow jack delayed a decision about relocating any military forces.

Dr. George Holland, an experienced physician, was sent by CSA commanders to evaluate the situation, and on September 8 he sent his report to Lt. Col. A. W. Spaight. His inspection, Dr. Holland wrote, "leaves no room for doubting that epidemic yellow fever exists in Sabine City . . . [and] the safety of the soldiers in your command who are still near Sabine City requires their immediate removal beyond the infected district."[2]

On September 8, Colonel Spaight sent permission for his company commanders to relocate their camp farther away from Sabine Pass, and two days later agreed to allow the men to be furloughed home for two weeks. Ten men were to remain at the new camp for guard duty while the rest were at home. John W. Hankamer, in his capacity as the company's 3rd corporal, was left in charge of the camp. A week later, the contingent left behind was rotated, with 1st Cpl. Charles Hankamer taking the place of his brother.[3]

Other soldiers from Spaight's Battalion were stationed near Sabine Pass and were at greater risk. Orders were issued to abandon the fort, but about thirty men chose to remain. Capt. K. D. Keith of Company B later wrote that he was "ordered to assume command of the post and to take care of the sick. . . . The fever was very fatal," he noted, and the number of troops "grew less every day. . . . Time passed—our principal business was to bury the dead."

Before the month was out, the troops who remained at Sabine Pass and survived the epidemic would face a second, and much more visible, menace.[4]

On the morning of September 23, 1862, three Union warships were spotted near the entrance to Sabine Pass: the steamer *Kensington*, the schooner *Rachel Seaman*, and the mortar schooner *Henry James*. Due to the shallow water at the entrance to the pass, it took another day to get the *Rachel Seaman* and *Henry Janes* "across the bar" and into effective firing range of Fort Sabine. The steamer *Kensington*, due to her deeper draft, had to remain offshore. A report submitted by Colonel Spaight the following day summarized the action:

Early the next morning the two sail vessels, having crossed the bar, took position and opened fire on our works, to which we promptly replied; but the shots from both sides fell far short. They then approached nearer, when a brisk fire from both sides was resumed and continued until dark. To the chagrin of officers and men, our shot still fell short, while the enemy was enabled, with his longer-range guns, to throw shot and shell around and into our works. . . . When night came on Maj. Irvine determined that it would be a fruitless exposure of the men and public property to attempt to hold the works another day.[5]

The ordnance and other property were removed, the guns were spiked [made unusable], and the troops were evacuated under cover of darkness. The only communication from Sabine Pass to the rest of the world was by courier, so news of the attack was slow getting out. At 4 a.m. on Thursday, September 25, even as the evacuation of Fort Sabine was underway, Captain Duncan was awakened with a message that "the Yankees had appeared at Sabine Pass." He sent word for his men to reassemble at their camp, but those messages had to be carried by hand to scattered locations, and a recall of the unit was not a speedy process.[6]

At seven o'clock that same morning, Col. X. B. Debray, commander of the CSA Sub-Military District of Houston, received his own alarming report by special messenger: Union vessels had entered Sabine Pass, the commander at Fort Sabine had requested assistance, and a "heavy cannonade" had been heard from the area. Reinforcements started toward Sabine Pass, but by then the Union forces had already achieved their first capture of a significant location along the Texas coast. Their foothold would, however, prove to be somewhat tenuous.[7]

After confirming that the fort had been abandoned, US Navy Acting Master Frederick Crocker, commander of the small Union force, led a shore party to demand the surrender of the town of Sabine Pass. According to a Union report, he was "met by a deputation of three citizens, who said the mayor had died two days previous, and that nearly all the citizens had left on account of yellow fever, which had been raging badly, but was then abating; after giving and receiving the necessary assurances of good conduct, etc. Captain Crocker returned on board, deeming it not prudent to allow anyone to land."[8]

In the aftermath of the loss of Fort Sabine and the key port at Sabine Pass, there was some inevitable second-guessing about the decision to disband most of Spaight's Battalion and leave Fort Sabine manned by a token force. The day after the surrender of the fort and town, Colonel Spaight prepared a report, concluding the outcome was determined not by the shortage of manpower but by the lack of guns with sufficient range to defend the fort from a naval attack. "It is now manifest that the result must have been the same, no matter what the number of troops here," Spaight wrote. "Great praise is due for the gallantry of the resistance offered with such wholly inadequate means."[9]

In his separate report on the battle, Colonel Spaight's superior, Col. X. B. Debray, supported Spaight's conclusions. "I concur with him in the belief that a large force could have done no more than Major Irvine's command, having no guns of sufficient range to answer those of the enemy."[10]

The Union won this round of the fight for Texas, and their next move was unknown to the Confederates. Would they press their advantage and push on toward the all-important railheads at Beaumont and Orange, or would fear of yellow fever blunt their advance? Would the Federals now shift their attention to other prime targets such as Galveston? CSA commanders quickly prepared plans to deal with possible threats in multiple locations, and the mounted troops of Company F figured prominently in their strategy at Sabine Pass.

15

REGROUPING

*I will observe the movements of the enemy ... and shall
lose no opportunity of inflicting injury upon him.*
—LT. COL. ASHLEY SPAIGHT, September 26, 1862

The men of Company F rejoiced when they were allowed to return home temporarily due to the yellow fever threat, but once the news of the Union attack on Fort Sabine reached Liberty County, it didn't take them long to return to duty. Within thirty-six hours of the CSA abandonment of the fort, they began to reassemble at their camp at Pine Island, and Lieutenant Colonel Spaight detailed his plans for his battalion. "I will observe the movements of the enemy and promptly report the result," he wrote, "and shall lose no opportunity of inflicting injury upon him."[1]

These soldiers knew they were heading back into harm's way from both the superior firepower on Union gunboats and yellow fever, and two days after Company F began gathering, Col. X. B. Debray confirmed the ongoing risk. "No permanent landing has been made [by the Union forces] and none will probably be made, owing to yellow fever, which is still raging," he noted. To make matters worse, some inhabitants of Sabine Pass had broken the quarantine and fled to the southern end of Beaumont. Colonel Debray feared "that the disease will spread over the whole town. If so, the trains are ordered not to stop at Beaumont."[2]

Risky or not, Company F's men streamed back to their Pine Island camp. On September 27 they continued south to their earlier location at Grigsby's Bluff, between Beaumont and Sabine Pass. The trip took all day, and it was well after dark before the weary men and horses arrived. The next morning was a Sunday, but it was definitely not a day of rest. Even as the troops worked on pitching tents and "fixing up" camp, word was received of more enemy activity.

During the previous night, a Union party in three boats "traveled to the mouth of Taylor's Bayou and attempted to burn the railroad bridge across that stream." A guard stationed there extinguished the fire, and the bridge was only slightly damaged, but the Federals "took off with them three citizens, one being the mail boy, who happened to be stopping at the house near the bridge." The scene of this latest action was about halfway between Grigsby's Bluff and the small town of Sabine Pass. By land, Taylor's Bayou was about ten miles south of Grigsby's Bluff, where Spaight's men were reestablishing their camp.

In response to this raid, 2nd Lt. George Duncan took twenty-five men from Company F to guard the vital bridge; they were joined by an equal number of men from Company A. On the following day, September 29, the remaining members of both companies were ordered to pack up and head toward Sabine Pass. Anticipating the need for multiple bases of operation, Company F left ten men at the camp near Grigsby's Bluff. Once again, John W. Hankamer was in charge of this group.[3]

Monday night found the main contingent bivouacked near Taylor's Bayou. It was a largely sleepless night, interrupted by several alarms that boats (presumed to be enemy craft) were in the area. Sunrise on Tuesday found the men tired and on edge, "all under arms on account of alarm." The brackish water in the bayou and Sabine Lake was not drinkable by their horses, and for the men's peace of mind, it was a good thing the direct connection between mosquito bites and yellow fever was not then understood. Their commanding officer noted, "Musketoes worse than I ever saw them."[4]

The final stage of their trip was delayed until Captain O'Brien's infantry company arrived by train from Beaumont to take over the task of guarding the railroad bridge. After supper, the cavalry troops headed south once again in the dark and at about ten o'clock reached a camp already established several miles from the town of Sabine Pass by Captain Marsh's cavalry company. Given William Duncan's comment from the previous day and the marshy terrain throughout the area, the "musketoes" were likely ferocious once again during this nighttime ride.

Wednesday marked the start of a new month, but more of the same for these troops. At about 11 p.m. on October 1, scouts arrived in camp with a report that men, presumably Union raiders, had landed near the abandoned Fort Sabine. The company saddled their horses, gathered their weapons, and started on the several-mile trip. They made the last part of the journey on foot and took up positions near a road "to await the enemy."

Two hours passed with no activity, so the weary troops returned to camp, where they "stationed men on two sides" to prevent a surprise attack. All was calm until shortly after noon on October 2, when a shore party from the Union gunboats landed, set fire to the train depot about a mile from the town of Sabine Pass, and then retreated to the safety of their ships.[5]

It was becoming clear that Lieutenant Colonel Spaight's plan to "observe and inflict injury upon" the gunboat-based Union troops was not going to be easy. In addition to the longer-range weapons of the Federals, which required the Confederates to keep their distance from the boats, Union sympathizers in the area also served as extra eyes and ears for the Northern troops. Lieutenant Colonel Spaight acknowledged that latter problem when he wrote to Colonel Debray on September 29, noting he "would have no little difficulty concealing my designs, or rather movements, on account of the unreliable character of a portion of the population in the vicinity of the Sabine Pass."[6]

While his three brothers were fighting mosquitoes and guarding against additional raids at Sabine Pass and Taylor's Bayou, John W. Hankamer was having his own challenges with one of those "unreliable portions of the population." He was staying busy leading the small detachment back at Grigsby's Bluff, and he wrote to his brothers Charles, Fritz, and George on October 3.

> I just came back from Tabors Bluff where I had been sent to take one James Taylor who had been taken prisoner at Beaumont and escaped. We did not find him, keep a lookout for him below, I think that he may have made his way to the blockade.
>
> I am going to send a wagon after the balance of our things at Pine Island in the morning, we are doing tolerable well here, only have to work mighty hard sometimes, but I suppose that you all have to do the same. I wish they would let me come down there, too. I would like, if I have to keep a strong guard, (as Col. Spaight has ordered me to) to keep it nearer our enemy, and I would like to be with you all anyhow. I would like to share all hardships with you all and dangers.
>
> I keep a guard here all night, and allow no one to come prowling around our camp without knowing his business. We had to ride our horses very hard on our trip . . . riding so much in the night.

James Gilbert Taylor, for whom John W. Hankamer asked his brothers to "keep a sharp lookout," was one of the known Union sympathizers in the area. An experienced river pilot, Taylor eluded CSA troops for two weeks and eventually slipped away to join the Federal blockade. On at least two subsequent occasions, Taylor used his knowledge of the tricky waters around Sabine Pass to guide Union ships during later operations against CSA forces.[7]

Even as the men of Spaight's Battalion were sparring with the enemy around Sabine Pass, early October brought more bad news from Galveston. On October 4, 1862, a group of Union ships, including four steamers with a mortar boat in tow, sailed into Galveston Harbor. They exchanged cannon fire with Fort Point, which guarded the harbor's entrance, and the Union gunboats disabled the Confederates' single artillery piece at the fort.

The Union force's commander, William B. Renshaw, then demanded an unconditional surrender, stating he would either "hoist the United States flag over the city of Galveston or over its ashes." CSA Col. X. B. Debray advised his superiors on October 5 that "Galveston cannot be defended, and a fight in the city would be a useless braggadocio." After a four-day truce to allow the evacuation of Galveston, the town was surrendered.[8]

As was the case at Sabine Pass, the Union's "possession" of the city was largely symbolic. Renshaw had heard rumors that yellow fever was present in Galveston, and in his initial report of the capture of the town, he explained his reluctance to engage in prolonged discussions with the remaining civilian authorities. He wrote, "I then thought of the great danger of contagion from yellow fever . . . deeming [the value to be gained from activities onshore] . . . secondary in comparison to the possibility of getting that fatal disease on board of us, and possibly killing many innocent people."

The reports of yellow fever later proved to be questionable, but they were an effective deterrent to even a token Federal presence on the island. After a brief show of raising their flag over the custom house in downtown Galveston, the Union sailors returned to their ships and continued the naval blockade. A small ground force charged with physically occupying a small part of the town didn't arrive until late December, but despite that delay, Galveston's usefulness to the CSA as a port was limited to occasional daring trips by blockade runners.[9]

As these events were unfolding in Galveston, the now-familiar nemesis of yellow fever once again altered the plans of Spaight's Battalion in the Sabine Pass area. After receiving word on October 5 that yellow fever had turned up in yet another military unit in the area, Captains Duncan and Marsh concluded it was time to relocate. They ordered their men to have supper and get ready to move out in short order.

The officers were determined to put some distance between their men and the most recent fever cases, so they started at dark, made it across Taylor's Bayou at 1 a.m., and rode on in the rain. They arrived back at Grigsby's Bluff at daylight, soaking wet, but the wisdom of the earlier decision to maintain a second camp in that area was confirmed.[10]

Company F's first ten days back on duty had been hectic ones, but the frequent shifting of locations was still in accordance with the plans for these cavalrymen by the area commander, Colonel Debray. On September 28, three days after the loss of Fort Sabine, he wrote:

> I have stationed the two mounted companies of Spaight's battalion between Beaumont and Sabine Pass at a point from which they can watch the movements of the enemy in the bay and bring prompt intelligence to Beaumont and Orange. Their orders are to drive off the herds of cattle from the vicinity of the bay, to push frequent scouts to the town of Sabine in order to watch the inhabitants, and to receive information to endeavor to cut off enemy's parties who may attempt to land to procure beeves.[11]

Perhaps these cavalry troops found it ironic they had joined the army only to spend part of their time performing one of the same tasks they did at home—chasing wild cattle across the coastal prairie and marshes. In this case, however, the purpose was a serious one—to deny the Union troops a source of fresh meat. Those duties were important, but before the month was over, the men of Company F would be reminded in a very personal way that they were also in a real, and very dangerous, shooting war.

16

UNDER FIRE

I am well as ever and sound as a dollar although the Yankees have had several shots at me with their rifles and a canon.
—JOHN W. HANKAMER, October 19, 1862.

In the early 1840s, a small settlement called Aurora was established on the western shore of Sabine Lake near the mouth of Taylor's Bayou. Twenty years later, the cluster of houses was more commonly referred to as "Sparks," taken from the name of one of the residents, John Sparks. The nickname also proved to be descriptive for a different reason when literal sparks flew in the early morning hours of October 15, 1862—and John W. Hankamer was right in the middle of the action.[1]

Company F had moved back to the Grigsby's Bluff area by early October, but small scouting parties referred to as "pickets" continued to make regular mounted trips back and forth to the Sparks vicinity. It was about a twenty-mile round trip by horseback, and a key objective was to keep an eye out for Union raiders intent on destroying a key railroad bridge across Taylor's Bayou.[2]

It may be difficult today to appreciate the vital role of that railroad, but in 1862 trains were the only way to move large quantities of men and supplies by land with relative speed. That fact was amplified in this swampy coastal area, where the only practical route for cargo between the docks at Sabine Pass and the rest of Texas was along the slightly elevated railroad grade that ran from the port northward to Beaumont.

The bridge over Taylor's Bayou was a key, and very vulnerable, point along the entire route. This wooden span was 220 feet long, and because Taylor's Bayou was navigable at this spot, the span was a drawbridge, with an opening thirty-six feet wide. As a result, it would be both difficult and expensive to reconstruct the bridge, especially in the midst of a war.[3]

Lieutenant Colonel Spaight was well aware of the strategic importance of the bridge and the entire rail line. He reminded his superiors on October 2 that the only other route to Sabine Pass was a seventy-five-mile trek over a "long and bad route by way of the Gulf beach" that was "almost impassable to wagons." Emphasizing that the railroad bridge and lower part of the road were at the mercy of Union gunboats, he urged that such heavy guns "as are to be had . . . be sent to the Sabine River and to Taylor's Bayou . . . without delay."[4]

Those requested heavy guns were also in demand elsewhere, so they were not available. Colonel Spaight's fears concerning his inability to protect the vital railroad bridge were soon justified. At five o'clock on the morning of October 15, two men from a group of pickets on duty near the railroad bridge area dashed back into Company F's camp with disturbing news: a boat had landed and fired on the patrol. Most of the pickets had "run off and they supposed W. Hankamer was killed." The order was given to "sound the bugle," and get ready to start for Sparks.[5]

The company arrived at the scene of the recent action at 10 a.m. and were both surprised and relieved to find John W. Hankamer and the rest of the pickets alive and well. That unexpected outcome was attributed to an irrefutable fact: the Union soldiers involved in the predawn skirmish had been very poor marksmen in the dark of night. The following day, Captain Duncan wrote to his wife about the incident, which was the first face-to-face contact between Company F and their Union adversaries.

> I had a picket guard of seven men at Sparks ten miles below here, and night before last the yankees came up there in a small boat about 3 o'clock—four of the pickets hailed them after they had landed.[6] The yankees assumed they were friends and told our party for one man to advance and they would do the same. My men not being certain they were yanks, one of them went near the yanks. When the yanks ordered him to surrender and shot at him at the same time—my men broke and all the yankees, about 8 or 10, fired at him without hitting. Two of my men who were boys ran entirely off and came to camp—the yanks supposing there was a cavalry co. near broke to their boat and put off.[7]

It's difficult to tell from that description which side in the brief skirmish was more flustered. In any event, the combination of nervous energy, poor marksmanship, and limited visibility at three in the morning allowed all participants to escape unscathed.

The grapevine was a very efficient means of communication between troops in the field and family members back home, so John W. Hankamer assumed correctly that news of his close call would soon reach Crackersneck. In an attempt to allay the fears of his family members, he offered his account of the incident, as well as a brief mention of another encounter later that day, in a letter to his sister Mina Wilborn.

> I am well as ever and sound as a dollar although the Yankees have had several shots at me, six with their rifles & five with a canon but it is all in luck and as God wills it, for I don't think it would be safe every time to let them shoot at me with six rifles at about 30 or 40 steps or with canon and shell at the distance of half a mile or 3 quarters, for they might accidentally hit me, as bad marksmen as I take them to be, for I'll warrant if they'll let me have six shots at that distance at them I'll hit one of them. But enough about that, our days are allotted, and we can neither lengthen nor shorten them.[8]

Despite the potentially grave consequences of this encounter, there was also a humorous side to the incident. Parts of Southeast Texas are infamous for a very heavy clay soil referred to locally as "gumbo." When it's wet, travel across the muddy ground is very difficult for man or beast, and feet, hooves, wagon wheels, or any other objects are easily mired in the extremely sticky goop. In his letter of October 16 to his wife, William Duncan closed his account of the pickets' close call with this short tale:

> Yesterday I went to examine the place [of the encounter between his pickets and the Union party] and found a shoe sticking in the mud left by one of the gentlemen in his haste to regain the boat, and one of the men that was with me found another in the same fix, which was a mate to the one I had, and I bought his shoe so that I have a pair of yankee shoes.[9]

In his dash to get back to the boat and flee the area, one of the Union sailors had gotten his feet stuck in the muddy bank and literally ran out of his shoes. Captain Duncan didn't share whether they were the right size for him, but given the difficulty in keeping both Southern soldiers and civilians in footwear during the war, it's certain these "prizes of war" were put to good use by someone.

This minor skirmish could be considered a draw, with the muddy shoreline giving a slight advantage to the Southerners. At this point in the larger conflict, however, the Union had a major advantage in terms of firepower from their gunboats. That leverage was confirmed later that same day when the predawn scrap between the pickets and the small boat crew at Sparks resumed with more participants on both sides.

Even as that brief predawn encounter was taking place, Acting Master Frederick Crocker was preparing a much more serious attempt to burn the all-important railroad bridge across Taylor's Bayou. Crocker's ire had been raised by an earlier failed attempt by one of his subordinates to destroy the bridge on September 26. Some Southern newspapers had reported that botched mission, and Crocker was determined not to have a repeat of that embarrassment.[10]

Sabine Lake's shallow water limited the use of Crocker's large gunboats, but he had the ideal vessel for this job—a shallow-draft steamer named the *Dan*, which had been recently captured from the Confederates in Louisiana. Crocker fitted the *Dan* with a 20-pound Parrott gun and a 12-pound boat howitzer; the term "pounds" in this case refers to the weight of the projectile the weapon could fire. The *Dan* then headed up the lake on October 15 with a crew of twenty-five men.

The Union's intentions were not a surprise, and they approached the bridge to find one company of infantry and two of cavalry from Spaight's Battalion in the vicinity. The CSA contingent, including Company F, was wary of the potential threat of the heavier guns on the Federal steamer and wisely kept their distance when they saw the boat approaching. Their caution proved to be justified.

The boat's heavy guns opened fire on the bridge from a distance of over a mile, and Crocker's report later noted his gunners had the Confederates "nicely in range." The Texans had no artillery of their own, and one of Spaight's officers later noted his companions "could not maintain their positions at the bridge as they had no chance but to stand and be shot at with cannon without being able to help themselves."

As was the case with the earlier predawn skirmish, there were no casualties of note on either side. A CSA officer who witnessed the action as his men pulled back later noted, "The yankees shot at them for half an hour as they were getting away without hitting anybody, though they came very near some. . . . One man was knocked down by a ball striking the ground at his feet. Another got his nose mashed."[11]

Once the Southern troops had withdrawn, the Union contingent burned the railroad bridge, along with several houses and two schooners in the same area. John W. Hankamer's letter about his close call earlier that morning reached home the following day, so it was probably hand-carried by someone traveling from camp back to Liberty County. His attempt to make light of the situation didn't do much to blunt the family's dismay about the incident, which had also been shared in a separate note from one of his brothers. John Stengler described the reaction of both parents in a reply on October twentieth.

> As much as I can see from your letter Wilhelm almost got shot by Yankees which was a great shock to us and made Mother very sick. . . . You have only been gone 3 weeks since last Friday but to me seems like 3 months. But, dear son, listen and pray to God and He shall keep you safe. . . . You make light of it in your letter but I know that it is hard on you. I hope that we will soon get better times.[12]

Better times would, however, prove to be elusive during the final months of 1862, for both the Stengler family and most of the residents of Southeast Texas. As the calendar moved from summer to fall, a new challenge arrived in the area from the north—but it wasn't Union troops.

17

ADAPTING

I have suffered these cool nights for want of some warmer clothes [more] than I have by the Yankees.

—JOHN W. HANKAMER, October 19, 1862

The early arrival of autumn in 1862 came as a surprise in Southeast Texas. Fall can be a pleasant season on Texas' upper coast, with an occasional cool spell providing a welcome break after the steamy months of summer. During October of 1862, however, the first of several "northers"—the local term for a cold front—was an overachiever.

When Company F mustered for the first time in late April, Texas was heading into the hottest season of the year, and the men were equipped accordingly. Perhaps they expected to make preparations for the coming winter based on a typical autumn, but when mid-October suddenly felt more like late November, the troops were unprepared for the sudden change.

As would be the case for much of the war, Company F's assigned post not far from home was a major plus; it allowed much-needed family support with clothing, food, medicine, and other essentials the CSA government was unable to provide. When winter arrived ahead of schedule, the Stengler household was quick to respond with help.

On October 15, Johanette Stengler wrote to her son Fritz: "As much as I can see from Charles and Wilhelm's [John William's] letters they would like to have their winter clothes. Now I would like to know what you and George would like to have in clothes and bedding. I think it best to put it all in a trunk and send it by railroad. Your father wanted to bring it by horse, but it is too much for one horse."

In a letter to his sister, Mina Wilborn, four days later, John W. Hankamer commented, "I have suffered more these cool nights for the want of some warmer clothes than I have by the Yankees, the heaviest coat I have is a thin linen jacket." The weather hadn't improved by the following week, and on October 25, Capt. William Duncan noted in his diary that a strong cold wind blew all day. The next morning was even worse. They had ice and frost, with "all of us freezing."[1]

The clothing and bedding sent from home were invaluable as fall progressed into winter. On December 3, John W. Hankamer wrote to Mina from Grigsby's Bluff, reporting, "The weather is quite cold and uncomfortable now, but we are still able to keep ourselves dry, by [putting] another tent on top of ours, but we can't have no fireplace in them, and we can't build a fire, so we have to depend on our clothes and blankets, for wood is very scarce."

Despite those discomforts, the men made the best of their situation. Fritz Hankamer wanted to add some music to life in camp and wrote to his parents in early December 1862, asking them to send his fiddle. John W. Hankamer assured his family on December 3 that "we are all well and in good spirits, and by playing a game of poker or running a horse now and then we pass of the time as well as could be expected, for we must do something to draw our minds from our troubles."[2]

"Troubles" of many kinds weren't limited to troops in the field. The Union naval blockade of Galveston that began in July 1861 was having a growing impact with each passing month, and many manufactured or imported goods were becoming either scarce or exorbitantly expensive. Many Texans took this challenge to heart, and residents adapted to shortages with a combination of ingenuity and hard work.

In September 1862, the *Galveston Weekly News* published an article by a writer who urged readers to "let it be fashionable, as well as economical, to 'Make Cloth!' It is now plain we must make our own cloth or do without it. We rejoice to learn from many parts of the State that the Texas women are going to work in earnest upon domestic manufactures, and that the old spinning wheel and hand loom are again being brought into requisition."[3]

The need for those efforts in homes across the state became apparent soon after the war started. Before the conflict, mills in Northern states were the primary source of cloth throughout the country, but with that supply cut off in the South, a critical shortage of fabric quickly developed. In addition to the usual market for the civilian population, the South suddenly needed uniforms on short notice for thousands of newly enlisted soldiers.

The CSA had good intentions for clothing its troops, but reality often fell far short of official guidelines. During their first year in service, each soldier was supposed to receive two caps and jackets; three sets each of trousers, shirts, and drawers; four pairs of shoes and socks; one greatcoat (or stable frock for mounted men); and one blanket. Most of those items were due to be replaced in the man's second and third year.[4]

Many of the original clothing records for Company F have been preserved, and they confirm the shortfall. For all of 1863, John W. Hankamer received one cap and coat, a pair of trousers, and two pairs of shoes. That same year, his brother Fritz was issued a cap and coat, two shirts, and a blanket. George Stengler and Charles Hankamer fared somewhat better, and all four men received some additional items in 1864, but still fewer than they were authorized.[5]

Johanette Stengler and the other women in her extended family were well aware of the needs. Less than three months after her sons joined the army, Johanette wrote to her sons Fritz and George: "I am sending you a shirt. . . . Can't you maybe get some material for shirts? Then bring it along. It does not make any difference whether it is white or blue. Here we cannot get even one yard. If you want to, I can make a nice shirt of the linen material which you had bought for a coat. . . . If you have torn some of your clothes, bring it along. I can mend it."[6]

Shortages of material also required some flexibility for uniforms. In an October 11, 1862, letter, Johanette Stengler told Fritz, "Your yellow pants are ready. I wish I could get material for shirts." The "yellow pants" may sound unusual, especially if Fritz wore them as part of his CSA uniform, but wives, sisters, and mothers used whatever material and natural dyes they had available. The official "Confederate gray" was rarely the norm when soldiers were clothed by family members rather than military quartermasters.[7]

Johanette Stengler's skills in both sewing and dyeing clothing were mentioned in several letters, including one to Fritz on April 26, 1863. "I would like to do some dyeing," she wrote. "I have dyed your old linen pants, also I have made your white shirt so it will fit better. . . . I want to dye your white shirt. I dyed John's and they look very nice."

Dyeing fabric was one of many practices that used centuries-old methods, especially when supplies of commercial products were limited. A variety of tints could be obtained from local plants, as Johanette Stengler confirmed in a note to her sons on May 15, 1864. "I want to dye the pants as soon as your father comes home and gets some bark for me," she wrote.[8]

These skills were invaluable in keeping soldiers clothed, but Johanette's efforts were hampered by both the scarcity of fabric and rising prices. In November 1862, Johanette told her sons Fritz and George that a neighbor was weaving shirt material and said, "As soon as I can have it, I will make some shirts for you. They will be better for winter. The material is heavy and expensive. She wants $2 a yard for it. There is none cheaper."[9]

Two dollars a yard was high in 1862, but Johanette would have been thrilled to find fabric at that price only ten months later. On September 15, 1863, she told her son Fritz, "Everything is so costly. They ask $10 a yard for trouser material." Those prices hadn't eased by the following spring. "Mrs. Maden sent word that she would weave cloth for us at $10 the yard," John Stengler wrote to his son Fritz. "If we get 12 yards which will make 4 shirts, maybe they would also weave pants material for me."[10]

At those prices, enough material to make four shirts would cost $120, nearly a full year's pay for a CSA private. Johanette Stengler and other family members soon realized they needed to replace outside sources of cloth with their own in-house production. In January 1863, John Stengler mentioned to his son Fritz that the elder Stengler was making a loom for John W. Hankamer, presumably for the use of John W.'s wife. In October of that same year, Mina Wilborn wrote to her husband, Charles, with an update on a blanket he had requested. "Your blanket will be in the loom Saturday," Mina told him, noting it would be ready "the last of next week or the first of the week after."[11]

The demand for cloth, and the challenges of life for rural wives during the war, are aptly illustrated by a letter Mina Wilborn wrote to her brother Fritz Hankamer on November 27, 1863. When a rumor reached the Crackersneck community that a supply of material was available in the town of Liberty, a group of five women set out on a trip across the prairie by horseback to get some of the precious cloth. Under the best of circumstances, the round trip would take them most of a day, and it proved to be a memorable ride—for all the wrong reasons.

> On the 16th [of November 1863], mother and I, and Mrs. Abshire, Mr. Ducas' daughter, Mahner's wife, we all went to Liberty. We had heard that we could get 7 yards of cotton cloth for each member in a family. You can imagine how happy I was. I figured I would get 42 yards and had it all cut up in my mind already. We went that long way. Mother's horse fell with her [part of text missing, but one of the other women dismounted to help] . . . and put mother back on her horse, then she made stirrups of her rope so she could get back on her own horse. Just imagine all this confusion. The next day mother got a terrible headache and I thought I would never make it back home and on top of all we did not get any cloth, because our men are in the militia.

Such experiences reinforced the need for self-reliance, and by the following year, Mina and others had become quite adept at weaving. "I will get more than 28 yards [of] cloth," she wrote to her brother Fritz on October 30, 1864. "It will come out of the loom tomorrow. It looks real nice." Mina was plagued by serious health problems, which made any physical labor very difficult for her. One solution was for her to team up with Caroline Higginbotham, a young neighbor who married George Stengler after the war, and the pair made efficient use of Mina's loom.

In April 1865, Mina mentioned one such project to Fritz. "I have broadcloth in the loom for pants, shirts and various needs," she wrote. "There are 47 yards in the piece. . . . Caroline is leaving it at our house. . . . Give my regards to George . . . [and] tell him that Caroline is weaving at my house, and has woven 20 yards since Saturday." This letter was written on a Wednesday, so those twenty yards had been produced in five days or less, a very impressive output.[12]

John Stengler also contributed his skills to the effort to clothe the troops. Before he left Germany in 1845, he wrote, "My intentions are to follow masonry or the shoemaking trade." While he never did either on a regular basis, his shoemaking skills proved to be invaluable during the war. Several letters mentioned his making and sending shoes to his sons in the army, although shoe leather was often even harder to find than fabric.[13]

That shortage of leather created real hardships throughout the South, including for the Stengler household. Several letters included requests from family members for their soldier-sons to watch for sources of either shoes or shoe leather. On January 28, 1863, Johanette Stengler wrote to her son Fritz with a request for his fifteen-year-old brother, John H. Stengler. "Could you get a pair of shoes for John?" she pleaded. "He has to go barefoot and it is so cold to be without shoes."

Since the Stengler and Wilborn families had herds of cattle, we might wonder why John Stengler didn't simply tan his own leather. Given his already overwhelming workload with crops, livestock, firewood, and other tasks on multiple family farms, it was simply a shortage of time and energy. The tanning process was both labor-intensive and time-consuming, and each batch of leather took six weeks or more of work.[14]

A letter from John Stengler to his son Fritz on January 24, 1863, provides insight into the family patriarch's unrelenting tasks. Two of the sons had written that their shirts were completely worn out, and Johanette had made some replacements but didn't have a reliable way to send them. "I would come myself and bring the shirts to you but cannot get away," John Stengler wrote. "We have had so much cold rainy weather which keeps me from doing anything in the field. I have a loom to make for Wilhelm. And all this time we have been chopping wood."[15]

Numerous accounts from the war describe CSA soldiers going barefoot for months at a time, and the shortage of shoes was so urgent that Texas commanders reassigned some soldiers with previous experience as cobblers to small factories to produce footwear. One such facility was established about fifty miles north of Beaumont in the small community of Town Bluff.

A soldier from Spaight's Battalion, William Ratcliff, was an experienced shoemaker, and he was detailed to return home, where he enlisted the help of his wife and children. Metal nails were not available to attach heels and soles to the shoes, so the family whittled wooden nails from red oak and then carefully hardened them in a fire. The resulting shoes were ankle-high, had square toes, and were made in a range of sizes, but there were no separate "left" and "right" shoes in a pair. He was expected to produce at least fifteen pairs of shoes a week, a quota he usually exceeded.[16]

Any footwear was very expensive, so even those basic models were in high demand. In April 1863, Charles Hankamer reported from Galveston that the cost of some "very common everyday women's shoes" was thirty-five dollars, about three months' salary for a CSA private. Those who could afford better quality goods had to pay even higher prices. On January 9, 1864, an officer bought a "thick pair of boots in Galveston for $100."[17]

Shoes and shirts weren't the only items in demand, and long-standing substitutes for other staples were pressed back into use due to wartime shortages. Mina Wilborn described one example in a letter to her brother Fritz on December 26, 1862: "You wrote some time ago I should buy soda or Saleratus, but we cannot buy any. I will send you some of ours and when you have used that up, burn corn cobs and use the ashes. . . . As soon as I get a pound of lye, I will cook potash for you which you can use instead of Saleratus, but do not take as much of it."

Saleratus was a leavening agent used in cooking before baking soda became widely available. Commercial versions started showing up in stores in the 1840s, but they were expensive, and during the war, the blockade hampered the supply in the South. An alternative could be made at home from potash, which was obtained by a process that began with leaching water through wood ashes. By February 23, 1863, Mina Wilborn had replenished her supply of potash, and wrote to Fritz that she had "made a Saleratus" and was sending it to him.[18]

The process of making candles was described in an earlier chapter, and homemade candles were important not only for the light they provided but also as a source of income in a time when cash was scarce. Throughout the war, family letters are sprinkled with examples of both an entrepreneurial spirit and a sense of humor. On December 22, 1862, one of the brothers wrote to Mina from Grigsby's Bluff, joking about the speculation prompted by a heavier-than-usual box that had just been delivered to their camp.

> Dear Sister: . . . McBride arrived yesterday about three o'clock, he brought that box of candles—we have not opened it yet, but opened the letter and found out what was in the box. I could not imagine what was in it, though I thought you had sent a lot of gold or silver, that was as near as I could come to guessing what was in it, but as it happened, it turned out to be candles.

They weren't gold or silver, but in those years, candles *were* a valuable commodity, so this package from home represented both useful items and a chance for some welcome extra income. A follow-up inquiry from Mina confirmed this dual purpose for her shipment. "Did you get the candles we sent with Mack?" she asked. "I did not write what you should sell them for. Sell them for as much as you can."[19]

A second letter to Mina, this one from John W. Hankamer, offers additional details about this project. "I have also received those candles, and bargained some at a bit a piece," he wrote. "I had better sell them up at that price than to be a long time selling them, for we don't know how long we may have [before we need] to move, and then I don't know how I could get along with them then, unless we moved but little ways. They are [a] ready sale at 8 to the dollar." With a cavalry private's pay at twelve dollars a month, the Hankamer boys and their sister had found a lucrative enterprise.[20]

Other do-it-yourself projects included a learning curve. On June 17, 1862, the wife of Company F's commanding officer wrote to her husband about a wine-making venture. "I was busy all day yesterday putting up the wine we made, it is very good," she said. "I put it up in bottles and stop it up very tight and in half an hour all the corks were out of the bottles. I had to put it in a jug, all but eight bottles that the cork did not work out, it is like Champagne. I seal the jug air-tight and the eight bottles and I shall not use it till you come."[21]

With many of the able-bodied males away in the army, women carried much of the load for keeping both soldiers and civilians clothed and fed. They did have some help from older men and young boys who remained at home, and letters in September 1864 from both Mina Wilborn and Johanette Stengler offered an example of family teamwork. Charles Wilborn was sidelined with a serious hand injury, and Charles Hankamer was home briefly on leave, but he was sick with "the fever." Eleven-year-old James Wilborn and sixteen-year-old John Henry Stengler harvested seven wagonloads of corn for the Wilborns and most of Charles Hankamer's crop, and then they helped the elder Stengler bring in almost four loads of corn. They then mowed two loads of hay and planned to "mow more if the good weather held."[22]

John Stengler also helped put food on the table for his family and others in the area. In February 1865, he was busy searching the river bottoms for his semi-wild hogs, and he wrote to Fritz Hankamer to describe the results. "I was at C. Baxter's yesterday to see if I could sell some hogs in Galveston, as you know I have found my hogs," he said. "I let D. Shelby have 3 of them. I owed him for some leather and paid my debt in that manner and got 100 pounds of wheat flour besides."[23]

John Stengler's swapping of three hogs for leather and flour illustrated another adaptation to the wartime economy—an increased use of the barter system. Noncash payments weren't limited to individual transactions. A notice in the *Galveston Weekly News* on January 14, 1862, advised customers, "Confederate States postage stamps are receivable at this office the same as money. We will go a little further—we will take corn, bacon, sugar, flour, or any article of merchandise in demand, at its market value, including postage stamps, in pay for what is due to us in these times."[24]

One item in very high demand for either purchase or barter was coffee, and shortages of that staple forced Texans to search—with limited success—for locally available substitutes. A visitor from Great Britain spent three months in 1863 traveling from Brownsville to Houston and on to Shreveport, Louisiana, and later wrote about this forced improvisation. He described "a peculiar mixture called Confederate coffee, made of rye, meal, Indian corn, or sweet potatoes." He observed that the lack of coffee "afflicts the Confederates even more than loss of spirits, and they exercise their ingenuity in devising substitutes, which are not generally successful."[25]

Other contemporary sources described additional coffee substitutes, including parched okra seeds, cotton seeds, corn hominy, peanuts, beans, and peas. It's probably no surprise that these efforts were described by one recent arrival in Texas as "wretched imitations." The key was to gulp the concoctions down quickly, the writer advised.[26]

Supplies of clothing, candles, and coffee were definitely important for day-to-day life, but they weren't the only things on the minds of both civilians and soldiers. As 1862 moved toward a close, reports from newspapers, letters, and the ever-present "grapevine" ran the gamut from encouraging to disconcerting, and the year's end included a surprising military development in Southeast Texas.

18

YEAR'S END

*Christmas is now at hand, but I rather think
we will have but a dull time of it.*

—JOHN W. HANKAMER, December 21, 1862

The autumn of 1862 brought both a large dose of reality—and one welcome surprise—to the residents of Southeast Texas. On October 11, 1862, shortly after the Union capture of Fort Sabine, Mina Wilborn wrote to her brother Fritz:

> I think it [the direct effects of the war] is starting here in Texas now. So far we have not experienced anything compared to many other places. I am happy to see by your letter that you are still in good cheer. . . . I heard that the Yankees want Galveston and what they want of the people has been surrendered and many are moving away from Galveston. Many of the poor folks stay.

Ten days later, shortly after her brother John W.'s close call with a Union patrol at Sparks, Mina replied to one of his letters. She was clearly aware of the frustrations her brothers felt by their adversaries' tactic of staying safely aboard their gunboats, except for brief raids close to shore.

> You write that you would like to get at the Yankees. I'm afraid they will visit you quite often now. It is terrible how they burn everything. . . . I wish this war would end, so all of you could be home again. . . . Sometimes I have good hopes because our army is doing good work in Virginia and other places and I think the Yankees will be whipped here too if they get off the ship. The Lord protect you if you get into a battle and may He give you strength and courage to bear it all. It is my most fervent wish that all of you come home safe and sound.[1]

On November 4, Johanette Stengler wrote to her sons Fritz and George, and she too was worried about recent developments. "I think we will have hard times yet before the war ends. Oh, beloved, beware of the Yankees. Take good care of yourselves that you do not get sick. If you need anything write, and I will send it as quickly as possible."

Although the arrival of sharply cooler weather in mid-October had created considerable discomfort for the troops, the fall chill also ushered in a much lower level of military activity for both sides at Sabine Pass. Mounted CSA pickets continued to make regular overnight patrols between Grigsby's Bluff and Sabine Pass, and Union boats still made occasional patrols up and down Sabine Lake, but by the end of October, a stalemate was beginning to develop in the area.[2]

Union forces had, after all, achieved their primary objectives along Texas' upper coast. They had captured Fort Sabine, cut off railroad access to Sabine Pass, and established control over CSA shipping via the pass and Sabine Lake. Meanwhile, other Union forces were blockading Texas' major port at Galveston and had obtained the surrender of that city, although the Federal navy lacked the ground troops to actually occupy the island.

It was not until they had taken control of water access through Sabine Pass that Union officers began to realize the importance of that unassuming location. On October 12, 1862, Acting Master Crocker, the commander of the small Federal force in the area, wrote about the topic in a letter to his superior, R. Adm. D. G. Farragut.

> The importance of Sabine Pass to the rebels appears to have been entirely underrated by us; the quantity of goods of all kinds and munitions of war that have been run in here has been enormous, and large quantities of cotton have been exported. There are now lying above [inland from Sabine Pass on the Sabine River] at least eight steamers and six schooners, large quantities of cotton, and quite a force of troops.[3]

Thanks largely to the Union gunboats and their superior firepower, nothing was seen or heard from the Confederate ships bottled up above Sabine Lake, or the reputed "force of troops." The small Union contingent at the pass seemed content to maintain its blockade of shipping and keep a mostly low-key presence from the relative comfort and safety of the gunboats. The final two months of 1862 were shaping up to be a period of uneasy status quo in the area.

There were, however, two factors that would soon work against the Federal stranglehold on this watery highway. Due to continuing fears about yellow fever, the Northern forces had failed to establish any presence on shore. A report in the *Galveston Weekly News* on October 15, 1862, noted, "The invaders keep close to their boats and seldom visit the shore."[4]

The second element in favor of the Confederates at Sabine Pass was the Union's heavy reliance on information from Northern sympathizers in the area, and that would ultimately be their undoing. US Navy Acting Master Quincy Hooper had been left in charge of the federal forces at Sabine Pass in early December, and thanks to some carefully placed disinformation, he made a critical decision.

On December 5, Hooper wrote he "had received positive information that the vessels under my command are to be attacked immediately by a strong rebel force." He asked for reinforcements and said he "could not make a successful defense" against such an attack. Pending the arrival of help, Hooper felt it prudent to withdraw his ships and men back across the "bar" at the mouth of Sabine Pass and into the open waters of the Gulf of Mexico.[5]

Less than three months after their celebrated victory at Sabine Pass, the Union forces suddenly gave up control of this key inland waterway, and with it, their potential beachhead for a move into the interior of Southeast Texas. By maintaining an offshore blockade, the Federals could still reduce the number of ships sneaking into Sabine Pass, but they no longer had any direct influence over activities on shore.

The Union's abandonment of inland waters at Sabine Pass in December 1862 was a welcome surprise for the CSA, but for the Stengler family members still at home at Crackersneck, there were other concerns on a more personal level. As the end of the year approached, their most pressing worry was the prospect of losing the last two adult men still at home due to an expanded military draft.

In April 1862, the initial CSA conscription law required military service for most white males between the ages of eighteen and thirty-five. On September 27 of that year, that range was expanded to include ages eighteen to forty-five. As 1862 drew to a close, John Stengler was forty-three, and his son-in-law, Charles Wilborn, had just turned forty. The law allowed some latitude for officials to decide when to call up additional men as needed, leading the family to hope that men in their upper thirties were more likely to be drafted before those in their forties.[6]

Rather than take their chances with the draft and risk being sent far from home as part of a larger CSA unit, some men chose to volunteer for a local state unit. The Texas State Troops were specifically designated only for the defense of the state, and although much of the initial focus for these companies was on defending the western frontier against attacks by native tribes, new militia companies were being formed throughout Texas. John Stengler was already part of one such unit in Liberty County, and in a letter on December 21, 1862, he provided a prediction to his son Fritz. "I believe all of us who are in the militia will in 3 or 4 weeks be in camp at Beaumont for instructions," he wrote. "I do not yet know if I will have to go, I do think that I will be excused on account of your mother's arm."

Johanette's chronic health problems and their ages (she was fifty-seven, John was forty-three) might gain John Stengler an exemption, but Mina Wilborn was very worried about the status of her husband, Charles. At age forty, he was certainly more vulnerable to the draft than his father-in-law, and his departure would leave Mina, in poor health herself, alone on their sizeable farm with five small children.

Should Charles Wilborn be required to leave home and join the army, his absence would also affect more than his individual household. The families of two of his brothers-in-law, John W. and Charles Hankamer, were already alone on their farms, and Charles Wilborn was doing all he could to help them, in addition to keeping up his own place.

Charles Hankamer was both aware and very appreciative of this help. Summer is a busy season for any farmer and rancher, and Joanah, Charles's wife, was home with two children under the age of two. Their farm was within a mile or two of the Wilborn and Stengler places, but not next door, so any help Charles Wilborn gave to Joanah also required time for travel back and forth.

On June 12, 1862, Charles Hankamer had been gone to the army for about six weeks, and he offered his thanks in a letter to Charles and Mina Wilborn. His note also confirmed that Charles Hankamer's priorities were focused on his family and not the war.

> I hear that our corn is fine only it wants rain, which I am afraid we will not get soon, and that Charles [Wilborn] has had his hands full of work since we have left. . . . I don't know how I will ever be able to pay him for all he has done for me or rather my beloved wife and children, but I sincerely hope that this unholy war may soon come to an end and let those who have family take care of them themselves.

With Charles Wilborn carrying much of the workload for three households, Mina expressed her fears about his possible conscription to her brother Fritz on October 11, 1862. After hearing rumors about the new law, she wrote, "I hope they do not all have to go. If they draft them up to 45 years, then Charles has to go too. That would make me sad. I heard that Act has not been passed."

The hopes of his wife notwithstanding, Charles Wilborn was a realist, and he was preparing for the worst-case scenario. In that same letter to her brother, Mina confirmed that her husband was putting things in order while he had the chance: "Charles has fenced the garden, field, and pasture. Today he is cutting wood. . . . He wants to get everything in as good shape as possible."

Charles Wilborn continued to stay busy right through the fall and into early winter. On December 26, Mina told her brother Fritz that "Charles has renovated our house. We have a new door. Much has changed since you have been home. . . . Fritz, Charles says come next Monday. He wants to kill a hog and you should help. I want you to help make the sausage and then I will give you one. I think if you will tell your captain about it he will surely let you go."

By late December, Mina was becoming increasingly convinced her husband would be drafted, and the prospect was daunting. "We heard this morning that all men who are at home yet have to go to Beaumont to drill for about 3 weeks or more. . . . If that is so then Charles will have to go also. I do not know what I will do or how I will manage if he has to go."[7]

Charles Hankamer was aware of his sister's concerns, and he wrote to her three days after Christmas to try to encourage her.

> I am glad to hear that you all remain in tolerable good health, but you seem to be mighty down in spirit, well times do look rather dark now, but I hope they are at its darkest now, you must liven up and

take it as easy as you can. I hope to heavens that your beloved Chas. will be lucky enough to skip the draft, for luck is the only thing now that I can see that will do any good, for no previous exemption will be acknowledged. Dear sister, anything that is my power to do to keep Charles with you I would do with pleasure, but nothing is all that I know of.

Charles Wilborn was facing several possible options and outcomes from an expanded military draft. He could do nothing and hope he wouldn't be called; volunteer for the CSA unit of his choice and perhaps join his other family members in Company F; try to find an opening in a state militia unit; or take his chances about his unit assignment if he were to be drafted. Charles Hankamer pointed out to Mina that volunteering for a CSA unit would mean signing up for the "duration of the war," while older men who were drafted would probably be placed in a militia unit that would serve for a shorter period and only within the state. Charles Hankamer's letter continued with some predictions to try to encourage his sister.

> [If I were Charles] I would risk the draft, and in case of the worst it won't be but for three months, [but] if he was to go into a volunteer company it would be for [the duration of] the war and it's just a mere chance if the draft takes him. From what I hear there is more than 250 men to draft the 80 out of, besides a good many will volunteer, so be easy, it's not to go out of the state, it's for the protection of our homes right here.
>
> There is no danger of the men that are now called on having to go into a regular battle, only if our state is invaded by a large force, and if that should be the case, every man that is able to bear arms will be called on.

Charles Hankamer closed his letter with a pair of intriguing predictions. When he wrote to Mina on December 28, 1862, the town of Galveston was still in Union hands, and Sabine Pass, while not physically occupied by Union forces, was still under the shadow of a naval blockade. His statements cause us to wonder if Charles had heard about upcoming Confederate military plans, or if he was merely trying to cheer up his sister. In either case, he ended his letter on a positive note, "Don't fear [our state being invaded by a large force], for even now I expect that Galveston is ours again and Sabine Pass will be in a few days more. Well, I must close, be of good cheer, hope for the best, and when the worst comes we must fight it out."[8]

While civilians waited for the outcome of the draft, they joined those already away from home in looking ahead to the rapidly approaching holidays. One of the advantages of Company F's camp at Grigsby's Bluff was its proximity to home for the soldiers, and throughout their first eight months of service, the men enjoyed a rather liberal leave policy. All of the Stengler family soldiers were back home for at least a short visit more than once during the last half of 1862, and that was an enormous help with the backlog of tasks on their farms.

These troops and their families shared many things in common with soldiers throughout history, including a strong desire to spend occasions such as Christmas and New Year's Day at home. Even with the relative calm in the Sabine Pass area, not everyone could be granted leave from his military post, so the approaching holiday caused both increasing anticipation and anxiety.

On December 18, Fritz Hankamer offered a cautiously optimistic prediction in a letter to his parents, but it was clear he was already learning about the vagaries of military life. "I think that if nothing unforeseen happens George will come home for New Year's Day," he wrote. "Maybe I will come too, but do not know for sure, one cannot depend upon it, you must not be looking for us until we are there."

Fritz's brother John W. Hankamer had his own prediction for the holidays, which he shared in a December 21 letter to Mina. "Christmas is now at hand, but I rather think we will have but a dull time of it, I wish I could spend that day at home, I would rather than anything, but there is no use talking, I know that won't be, but I hope this war may soon end, I would like mighty well to be home again." Family members at home were also adjusting to the idea of a disappointing holiday. "It does not look as if you could come for Christmas and I had been so happy in anticipation," Mina wrote to Fritz on December 21. "We have to become reconciled to this."

Lieutenant Colonel Spaight, recognizing that his men would be disappointed to spend their Christmas in camp rather than at home, did what he could to offer a little holiday cheer by sending some blankets and a few items of clothing for the "most needy" men in the unit. On Christmas Eve, 1862, he wrote from his headquarters in Beaumont to Capt. William Duncan, commanding officer of Company F. He apologized he was unable to send any eggs for a Christmas nog for all the men, and he closed his letter with a rather somber prediction.

> Dear Sir:
> I am sorry to say no eggs have come either for me or to spare you. I wish I had enough eggs to give the entire company a nog.
> I send by the *Sunflower* [a steamboat] a corn sack, 8 carpet blankets, and 1 real blanket with the names of the 8 men on there. Tell them it is a Christmas present. I have four pair pants—3 or 4 shirts and some few socks. I wish to give them to the most needy. See who needs them most and let me know.
> Of course, there could be no harm in a good [illegible] all around if it could stop at that.
> No news here. All my calculations about the close of the war are at fault. I have all along believed that if not closed this winter in time to begin a cotton crop that no man could make a rational prediction as to its duration. I now see no signs of its closing this winter and incline to the opinion that it will only stop with the utter ruin of both parties. A pleasant anticipation!
> Your true friend,
> A. W. Spaight [9]

His commanding officer may not have been able to come up with any eggs for a Christmas nog, but Captain Duncan was determined to offer at least a token holiday treat for his men. He noted in his diary on December 24 that he had located some scarce eggs in the local area and paid a premium price for them. Christmas Day for Company F included the usual routine of roll call for the troops, but sometime during the day, their commanding officer "made a small nogg out of 2 bottles of liquor, gave the men a taste around. No more liquor."[10]

One of her brothers wrote to Mina on December 28 from Camp Spaight (Grigsby's Bluff) and shared his assessment of their first Christmas of the war. Perhaps he was concerned his parents would look askance at any reports that reached home about the Christmas nog, so he assured his sister it was only a token helping. In response to Mina's previous concerns about her brothers sleeping in a cold tent during the winter, he also offered news of an upgrade in accommodations.

> Dear sister. . . . I tell you we had about as poor a Christmas this year as ever I wish to have, that is we had an awful dull one, but I hope you had a better one at home. Well, the Capt. give us an eggnog but it was not enough to make anyone drunk, he didn't give but about one swallow a piece. . . . You want to know whether our tent was up yet or not, well I have written one letter to you since we moved but perhaps you did not get it. Well, we have built us a house and taken the tent down.

The day after Christmas, Mina wrote to Fritz, confirming that none of the brothers was able to secure leave. "Christmas is passed and not one of you was home," she wrote. "I hope you had a nice Christmas. I believe you felt like we did. All of you would rather have been home. O, how I and Charles and the children wished you could have been with us. You could have eaten with us. We did not have anything fancy but as good as possible."

Before the week was over, Mina's attention would be focused on more urgent matters. In a letter dated December 30, 1862, she confirmed that her husband, Charles, had received the summons she had been dreading.

> Dear brothers Fritz and George—Charles has been drafted. That is what Henry Braun heard in Liberty yesterday. . . . Charles has to leave soon, that is what I had been afraid of all along. . . . Excuse me for not writing more but I feel too bad. Hearty greetings from all of us, your loving sister. . . . Charles has to leave by Friday. He received orders. Answer soon.

The handwritten draft notice for Charles Wilborn was dated December 30 and was brief and to the point: "Charles Wilborn—This is to inform you that your name was drafted, you must be at Liberty next Friday ready to start, bring your gun with you. Dec the 30 1862. Bring cooking utensils."[11]

On New Year's Eve 1862, John Stengler confirmed Mina's news in a letter to Fritz. Although fifteen-year-old John Henry Stengler was still living at home with his parents, Charles Wilborn's departure would leave the elder Stengler as the only adult male in the extended family's four separate households. John Sr. acknowledged that reality and closed his note with a New Year's greeting for his sons.

> It is hard for us that everybody out of this family is gone except I. . . . Dear Sons Carl, Wilhelm, Fritz, and George, your mother and I wish all of you Happy New Year and hope that God keeps you in good health and hope that this year peace will come and that you soon can come home. Many greetings from your loving mother and father. John Stengler.

As the final day of 1862 drew to a close, the family's attention was understandably focused on Charles Wilborn's impending departure. They would soon learn, however, why none of their soldiers had been able to take leave for the holidays. A major development in the war—the largest battle fought thus far in Texas—was literally just over the horizon.

19

"THE HEAVY ROLL OF ARTILLERY"

I know you must have heard the heavy roll of artillery, we could hear it here plain.
—JOHN W. HANKAMER to his sister
Mina Wilborn, January 4, 1863

Maj. Gen. John B. Magruder was a man on a mission. When he was named commander of the Confederacy's District of Texas, New Mexico, and Arizona in late November 1862, he "found the harbors of this coast in the possession of the enemy." He immediately began planning to try to change that situation.[1]

When a small flotilla of US Navy ships entered Galveston's harbor in October 1862 and threatened to shell the city unless it was surrendered, the meager Confederate defenses on the island were unable to counter the threat. Under the circumstances, capitulation after only a token fight for Texas' most important seaport had been a prudent decision. The infrastructure of the town may have been saved, but its diminished usefulness to the CSA was significant from both a military and economic standpoint.

By forcing the evacuation of many of Galveston's citizens and maintaining control of the harbor, the Union effectively shut down almost all of the shipping in and out of the port in the autumn of 1862. The only goods that continued to reach the island came via daring blockade runners. Even so, the Union hold on the island was tenuous for lack of one essential resource—troops to secure the town itself. When the Confederates left the city, they merely pulled back several miles and took up entrenched positions at Virginia Point, on the mainland end of the wooden railroad bridge that was Galveston's connection to the rest of Texas.

The difficulty of holding control of Galveston without adequate land-based troops was a serious concern for US Navy commanders. On October 14, Adm. D. G. Farragut wrote to Commander Renshaw, who was in charge of the Union forces at Galveston. Farragut congratulated his subordinate "on the easy conquest you made of Galveston," but then noted, "I fear that I will find difficulty in procuring the few troops we require to hold the place. I informed the Secretary I could take the whole coast if I had only a few troops to hold it."[2]

Assistant Secretary of the Navy Gustavus V. Fox offered Admiral Farragut some hope of ground troops in a message on November 7. Commending Farragut for the capture of both Sabine Pass and Galveston, he noted, "Your people seem to be doing agreeable service down on the coast of Texas. An army force is preparing on a large scale to move into and take possession of that country."[3]

"Preparing to move" proved to be a relative term, and by mid-November, the situation had not changed. US Maj. Gen. B. F. Butler, apparently despairing of any help via normal military channels, sent a plea from his headquarters in New Orleans to Senator Henry Wilson, chairman of the Senate Committee on Military Affairs. "We want more men," he wrote. "We are now casting about for a regiment to send to Galveston—which the Navy has opened to us. . . . Reinforcements have been promised us, but they have not come."[4]

During that same month, Navy Capt. J. M. Wainwright also pressed his case for troops from his base aboard the steamer *Harriet Lane* in Galveston harbor. He reminded General Butler on November 14, "Though the town is under our guns, we have no force to occupy it and feel the want of some troops badly. This place can be easily held by a regiment with the aid of one or two vessels in the harbor."[5]

In early December, there was finally a hint of progress for Union commanders. From his office in New Orleans, General Butler provided an update to Edwin Stanton, secretary of war: "The 1st Texas Cavalry (U.S.) has been recruited without bounty or expense to the Government to the number of about 150 men. I am about sending it to Galveston, where it is expected to fill up its ranks from the same class of people who have enlisted in it here." Although it may sound like a misnomer, the 1st Texas Cavalry (US) was a Union force. These soldiers were expected to form the core of a larger unit that would be recruited from Union sympathizers, once these troops landed in Galveston.[6]

While Federal officers up and down the chain of command searched for ground troops to secure their foothold in Galveston, CSA General Magruder was moving ahead aggressively with his plans to retake the city. Like his Union counterparts, Magruder recognized that a key aspect of the situation had not changed since the Federal capture of the port in October. The Union still had no viable presence on the island itself, but it held the advantage with its heavy naval guns on ships stationed in the harbor.

Magruder needed a naval force of his own, but with no chance of help from outside the immediate area, his options were limited. His commanders chose an unorthodox solution using an item readily at hand—cotton. When tightly compressed into bales for shipment, cotton is a very dense material, and when stacked several layers high and wide on the deck of a steamer, the bales provided surprisingly efficient protection against enemy fire for both boat and crew.

Using this technique, frenzied work began on Christmas Day and went on around the clock to convert two river steamers, the *Bayou City* and the *Neptune*, into "cottonclad" gunboats. Two smaller vessels, the *Lucy Gwinn* and the *John F. Carr*, would accompany them as tenders, supplying wood for the gunboats' boilers. This pair of fighting ships were lightly armed; the *Bayou City* had a single 32-pound rifled gun, while the *Neptune* carried two 24-pound howitzers.

In addition to their usual crews, the two cottonclads would each carry 150 sharpshooters, volunteers from infantry and cavalry units. They were armed with both shotguns and the highly prized Enfield rifles, weapons that were in short supply in Southern ranks. The sharpshooters' task was to drive Union gunners from their positions on their ships, and then board and capture the Federal gunboats if the Confederate craft could either ram them or draw alongside.[7]

The second phase of Magruder's plan involved using the railroad bridge connecting the mainland to the island to move his ground troops and artillery to points within range of the Union gunboats. Compared to the Union armament, the CSA was at a distinct disadvantage. Their weapons consisted of six siege pieces, including one heavy gun mounted on a rail car, and fourteen smaller artillery field pieces.[8]

Arrayed against the Confederates was a small but impressive Union fleet: the steam-powered gunboats *Clifton*, *Harriet Lane*, *Westfield*, *Owasco*, and *Sachem*, along with six other transport and support vessels. Among them, they carried at least thirty heavy guns.[9]

Galveston had been largely abandoned after the initial Union foray in October, but the remaining population was rife with informants for both sides. It was no secret, then, when Union Commander Renshaw received a Christmas gift of sorts on December 24.

Three companies—a total of about 260 men—of the 42nd Massachusetts Volunteer Regiment reached Galveston Harbor from New Orleans on Christmas Eve. They landed on the island the following day and immediately began fortifying a warehouse on Kuhn's Wharf, at the foot of Eighteenth Street. That position put them within easy range—and therefore under the protection—of the heavy guns on the Union ships. By erecting a stout barricade between their position and the center of town, and by pulling up all but one easily removable plank connecting the wharf to the shore, they were unapproachable from the land.[10]

Once they had established a defensible position on the pier, these soldiers finally provided a Union presence on the ground in Galveston. Effective control of the city, however, was more illusion than fact. One of the unit's officers noted that "patrols were sent through the city by day, pickets were posted at the corners of main streets, and a lookout kept from the cupola of Hendley's buildings, which commanded a view of the whole city and suburbs. At night, however, the pickets were drawn in near the head of the wharf."[11]

After dark, Confederate patrols were able to roam through the city at will. This freedom of movement was so relaxed that only a few days before the upcoming battle, CSA General Magruder made a nighttime inspection of key points around the island and the town. He was accompanied by a party of eighty men and supported by three hundred more as he passed through the city of Galveston."[12]

The initial Union ground force on the island may have been small, but CSA officers were concerned about reports that these soldiers were

FIGURE 10. CSA Cottonclads on their way to Galveston, December 31, 1862, from C. W. Raines, *Six Decades in Texas, or Memoirs of Francis Richard Lubbock*. Courtesy of Rosenberg Library, Galveston, Texas.

only the vanguard of a more substantial contingent. Within the next few days, additional Union troops and supporting artillery were expected to arrive in Galveston, and that would represent a significant shift in the military balance. The end of December brought a full moon, certainly not an ideal time for a nighttime attack, but the impending arrival of a large Union force dictated quick action by the Southerners.[13]

The limited means of communication available in 1862 made coordination between the makeshift CSA gunboats and the ground forces attempting to sneak into town under cover of darkness difficult at best. The solution was to rely upon the most basic of tactics and signals. The Confederate gunboats were to move down Buffalo Bayou from Houston to a point as close to Galveston's harbor as possible without being detected. They were then to wait until they heard cannon fire from the town before starting their waterborne attack on the Union fleet.[14]

On New Year's Eve 1862, the Confederate ground troops began their move from the mainland across the two-mile-long causeway to the island and then into the city itself. Some of the heavier artillery pieces had to be moved nine miles over "very difficult roads," and the desire to maintain an element of surprise meant they could not get underway until nightfall. Some of the units eventually approached within two blocks of the wharf where the Union infantry waited, and it was long past midnight before all the CSA forces were in position.[15]

The impending attack was hardly a surprise. At 1:30 a.m., the bright moonlight enabled two Union vessels to spot the lurking Confederate gunboats, and the signal "enemy afloat" was flashed to the Federal fleet. Shortly thereafter, the Union troops on Kuhn's Wharf were alerted by their pickets that "the artillery of the enemy was in possession of the market place," and a second signal was passed among the fleet—"enemy on shore."[16]

As the moon began to set at about 3:00 a.m., darkness and an uneasy calm settled briefly over the town and harbor. The agreed-upon signal for Southern forces to commence the attack was a round fired from the center cannon in their line in town, and General Magruder, a hands-on commander, personally fired the opening shot.[17]

That initial shell was promptly followed by a vigorous exchange of artillery and rifle fire from both sides. Theo Noel was part of the CSA force entering downtown Galveston and later described the response by the heavy guns on the Union ships to Magruder's first shot.

> Great Heavens! A flash, and the whole surface of the water was lighted; and like lightning it kept flying from right to left with such rapid succession that one could hardly discern the pauses or intervals between each broadside. Then came the thundering sound—no, thunder bears no analogy to the sounds that there met our ears—the ground on which we stood fairly quaked, as broadside after broadside was poured into the city.[18]

The combined barrage of dozens of heavy naval guns and field artillery pieces was clearly heard at Company F's camp at Grigsby's Bluff south of Beaumont. The straight-line distance from Galveston to that camp was about fifty miles, but it was across either open water or flat, marshy terrain, so the sound carried well in the predawn darkness.[19]

The noise of the battle would have been even more audible—and worrisome—at the family's homes near Crackersneck, which was about forty straight-line miles northeast of Galveston, much of that distance across the open waters of Galveston Bay. Many years later, a project to interview former slaves from Texas included the reminiscences of Jacob Branch. At the time of this battle, he was a child living in Chambers County near Double Bayou, about a dozen miles closer to Galveston than Crackersneck.

Jacob had gotten up as usual at the "crack of dawn to milk" when he felt a shock that shook the earth. He described a surreal scene of fish jumping out of the water and turtles and alligators running out of their ponds. He and his half brother Eleck ran into their house on the Elisha Stephenson farm and saw "all the dishes and things jumped out of the shelf." At the time, of course, they had no way of knowing what was taking place, but he commented later that "they plumb [ruined] Galveston."[20]

That secondhand description of the effects of the short battle on the city was later confirmed by a visitor with an experienced eye in such matters. A British military officer who visited Galveston four months after the fighting observed, "Its houses are well built; its streets are long, straight, and shaded with trees; but the city was now desolate, blockaded, and under military law. Most of the houses were empty, and bore many marks of the ill-directed fire of the Federal ships during the night of the 1st of January last."[21]

At the time of the battle, there was no direct telegraph communication between Company F's post and the rest of the world, so those men had no immediate information about what the distant cannon fire signified. Their reactions likely ranged from curiosity to concern, but lacking any news, life in camp on New Year's Day went on as usual, and the company drilled after the midday meal.[22]

For their comrades in Galveston, life was anything but routine as the sun began to rise on New Year's morning. The Confederates' artillery and infantry, without the benefit of earthworks or other defenses, were receiving what Magruder later described as a "tremendous discharge of shell, followed with grape and canister." Unable to approach the Union troops on the wharf by land, the CSA plan called for infantry units to wade into the shallow water of the bay and use scaling ladders to assault the wharf.[23]

The attack was nearly a disaster for the Confederates. The scaling ladders proved to be too short, and the soldiers were left floundering in the water under withering fire from the wharf above. With the gradual

FIGURE 11. Capture of the USS *Harriet Lane*, January 1, 1863. Courtesy of US Naval History and Heritage Command.

arrival of daylight, Union gunboats were able to identify their targets on shore from a range of fewer than three hundred yards, and it began to appear the land assault might fail.

It was at this critical juncture that a dramatic change in the situation occurred. According to a report filed after the battle by CSA General Magruder, "At this moment, our fire still continuing, our gunboats came dashing down the harbor and engaged the *Harriet Lane*, which was the nearest of the enemy ships, in the most gallant style, running into her, one on each side, and pouring onto her deck a deadly fire of rifles and shotguns."

One of the two CSA cottonclads, the *Neptune*, was quickly damaged and soon sank in shallow water. The main gun on the second cottonclad, the *Bayou City*, exploded after firing only three rounds. On its second attempt to ram the much larger *Harriet Lane*, the two vessels became locked together, and the CSA boarding party quickly poured over the side and took control of the Union ship.[24]

The Union ship *Owasco* attempted to come to the *Harriet Lane's* aid but was driven off by rifle fire from the Confederate sharpshooters. Before the naval battle had even begun, Captain Renshaw's flagship, the

Westfield, ran aground in the dark in the bay's notoriously shallow water, and its guns were not a factor in the battle.[25]

By about 7:30 a.m., a three-hour truce was declared while Union naval commanders weighed a demand for their surrender. According to a CSA report, "All the enemy's vessels were immediately brought to anchor, with white flags flying." Subsequent Confederate and Union reports disagreed about whether the flags indicated a temporary truce or a surrender, but after spotting the white flags on their ships in the harbor, the Union infantry on Kuhn's Wharf surrendered. Thanks almost entirely to the success of one improvised cottonclad gunboat, Magruder's forces had defeated a much superior naval force. Before the morning was over, the city was back in Confederate control.[26]

The final tally revealed the Confederates had captured a key gunboat, the *Harriet Lane*, two unarmed supply ships, the *Cavallo* and the *Elias Pike*, and the schooner *Lecompte*. Some four hundred Union officers, sailors, and soldiers were either casualties or captives, including all of the infantry stationed on shore. Confederate casualties were reported to be twenty-six killed and 117 wounded.[27]

A second gunboat—the Union flagship *Westfield*—was still aground when fighting ceased, and Union Commander Renshaw was determined not to leave it intact for use by the enemy. A plan to destroy the ship once all hands had abandoned ship went awry, resulting in the deaths of Renshaw, two other officers, and several sailors when the magazine exploded prematurely.[28]

To the disgust of CSA officers, as the three-hour truce was nearing its end, the remaining Union ships simply sailed out of the bay. They were soon out of reach of Confederate shore batteries and headed back to New Orleans, where their officers would face withering scorn from superiors, peers, and the Northern press. *Frank Leslie's Illustrated Newspaper*, published in New York, included a full-page illustration of the "Destruction of the U. S. Flagship *Westfield* and Capture of the *Harriet Lane*, at Galveston, Texas." An accompanying story noted, "We illustrate today one of the most annoying events of the war, since it would appear to have been the result of a surprise, for which our military authorities should have been prepared."[29]

Although five Union ships and their personnel managed to escape from Galveston, the defeat was a significant setback for Northern plans for both Texas and the Gulf Coast. According to Gustavus V. Fox, assistant secretary of the Navy, "The Galveston disaster is the most melancholy affair ever recorded in the history of our gallant navy . . . [and] our prestige is shaken."[30]

Near the end of the war, Union Gen. N. P. Banks offered his thoughts about the importance of this battle. "I regarded the loss of Galveston in its consequences . . . as the most unfortunate affair that occurred in the department during my command," he said. "Galveston, as a military position, was second in importance only to New Orleans or Mobile."[31]

Thanks to limited communications, the men of Company F at Grigsby's Bluff had no knowledge of these events on the day they occurred. Shortly after 10:30 p.m. on January 1, a man from the steamboat *Sunflower* arrived in camp with a message from Lieutenant Colonel Spaight: Company F was to board the *Sunflower* and "proceed to Beaumont, then to Houston with all dispatch."

The troops were roused out of bed and told to get ready to move out. They were apparently anxious for some action since their response to this news was reported to be, "All glad." Within two hours, shortly after midnight, they were headed for the *Sunflower*, leaving about a dozen men behind to keep an eye on their camp. The obvious sounds of distant cannon fire hours earlier, along with the skirmishes in their immediate area only two months earlier, made them wary about the ongoing threat of another attempted Union offensive.

It now seems likely their orders to head for Houston were issued before the outcome of the Galveston fight was known, and the message was delayed in reaching the unit. After Company F was loaded on the steamer, the boat made another stop to load additional men from Captain Keith's company, which was camped about a mile away from Company F. Before they could get on board, an additional message was received, ordering them all back to camp. The fight at Galveston was settled, at least for the time being.[32]

The first reports about the actual battle finally reached Company F's camp about thirty-six hours later. After darkness had fallen on Friday, January 2, a relative of one of the company's officers arrived bearing a newspaper with an account of the fight. That version of the Confederate victory quickly spread through the camp, and on January 3, John W. Hankamer shared his secondhand report of the battle in a letter to his sister, Mina.

> Dear Sister: . . . a terrible fight taken place at Galveston on New Year's Day, but I reckon you have heard of it before now. I know you must have heard the heavy roll of artillery, we could hear it here plain; our men took and destroyed four of the enemy's vessels and they destroyed one to keep it from falling into our hands; our men also took six hundred prisoners.[33]

It is true in many situations in life that timing is everything, and that was definitely the case for the Confederates' efforts to retake Galveston. The day following the battle, another Union ship appeared just outside the harbor. The captain was unaware of what had transpired barely twenty-four hours earlier and was nearly lured into a trap. Aboard the vessel were additional troops, perhaps one thousand in number, sent to help hold the island, along with more artillery. A ruse to convince the ship to enter the harbor failed, and it escaped back to New Orleans.[34]

It's impossible, of course, to predict the impact if those additional troops had reached Galveston even forty-eight hours sooner. That said, Maj. Gen. N. P. Banks, the Union Army commander for the area, had a strong opinion about the importance of these reinforcements, along with the North's failure to destroy the railroad bridge connecting Galveston with the mainland. More than a year after the battle, Banks wrote to the secretary of war, saying, "Had the troops sent for its occupation arrived a day or two earlier, or in sufficient time to have destroyed the bridge, the attack would have been defeated."[35]

There is yet one more example from Galveston of how even the smallest details can have an enormous impact on historical events.

The Union may have lost control of Galveston on January 1, 1863, but Admiral Farragut didn't accept the defeat as anything but a temporary setback. Two days later, on January 3, he ordered Comm. H. H. Bell to take the USS *Brooklyn* to Galveston "as soon as your ship can be gotten ready," to "ascertain the true state of things at that place." If, upon his arrival, Bell found things "favorable," he was to "retake Galveston or at any rate send the gunboats up into the harbor and retake the *Harriet Lane*, if possible." He was also ordered to "shell the troops out, if any appear." By January 12, the gunboats *Sciota, Cayuga, Hatteras, New London, and Clifton* would join the *Brooklyn* near Galveston.[36]

CSA General Magruder fully expected another Union attempt at Galveston, and shortly after the battle was over, he put men to work fortifying the town. They began adding new earthworks, blockhouses, and guns, including those captured from the Union ships on January 1. They were not, however, ready for a major assault when this new Federal flotilla appeared just offshore.

Commodore Bell used the rifled guns on the *Brooklyn* to shell CSA parties working on fortifications along the shore on January 7, 1863, and with the arrival of more Federal ships, additional rounds were fired at CSA positions on Saturday, January 10. These shots were primarily for intimidation, and now that the new Union flotilla had assembled, a concerted attack was planned for Monday, January 12.[37]

A report written from one of the ships on the evening of January 10, 1863, described the confidence of the Federal sailors. "When the bombardment is renewed it will be terrific. Galveston is a doomed town; the disgrace attending the capture of the *Harriet Lane* must be wiped out, and vengeance upon its butchers and captors will be awful."[38]

This optimism would prove to be premature.

Late in the afternoon of January 11, as the Union ships awaited the attack on Galveston, the top of a distant sail was spotted peeking over the horizon in the Gulf of Mexico. The identity of this vessel was not known, so Commodore Bell ordered one of his gunboats, the USS *Hatteras*, to investigate. The mystery ship changed course, headed back the way it had come, and both vessels disappeared out of sight as daylight faded into evening.

As darkness fell, the crews of the remaining Union ships suddenly heard distant sounds of heavy guns, and Commodore Bell immediately sent three of his gunboats in that direction. Nothing was found until about 11:00 a.m. the following day when the wreck of the *Hatteras* was spotted, its hulk sitting on the bottom in shallow water. Six of the crew reached Union ships off Galveston later that day in a small boat and reported that their craft had been sunk in a short engagement the evening before. All but two of the remaining crew members from the *Hatteras* were picked up by the enemy vessel, which then disappeared into the night.

The mystery ship was later identified as the CSS *Alabama*, the Confederacy's most feared warship. After the brief fight, the *Alabama* sailed away into the vast expanse of the Gulf of Mexico and on to Jamaica, where the captured crew from the *Hatteras* was released ten days later.[39]

The *Alabama's* presence near Galveston on January 11, 1863, was not a coincidence. The ship's captain, Raphael Semmes, had learned from captured Northern newspapers that Galveston had surrendered to Union forces and steps were underway for an invasion of Texas. Galveston would reportedly be the rendezvous point for the large fleet required to move "not less than 30,000 men," including cavalry and light artillery, and news stories also helped Semmes predict when the Federal fleet would reach Galveston.

Due to the shallow water at the entrance to the harbor, Semmes expected most of the Union ships "would be obliged to anchor, pell-mell, in the open sea." This would provide the *Alabama* an opportunity to "surprise this fleet by a night attack, and if possible, to destroy it, or at least greatly cripple it."

As the *Alabama* neared Galveston on January 11, the lookout high atop its masthead was instructed to watch carefully for the first sighting of "an immense fleet anchored off a light-house." When it was spotted, Semmes planned to "haul off and await the approach of night" before he "ran in and made the assault." When the lookout reported "five steamers which looked like ships of war" instead of a huge fleet of transports, Semmes realized something was amiss. Shortly thereafter, when a shell thrown by one of the steamers burst over the city, he realized the Confederates must have retaken Galveston, and the Union invasion plans had changed.

Semmes was faced with a dilemma. He later wrote, "I certainly had not come all the way into the Gulf of Mexico to fight five ships of war." When one of the Union steamers was seen heading in his direction, Semmes quickly decided to lure it away to a distant location, where he could engage it in a one-on-one fight. The *Hatteras* was to be the loser of that encounter.[40]

Once again, a small detail affected the course of the war. Bell, thus alerted that the notorious *Alabama* was roaming the waters of the Gulf of Mexico, sent another of his ships to New Orleans to sound the alarm. His forces now depleted by two fighting ships, Bell called off his planned assault on Galveston.[41]

Bell's commanding officer, R. Adm. D. G. Farragut, was left with the unpleasant task of informing his superiors of this latest setback. On January 15, 1863, Farragut sent his report to Gideon Welles, secretary of the Navy, and its opening sentence summed up the events of the second week in January: "Sir: It becomes my painful duty to report still another disaster off Galveston."[42]

Bell remained on his ship offshore at Galveston, observing the continued Confederate work to fortify the island. On January 24, he forwarded a frank assessment to Admiral Farragut in New Orleans, noting that Galveston's defenses could be called "formidable to anything we might send against them . . . [and] there does not appear to be the least chance of success for any uncombined naval and land attack that could be made."[43]

In addition to the actual loss of a valuable ship, the *Hatteras*, and the missed opportunity to retake Galveston, the impact of these events on the morale of the Union Navy was significant. On January 29, Rear Admiral Farragut advised the secretary of the Navy that when the USS *Clifton* returned from Galveston, he found the officers and crew to be "so demoralized . . . with many of the crew deserting" that he had to keep the ship at New Orleans.

Farragut's summary of the current state of affairs for naval operations in the western Gulf of Mexico was even more dismal. In his opinion, "The shameful conduct of our forces at Galveston has been one of the severest blows of the war to the Navy; the prestige of the gunboats is gone in that quarter until it is again reestablished by some corresponding good conduct on our part."[44]

The immediate threat to Galveston—and the rest of Texas—was over. The troops of Company F and the rest of Spaight's Battalion had been distant bystanders to this Confederate victory, but that was about to change. General Magruder's next target involved the Union blockade at Sabine Pass, and the men of Company F would soon get their chance to play a direct, and much different, role.

20

FROM SADDLES TO STEAMERS

*William and Fritz are both at Orange with 24 of
our men ... to go on board of our gun boat ...
for the purpose of retaking this place.*
—CHARLES HANKAMER, January 11, 1863

The troops in Spaight's Battalion may have missed the battle for Galveston on New Year's Day of 1863, but they would soon have a chance to put their months of drills to use. After the Confederates' victory at the island city, CSA General Magruder intended to move quickly to build on that momentum. His next objective was to break the Union blockade of Sabine Pass on the Texas-Louisiana border.

As had been the case at Galveston, the Union held a major advantage in the number of naval guns in the Sabine Pass area. Based on their recent success at Galveston, the Confederates planned to offset their shortage of heavy weapons with a combination of small arms and improvised cottonclad gunboats. A key element in this strategy required the cottonclads to approach within rifle range of their opponents, and then rely on the shipboard sharpshooters to drive the Union gunners from their posts. Once the superior firepower of the blockaders had been neutralized, boarding parties from the CSA cottonclads would take control of those vessels.

Preparations for the operation were already underway in December 1862 at a shipyard in Orange, Texas, on the Sabine River east of Beaumont. The Confederate "flotilla" would consist of only two vessels, which were river steamers retrofitted as gunboats. Their makeshift protection from the Union gunners would rely upon materials readily available in the local area—dense bales of cotton stuffed tightly between a double wall of heavy oak beams.

The larger of the two vessels, the *Josiah H. Bell*, was a 171-foot-long sidewheel steamer that had been used to haul everything from cotton to locomotives for the Texas and New Orleans Railroad's expansion in Southeast Texas. Due to the shortage of heavy weapons, the *Bell* was armed with only one heavy gun, but it was a *big* one, a 64-pound rifled cannon. The *Bell's* most important asset, however, was not a gun at all, but the three boilers in the engine room, which supplied a 450-horsepower steam engine. The second member of this mini flotilla was smaller than the *Bell*. The 135-foot-long *Uncle Ben* was also a side-wheeler with twin smokestacks; it was fitted with a pair of 12-pound smoothbore field guns and a single 6-inch rifled gun.[1]

Men from two artillery companies would handle the fleet's total of four large weapons on the pair of ships. On January 4, a call went out for volunteer riflemen from the ranks of Spaight's Battalion to serve as sharpshooters on the gunboats. John W. and Fritz Hankamer were among those selected, meaning for at least one battle, these cavalry soldiers would trade their saddles for a place on the deck of a cottonclad steamer. They were assigned to the *Uncle Ben*.[2]

The shotguns normally carried by these cavalrymen were unsuitable for this assignment, so on the night of January 5, the volunteers received orders to obtain muskets and bayonets from the infantry troops camped nearby in Captain Keith's unit. Thus armed, the sharpshooters boarded a train and headed for Beaumont and eastward to the town of Orange. On January 11, 1863, Charles Hankamer wrote to his sister from Sabine Pass with an update.

> We are here at the Pass, the most hateful place I've ever been at, a place where we will never hear from anywhere. . . . William and Fritz are both at Orange with 24 of our men and the same number from every Company in the Battalion, to go on board of our gun boats that are fitted up for the purpose of retaking this place, but the enemy left here before the boats were ready, so we came to town and taken possession, but if our boats don't come down in a day or two I don't know how long we will keep position, for the enemy's vessels are swarming outside the [bar] and from their movements

goes to show that they will come in. If they should come before our boats comes down it will be no trouble for them to shell us out, for we have nothing here larger than a shotgun.[3]

Rumors of the impending action had also reached family members back at Crackersneck. On January 15, 1863, John Stengler wrote to his sons Fritz Hankamer and George Stengler to express his concerns. "Much beloved sons, we have for some time now been in much worry over you, since John Brown was here on the 4th, [he] told us that Fritz and Wilhelm were now on a ship and that George and Karl had ridden to Sabine Pass to chase the Yankees away from there."

This letter from John Stengler also offered a reminder of the many ways individual and family milestones were disrupted by the war. "Beloved son George: Today is your birthday," John wrote. "I congratulate you, I pray that God may keep you in good health in your 21st year and that He will be with you and protect you in all dangers. Pray to Him for protection. . . . I wish that you could once come home, it is close to 4 months since you were here."

Their father's sources were correct regarding the mid-January military activity. In the predawn hours of January 21, the *Bell* and *Uncle Ben* finally got up steam and headed out of Sabine Lake and then into the open waters of the Gulf of Mexico. This move was hardly a surprise to Union commanders, but hints of a CSA attack on the Federal blockade had worked in favor of the Confederates. Six weeks earlier, Union Navy Commander Law was sent to Sabine Pass to assess the situation. He found "much uneasiness" aboard the Union ship on duty in the area, the *Rachel Seaman*.

The source of those worries was "reports of movements of the rebels," who were said to have at least four armed boats, several of them cottonclads, plus other vessels. These would reportedly be assisted in an attack on the *Rachel Seaman* by a land force of about five hundred men and light artillery pieces. As a result of those concerns, the Union Navy pulled back from Sabine Lake to positions offshore and thus gave up effective control of the town of Sabine Pass and the surrounding land and inland waters.[4]

The Union blockading force now spent most of its time patrolling offshore in the gulf, and while its firepower was certainly adequate to take on unarmed blockade runners or CSA ground troops, it was no longer an overwhelming adversary for the pair of Confederate cottonclads. Only a few days earlier, the Federal force in the area had been reduced by a third with the departure of the *Rachel Seaman*, which had been sent to Pensacola for repairs. According to its master, that vessel was "leaking so badly in her upper works in a rough sea as to damage his ammunition and materially injure the health of the crew."

The remaining blockaders consisted of a pair of ships, including the *Morning Light*, a large three-masted, square-rigged sailing ship carrying eight 32-pound guns. Despite its somewhat gentle name, those weapons made this converted merchantman a formidable opponent for the small Texas fleet.

The *Morning Light* was accompanied on blockade duty by the *Velocity*, which was armed with two 12-pound howitzers. Its name suggested a speedy ship, but the *Velocity* was not much of a threat. Just three days before the impending battle off Sabine Pass, it had been described by Commodore Bell as "a miserable little craft, badly found, and scarcely able to keep the sea."[5]

An eyewitness account written later for the *Houston Telegraph* reported that the two CSA cottonclads headed through Sabine Pass at about half past six on the morning of January 21, 1863, with the *Bell* in the lead. They were soon spotted by both Union ships, which "made all sail and tried to get away, but it was no use. Heaven favored us," the Southern correspondent noted, "and frowned upon them in the shape of a very light breeze."

Under those conditions, the two sail-powered Union ships were at a distinct disadvantage compared to the Confederates' steam-powered gunboats. Two hours later the chase had covered twenty miles of open water, and the CSA ships had closed the distance to about two miles. At that point the breeze began to pick up, briefly raising Union hopes they might escape, but the advantage remained with the Texans. According to an eyewitness on board the *Bell*, "We were going at the rate of 7 miles an hour and the enemy about 5."

An exchange of fire by both sides ensued, resulting in little damage to the Southern craft, and the extra maneuverability provided by their steam engines offered a significant advantage. Several long-range shots from the *Josiah Bell's* 64-pounder caused considerable damage to the Union's *Morning Light*, and by 11:00 a.m., the *Bell* had closed the distance enough to allow the sharpshooters' rifle fire to begin to take effect.[6]

FIGURE 12. This sketch of the capture of the USS *Morning Light* appeared in *Frank Leslie's Illustrated Magazine* shortly after the battle. The bulky shape of the cottonclad *Josiah Bell* is shown on the left side of the drawing. Courtesy of New York Public Library.

As had been the case three weeks earlier at Galveston, withering, well-placed rifle fire by soldiers on the Southern ships proved superior to heavy naval weapons by driving the Union gunners from their posts. The *Morning Light*, unable to defend itself, struck its colors and surrendered shortly after 11:00 a.m. The smaller *Velocity* soon followed suit.

The brief offshore fight ended in a lopsided CSA victory. The Confederate soldiers and sailors sustained only one minor wound and little damage to their two cottonclads. Union casualties were one killed and nine wounded, with 107 captured.[7]

Of even greater importance was the Federal loss of the two vessels, ten heavy guns, and a considerable quantity of ammunition and other supplies. The mood among the Southern troops following this success was described as, "Great rejoicing on our side," although the CSA's gains would soon prove to be more psychological than tactical. This naval victory, combined with the retaking of the town of Galveston only three weeks earlier, boosted Confederate confidence and struck a serious blow to Union morale.[8]

After Union Admiral Farragut received word of the battle, he had the unpleasant task of informing Secretary of the Navy Gideon Welles of the outcome. On January 21, 1863, he wrote, "I have received dispatches by which you will see that our disasters on that coast are not yet ended." In a separate message the following week he lamented, "There will be no end to this Galveston success until we make a clean destruction of one of their vessels. . . . They are growing bold."[9]

From a military standpoint, the Texans were unable to achieve maximum advantage from their success. Both of the captured vessels were sailed back toward the port of Sabine Pass, but the *Morning Light* drew too much water to readily negotiate the shallow water at the mouth of the pass. The small contingent of CSA naval officers who had successfully prosecuted the battle argued that it would be feasible to kedge, or drag, their prize "across the bar" and into Sabine Lake. To their dismay, that suggestion was overruled by a major who had been sent from General Magruder's staff in Houston to oversee the whole operation.

As a result, while some of the supplies on board the *Morning Light* were laboriously removed and shuttled ashore, none of its heavy guns could be salvaged by the CSA before additional Union warships arrived on the scene. About forty-eight hours after the battle, the Southerners set the captured vessel ablaze, rather than risk losing it back to the Union. What was left of the burned hulk sank in ten feet of water.[10]

The long-term military implications of the battle were relatively unimportant for both sides, but there was considerable relief at the outcome back in Liberty County. Only three days after the fight, John Stengler wrote to his son Fritz, "We had [a letter] from Karl and George wherein I see that you and Wilhelm are on the boat and that you are still in good health which makes us very glad." Later that week, on January 28, John Stengler expressed further thanksgiving in a letter to his sons Fritz and George. "Dear son Fritz, you cannot imagine how glad we were over your battle," he wrote. "I thank God for so graciously keeping you and that not one of you was wounded in the battle against the Yankees."[11]

As January 1863 drew to a close, the family's attention was diverted from the recent success at Sabine Pass to implications of the war that were much more personal. Charles Wilborn had left home to report for military service.

21

AN EXPENSIVE SOLUTION

It is hard for us that everybody out of this family is gone except I.
—JOHN STENGLER, December 31, 1862

During January 1863 much of the family's attention was focused on military developments close to home, including the Confederates' retaking of Galveston and the gunboat battle near Sabine Pass. Even with those events dominating the headlines in Texas newspapers and local conversations, there was an additional concern for the Stengler and Wilborn households—Charles Wilborn's departure for military duty.

The delivery of Charles's draft notice on December 30, 1862, was not really a surprise, but that didn't lessen the impact of his absence on the extended family. The following day John Stengler wrote to his son Fritz: "It is hard for us that everybody out of this family is gone except I." When that letter was written, John Stengler was about to turn forty-three; his son-in-law Charles Wilborn was not much younger at forty.

The absence of "Everybody in the family except I" reflected in part John Stengler's concern about the large workload from the combined family farming and livestock operations, tasks that would now fall primarily upon himself and the wives in the households. There was one other source of help—the Stenglers' youngest son. John Henry Stengler was fifteen and could certainly be useful around the farm, although he was already voicing his desire to join his brothers in the army.

The impact on the extended family of Charles Wilborn's departure was also magnified far beyond the loss of one able-bodied male. Charles had grown up on the ranch of his stepfather, Silas Smith, and thus had, by far, the most agricultural experience of anyone in the family. His wife,

Mina, and at least two of their young children also had serious health problems, leaving her unable to do much, if any, of the physical labor on their farm.

A few days after Charles Wilborn reported for duty, John W. Hankamer wrote to his sister, Mina, and tried to offer some encouragement.

> Dear sister, it grieves me very much to hear that Charles should have to go, I could weep with you, I feel it so, but I know it would do no good. . . . [T]he only consolation we have is that the quicker we go into it the quicker we get through it. I would have liked it the best in the world to have gone up to see him at Beaumont, but they would not let more than one go, and Charles [Hankamer] went; they started to Concord this morning on foot, they hired two wagons to carry their baggage. . . . I don't think Charles will be kept in much longer than a week or two only, just long enough to be mustered in.[1]

The following week, Charles Hankamer also wrote to his sister and offered both encouragement and a suggestion to help with her tasks on the farm.

> Dear sister, . . . I am glad to hear that you have heard from your beloved Charles, I wish you would send me the directions, I want to write to him but I [do not know] how to back [address] my letters. I've not heard anything from him since I saw him, only that they started the next day in a wagon, that is they hauled their things and walked themselves, but it is but a short distance from Beaumont to Concord. It is hard for me to hear that Mrs. Martha White would have the hardihood to refuse you [the use of] a Negro [one of the White's slaves] for a short time. . . . [W]ell, I don't know what you had better do, but if you can get one [of] Jim White's [slaves] for a short time take him, and I think I will be at home in a week or two. Take it as easy as you can and compare yourself with those that are still worse off than you are. I am pretty certain that Charles will be back in a short time. My very best regards to you and the children. Kiss them for me from your ever more and sincere brother, Charles H.[2]

Mina wrote to her brother Fritz on January 24, 1863, and her letter offered a sense of her emotions about her husband's departure. She was not, however, insensitive to the hardships faced by her relatives who had been serving for the past nine months.

Dear brother, I do not suffer as all of you. You are cold and wet these nights [and] have to stand guard. I suspect not the right food either. God alone knows when this war will end. No human knows.... First you four were taken into the service. It is four months Monday since I last saw you, now Charles is also gone. Sometimes I can hardly bear it. The man who writes the few lines for Charles never writes how Charles is. I wish Charles himself could write.

Was Charles Wilborn unable to read and write, or was he in a location where he did not have a chance to pen a letter? The former seems likely, and it would not be unusual, especially given Charles Wilborn's upbringing on the frontier of pre-statehood Texas.

That same day, John Stengler wrote to his son Fritz, confirming that the elder Stengler also felt the increased pressure of tasks in the absence of the family's other adult men. "[I] have so much work to do that I do not know where to start," John said.[3] The difficulties faced by these families due to the departure of Charles Wilborn and their other sons and husbands were not unique; other households, both North and South, found themselves in similar circumstances during the war. A British military officer who traveled through East Texas in May 1863 later wrote, "All the villages through which we passed were deserted except by women and very old men; their aspect was most melancholy."[4]

That reality didn't lessen the challenges facing the Wilborns, so the couple decided to solve their problem by turning to one of the most controversial practices of the Civil War era—Charles and Mina decided to hire a substitute to take his place in the army.

The system of using paid substitutes for men who didn't want to serve for a variety of reasons was utilized by both the North and South in the early years of the war. The CSA Congress authorized the practice when it instituted the conscription system in April 1862. Paid substitutes were individuals who were otherwise exempt from military service (often due to their age) or those who had not yet been drafted.

The substitute system was often derided as a way for wealthy individuals to avoid military service, and in many cases, that criticism was warranted. There were, however, situations like the Wilborns' where conscription of the head of the household placed a serious hardship on the family; hiring a substitute offered a possible solution to their problem.[5]

It was also an expensive one. The price paid for a substitute varied from place to place and at various times during the war. Individuals seeking a substitute sometimes advertised in local newspapers, with prices ranging at times to several thousand dollars. The ever-present grapevine could be used to bring interested parties together, and in large cities, especially in the North, a lucrative business of substitute brokers quickly developed.[6]

On January 28, 1863, John Stengler informed his sons Fritz and George about the decision.

> Charles brought your letters, he came home last Sunday, he hired a substitute, he has to pay him $575, he goes tomorrow to pay the money. . . . Much beloved son Fritz: I loaned your $300 to Charles and the $100 of George's money. Your mother today turned it over to Mina and told her that you and George had given me permission to loan the money to a relative at 10% interest. You can arrange the note whichever way you want, if you want the $400 all on one note or a separate note to each.

It's clear from this letter that the Wilborns didn't have all of the cash for the $575 substitute fee and were forced to ask for a loan from other family members. To put this in perspective, a private in the CSA cavalry was paid twelve dollars a month, so $575 was the equivalent of four years' pay for that enlisted rank.

Although John Stengler's suggestion that his daughter and son-in-law repay the loan at 10 percent interest may sound rather harsh, there was a reason for his proposal. Both George Stengler and Fritz Hankamer were single and had been living at home with their parents when they left for the army. The young men prudently sent most of their military pay back home for safekeeping, and as a subsequent letter confirms, had authorized their father to loan those funds out at his discretion, to earn a little additional income while they were away. It quickly became clear, however, that they did not intend to profit at the expense of a family member.

Charles Wilborn returned home shortly after hiring his substitute, as confirmed by a letter from George Stengler to Mina on February 12, 1863. In that same note, George put to rest any ideas about collecting interest from his sister and brother-in-law.

Father arrived here night before last between 8 and 9 o'clock in the night, I was glad to see him. I wish Charles could have come down when he was up there at the bluff, I should like to have seen him very much. I am glad to hear that he has got back home again and I expect you are somewhat glad too that he is back again. He had to pay right smart for his substitute, but it is better for him to pay a little for a substitute and be home than to be off and you down sick all the time and some of the children sick too half of the time. . . .

I heard Charles had borrowed some money that I had at home, that is all right, I'd rather have it loaned out than to have it lying up doing nothing, and about giving us your note, I expect you had better give me mine in my name and Fritz's in his name. It don't make any difference with me how it is fixed, any way will do me because I know it is all right, and about the interest, you needn't to bother your head, because I don't want no interest for my fraction of it, and I rather you would keep it until I want it because I expect it [will] be a long time before I shall have any use for it, now till the war ends.

In hindsight the investment in the substitute fee proved to be a poor one, with or without any interest. About three weeks after Charles paid the fee and returned home, Mina provided an update to Fritz Hankamer.

Dear brother, we heard that the entire militia will be sent home. Had Charles known it, he could have saved his money. But of course we did not know it. I am sorry that we went into debt again, but I can't help it. But better that than he should have been gone three months. We have not written the note yet for the money from you and George because we do not know how you want the note written. We will wait till we hear from you.[7]

Subsequent letters back and forth confirmed that neither Fritz nor George wanted any interest paid on their loan to their sister and her husband for the substitute fee, and the question was put to rest to everyone's satisfaction. Fritz offered this clarification about their money being held for safekeeping by their parents: "I told Father that if he could get a chance to loan it out . . . to get as much interest as possible, but I don't want any from you or Charles."[8]

At least six men who enlisted in Company F in April or May of 1862 also subsequently decided to hire a substitute. Their time served in the unit ranged from three to ten months. In one case, the company's 2nd corporal obtained a substitute after eight months in the army; only three months later, the substitute hired his own replacement. All the men hired as substitutes were above the age subject to the draft at the time they were hired.[9]

Ultimately, Charles Wilborn's expensive substitute gained him only a few months back home. By the end of 1863, the substitute system was abolished by the CSA Congress, and in February 1864, all men who had paid a substitute were required to report for duty themselves.[10]

In the meantime, letters back and forth between those at home and the men still away in the army confirmed the value to all of them in having Charles Wilborn back at home. On May 29, 1863, Mina Wilborn replied to an earlier letter from her brother Fritz. "You write about father and Charles coming to [see] you. I think father will come . . . but Charles cannot come now," she wrote. "He has to work his corn and when he has finished his, he has to work Wilhelm's and then Karl's. You know how it is with field work. It has to be done, as much as he would like to come to see you."

The help extended by Charles Wilborn to his in-laws continued during the busy growing season and into the summer. On July 31, 1863, Charles Hankamer wrote to his sister, Mina: "I am glad to see in my letter [from his wife, Joanah,] that Charles managed to save my fodder, I did not expect it, though I am right glad of it, she says further that my potatoes seem to be first rate, but I supposed it is very dry there yet, for Joanah says that she has not had a good rain since I left."

Perhaps rumors of the impending end of the substitute system were already circulating by the summer of 1863, or the family simply wanted to reduce the risk that Charles Wilborn would be required to return to the army, even after having spent the money for his replacement. In any case, Fritz Hankamer wrote a request on July 23, 1863, for an exemption from military service on behalf of his brother-in-law. He directed his letter right to the top, to the commanding general of CSA forces in Texas, and his plea offers some details about the medical complications facing the Wilborn household.

General Magruder Commanding—Dear Sir, I address you with a few lines concerning my Brother in law who has been drafted and his whole family being afflicted with the scrofula, or King's Evil as it is generally known, his wife has been disabled for ten years and is not able to do anything, she has to get about on crutches for ten months at a time when perhaps she will at times get a little better, her eldest son ten years of age is so nearsighted that he is not able to do anything for he can't see. The second child a girl about eight years old is almost entirely blind for she has to be led about in the house since February last. [The doctor] is tending on her and the other little children are very nearly as bad off, for one is crippled in his leg so he cannot get about much, it doesn't pain him at all times but he suffers a great deal at times, besides there are four of us who are gone in the service, two of my brothers are married and he has been helping them along and two of my brothers volunteered better than a year ago. Dear sir, if you could give him some showing so he might stay at home I would be very thankful for your kindness, for I don't know what his family will do if he leaves home. Dear sir, if you wish to have it certified I can get anyone that knows the condition of his family to certify that this is the fact, I would thank you a thousand times to give him a showing to stay at home, if it be possible direct your answer to Charles Wilborn . . . for I will return to my command in a few days. I have been sick or I would not have been here now. From your humble F. Hankamer. Please direct your answer [to] Charly Wilborn, Liberty Post Office, Texas.[11]

Fritz Hankamer's letter paints a bleak picture of the health of Charles Wilborn's family. Scrofula is a form of nonpulmonary tuberculosis that involves the neck and lymph systems and is a disease that had been known since ancient times. It was sometimes called the "King's Evil" in Europe, due to a belief in previous centuries that a touch from the king could cure the affliction. Despite those seemingly serious problems in his household, the request for Charles's exemption was denied. It appears his use of a substitute ended in August 1863, and family letters confirm he was back on duty by late that summer.[12]

On September 20, 1863, Mina Wilborn wrote to Fritz, "I wish Charles would get a furlough. I have not heard from him since the 10th. I heard they are at Sabine Pass. I think they will be there for six months or longer. The Lord only knows."

In the end, the Wilborns' considerable financial investment in a substitute for Charles gained him very little time back home. His duties with the militia did keep Charles in Southeast Texas and relatively close to home, whereas the future assignments of his relatives serving in Company F were much more unpredictable. As the Hankamer and Stengler brothers began their second year of military duty, they made the first of several moves to new duty stations, and the change would prove to be a mixed blessing.

22

EAGLE GROVE

We are stationed at Eagle Grove, about 5 miles below town in a very pretty place just at the railroad bridge.
—JOHN W. HANKAMER, April 12, 1863

The arrival of spring in 1863 marked the beginning of a second year away from home for the men of Company F. Virtually all that time had been spent within a few miles of Sabine Pass, Texas, and while that location was relatively close to their families—and far from major battles in the East—it was hardly an appealing duty station.

On February 27, 1863, the commanding officer of Company F commented about the seemingly constant wet weather, noting, "Every part of this town is shoe mouth deep in mud." The following week, George Stengler summed up his impressions about the area in a letter to his sister, Mina. He wrote that "there is plenty of musketoes here and plenty of water all over the place, this is the ugliest mud hole I ever seen, you bet if this war ever ends this place won't hold me."[1]

Given that description, it's no surprise that these troops welcomed a change in location, even though Galveston was no longer a thriving commercial center. Following its surrender to Union forces the previous autumn, many of the residents who could afford to do so had left the city, and the continuing Union naval blockade made life difficult for those who remained. Despite those changes, Galveston certainly held much more appeal to the men of Company F than Sabine Pass.

An increased Union naval presence just offshore made CSA General Magruder nervous about another Federal attempt to capture Galveston, so he ordered the reassignment of additional forces to the area. Those troops included Spaight's Battalion, which was relocated from Sabine Pass to man fortifications on the outskirts of the city at Virginia Point and Eagle Grove.

Those positions were located at each end of the all-important railroad bridge connecting Galveston to the mainland, and about five miles west of the city's center. Since the Union blockade had severely reduced the flow of goods into the town by sea, the trains were a critical lifeline for supplies for the island's residents. The tracks were also an important conduit to the interior of the state for items blockade runners managed to sneak into Galveston.

Company F received its orders on Thursday, March 19, 1863. On the following Monday, the soldiers learned the unit was to be "dismounted," meaning they would be converted from a cavalry unit to an infantry company. This information was greeted with far less enthusiasm than the news about their new location. Their horses were deemed to be of little value for their new mission to guard the railroad bridge, and providing forage for the animals would place serious strain on the CSA supply system. A story in the *Houston Tri-Weekly* two months earlier mentioned the shortage of corn needed to keep thousands of cavalry horses in good condition until the crop for that year could be grown and harvested.[2]

The men broke camp at Sabine Pass, loaded their equipment into wagons, and returned home to Liberty County with their horses. They were given a week to complete those arrangements before reassembling on the shore of Trinity Bay near Anahuac, where they would board a boat to Galveston. Due to delays caused by weather and problems with their ferry, they did not reach Virginia Point until April 8.

The following day, Company F established its new camp at Eagle Grove, near the island end of the railroad bridge. The company shared that position with the men from Captain Marsh's Company A, while the remainder of Spaight's Battalion was positioned at Virginia Point on the mainland end of the causeway. The name "Eagle Grove" was taken from a grove of oak trees, which for many years provided a nesting place for a bald eagle. The eagle presumably found a new home, but the grove was destroyed during construction of the railroad bridge in the 1850s.[3]

On April 12, 1863, John W. Hankamer wrote to his sister, Mina, and described their new post.

We are stationed at Eagle Grove, about 5 miles below town in a very pretty place just at the railroad bridge where the cars pass within 200 yards of us; there is a train passing here just now coming from Houston, and soon one will be back going to Houston, and I must be in haste to get through writing, for I want to send my letters by her. We are all in fine spirits and enjoy this place a great deal more than we did Sabine Pass, although we are not allowed to go to town only two a day, but then it is so far to go on foot that none of us care a great deal about walking it very often.

In today's world, we might not consider a campsite near a railroad bridge a desirable location, but in this case, easy access to the trains was a plus. The officers, if not the enlisted men, occasionally used the trains to travel into Galveston; even better, the "cars," as the trains were often called, offered the potential for better mail service to and from home.[4]

The young men's mother was pleased with the reported improvement in their situation as well. On April 26, 1863, Johanette Stengler wrote to Fritz: "Dear son, we are so happy that you like it better there. There you are in a dry place, which is better because you have no houses to stay in." Mrs. Stengler also considered the possibilities provided by her boys' proximity to a real city. In response to comments that they might occasionally be allowed to walk into town, she told Fritz to be on the lookout for some supplies she needed, because "I would like to do some dyeing."

The availability of goods for sale in Galveston must have appealed to family members in rural Liberty County, but due to the blockade, prices put many items out of reach for most buyers. On April 29, Charles Hankamer offered an update for Mina and Charles Wilborn, writing that "a man can buy most anything here in the clothing line but it is awful high. I priced some shoes, very common every day women's shoes, which was 35 dollars, that begins to look to me like it is almost impossible for me to get shoes at all for Joanah."

The brothers' duties at Eagle Grove offered the men some free time, as indicated by a request Fritz sent to his mother. She replied, "I cannot send you [so] many fishing rods, as we have to send them by mail. I can send you more the next time."[5]

Despite these promising reports, Eagle Grove was far from perfect.

Two days after the unit's arrival, one officer noted that the house flies were "very annoying," and fleas were also a problem. The welcome addition to their diet of fresh seafood from Galveston Bay also proved to cause unexpected trouble. Captain Duncan's diary noted he ate oysters at least twice during his first week on the island, and he soon regretted the decision.[6]

His men may have enjoyed the same dubious treat because shortly thereafter both their commanding officer and many of their peers became seriously ill. This crisis was confirmed by several entries on the "morning report," a document that was prepared by every army unit to record key facts about the unit's status. The report included a daily tally and a monthly summary showing the number of men present for duty or absent for specified reasons, the names of soldiers on special details or leave, the unit's location, and comments about any unusual events.

The accuracy of morning reports was taken very seriously because they could affect a soldier's pay by noting the dates of changes in rank and any disciplinary actions. Each day's entry on the form was signed by the unit's commanding officer and first sergeant, or someone acting on their behalf.

The morning report for Company F for April 1863 confirmed that the unit had experienced a significant medical problem. It showed the number of men listed as "Present but sick" averaged about twelve per day for the first half of the month, but on April 18, the number of sick jumped overnight from sixteen to thirty.[7]

The culprit may have been the raw oysters, which at some times of the year could carry a variety of pathogens. Other maladies plagued the unit at their new camp as well, with several men coming down with measles. Three weeks after they arrived at Eagle Grove, Charles Hankamer described the unit's health woes in a letter to Mina and Charles Wilborn.

> We have had a great deal of sickness in our Battalion since we have been down here, not so many that are dangerous in ours and Marsh's company that are quartered here on the island as in the other three companies that are quartered at Virginia Point. . . . [O]ne or two are lying at the point of death there now, the worst case we have is Silas [Smith Jr.] with the yellow [jaundice] at the hospital, and three

or four in camp here with the measles. We have had more sickness here at one time than at any other place since we have been out, but I hope that as soon as we get [acclimated] we will be as healthy here as anywhere.[8]

Perhaps the brothers in Company F were satisfied to eat some of the fish Fritz Hankamer was catching instead of raw oysters and thus avoided the problems afflicting so many of their peers. On April 29, Charles Hankamer noted, "All in our mess are well, but it is the only mess in our company that has no sick ones in it."

Although this use of the term "mess" may not be as familiar today, during the war troops generally lived and ate in small groups of about four to ten men called a "mess." Members of a mess were often either relatives or at least acquaintances before enlisting, and they took turns with the cooking and cleanup of meals. When they were assigned to the same camp, the Hankamer and Stengler brothers were part of the same mess. An example of these shared chores is found in a November 26, 1863, letter from George Stengler: "I must close, for it is my cook day today and I will have to go to getting dinner."[9]

The culinary skills of these young soldiers were often tested by both the limited variety and the uncertainty of food supplies. During their first summer in the army, Charles Hankamer described some of those challenges to his sister, Mina. "One beef [steer] has to last us, and another company with a camp close to us, two days," he wrote. "They get a beef one time and us the next . . . [and] we have flour only once and a while, nor don't know one day what we will have the next."[10]

The ability of the CSA to supply troops through official channels varied considerably throughout the war. A letter to Company F's commanding officer from battalion headquarters in Beaumont on January 4, 1863, illustrated how tenuous the supply lines were at times.

> Sir: Owing to a dispatch from Galveston the train could not go down yesterday. I informed the Col. that you would be out of supplies, but he said you could borrow of Capt. Marsh [commander of another company in Spaight's Battalion]. We have had but one train from Houston in eight days. The conjecture is that we are entirely out of supplies. I have to purchase flour today at $50.00 a hundred for

your company—if we do not get a train from Houston today. I am afraid that we will have some difficulty in obtaining supplies. I hope you will be as prudent as possible until we get communication with Houston.[11]

On some occasions shortages could create an opportunity. In April 1863, less than two weeks after Company F arrived at Eagle Grove, the commanding officer wrote to his wife at their home in Liberty County. "I want you to go to raising chickens—they are scarcer here than anything else," William Duncan wrote. "I do not know what they are worth but I am certain no sort of a chick could be had for less than a dollar. Stop eating eggs and go to raising chickens. You all live well enough without eggs."[12]

The potential market for chickens (and eggs) in Galveston continued into the next year and also attracted the attention of Mina Wilborn. In a letter to her brother Fritz, Mina asked him to take a message to a local man, Mr. Baxter, who made trips by boat back and forth between Galveston and Liberty County. "Ask him if it is agreeable with him if Charles brings [the chickens] next week, and ask him if he also takes eggs," Mina wrote. "There are others who also would like to send eggs [and] chickens and [ask] if he would take them or not."[13]

By the summer of 1863, the food situation had gotten so bad on the island that what was later described in official records as the "Mutiny at Galveston, Texas" occurred among some of the troops. On August 4, 1863, Lt. Col. E. F. Gray of the Third Texas Infantry submitted the following report to his superiors:

SIR: I would respectfully and earnestly call the attention of the general commanding to the character of the provisions being issued to the troops of this regiment, and I presume, to all at this post.

The only issue now given consists of beef, molasses, and cornmeal. The latter . . . is sour, dirty, weevil-eaten, and filled with ants and worms, and not bolted [unsifted, so it had a very coarse texture], and the troops without the means of [sifting] it themselves, it becomes wholly superfluous to add that it is exceedingly unwholesome. . . . Accompanying this communication, I send a sample of the corn-meal issued to this regiment. A casual examination will satisfy you of its unwholesomeness.[14]

During the next two years, prices for many items in Galveston increased to previously unimaginable levels, including butter at nine dollars a pound and flour at two dollars a pound. Coffee, if available at all, could command as much as thirty dollars a pound! For some perspective, a pound of butter and a pound of flour at those prices would take all of a CSA cavalry private's pay for a full month.[15]

Company F's stay at Eagle Grove proved to be a short one, so they avoided experiencing the worst of Galveston's food supply woes. In a letter dated April 29, 1863, Charles Hankamer told the family:

> There is a good prospect for us not to be kept here very long, for you have doubtless heard of our defeat in the state of Louisiana, we have sustained a heavy loss there. . . . The last news we had from there give us an account of the loss of about half of the Brigade which was about 5,000 strong before that fight. Why in the world they have not been reinforced long before now is a mystery to me. There is plenty of men in Texas that could of bin there before now, all the regiments and battalions down here that I have heard from has orders to be ready to march in a moment's warning, but none has marching orders that I know of.[16]

A few days later, on May 2, John W. Hankamer offered an update on both the medical situation and the uncertainty about the unit's move to Louisiana or elsewhere.

> We are all well except George and Fritz, they have got a bad cold, but they are better now, we have a great many cases of measles in camp now, but none of us have taken them yet. We have yesterday for the second time received orders to keep ourselves ready for march, but I don't know where to, nor do I think we will leave here soon, but we don't know what will be done.

Family members back home had expressed concerns about what might lie ahead for Company F and the possibility that Charles Wilborn might be drafted again after only recently returning home. Fritz tried to provide a little reassurance—mixed with a touch of bravado—for his sister.

> Dear sister, you wrote that you was uneasy about the conscription but I don't think there is much danger about that, for we are enough

for what few yankees there is in Louisiana, if they will only let us go to them.... [Y]ou might laugh at this but I tell you if they take us to Louisiana you will soon hear of the yankees running and us right after them, won't we make them git.[17]

Four days later, Fritz and the rest of the men in Company F learned they would have their chance to "make the yankees git." Shortly after breakfast on May 8, they were told to "get ready to march in 48 hours to Louisiana." A flurry of activity for the next two days helped mask sad news recorded in Captain Duncan's diary. "Some of the sick very bad off," he wrote. "Heard that S. Smith in hospital would die."[18]

Silas Smith Jr. was Charles Wilborn's half-brother, and thus Mina Wilborn's brother-in-law. Charles and Silas Jr. had grown up together on Silas Smith Sr.'s ranch in Liberty County, and it was there Charles acquired his knowledge of cattle ranching. Silas Jr. had joined Company F at the same time as the Stengler and Hankamer brothers the previous year. He was also the brother of John W. Hankamer's wife, Lurenda Smith Hankamer.

On April 13, only five days after arriving at Eagle Grove, Silas Smith was sent to the hospital at Virginia Point. He was reportedly suffering from "yellow jaundice," a vague term that covered a variety of conditions, and he was still in the hospital when his companions departed Eagle Grove. On May 12, 1863, Silas Smith Jr. became the first member of the extended Stengler family to perish during the war. As was the case for so many others during the conflict, he was a victim not of enemy fire, but of illness.[19]

Company F's situation offers an example of how sickness impacted military operations. The morning report for May 10 showed the company had eighty-three men enrolled, including four officers, but only fifty-three were "present for duty." The thirty who were not "present for duty" included seventeen who were listed as "present but sick," with the remaining thirteen on sick leave, other leave, AWOL, or detached service. Less than two-thirds of the company was reasonably fit for action.[20]

On May 10, 1863, two days before Silas Smith died, the men of Company F boarded a train for Houston. They arrived as darkness fell, slept near the tracks, and were up by three the next morning. As proof that some things don't change very much from one generation of soldiers to the next, one of their first orders of business in the predawn hours was duly noted as, "Drank coffee."[21]

Barely one month after arriving at Eagle Grove, Company F was on the move again. In retrospect, its next assignment would prove to be both longer and much more difficult than these men may have anticipated. For the first time since joining up, they would also be part of a much larger military campaign, facing a potentially potent Union force in unfamiliar territory. Based on a description of another CSA unit leaving Galveston the previous week, these Texans were not nearly as well equipped as their upcoming foes. Arthur J. Fremantle was a British military officer who was visiting Galveston earlier that same week, when another CSA unit departed for Louisiana. He described the haphazard variety of their uniforms and weapons:

> I saw Pyron's regiment embark for Niblett's Bluff to meet [Union General] Banks. This corps is now dismounted cavalry . . . about four hundred men . . . dressed in every variety of costume, and armed with every variety of weapon; about sixty had Enfield rifles; the remainder carried shot-guns (fowling-pieces), carbines, or long rifles of peculiar and antiquated manufacture. None had swords or bayonets—all had six-shooters and bowie knives.[22]

A similar description likely applied to Spaight's Battalion, but the lack of standardized weapons and uniforms was not foremost in the minds of these men as they headed to Louisiana. For the first time since enlisting just over a year earlier, Company F was leaving Texas.

23

"A COUNTRY LAID IN WASTE"

This whole country is laid in waste by the enemy, it is dreadful to look at. . . . [S]uch havoc has never been heard of before.

—JOHN W. HANKAMER, June 30, 1863

The first two years of the Civil War in Louisiana were not good ones for the Confederacy. In late April 1862, barely one year after the first shots were fired at Fort Sumter, New Orleans surrendered to Union forces. The loss of the largest city in the South—and one of its most important ports—was followed within days by Federal possession of the state capital, Baton Rouge. In April 1863 Union Maj. Gen. Nathaniel Banks launched an expedition up Bayou Teche, which runs for 125 miles from the southern Louisiana coast to the central part of the state. Banks succeeded in driving Confederate forces under Major General Taylor out of southeastern Louisiana, and additional Southern troops were ordered to that area in May 1863.[1]

Those reinforcements included Company F, and the men's journey to their initial destination, near Vermilionville (now Lafayette), Louisiana, would cover about three hundred miles. In theory, the first part of the trip by train—from Galveston to Houston and then east to Orange, Texas—should have been relatively easy. In reality, it was plagued with engine breakdowns, more delays when cars ran off the tracks, and an unscheduled overnight layover at Liberty.

That stop was advantageous for some of the soldiers; the morning report noted that six men, including Fritz Hankamer, were "left at Liberty, sick." Two of Fritz's brothers, George Stengler and Charles Hankamer, were also ill, and their trip ended at Beaumont. One private was assigned as a nurse to stay with them and another ailing soldier. The unit was now short by at least nine additional men before it even departed Texas.[2]

On its fifth day after leaving Galveston, Company F boarded a steamboat for a ten-mile trip up the Sabine River from Orange. The weary travelers finally set foot on Louisiana soil around nightfall on Thursday, May 14, 1863, at Niblett's Bluff. Located on high ground on the east bank of the Sabine River, Niblett's Bluff was an important river crossing on the route between Houston and Baton Rouge, but before the Civil War the small settlement hardly excited much interest. By 1863 it hosted a small but vital supply depot and a rudimentary military hospital, and this was the last permanent CSA facility the men would see until they returned to their home state.[3]

After spending a rainy night near the Sabine River, Company F finally received some welcome news on the morning of May 15—they were to be "remounted." The return to their previous status as a cavalry unit would prove to be very fortuitous in the weeks ahead. During their time in Louisiana, both cavalry units in Spaight's Battalion, Companies A and F, were reassigned as part of George W. Baylor's cavalry regiment. That unit soon became part of James P. Major's cavalry brigade, under the overall command of Maj. Gen. Richard Taylor.[4]

Lieutenant Sheldon and fifteen men from Company F returned to Liberty County to bring back the unit's horses and associated gear, and then their travels into Louisiana finally got underway. Details about the trip are sketchy, but they probably followed the same general route that had been used for several decades by cattlemen moving their livestock from Southeast Texas into Louisiana. Even after many years of use, the primitive road still offered a difficult and dangerous journey.[5]

The terrain in southern Louisiana was similar to Southeast Texas, a flat, low-lying jigsaw puzzle of open prairie, marshland, and dark woods interspersed with a confusing tangle of sluggish bayous, unpredictable rivers, dense thickets, and murky swamps. By early May, summer was already well underway, and the countryside was well-populated with venomous snakes, alligators, and clouds of mosquitoes.

Company F made the trip without any recorded incident and three weeks after leaving Houston finally reached its destination near Vermilionville, Lafayette Parish, Louisiana. Its new post, dubbed "Camp Texas,"

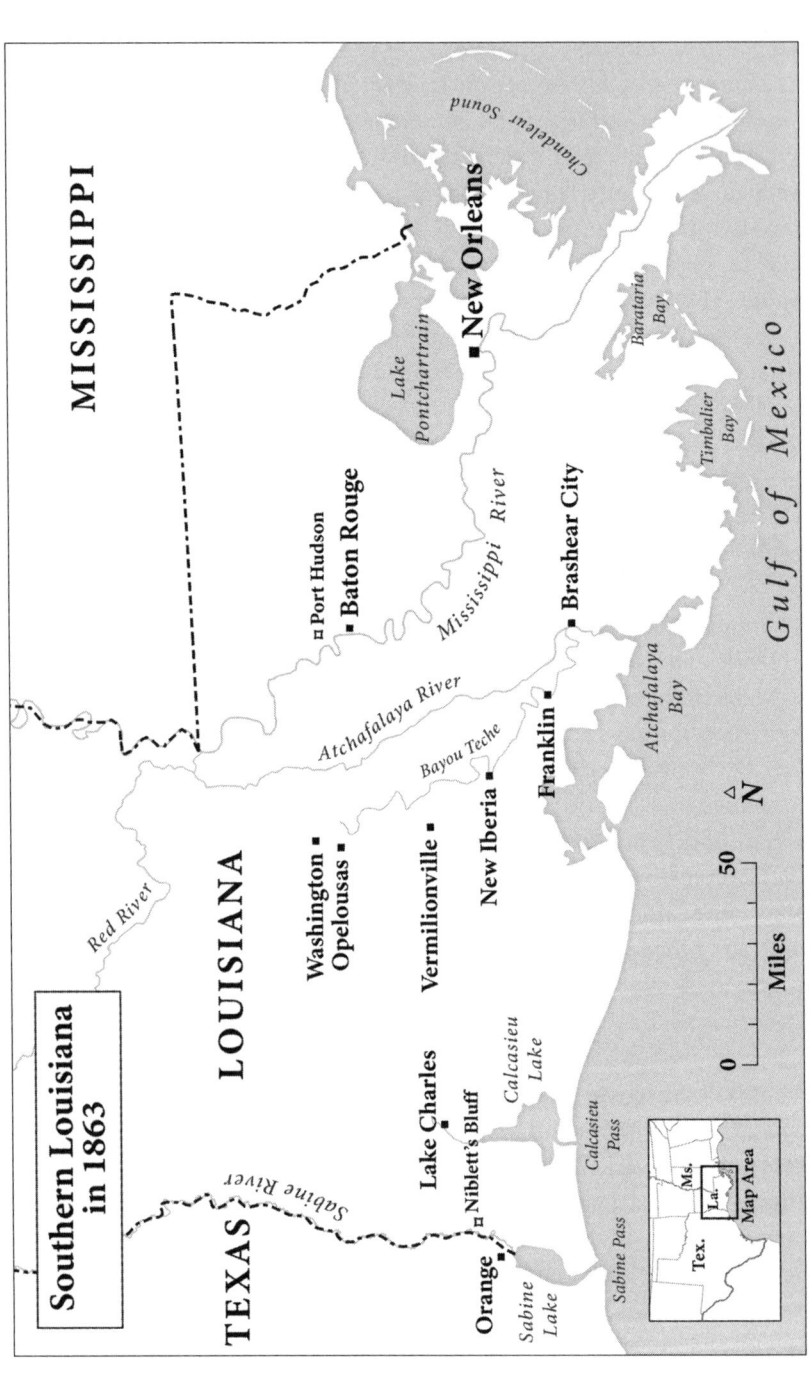

FIGURE 13. Southern Louisiana in 1863.

was about sixty miles west of Baton Rouge, and John W. Hankamer wrote to Fritz Hankamer and George Stengler from there on June 4, 1863. His two brothers, along with Charles Hankamer, had been left behind in Texas, too sick to travel, and John W. had some advice once they were well enough to rejoin their unit.

> I should advise you not to come until you are both sound and well . . . and get as many more of the boys of our Co. as you can to come with you, for if there is not a good many of you they won't give a pass at Niblett's Bluff, or else you can't get here. . . .
>
> [B]ring provisions enough with you to last you about three days this side of the Sabine, for after you leave the big woods you can't get anything more until you get . . . this side of Nezpique; there is not much danger now of conscripts on the route, for they lie low ever since the Yankees left, but it is very well to be on your guard, and if you are, there will be no danger . . . [and] ride your horses slow and give them as good a chance as possible, for it is a hard ride without corn.[6]

John W. Hankamer's warning about "conscripts" referred to renegades who, according to an August 1863 article in a Houston newspaper, "have taken to the woods and bottoms and evaded the enrolling officers, and declared it to be their intention not to fight for either Federal or Confederate Governments." Sometimes referred to as "Jayhawkers," these outlaws posed a danger to civilians, soldiers, and supply trains moving between the Texas border and towns and camps across southern and central Louisiana. The article warned that these desperados "plunder good citizens and murder alike citizen and soldier. They are said to be 300 or 400 strong . . . and are principally armed with double-barreled shotguns."[7]

The CSA began taking steps to combat the Jayhawkers, but they met with only mixed success, since troops needed for that effort were also in demand elsewhere. A small garrison was stationed at Niblett's Bluff, and the post's provost marshal enforced restrictions on all travelers passing through the area. During the summer of 1863, that officer was directed to "cause all persons passing through the place to give a strict account of themselves, and will detain all suspicious characters, so as to keep the place free of marauders and spies."[8]

CHAPTER 23

After safely arriving in Louisiana, Company F spent the first half of June near Vermilionville, then relocated southeast toward the Louisiana Gulf Coast. They missed a significant fight on June 23 near Brashear City (present-day Morgan City), but during their move, they passed through areas that had been severely impacted by fighting. On June 30, 1863, John W. Hankamer penned a letter from "St. Mary's Parish, LA," about fifty miles south of Baton Rouge, to his sister, Mina Wilborn. In addition to providing news about recent events, it included some of the strongest emotions about the war found in any of the family letters.

> Dear sister: . . . [W]e have been now 7 days on the march and are encamped about 9 miles from Berwick Bay [on the Atchafalaya River near present-day Morgan City]. . . . We are ordered to Berwick's Bay I don't know whether we will go or not but our troops are crossing over all the time now, and are on their way to New Orleans, which will be in our possession before 2 weeks more, or else there will be a great deal of blood spilt in the attempt; a fight occurred here last week in which a great deal of property was captured by our men. . . .
>
> [Brashear City] is in our hands . . . [and] fighting is going on every day more or less. . . . [T]his whole country is laid in waste by the enemy, it is dreadful to look at, houses and fences are burned down or tore down and destroyed, crops were left to the mercy of anything that would go to it, such havoc has never been heard of before, people were robbed of their money, clothing and everything else and where ever the owners were gone the houses were pillaged and burned, such a set of ruffians ought not to be taken prisoners but shot wherever found, but they are paying now for their raid through this country with their lives. . . .
>
> [I]t makes me mad to see the desolation of this people and I long for an opportunity for revenge for part of the wrong they done here and are doing daily where ever they go.[9]

Barely two weeks after John W. Hankamer wrote to describe the Confederates' capture of a large Union supply depot at Brashear City, George Stengler wrote to Mina Wilborn from New Iberia about a major development in the war. On July 16, 1863, he noted, "It is reported here that Fort Hudson and Vicksburg has both gone under." George's news was correct, and the surrender of CSA forces at Vicksburg, Mississippi, and

Port Hudson, just north of Baton Rouge, gave the Union control of the Mississippi River. That development effectively cut off states west of the Mississippi from the rest of the Confederacy, and more important to the men in Company F, it freed up additional Union resources to devote to Louisiana and Texas.

CSA troops hastened to complete the removal of captured items of value from Brashear City, and on July 20, they began a hasty withdrawal westward ahead of advancing Union forces. Their first challenge was to get across the Atchafalaya River, and after arriving at the water's edge at 11:00 p.m., Company F spent the entire night standing in the mud, waiting for a boat. They finally crossed the next morning on a ferry, making their escape by only a matter of minutes. As they rode away, they could hear the cannons of approaching Union gunboats.[10]

Before he knew Company F was being sent to Louisiana to help counter a possible Union invasion of Texas, Fritz Hankamer was optimistic about their prospects. In a letter to Mina, he predicted, "I intend to go down to New Orleans and take a look at the place after we run the yankees away."[11]

Three months later, at the end of July, Company F had yet to see any Union troops (other than prisoners), Fritz had not taken his look at New Orleans, and two of his brothers found themselves on an ironic assignment for the CSA. Charles Hankamer and George Stengler's military duties in Louisiana were certainly important, but they weren't much different from their daily routine at home before they joined the army—they were herding beeves.

24

PICKETS, PASTURES, AND POSTMEN

*I believe I have seen more men in the last week than
I have ever seen before in all my life, it has been almost
impossible to travel on the roads, or get through
the streets for men and wagons.*

—CHARLES HANKAMER, July 31, 1863

After two months in Louisiana, the men in Company F may not have seen any military action, but Charles Hankamer still had some new experiences to report. On July 31, 1863, he wrote to his sister, Mina, from New Iberia, Louisiana, about sixty miles southwest of Baton Rouge. Union and Confederate forces were sparring for control of southern Louisiana, and Charles's letter included a vivid word picture of the hustle and bustle that is part of a large military campaign.

> Most all the government stores are moved from here, and they are now moving the sick, there has been as many as fifteen hundred here at one time, but there is not so many now. I believe I have seen more men in the last week than I have ever seen before in all my life, it has been almost impossible to travel on the roads, or get through the streets for men and wagons; you can get an idea, it taken from 15 to 20 big beeves every day [to feed these men], but they have all passed through now, at [least] the bulk of the army has.

At least one aspect of his situation was familiar, and Charles's skills as a cattleman in civilian life had been noted by his military commanders and put to good use. "I am still here and have a thousand beeves in my charge," Charles said. "I have 13 men with me, about what it will take to drive them, for I look for orders every day now to move the drove. I have them in a large pasture now, about 5 or 6 miles from [where the unit was camped]."

A herd of a "thousand beeves" was a lot of cattle, even by Texas standards, and that beef on the hoof was a vital resource for the Confederate units in the area. In a time and place where refrigeration for fresh meat wasn't available, salt to preserve meat was often scarce, and supplies of other rations could be uncertain, those cattle provided a key part of the diet for the troops—and there were a lot of mouths to feed.

As Charles's letter indicated, there had been plenty of military activity in the area, and many of the troops in southern Louisiana had been involved in significant fights during June and July. One reason for Company F's absence from action may have been the unit's health woes that began in Galveston in late April. From the time they left Galveston Island in early May through much of the summer in Louisiana, Company F was chronically shorthanded due to sickness.[1]

Some of the men, including Fritz and Charles Hankamer and George Stengler, had remained in Texas to recuperate when the unit departed Texas, and several of them did not return to duty for a month or more. Their commanding officer, Capt. William Duncan, had also left the unit for several weeks in May and June to recuperate at home. Charles Hankamer and George Stengler's assignment herding beeves may have stemmed both from their recent return from that extended leave and their previous experience with livestock.

By early August, George Stengler had joined Charles Hankamer in keeping an eye on the army's "meat on the hoof," while the majority of Company F served as pickets (roving patrols or outlying perimeter guards) in the general vicinity of New Iberia. The first of September brought changes for the company, including a pleasant surprise for John W. Hankamer: he was promoted to 4th sergeant for the company. The new rank brought additional responsibilities, but also a welcome increase in pay; a sergeant earned seventeen dollars a month, compared to thirteen for a corporal and twelve for a private.[2]

A September 7, 1863, letter from Charles Hankamer to Mina Wilborn illustrated a common complaint from soldiers away from home—the lack of mail.

> Dear Sister—Again I seat myself to address you with a few lines but not in answer to any that I have received. . . . [I]t has been two

months since last Friday since I left home and have got but two very short letters from you yet . . . [and] you know that time passes off mighty slow. These two months have been the longest to me, of any that I experienced since I've been out.

Charles Hankamer's comment about the lack of mail echoed a similar complaint from his brother George Stengler, who wrote to Wilhelmina Wilborn from New Iberia, Louisiana, on August 9, 1863. He noted he hadn't "yet seen the scratch of a pen from you since I left, but I am looking for letters now daily."

There's no question the official postal system had plenty of challenges. In February 1861, two months before the start of hostilities, the Confederacy established its own Post Office Department, and the new service officially began operating on June 1, 1861. Southerners who had worked for the US postal system were recruited for the new CSA service, and many accepted, so their skills were invaluable to the new department. Even with the help of those experienced hands, there were plenty of hurdles in getting the new system up and running.

Until new stamps could be ordered, printed, and delivered, local postmasters resorted to a variety of measures to keep the mail moving. Temporary "provisional" stamps were printed locally in at least fifty-three cities and towns, but in most cases, local postmasters simply collected cash for the postage, marked the envelope "paid," and handstamped the postmark. An example is shown in figure 14.[3]

In addition to challenges posed by the start-up of a new postal system, soldiers and family members soon faced an additional problem—the scarcity and cost of writing paper, envelopes, and ink. Charles Hankamer confirmed this was already a problem during his first two months away from home. On June 12, 1862, he wrote to Mina and Charles Wilborn from his camp at Grigsby's Bluff, south of Beaumont, Texas. "Dear sister and brother-in-law: You complain at me for not writing to you oftener than I do," he said, "but you know the reason why, it is not for the want of love toward you and Charles and your beloved children. You know that paper is very scarce."

As time went by, items such as paper, pens, and ink became even harder to find—and were increasingly expensive. On November 6, 1862, John Stengler advised Fritz, "Tell George, Charles, and William that I would like to

FIGURE 14. An example of "manuscript postage" used before CSA stamps were available. The postmaster simply wrote "Paid 10 cents" on the postmarked envelope. Courtesy of Julia Duncan Welder Collection, Sam Houston Regional Library and Research Center, Texas State Library and Archives Commission.

write to them but paper is so dear, I paid 2 dollars for a quire, should one of you want paper, write and I will buy it." A "quire" usually included twenty-four sheets of paper, so a dollar would only buy a dozen pieces. In January 1863, another soldier in Texas said writing paper cost ten to twenty cents a sheet in Houston, and with an army cavalry private earning twelve dollars a month, paper at that price was very "dear" indeed.[4]

Mina Wilborn suggested one solution to her brother Fritz: "I wish you could write a few lines to me. All four of you could write on the same piece of paper. Read my letters to Wilhelm, Karl and Fritz." Another technique was to squeeze as many words as possible onto a single sheet. Mina Wilborn probably held the family record for this approach with a December 26, 1862, note to her brother Fritz. Her letter, composed on a three-by-eight-inch scrap of paper, contained three hundred words. Other people adapted to limited writing supplies by making their own envelopes. Celima Duncan wrote to her husband on December 12, 1862, and complimented his homemade stationery. "The envelopes you made are very nice and well made. I think I shall make me some, for they are getting very scarce here."[5]

CHAPTER 24

Even when letters were written, mail service was spotty and slow delivery was the norm. The postal department's challenges were compounded when units changed locations, as occurred after Company F relocated from Sabine Pass to Galveston Island. On April 29, 1863, Charles Hankamer wrote to his sister, Mina.

> I seat myself to address you with a few lines again without having heard a word from you or anyone from home, though I have written twice before now, and directly after I came here, and it is three weeks today since we left Liberty since I last seen my dear wife and children, and three weeks last Monday since I last seen you or even heard from any of you. . . . I could be content if I could only hear from you all, but this wears me out.

Except for their seven-month assignment in Louisiana, the soldiers in Company F were assigned to duties within about one hundred miles of their homes. That allowed friends or family members to visit their camps occasionally, and there was rarely a month when at least one member of the unit wasn't on leave. During such trips, the travelers often served as unofficial postmen, although some may have needed an extra pack animal to handle all the requests to carry letters and packages back and forth.

A December 3, 1862, letter from John W. Hankamer at Grigsby's Bluff to his sister, Mina, at Crackersneck offers an example of this system. "I received your letter yesterday when I returned from picket. Alfred Weed came back [from home] the day before, I do not know who I will send this with yet, but there are several going home, and I expect that I will be able to send it today or tomorrow. I would put your money in here if I knew exactly who would carry it."

Using trusted friends or relatives to carry letters containing cash rather than risking them to the mail was a common procedure. In February 1865 John Stengler asked his son Fritz to check on the price of some items in Houston, where Fritz was stationed. If Fritz found the supplies at a good price, John wrote, "I can then send the money with George when he comes home so you can buy them."[6]

Letters were valuable, but the ultimate mail call included the combination of a note and a package. The first surviving record of such "care packages" for these family members was one sent by Mina Wilborn to her brothers on June 9, 1862. She suspected the contents would likely have fared better with personal handling rather than normal mail channels. "I am sending you some cake made of our fine flour," Mina wrote. "It may be all to pieces by the time you get it." "All to pieces" or not, a cake made of "fine flour" was certainly a welcome surprise for these young men surviving on their limited rations and shared cooking skills.

Even with a personal courier, the combination of the steamy Louisiana summer weather and long transit times conspired against a well-intentioned surprise for Capt. William Duncan in August 1863. He wrote to his wife thanking her for sending a generous box of treats, and either Mrs. Duncan baked an exceptionally good cake, or her husband was *really* desperate for a change in his menu.

Whichever the case, he wasn't deterred by the condition of the contents. "I received the box by Colonel Spaight," he wrote. "Everything is in good order but the cake, which was spoilt, having become very moldy. I ate some of it. The butter is perfectly sweet and firm. The pomegranates nice as ever and the cordial delicious. The preserves look fine—I have not tried them."[7]

The unreliability of regular mail channels fell to new lows during Company F's time in Louisiana. Those problems were compounded by the unit's numerous changes in location, but William Duncan also believed something underhanded was afoot. On August 20, 1863, he wrote to his wife, "I know some scamp takes my letters out of his office and destroys them. I heard of one that was in the office at New Iberia, but when I sent to the office, there was no letter for me."

Such difficulties led the men in Company F and a second cavalry company stationed with them in Louisiana to take serious measures—they hired their own private mail carrier. Captain Duncan explained the plan to his wife in an August 1, 1863, letter written from Grand Lake, Louisiana.

> We are trying to make arrangements with Mr. James Tucker to carry letters once a month for our two companies—mine and Capt. Marsh's. If said arrangements is made, there will be some certainty of your getting a letter once every month from me and I from you. . . . Mr. James A. Brown is going to furnish Mr. Tucker with a pack horse—so he will be able to carry what we want to send. . . . Mr. Tucker is to bring our letters from home once a month, and we pay him eighty dollars for the trip.

Three weeks later, William Duncan expressed his hopes for the new system in another letter to his wife. "Our mail carrier Tucker I expect here in about ten days, and then I will get letters again. He was to leave Texas today ... [and] if he continues to take our letters back and forward, I shall think we have done one of the best things in the world in securing his services—as it is almost impossible to get letters by mail. There are so many letters coming to an army that they cannot be managed properly—and go astray and get lost."[8]

We know this private mail system for Company F was used for at least two months, because several letters between the soldiers and family members mentioned sending items with Mr. Tucker. Even so, a courier traveling by horseback over that route required nearly two weeks for the trip, certainly not fast enough to bring timely reports about major developments preparing to unfold in Southeast Texas.

As the summer of 1863 drew to a close, Union political and military leaders had ambitious plans for an invasion of Southeast Texas. If that campaign proceeded as planned, the Stengler, Hankamer, and Wilborn farms would be squarely in the center of the area contested by Union and Texas forces. Spaight's Battalion and other troops previously stationed along the upper Texas coast were now many days' ride away in Louisiana—and fewer than fifty CSA troops remained to defend the key port at Sabine Pass.[9]

25

RAISING THE FLAG IN TEXAS

I was informed... that that there were important reasons why our flag should be established in Texas with the least possible delay.
—MAJ. GEN. N. P. BANKS, US Army, August 15, 1863

August of 1863 marked a major shift in Union priorities for not only Texas but the entire Gulf Coast, and Sabine Pass was suddenly the focus of the discussion. Why the renewed Union emphasis on this sparsely settled corner of the state? The answers were based primarily on politics and economics rather than military objectives.

The French had invaded Mexico in 1863 and established a puppet government, raising concerns about renewed European influence in the region and even the potential for direct French support of the Confederacy. In the United States, prominent businessmen and politicians were lobbying hard for a reliable source of Southern cotton, which New England textile mills urgently needed. The South, meanwhile, was obtaining vital revenue for its war effort by shipping cotton overland across Texas to Mexico, where it was sold to buyers from England and Europe. Returning Texas to Union control would ease all of those concerns, and thus that goal was suddenly a high priority in Washington.[1]

Maj. Gen. N. P. Banks, commander of the US Army Department of the Gulf, received his orders on August 15, 1863.

> I was informed ... that there were important reasons why our flag should be established in Texas with the least possible delay and instructing me that the movement should be made as speedily as

possible, either by sea or land. I was informed . . . there were reasons other than military why those directed in Texas should be undertaken first; that on this matter there was no choice, and that the views of the Government must be carried out.[2]

Banks's superiors gave him the authority to determine how to gain military control of the state, and he made "immediate preparations for a movement via the coast against Houston, selecting the position occupied by the enemy on the Sabine as the point of attack." He reasoned that Sabine Pass was the nearest point in Texas to his base of supplies and reinforcements in Louisiana, and it would allow efficient transportation of his forces by water. If Sabine Pass could not be taken quickly, his subordinate commanders were instructed to land anywhere they deemed best along the coast southwest of the pass.[3]

Regardless of the initial point of entry, the primary objective was to take control of the railroad that ran between Beaumont and Houston. Once that vital transportation link was secured, Banks envisioned a quick overland move to Houston. Within ten days of the landing, he expected to have "20,000 men at Houston, where, strongly fortified, they could have resisted the attack of any force that it was possible to concentrate at that time."[4]

Banks also noted, "The occupation of Houston would place in our hands the control of all the railway communications of Texas; give us command of the most populous and productive part of the State; enable us to move at any moment into the interior in any direction, or to fall back upon the Island of Galveston, which could be maintained with a very small force."[5]

On October 22, 1863, General Banks submitted a follow-up report to President Lincoln, defending his plan for the campaign. A map accompanying that report showed if the alternative landing site on the coast below Sabine Pass were used, his "proposed line of march" ran to the town of Liberty and would have passed very near the small settlement of Crackersneck.[6]

It's impossible to say in hindsight what impact a successful Union invasion and occupation of Texas might have had on the overall length of the war. There's little doubt, however, that the movement of thousands of troops and a fight across Southeast Texas for control of Houston and

Galveston would have severely affected the civilian population, including the Stengler, Hankamer, and Wilborn families in Liberty County.

That prediction is supported by two contemporary accounts of the effects of similar fighting in nearby Louisiana. The previous chapter quoted a June 30, 1863, letter from John W. Hankamer, who had witnessed the devastation after Union and Confederate troops had fought across St. Mary Parish in southern Louisiana. His comments bear repeating, given the risk of similar outcomes in Liberty County if Banks's plans for Texas had succeeded.

"This whole country is layed [sic] in waste by the enemy," Hankamer wrote. "It is dreadful to look at, houses and fences are burned down or tore down and destroyed, crops were left to the mercy of anything that would go to it, such havoc has never been heard of before."

Union Gen. N. P. Banks described similar destruction elsewhere in Louisiana, but he laid the blame on CSA forces. Explaining the difficulties of an overland march by Federal troops across central and northern Louisiana into Northeast Texas, he noted, "The resources of the whole of this country are completely and thoroughly destroyed by the enemy.... [It is] a country utterly depleted of all its material resources."[7]

Regardless of which side was responsible, a similar fate could await the residents of Liberty and Chambers counties if the Union invasion succeeded and opposing armies fought across Southeast Texas. Two previous Union attempts to capture Galveston and Sabine Pass had failed when its quick naval victories had been reversed due to the lack of ground troops to secure those gains. General Banks did not intend to make the same mistake a third time, and his plan included overwhelming naval and ground superiority for the upcoming attack.

The Union was assembling an impressive armada. Four gunboats would lead the attack, while some two dozen other ships would transport about five thousand troops, five artillery batteries, and their supplies. Once the initial landing was completed, the transports would return to Louisiana to ferry thousands of additional ground forces for the move against Houston.[8]

The Confederates' defense against this powerful force was Fort Griffin, manned by fewer than fifty troops. Located about two miles inland from the Gulf of Mexico, the fort guarded water access via the Sabine and Neches rivers to the interior of Southeast Texas and the all-important railroad between Beaumont and Houston. As those rivers flowed south, they merged to form Sabine Lake, which then emptied into the Gulf of Mexico. A critical factor in an assault on Fort Griffin was the channel that connected the lower end of Sabine Lake with the gulf.

Navigation of that winding passage was complicated by sandbars, shallow water depths that fluctuated with the tide, and an oyster reef that divided the waterway into two even narrower channels. These challenges created a nightmare for ship captains and provided regular employment for experienced river pilots.

The terrain in this area is primarily low-lying marshland, and the new fort was strategically placed on the scarce high ground, overlooking the area where the oyster reef split the waterway. The position provided a commanding field of fire almost directly down the western channel. Two skilled military engineers, Col. Valery Sulakowski and Maj. Julius Kellersberg, directed the design and construction of the fort, with work beginning in the spring of 1863. Although not fully completed by September, the fortification was still substantial. Five underground "bombproofs" and four magazines were protected by a combination of four feet of earth, two feet of solid timbers, and two layers of railroad iron.[9]

Finally, the armament of the new fort had been upgraded from the limited firepower available the previous year at Fort Sabine, which had since been abandoned. Fort Griffin's design allowed for the efficient use of six large guns, but as work progressed on the fortification, only four were available. Artillery pieces were in short supply throughout the Confederacy, and finding two more cannon seemed to be an insurmountable task. The solution turned out to be right under the feet of the troops at Sabine Pass.

A local fisherman told Major Kellersberg that when the previous fort was abandoned to Union invaders, two large guns were sabotaged and then hastily buried to prevent their falling into enemy hands. Digging into the muddy ground and probing with long poles, CSA builders eventually unearthed just what was needed—a pair of 32-pounder cannon.[10]

Almost everyone except Major Kellersberg believed the two guns were damaged beyond repair. In addition to being severely rusted, the rescued artillery pieces were missing essential parts and had been "spiked" to prevent further use. Kellersberg refused to be deterred. He had the guns shipped to Galveston and supervised their overhaul in a frantic, round-the-clock effort. They were returned to Sabine Pass by mid-August, which would turn out to be barely three weeks before the upcoming battle.[11]

With the addition of those salvaged cannon, Major Kellersberg had his six big guns for the new fort. Now the engineer and Lt. Dick Dowling, who would command the defense of the fort, faced one last problem, but it was a big one—they were critically short of ammunition. That need was solved on September 1 when Dowling learned that between one hundred and two hundred solid (nonexplosive) cannonballs for a 32-pounder were being used as ballast on the CSA cottonclad *Uncle Ben*.

Ironically, those crucial pieces of shot were aboard the Union's USS *Morning Light* when it was captured near Sabine Pass eight months earlier. The CSA failed to salvage the vessel's heavy guns after that sea battle, and it was set afire shortly after its capture to keep it from being reclaimed by Union forces. There was no immediate need for the abandoned metal in the burned-out hulk, and it was eventually consigned to the lower reaches of the *Uncle Ben*. There it remained, nearly forgotten, until it suddenly became immensely valuable. The cannonballs were transferred to Lieutenant Dowling, and his gun crews would soon put them to use.[12]

Now armed and equipped, Dowling's gunners were not idle during the hot, steamy days of early September. As work on the fort continued at a frenzied pace, Dowling directed his artillerymen to drive painted wooden stakes into the channel and then use them as markers for target practice. Major Kellersberg aided their efforts by painting a white line on the barrels of the cannon, and the gunners used those stripes to perfect their aim at the wooden stakes.

A little white paint and a few wooden posts would not normally be significant elements in a battle that would pit several dozen men in a small fort against four gunboats carrying over two dozen naval guns and hundreds of sailors and soldiers. This battle, however, would not be a typical one, and the CSA gunners' ability to quickly shift their fire between the known points marked with those wooden stakes would prove critical during the upcoming fight.[13]

Thus, the stage was set for the battle for control of Texas. The outcome would be determined by a series of events so improbable they almost defy belief.

The Union flotilla began gathering off the southern Louisiana coast on the morning of Saturday, September 5, 1863. US Army Gen. William B. Franklin would be in charge of the ground forces, while US Navy Acting Volunteer Lt. Frederick Crocker would direct the naval elements. During a final conference between Franklin and Crocker, General Banks's carefully-crafted plan underwent some significant changes. The four gunboats would begin the attack, assisted by about 180 army sharpshooters divided among the four vessels. Once this initial attack had "driven the enemy from his defenses" and any CSA gunboats had been destroyed or driven off, the transport ships would advance and land the ground troops.[14]

With the plan now finalized, the Union vessels got underway. There was widespread speculation among the troops that they were headed for either Mobile or Galveston, but once their course was set, it became clear they were bound for Texas. General Banks had insisted on strict secrecy for the campaign, believing surprise was vital for a successful attack on Sabine Pass. As a result, only a few high-ranking officers knew any details about the expedition's plans. As events unfolded over the next several days, it soon became clear the Confederates had a few surprises of their own.[15]

26

A "MOST EXTRAORDINARY FEAT"

This seems to me to be the most extraordinary feat of the war.
—CSA MAJ. GEN. JOHN B. MAGRUDER,
September 9, 1863

The morning of September 6, 1863, offered an impressive scene a few miles off the southern Louisiana coast. Over two dozen ships were heading steadily westward across the Gulf of Mexico, and Maj. Elias Porter Pellet of the 114th Regiment, New York State Volunteers, noted a confident, even festive, atmosphere among the troops.

> The sight was a gallant and inspiring one; twenty-three steam transports and three gunboats stretching away in two lines over the smooth surface of the Gulf under a cloudless sky; the decks of the vessels and the rigging up to the tops crowded with soldiers, laughing and chatting, and everybody speculating good-humoredly upon the events of the coming week. . . . [T]he stirring strains of several bands lent interest to the scene.[1]

That optimism was shared by the Union's top commander in the region, Maj. Gen. N. P. Banks. "Nothing was wanting to secure the success of the expedition," he wrote. "The troops were in good condition, the weather fine, the sea smooth, and the enemy without suspicion of the movement."[2]

To avoid detection, the Union flotilla was instructed to remain far enough from the coast during the daytime to be unseen from land, then approach Sabine Pass under cover of darkness in time to launch a quick attack at dawn on Monday, September 7. Their biggest challenge would be finding such a precise point on the water in the dark during a time when nautical navigation and communications were decidedly primitive by today's standards.

The Union officers' solution was a clever one. One gunboat, the *Granite City*, had been sent ahead of the rest of the fleet with two pilots who had experience in the Sabine Pass vicinity. The *Granite City* was to contact the Federal ship already on blockade duty and inform that vessel's captain about the upcoming operation. The *Granite City* would then anchor "exactly at the mouth of the channel and by night show a light from the seaboard side of his vessel, by which the fleet could, on their arrival, be guided to a proper anchorage."[3]

The Confederates were accustomed to seeing one or two ships on blockade duty, so the presence of a Union warship would not cause undue alarm. Once in position, the *Granite City's* light facing toward the open gulf would not be conspicuous from land, but it was a critical part of the Union strategy. As the US Navy's Lieutenant Crocker later explained, "There was no other way to ascertain the exact position of the pass in a dark night."[4]

Everything was unfolding according to plan until the *Granite City* approached Sabine Pass on the afternoon of September 6 and found no sign of the expected blockading vessel. Speculation soon produced some ominous possibilities. Might the missing Union ship have been captured or sunk by the same CSA cottonclads that had already snared two other blockaders off Sabine Pass earlier that year? Had the Confederates somehow learned of the planned attack and laid a trap for the approaching *Granite City*?

According to a report compiled by Lieutenant Crocker, the master of the *Granite City* later stated that shortly after arriving near Sabine Pass he "discovered a large man-of-war steamer, painted lead color, which his fertile imagination transformed into the dreadful *Alabama*." That much-feared Confederate warship had already sent other Union ships to a watery grave, and the captain of the *Granite City* "thereupon got underway and left." He didn't stop until he had reached presumably safer waters, miles to the east.[5]

So, where *was* the missing Union vessel expected to be on duty near Sabine Pass? That ship was the USS *Owasco*, and due to the secrecy shrouding the Sabine Pass expedition, its captain had not been informed of the impending campaign. The ship's supply of coal had begun to run low, and following standard procedures, the *Owasco* had simply headed down the coast to Galveston to reprovision. Its replacement would not arrive on station near Sabine Pass until the following day, and by then the damage was done. One might wonder if the plan could unravel any further, and the answer is "absolutely."[6]

An advance division of the fleet comprised of Union ships that would lead the initial attack steamed carefully westward on the night of September 6, all eyes alert for the expected signal light on the *Granite City*. This group, headed by Lieutenant Crocker and General Weitzel, included the gunboats *Clifton*, *Arizona*, and *Sachem*, plus four transports carrying about one thousand infantrymen and two artillery batteries. They saw no signal light, and Crocker finally concluded they had somehow overshot their destination. The group reversed course and sailed back to the east, but after failing once again to spot their signal, the ships eventually ended up off the southern Louisiana coast, about thirty miles east of Sabine Pass.[7]

Sunrise on September 7—the expected time for the surprise attack—found the Union task force scattered and confused. The advance group headed by Lieutenant Crocker finally located the *Granite City*, dozens of miles from Sabine Pass. His attempt to head off the remainder of the flotilla carrying General Franklin and the bulk of the army troops failed. That group arrived off the coast near Sabine Pass at 11:00 a.m., expecting to find the area already under Union control.

They were dismayed to find Sabine Pass undisturbed and still in Confederate hands. Even more puzzling was the absence of the *Granite City* and the other ships in the advance landing party. With the midday arrival of General Franklin's ships visible to lookouts at the pass, any element of surprise was lost.

General Franklin, having no means of communicating with his missing gunboats, decided to wait for developments. His mood was almost certainly as dark as the night sky by the time Lieutenant Crocker arrived around 9:00 p.m. The remaining ships in the flotilla straggled in during the next several hours, and this time they had no difficulty finding their destination. Stealth was no longer an issue. With so many ships' lights illuminating the gulf just offshore of Sabine Pass, the area was said by one observer to resemble a sizeable city.[8]

The Union commanders faced a critical decision as sunrise approached on Tuesday, September 8. Having lost the element of surprise, should they continue with the attack? Given their instructions from Washington about the urgency of "planting the flag in Texas," both Lieutenant Crocker and General Franklin were disinclined to give up without a fight. Now, however, there was one more complication—the anticipated weakness of the Confederates' defenses at Sabine Pass was unexpectedly in question.

Crocker had successfully captured this area with little trouble the previous September and had started the current venture expecting another easy conquest. The captain of the USS *Cayuga*, which had arrived back on blockading duty to replace the missing USS *Owasco*, injected an element of uncertainty into Crocker's plans. The captain was unable to provide any details about the current fort or number of troops stationed there, but he believed they were "stronger than we expected."[9]

A personal reconnaissance of the pass was therefore deemed necessary, so shortly after daylight on Tuesday morning, Crocker took the gunboat *Clifton* across the bar and into the lower end of the channel. Instead of the primitive mud fort located there during his previous visit, Crocker was surprised to find a new and "very formidable earthwork, mounting six guns, some of them apparently very heavy." He also noted a small cottonclad steamer, presumably a gunboat, but he saw very few troops.

In an attempt to determine the actual strength of this fortification, Crocker continued upstream within easy range of the fort's guns, expecting to draw fire. The *Clifton's* foray was met with silence. The Union commander then tried "throwing a number of shells" at the fort, firing a total of twenty-six rounds during the next hour. Again, there was no response.

A high-stakes game of cat-and-mouse was underway, and Lieutenant Dowling's men were safely hidden out of sight in the fort's underground "bomb-proofs." While the CSA gunners waited calmly in their bunkers, the barrage from the *Clifton* did no damage of any importance to the sturdy fortification. Puzzled by the continued lack of activity at the fort, Crocker withdrew downstream, signaled additional Union vessels to join him inside the entrance to the pass, and arranged another conference with his army counterparts.[10]

They had plenty of time to discuss their plan. Due to the shallow water, it took most of the day to get the remaining three gunboats and some of the troop transports "across the bar" and into the lower end of the channel. The remaining vessels, which drew too much water, remained in the gulf outside the pass. Shortly after noon, while efforts to get ships across the bar were continuing, Lieutenant Crocker, General Franklin, and General Weitzel took a small boat and conducted a firsthand inspection of potential landing places for infantry troops along the shoreline. The results were not encouraging.

According to General Franklin's after-action report, their small boat grounded in the mud while it was still 125 feet from shore. Sailors who climbed overboard and tried to wade to the bank were soon mired above their knees in the muck. The officers concluded that any soldiers carrying muskets and rations who attempted the same feat "would have sunk to their middles." Only one potential landing spot was noted. At the site of the old abandoned fort, there was a near-vertical bank where there was enough water for small boats to approach the shore and offload the troops.

Armed with that information, the Union officers revised their plan once again. Crocker's four gunboats would be divided into pairs, with the *Sachem* and *Arizona* starting first, steaming up the Louisiana (right-hand) channel. Once they drew fire from the fort, the *Clifton* would move up the Texas (left-hand) channel to a point where its guns could engage the fort at close range. Sharpshooters on all three gunboats would attempt to drive the fort's gunners from their posts.

The fourth Union gunboat, the *Granite City*, would follow the *Clifton* up the left-hand channel, but would lag behind. The *Granite City* would support the landing of five hundred ground troops carried by the transport *General Banks*, which would be last in line, following the *Granite City*. After going ashore near the site of the old abandoned fort, the ground troops would assault the new fort by land. Figure 15 illustrates the position of key elements at the start of the battle.[11]

The success of this plan hinged on a key point. Lieutenant Crocker and General Franklin did not believe the soldiers in the fort, with their limited number of weapons, could shift their guns quickly enough to cover all those targets before they were driven from their posts by the

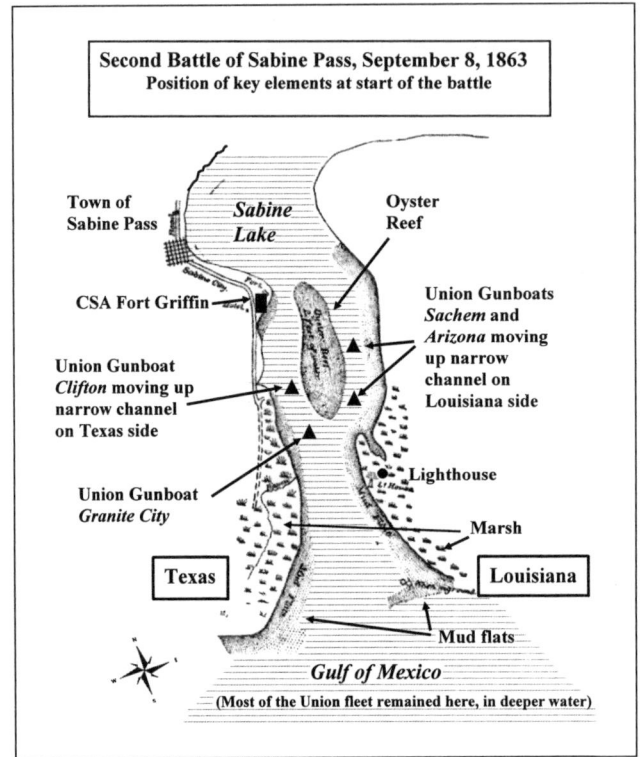

FIGURE 15. Map of the Second Battle of Sabine Pass, September 8, 1863. Adapted from "A Tracing by G. D. Elliott, Asst. Engr. Department of the Gulf," in the *Official Records of the Union and Confederate Navies in the War of the Rebellion*, vol. 20: 530.

combined fire from the ground troops, the sharpshooters aboard the four gunboats, and the gunboats' twenty-seven large guns.[12]

Shortly after 3:30 p.m., Crocker gave the signal to begin the attack, and the USS *Sachem* and USS *Clifton* began their advance up the channel toward Fort Griffin. For the first few minutes, there was no break in the eerie silence from the fortification—the only shots were those fired by the Union gunboats.[13]

Lt. Henry C. Dane was a signal officer assigned to the *Sachem* and was expected to remain at the side of the gunboat's captain. As the *Sachem* progressed up the channel on the right-hand side of the large oyster reef,

Dane noticed "some poles set in the mud," and pointed them out to the master, Acting Volunteer Lt. Amos Johnson.

"Well, what of them?" Johnson replied gruffly.

According to Lieutenant Dane, an answer was soon forthcoming. The moment the *Sachem* passed the first pole, "a flash of flame shot from the parapet [of the fort], a white cloud rose over it, and 'wh-i-ng' went a shell fifty feet about our heads." The first several shots were a little high, but each succeeding one was closer to the mark. Lieutenant Dowling and his artillery company known as the Davis Guards had been biding their time until the Union vessels reached those painted poles they had been using as aiming points during target practice.[14]

The CSA gunners were soon inflicting severe punishment on the *Sachem*, and when it had traveled about halfway up the edge of the oyster reef, the ship ran aground. The gunboat was now a stationary target, and a shot soon passed through the ship's boiler, disabling the vessel and causing a flood of boiling water and steam to pour through the ship.

The *Sachem's* fight was all but over, and many of the crew who were not already casualties began jumping overboard. The *Arizona*, which was following the *Sachem*, soon began having engine problems due to the mud and shallow water. Its captain, fearing a fate similar to that of the lead ship, ignored repeated signals from the *Sachem* for help, and with some difficulty, he backed the *Arizona* down the channel to safety.[15]

On the opposite side of the oyster reef, the *Clifton* was not faring much better. Once the *Sachem* had been disabled, the CSA gunners quickly swung their guns to give their full attention to the *Clifton*. A shot from the fort soon severed the *Clifton's* tiller rope, which made it impossible to steer the vessel. The ship ran fast aground and became another stationery target for the Confederate gunners.

The *Clifton* and the fort continued a vigorous exchange of fire for about thirty minutes, but the advantage was definitely on the side of the CSA troops in their fortified position. Under concentrated fire from the fort, the *Clifton* soon suffered the same fate as the *Sachem*—it was disabled when its steam chest was hit by a shot that released a burst of steam and hot water, driving sailors from the ship's interior and sharpshooters from the deck. Fearing the vessel would blow up, many of the men jumped overboard and swam or waded to shore, where they surrendered, and an officer hauled down the vessel's flag.[16]

FIGURE 16. The Second Battle of Sabine Pass, September 8, 1863, as depicted in *Harper's Weekly* magazine, October 19, 1863. This view is looking north, up Sabine Lake toward Fort Griffin, which is on the left bank; the lighthouse on the right is on the Louisiana shore. Courtesy of US Naval History and Heritage Command.

With surrender signals displayed by both the *Clifton* and *Sachem* and the *Arizona* in apparent retreat, the fourth gunboat, the *Granite City*, withdrew as well. No attempt was made to land the five hundred troops aboard the *General Banks*. Aboard the *Sachem*, signal officer Dane was true to his assignment and kept detailed records. He noted, "It was just one hour and twenty-nine minutes from the moment the *Sachem* fired her first shot to that when Captain Johnston struck his flag." The Second Battle of Sabine Pass ended none too soon for the defenders at Fort Griffin. According to one of the soldiers in the Davis Guards, the defenders were down to about forty charges of powder for their large guns when the fight was over.[17]

Lieutenant Dowling and his men were quickly hailed as heroes in Texas and across the Confederacy. The day following the victory, Maj. Gen. John B. Magruder wrote, "This seems to me to be the most extraordinary feat of the war." Nearly twenty years later, Jefferson Davis, the former president of the Confederacy, offered his own opinion of the fight:

"The success of the single company which garrisoned the earthwork is without parallel in ancient or modern war."[18]

As one would expect, there were strong opinions of a much different type in the North. *Frank Leslie's Illustrated Newspaper* noted, "The movement made to at last occupy and hold Texas seems to have been conceived in the same blundering spirit which has hitherto made Texas, in our military annals, synonymous with disaster and disgrace."[19]

In the aftermath of the battle, there was no shortage of second-guessing among the Union ranks. A report three days after the battle included one Union officer's perspective on the series of errors that resulted in the defeat, assessing, "a combination of those unfortunate accidents which no human foresight or determination can prevent or overcome, turned victory into defeat."[20]

This latest Union effort to gain a solid foothold in Texas had indeed resulted in both "disaster and disgrace," but CSA officers were not ready to relax their guard. Another attempt by the Federals was expected, but it was not clear whether this would be overland from Louisiana or another attack along the coast.

That unease was reflected in a letter from Johanette Stengler to her son Fritz, written a week after the CSA victory. She had received a reasonably accurate report of the capture of Union ships, guns, and troops, but was far from convinced their worries were over.

"I can tell you it looks very bad here," she wrote. "We have heard that at Sabine Pass there are many ships and Yankees. We already have two ships, 15 cannons, and how many Yankees I don't know.... Dear Son, I heard that you all would come back to Texas. I hope it is true, because I hope you do not have to stay in Louisiana when the enemy is here."[21]

The men of Company F would have been happy to return to Texas and help defend their home territory, but their time away was not yet finished. The coming months would include both routine and ironic assignments, along with narrow escapes and heroism under fire. Once the long-awaited order to return to Texas finally came, their anticipation of seeing home was quickly tempered by an unexpected ordeal that had no connection with Union forces. Merely surviving the trip back to Texas would prove to be perhaps their greatest challenge of the war.

27

FIRE AND ICE

During this month, we have had hot times with the enemy.
—MORNING REPORT FOR COMPANY F,
October 1863

The men of Company F missed the Federal attack at Sabine Pass on September 8, 1863, but that Confederate victory did not remove the threat of a Union invasion of Texas. If anything, the pressure on Union General Banks to gain a foothold in the state had increased, and he wasted no time making his next attempt. Banks's new plan involved a land campaign across Louisiana toward the Lone Star State, a route that would soon draw the cavalrymen from Liberty County into the action.

For this expedition, Banks assembled a force large enough to overwhelm any resistance, putting it under the command of Maj. Gen. W. B. Franklin. Some sources estimate this army numbered thirty thousand men, and the task of opposing this Federal advance fell to CSA Maj. Gen. Richard Taylor. He had some 8,400 men, many of them thus far untested in battle.[1]

On September 13, only five days after the Union defeat at Sabine Pass, the first troops for Banks's new initiative began crossing the Mississippi River at New Orleans. It took three weeks to move this huge assembly of men and wagons about eighty miles by ferry, train, and road to Brashear City. From that point Banks planned a steady advance to the northwest, roughly following Bayou Teche. This was the same general route some of these troops had taken several months earlier, so they were familiar with the terrain.[2]

Due to the vastly superior size of this Union army, the Confederates' strategy was to stay out of range of the main Federal force and try to slow their advance with brief harassing strikes at their enemy's flanks. Some of their first contacts were noted in Company F's morning report for October 6: "Heavy skirmishing with the yankees at New Iberia, La." This campaign had just begun, and the intentions of the Union commanders were still unclear to the Southerners. CSA General Taylor wrote to his headquarters, "There is no doubt that the enemy is advancing in very large force. Whether it is his intention to march to the Red River Valley before going to Texas has not yet been developed."[3]

Whatever the Federals' plans, it didn't take long for the Confederates' strategy to begin to have an impact. On October 14, Union General Franklin commented about his position along Vermilion Bayou, "This is an uncomfortable place, as the enemy is continually trying to find a weak point in our lines with his cavalry." Three days later, Franklin complained to his headquarters, "Enemy is very pertinacious and annoying."[4]

The Confederates' unwillingness to make a head-to-head fight against the much stronger Union force was a logical decision, and it caused General Franklin to question the value of such a large army. On October 24, he wrote, "It is useless . . . to march this large force any farther with any expectation of getting a fight from the enemy." His message also revealed his concerns about supply difficulties.

"There is no enemy in front who can be attacked by this expedition, and . . . it is impossible to stay here long," Franklin wrote. "There is very little forage in the country, and a move somewhere must soon be made. . . . I think that we must get nearer to New Iberia or the Mississippi River." A shift toward either of those locations would represent a halt in the army's advance toward Texas, and by November 1, messages from General Franklin indicated that the Federals' Texas Campaign had stalled. "I have been obliged to return to this place, Carrion Crow Bayou, on account of scarcity of forage and doubt about supplies. The roads are getting exceedingly bad."[5]

While the Union commander fretted about supplies, his Confederate adversaries continued their strategy of opportunistic jabs. Company F's activities during October were summarized by a terse comment in the unit's morning report, "During this month we have had hot times with the enemy." Similar activity continued into early November, with the morning reports for Company F noting, "Heavy skirmishing near Bayou [Bourbeau] St. Landry Parish, La," and "Squadron in a fight at Bayou [Bourbeau]."

The latter was a very succinct description of one of Company F's most significant military actions during the war. The Battle of Bayou Bourbeau was fought on Tuesday, November 3, 1863, about eight miles south of Opelousas, Louisiana. Estimates of the Federal force vary widely, but a credible figure would be about 1,800 men. The Union troops involved in the fight were camped on the west bank of Bayou Bourbeau and were the rear guard for Franklin's main army, which was located about four miles farther south.[6]

The Confederate force, under the command of Brig. Gen. Thomas Green, included perhaps three thousand to four thousand men, both cavalry and infantry. For many of them, it would be their first battle of the war. During the morning, the infantry units marched south from the small town of Opelousas, following a road bordered on the right by open prairie and on the left by woods that followed the winding course of the bayou. By about 11:00 a.m. they had reached a point within range of their planned attack but still out of sight of the Federals' camp.[7]

Occasional skirmishing during the previous twenty-four hours between the Texas cavalry and Union pickets had provided a distraction, with the Federal troops' activities in camp interrupted by repeated "calls to arms" at all hours of the day and night. Shortly before noon on the third, the Union troops were back in camp after being rousted from bed before daylight by yet another false alarm. They were preparing to have a meal, waiting for their turn with a visiting paymaster, and casting absentee ballots for a state election being held back home.[8]

When the Confederate attack was launched, the Federals were caught by surprise. An eyewitness report published the following week in a Wisconsin newspaper noted, "During all this time, and until the final clinch, we all supposed it to be a mere guerrilla annoyance, that no serious attack was contemplated—and felt quite as safe as if in the streets of Madison."[9]

Company F was part of a cavalry contingent that attacked the left flank of the Union position. The Wisconsin newspaper report continued, "I saw a vast line of cavalry sweeping down upon the camp, which had not an armed man in it—saw them gobble up the pickets, and come on with the velocity of the wind." Union Maj. Gen. C. C. Washburn later reported his men were "assailed with terrible energy by an overwhelming force in front and on both flanks."[10]

FIGURE 17. Sketch of the Battle of Bayou Bourbeau (also known as Grand Coteau). This sketch appeared in *Frank Leslie's Illustrated History of the Civil War*. Courtesy of Alamy.com

The fight lasted about three hours and was considered a Confederate victory. A relatively small number of soldiers died in this battle—twenty-five Union and twenty-two Confederate. Total casualties from this engagement were 716 killed, wounded, missing, or captured on the Union side, compared to 180 from the South. The following day both sides agreed to a truce, and most of the wounded prisoners were exchanged. On November 4, CSA Major General Taylor submitted a report, stating that "the enemy to my front are retreating to Berwick Bay. . . . The expedition to Texas by land is abandoned."[11]

Following the battle at Bayou Bourbeau, some of the Confederates lost interest in Louisiana in general and fighting in particular. John W. Hankamer and a fellow soldier were detailed on an overnight trip on November 9 to "hunt up some of the absentees." In addition to deserters hanging out in Louisiana, there were even more absentees back in Texas. General Green, commander of the Texas cavalry units then serving in

Louisiana, said he had "about 2,000 men of my division now in Texas, who have either gone there on sick furlough and never returned, or who have skulked and gone off without leave."[12]

On November 19, Company F's commanding officer wrote to his wife with an interesting comment about the military situation and an opinion the officer almost certainly shared with his troops. "All the news I have from the yankees in Louisiana is they are falling back [eastward]," Duncan wrote. "I hear they [other Union forces] are in Texas near Corpus Christi—if such is the case the militia will have an opportunity of doing something. I hope if Texas is invaded that we will be ordered back, for I would rather fight yankees in Texas than in Louisiana."[13]

This information about Union activity in South Texas was accurate. Even while Franklin's overland expedition across Louisiana was spluttering toward a conclusion in late October, his superiors had not abandoned their determination to secure a foothold in Texas. On November 2, 1863, the day before Franklin's army was suffering an embarrassing defeat at Bayou Bourbeau in Louisiana, their overall commander was celebrating a Union victory hundreds of miles away in Texas.

General Banks was aboard his flagship anchored just off the southern tip of Texas. On October 27, he had departed Louisiana in command of another naval expedition to the Lone Star State, and this time he was finally able to send a long-awaited message to Washington: "The flag of the Union floated over Texas today. . . . Our enterprise has been a complete success."[14]

Two days later Union forces occupied Brownsville and the coastal port of Brazos Island, and the Federal navy and army turned their attention up the coast toward Corpus Christi. Numerous messages between Union officers made it clear their ultimate goals were Houston, Galveston, and control of the entire Texas coast.[15]

General Banks also had the attention of CSA commanders, and a week after Captain Duncan wrote to his wife about his desire to return to Texas to fight, the top Confederate officer in the state was doing his best to grant that wish. On November 27, General Magruder sent an urgent request to his commander, Gen. Kirby Smith.

> Re-enforcements are necessary, and I urgently request, general, that you will send me Green's and Major's brigades of cavalry and the

batteries attached to them, as all these troops are Texans, and such other troops as can be spared from General Taylor's army, Louisiana not being seriously threatened at present. . . . I regard this portion of Texas as the heart of the Trans-Mississippi Department, and, scattered as my ill-armed forces necessarily are . . . I fear we shall lose vital points which can never be recovered.[16]

General Magruder wasn't the only high-ranking CSA officer who wanted those Texas cavalrymen sent back to Texas. Brig. Gen. Thomas Green commanded these troops, and on December 4, he dispatched a message to Magruder. "I have been watching with great interest for all the news in relation to the movements of the enemy in Texas since the invasion by Banks," Green wrote, "and I assure you I am exceedingly anxious to be ordered there with my division of cavalry, to assist in defending my own state."[17]

Unknown to either officer, this request had already been approved at higher levels. On December 2, General Magruder was notified orders were being issued for Green's division of cavalry to head for Texas. They were to proceed westward "forthwith" via Niblett's Bluff, and General Magruder was directed to position supplies for those troops along their route "as far as possible."[18]

Rumors of Company F's possible return to Texas had been shared in letters home, and while Johanette Stengler was glad to hear about those prospects, she was concerned about her sons' situation in the meantime. In a letter to Fritz Hankamer on November 28, 1863, she noted:

> You wrote that maybe you would return to Texas soon. I have heard that you have not enough to eat, that is bad. That worries me and you have no warm clothing and it is very cold. I sent you and George each two undershirts and your gloves and 6 blocks of tobacco for you and Wilhelm with Captain Duncan. He has been gone a long time but I heard that he is still on the [Niblett's] Bluff. . . .
>
> I wish you had written what clothing you want. . . . I will send you two heavy shirts, your new woolen pants, your vest, a pair of socks, a pair of drawers, a handkerchief, I believe you have none, and a pair of new shoes which your father made for you. I would have liked to send you a quilt, but I do not know how you can carry all this. . . .
>
> I hope that you will all soon have warm clothing. Take good care

of yourself so you do not get sick. I have to close because I am coming to the end of the paper. I commend you unto the care of the Lord. He is my sole Comforter. . . . Farewell until we see you. I expect you any day. I heard that you all return soon. Do not leave Charles and George behind.

Johanette Stengler had heard that Captain Duncan had been back in Texas, and she hoped to use him as a reliable way to transport the clothing to her sons. Based on the date of her letter, it seems unlikely her shipment caught up with him before he left Niblett's Bluff to return to Louisiana. His diary does show he brought letters, money, and other items from home for some of his soldiers and fellow officers.[19]

With the arrival of winter, the problem of staying warm was becoming a high priority for the troops in the field, and that situation was understood by the family back home. On November 30, 1863, Mina Wilborn expressed those concerns to her brother Fritz. "I know you have hard times where you are," she wrote. "Do you have enough wood to build a good fire when it is cold and where do you get the wood? There isn't much wood where you are. Write me about it, I can imagine how everything is with you."

Mina Wilborn's imagination about how her brothers were faring may have been as reliable a source as the rumors circulating throughout southern Louisiana. According to one report, the troops were going to "move against the Yanks" in Louisiana, while others said they were headed back to Texas. The speculation about their upcoming assignments was no more consistent than the weather, and over one week's time, conditions changed from "everything frozen" to "very warm" and then back to "slept too cold for comfort."[20]

If the wild weather swings weren't bad enough, the troops were also plagued by a stint of very wet weather. By Saturday, December 12, after several days of rain, "everything looked like a flood. Bayou Vermilion out of its banks and running upstream," William Duncan wrote in his diary. There was, however, yet another promising rumor when some men from Captain Marsh's company arrived in camp with "news we were all to go to Texas soon."

"Soon" proved to be a relative term. The slow communications that were common at the time were a source of both frustration and worry for General Magruder, who was anxiously awaiting the arrival of these reinforcements back in Texas. Despite a message to Magruder from his commanding officer on December 2 that General Green's cavalry division was being ordered back to Texas "forthwith," orders for Company F to get underway didn't filter down for another two weeks. Its actual departure date was eventually set for Thursday morning, December 17.

The men spent Wednesday "preparing for the march," and despite their eagerness to head toward their home state, the weather made the tasks of organizing and packing gear very difficult. It rained long and hard during the day, and a northerly wind was an ominous indicator that more cold weather was in the offing.

The second half of December would turn out to be one of the coldest ever recorded up to that time throughout Louisiana and much of Texas. Accounts from civilians and soldiers from both Northern and Southern units commented on the combination of bitter temperatures, ice, and even snow. Ponds were frozen solid and travel conditions were terrible, but troops from Texas were urgently needed back in their home state. Captain Duncan wrote to his wife on the sixteenth from Vermilion Bayou.

> I expect to march in the morning with the company for Texas. . . . Major's Brigade is being ordered off, and we being with it will go without orders to the contrary. . . . I do not know how long we will be on the road but on account of bad roads I expect it will take a long time to get to Liberty. Whether I will get a chance to stop or not I cannot say. I would give anything in reason if I could get to take a New Year's dinner with you. I expect we will go straight through to Houston if the enemy is advancing. Look for me when you see me.

Their departure on the seventeenth was an early one, with Duncan noting, "Got up at 3 o'clock. Very cold and everything wet; got ready, eat & started little after sunrise, off for Texas. Found the prairie almost entirely covered with water. So cold that I thought I would freeze. Stopped & put on another pr. flan. drawers & another pr. socks, which helped. The cart [carrying his gear] crossed one fork Plaquemine Brule & camped."[21]

Duncan's comment that he tried to stay warm by putting on extra layers of clothing was undoubtedly a technique also used by his men if the additional items were available. Family members certainly anticipated

CHAPTER 27

that need, although some of those efforts were sent too late to help. On December 16, Johanette Stengler wrote to her son Fritz Hankamer, the day before Company F began its march back to Texas.

"Dear Son," Johanette said, "you write that you do not want so much clothing, but it was too late, I had already sent it. I think you will need it but it might be too much for you to carry. I hope your shoes fit. I do not think that they are too small but your father had lost your measurements. He also made a pair for Charles but I do not know whether they fit him."

We don't know if the extra clothing she sent in late November reached her sons before they left for Texas, but given the weather, it would have been a potential lifesaver. The hardships her sons would face during the next two weeks were almost beyond imagination for these Texans, and the extreme weather was no respecter of rank. On December 17, General Green wrote to General Magruder from Mermenton [Mermentau], Louisiana, about forty miles east of Lake Charles. He advised that Major's brigade left Vermilion Bayou on the morning of December 17, and Green's brigade was stuck "water-bound" between two bayous. General Green noted, "It is so cold, my fingers are stiff, and I cannot write a legible hand." An account by a Union officer recorded similar conditions in southern Louisiana during this same time period.[22]

"Water-bound" was an ongoing problem. Bayous were out of their banks, and bridges were often underwater or completely gone. At one crossing, Company F was up before daylight, hoping to be the first to get their wagons over the flooded bayou. That wish was a futile one. They finally started crossing their wagons and horses about an hour before sunset, completing the grueling job in the dark at about 10:00 p.m. Rain compounded their misery, and lacking tents or other gear for a warm camp, they pushed on ahead for another six miles. An entry in Captain Duncan's diary noted they were "all worn out."[23]

Part of the reason for the extremely long days was continuing pressure from higher levels in the CSA. Two days before Company F began its trip back to Texas, General Magruder sent the following message to General Green in Louisiana: "Hasten on your command as rapidly as possible. The enemy, in force, is pressing on all sides." Magruder continued with another order that would be a disappointment to troops returning to their home state after an absence of seven months: "Give no furloughs or leaves of absence. There is no time for them now. Furloughs will be allowed after the fight."[24]

General Magruder's desire for the troops to "hasten" their return to Texas was understandable, but the weather and terrain failed to cooperate. The unrelenting cold and rain continued, and the roads were described in a single word, "Horrible." One of the men succeeded in obtaining some badly needed corn for their horses, which were described as "starved." Given the terrible conditions, the name of a nearby landmark—Bayou Serpent—must have seemed appropriate.

The night of December 22 brought yet another rainy stop, but at least the men found a campsite in an area of pine woods that may have offered some token shelter. The following day, with the rain continuing to fall in "torrents" for half the day, Company F passed through Lake Charles and slogged ahead to the Calcasieu River before sunset. Crossing this major waterway required nearly six hours. After it was finally completed at 11:00 p.m., the weary troops pushed on for another four miles before making camp. Duncan wrote that he went to bed at 3:30 a.m. with their "horses starving and nothing to eat. I in same condition and everything wet."

December 24 brought yet another early start, but a small gift of sorts. At a place described as "Abel Lyons," probably the name of a local resident, they obtained some corn and stopped and fed their horses. They then pushed on again to a point within about seven miles of their intermediate destination, Niblett's Bluff. Sunrise on Christmas Day found the men already up and ready to move, and after a few mouthfuls of a token breakfast, the day's travel was marked by the first promising development in a week of misery—their arrival at Niblett's Bluff. That small settlement and army depot on the Louisiana bank of the Sabine River were presumably able to provide badly needed rations for both men and horses.

By nightfall, Company F had completed crossing the waterway and set up camp, and there was likely a sense of relief that they were finally back on Texas soil, soggy as it was. Their holiday was a token one at best. Captain Duncan had purchased two quarts of whiskey at Niblett's Bluff and noted in his diary, "Gave my Co. a drink round for their Christmas. I ate some of the little cakes I brought from home and gave some of the men a taste. That was our Christmas."

The men may have been glad to be back in Texas, but the change was merely symbolic as the unrelenting rain and severe cold continued to make travel both miserable and dangerous. They had no tents for shelter during their brief overnight stops, and William Duncan, who had traveled throughout the region for years as a livestock broker, wrote, "Never saw the like of water." Their wagons bogged down constantly, and at least one cart was finally abandoned altogether. On December 27, their progress was halted once again by a flooded creek where they had to build a bridge before continuing. Word reached them "to hurry on to the railroad line," where they were to take the train toward Houston.

It took the men five more days to reach the railroad at Carter's Station, east of Liberty. It must have seemed impossible for conditions to get any worse, but after a very limited respite from the cold, the predawn hours of December 31 brought a bitter north wind that "blew a gale." William Duncan wrote, "everything frozen" at daylight, and by midday, it was the "coldest weather I ever felt."[25]

Another observer in Southeast Texas corroborated that opinion. James Madison Hall wrote in his journal that on December 31, the ground was covered with two inches of snow, and his mill pond was "frozen entirely over one inch thick." The cold was so extreme that night, noted Hall, "it froze all the little woman's eggs in my room, although I kept a large fire in it throughout the entire night. It is decidedly the coldest spell of weather that I have ever experienced in the State of Texas, after a residence of 28 years." The extreme cold would not relent for another nine days.[26]

Despite the bitter cold, Company F was at least spared additional travel by horseback. They camped near Carter's Station, a few miles east of Liberty, until January 6, when a train finally arrived to take them to Houston. William Duncan wrote a brief note to his wife the next morning, telling her they were "camped in the woods near Houston. I expect we will leave here in a day or two for some place on or about the Brazos." That would be in line with an earlier message to a senior CSA officer bringing his troops to Texas from Louisiana. He was told, "Move your command as rapidly as possible to Columbia, Texas," which was about fifty miles southwest of Houston.[27]

If Company F had continued toward Columbia, they may have found living conditions even worse than what they had experienced during the past month, if that was possible. The Fourth Texas Cavalry had also been assigned to Louisiana for much of 1863 and returned to Texas a few days ahead of Company F. On January 5, 1864, they were camped on the open prairie near Harrisburg, south of Houston, and Theo Noel, one of their soldiers, later described their ordeal.

"All will remember the suffering endured by the men of the command, through the coldest spell of weather that Texas had experienced for many years," Noel wrote. They were "without tents or shelter of any sort. . . . For seven days the whole country was under water, not a dry spot was to be found on which to sleep, much less build a fire to warm or cook with. Every night ice was formed on the ponds and horse tracks from one [to] two inches thick." On January 9, 1864, this unit moved to Brazoria County, near the Brazos River, "on one of the coldest days that we had yet experienced. On this trip many of the boys' feet were so frozen that their toe nails came off."[28]

Those troops endured such terrible conditions because of the continuing threat of a Union advance on Houston and Galveston by Federal forces that had occupied parts of the South Texas coast. Those concerns also increased the likelihood that additional locally raised Texas State Troops would be needed to bolster the ranks of CSA regular army units. Among those likely to be affected were the remaining adult males in the Stengler, Hankamer, and Wilborn households, along with one other family member who was determined to do his duty, despite his age.

28

SOLDIERS YOUNG AND OLD

Oh, if you could only see him. He looks like a real soldier.
He uses your father's big knife and pistol and his gun.
He rides our mare. . . . He is so young to be a soldier.
—JOHANETTE STENGLER, September 15, 1863

By the fall of 1863, John Henry Stengler was determined to be a soldier. At age sixteen, he was not yet subject to the draft, but family letters say he was serving in a local Texas militia unit by mid-September 1863. Perhaps the recently attempted Union invasion at Sabine Pass, only a few miles from his home, tipped his decision to enroll in a unit designated specifically for the defense of Texas.

John Henry was the youngest son of John and Johanette Stengler, and the last of their children still living at home when he decided to follow his four older brothers into uniform. On September 15, 1863, Johanette confirmed his departure in a letter to Fritz Hankamer, and she provided a rather poignant description of her teenage soldier.

> Our John is gone too. I believe the company is at the Sabine Pass, but 10 men had to stay here. They have to patrol from Beaumont to the station house and 3 have to ride to Liberty every day. John has been home twice. He is hale and hearty. He seems to like it, but I think he would rather be at home. I wish so too because I miss him very much. All my help is gone. We cannot do anything about it because almost all are gone. Charles [Wilborn] and Alfred are gone too. . . .
>
> Dear Son, John would like to use your double-barrel shotgun. He has our small one but it does not serve the purpose. If you will let him use it, he will take good care of it. Oh, if you could only see him. He looks like a real soldier. He uses your father's big knife and pistol

and his gun. He rides our mare. I hope the good Lord will keep him safely. He is so young to be a soldier.

Two other family members also served in the Texas State Troops at this same time. Charles Wilborn was enrolled in Company B by August 1863 and later served in Spaight's Battalion. Comments in several letters tell us the oldest man in the family, John Stengler, also served at least intermittently in a local militia unit, although more details are not known.[1]

A separate letter in September from Mina to Fritz Hankamer confirmed that her husband Charles was once again on military duty. "I wish Charles would get a furlough," she wrote. "I have not heard from him since the 10th. I heard they are at Sabine Pass. I think they will be there for six months or longer. The Lord only knows. The Yankees will try to see what they can do to us. I think all our people who were sent from Texas to Louisiana will be sent back here which would be as it should be."

Mina also passed along some additional details about the young John Henry Stengler's duties. "John has been home twice," she wrote. "He, Abshire, and 8 others have to protect the telegraph cable. It has been cut two times already. I wish they had left Charles there, too, then he would have come home sometimes too." The telegraph line in question followed the railroad from Houston to Beaumont and was a vital communications link for CSA commanders. Mina's comments about the line having been cut twice strongly suggest activities by Union sympathizers in the area.[2]

The young John H. Stengler's early entry into the militia—and Charles Wilborn's ongoing service—were likely influenced by the continuing threat of a Union takeover of the Texas coast. Despite the CSA's dramatic success in repulsing Union forces at Sabine Pass in early September, it was widely believed the Northern leaders would soon make another attempt somewhere in the state. The Confederacy was woefully short of enough regular army troops to defend hundreds of miles of Texas coastline, and thus the role of Texas units had assumed much greater importance.

That role was confirmed in late 1863, following the successful Union invasion of the Lower Rio Grande Valley. A circular issued by General Magruder's headquarters on December 3 noted that the "threatened condition of Galveston and Houston render it imperatively necessary that every man should be in the field." This appeal also called for "all mounted companies and organizations for local defense" across the southeastern and south-central parts of Texas to report to Houston as rapidly as possible.[3]

Military commanders certainly had plenty of challenges, but soldiers and their families were often more interested in the details of day-to-day life. Back on September 20, 1863, Mina wrote to her "Dear and Beloved Husband" describing the situation at home and noting that a neighbor had sent a man over to cut some wood for her. She continued with some practical matters for Charles.

> I would like to send you your [mosquito] bar and tobacco but if I should fail to send these things, write and let me know what you want and I will try to get someone to take it over to you, for I won't know when John will go over. Dear Charles, try and get off and come home as soon as you possibly can [even] if it is only for a few days. . . . I hope that God may be with you and protect you and keep you in good health and fetch you back home safe before long. Me and the children send our love and regard to you, and Mother's family also. . . .
>
> Dear Charles something more, I heard that the major had hired a shoemaker for to make shoes for the battalion, you have to pay 6 dollars a pair I heard, I think you better try and get a pair made if you can. I sent you some tobacco, this is all I can send to you at present. Mina Wilborn.

This letter confirms the financial strain Mina felt as the war continued. A pair of shoes at six dollars would take two weeks of her husband's army pay, but such items were very difficult to obtain. On the same day as this letter from Mina to her husband, her mother was writing separately to Fritz Hankamer with more confirmation of the Wilborns' difficult circumstances.

"Dear son, Mina told me that she has no money," Johanette wrote. "She has to send for the doctor so often for Martha, and that costs so much. I think she wants some of yours if she may have some. I think you will let her have some. Oh, I wish that Charles was home again. We have not heard from him."[4]

With the arrival of autumn, Mina and her husband, Charles, seemed resigned to the likelihood that he would not be returning home from the army in the immediate future. On October 19, 1863, she wrote to her husband confirming that she was working on an item he would need for the coming colder weather. "I am getting along very well, everything about the place is doing well as could be expected," she said. "I will soon have your blanket ready for you, and I hope you will get to come home for it yourself."

Charles was also preparing for the change in the weather, as well as hoping to get a renewed supply of a popular item. He sent Mina a request that was apparently on behalf of someone else in his unit since this item was to be made smaller than his size. "Dear wife: I have something more to write to you about. Them caps, knit one about 8 stitches smaller than mine, and send me some tobacco, the first good chance you have. . . . This from your loving husband, Charles Wilborn."[5]

As the end of the growing season approached, Charles Wilborn was keenly aware of the need to get his crops harvested. On October 27, 1863, he sent a letter to his wife, telling her to "write to me when harvest is and I will try and come home for a few days. You must do the best you can about meat and all things. . . . You will please send me one pound and a half of coffee . . . if you can spare it."

Two days later, on October 29, Mina replied to Charles, commenting on his request for several knit caps, asking his advice about the purchase of some much-needed salt, and updating him on the whereabouts of some of her brothers.

> Dear Husband. . . . You wrote you wanted three caps knit. I can't knit them on the account of my arm, it pains me so bad when I knit, and another thing I have not wool enough, it took nearly all for your blanket. Your blanket will be in the loom Saturday. I want you to try to come home the last of next week or the first of the week after, I will have your blanket ready then. I could send it but I rather you would come home if it's only a few days, ask the captain and tell him I thought he would let you come. . . .
>
> I would like for you to write how much a pound I shall pay for the salt. . . . I will send your half pound coffee . . . and when you come home after your blanket you can take the rest. When I heard from Charles [Hankamer] and George [Stengler] they were still herding beeves at Washington [Louisiana], and the rest [of the boys] it is hard to tell where they are now, the last we heard from them they were at

Vermilionville.... Try and come to get you some bedclothes, I know you are cold. I feel bad about you, it is very cold.

The next surviving family letter wasn't written until late November, when Mina sent a note to her brother Fritz in Louisiana.

> I had a few lines from Charles too which were written yesterday, he is well. They have to guard oxen, that is Captain Wooten's company does. They are from Beaumont. How long they stay or where they will go, I do not know. Our brother John is not with the company as yet. He and others still have to watch that the telegraph cable will not be cut. I hope he stays there.
>
> Charles writes they have enough to eat, also enough for their horses and also a good place for camp, but much work. The oxen have to be watched day and night. Charles did not mention about the oxen but others have told me. John does better where he is.
>
> I had a health testimonial from the doctor and confirmed by the county clerk about the condition of our family, also a petition signed by our neighbors sent to General Magruder, but it did no good. He ... will not let Charles come home.... Dear brother, you cannot imagine how quiet it is at our mother and father's house and they being alone. Our children go over there often, in particular, Andrew [age five]. He spent two overnights already there.[6]

General Magruder—and his subordinates who handled requests such as the Wilborn's—were not inclined to release any soldiers from duty in the autumn and early winter of 1863. On December 3, in response to reports that Union troops on the lower Texas coast had "turned their attention to Galveston," state troops in the Liberty area were ordered to proceed "as rapidly as possible ... by forced marches to Galveston." CSA Brigadier General Slaughter was put in charge of Galveston with instructions to "defend that place to the last."[7]

The civilian population had plenty of cause for concern about this new threat as well. After more than two years of fighting in much of the South, sources of supplies for both sides were wearing thin, and Union officers had their eyes on the unscathed farms, forests, and fields in East Texas. On December 12, 1863, Union General Banks wrote to the general in chief of the US Army describing Banks's plans for Texas. "My desire is to occupy Galveston Island, if it can be done within a reasonable time," he said. "This will give us the entire coast. . . . Eastern Texas offers us recruits, horses, forage, and supplies of every kind. All other parts of this department have been stripped by the two armies of everything necessary for their support."[8]

"Eastern Texas" included Company F's home territory in Liberty County, and plans by the Union to tap the area to support the Union Army certainly did not bode well for farmers, ranchers, and other residents.

News of Union activity in South Texas managed to filter down to the lowest ranks and youngest soldiers. On December 2, 1863, the young soldier John Henry Stengler wrote to his brothers from Carter's Station, on the railroad line between Liberty and Beaumont.

> Dear brothers: As for news, I know some of the Yankees have taken Brownsville and Corpus Christi and it appears like they come a little closer to us all the time. . . . I heard that your battalion would soon be back in Texas again. I am in hopes that you will. I am in hopes that this war will soon end and that you can stay . . . home. I am still stationed here close to Carters guarding the telegraph line but I don't know how long I will stay here, for I have heard that they were going to take me away and put some other man here, they have exchanged the most of us. . . . On their place the company is now herding beeves close to Joseph Healcars.
>
> It will be a week Sunday since I have been at home, but I expect to go home Saturday. . . . I know nothing more to write. . . . [E]xcuse any bad handwriting and for not writing more.

The young soldier's sister back home at Crackersneck didn't have any news about military activity, but Mina Wilborn had been focusing on items of more immediate importance to her family. A top priority was a leave of absence for at least a short visit home by her husband, and Mina had devised a clever strategy to make that possible. In an earlier letter, Charles Wilborn had asked Mina to knit several caps, and one of them was apparently for his commanding officer.

With the arrival of colder weather, Mina saw the possibility of gaining a little leverage with that cap, and she explained her plan on December 6, 1863.

> Dear Husband. . . . I sent you a half pound coffee. . . . I expect you have got it by this time. . . . I heard you were to be along yesterday

> with the beeves and I was preparing for you. Try and come home. I have got that cap done that the captain spoke for. I knit it on purpose so you could come home. I will not send it by anybody else and if the captain wants it he will have to detail you to come after it.

Mina then continued with an additional reason for the captain to allow Charles to make the short trip back home, and she included some other practical information.

> I know your horse looks bad and the other one is in very good order, you can make that an excuse to come after him. . . . Dear, if you can't get to come home write as soon as possible, I would like to hear from you. . . . [E]verything about the place is done as well as can be expected. Me and the children send our love to you, write soon . . . your ever-loving wife, W. Wilborn.

Perhaps the combination of the extremely cold weather and the lure of the knit cap for the captain did the trick, since a letter from Mina Wilborn to her brother Fritz on December 18 noted that Charles Wilborn was back home at least briefly. As usual, he took the time to look after chores at his relatives' farms as well.

"Charles fed two of your sows and 23 shoats yesterday," Mina wrote. "He could feed them without getting the dog to round them up." The often-uncooperative semi-wild hogs must have been feeling the effects of the cold and were glad to get an easy meal by staying closer to the farm.[9]

Charles Wilborn's visit home was a brief one, since he wrote to Mina again on January 4, 1864, from Jefferson County, Texas. His letter illustrates the challenges facing many farm wives while their husbands were away during the war, and the list of things that needed to be done was daunting.

> Dear and beloved wife. . . . I am well at this present time, only my arm it is tolerably sore with this vaccination. . . . Dear wife perhaps you can get to hire a hand of John White, try and . . . get him for 4 months, that is if you can get him at a reasonable price, and if you can get him, put him to splitting rails, and let him split about 2000 rails, have them split where I split the last ones, your father can show him where it was.
>
> And if you get him, give him two weeks to split the rails and stack them, and after he is through and [if it] is dry enough, have him to put the manure between the two old rows and then let him

commence back of the cow pen and then . . . all over the field; I know you will have to see to it yourself for I don't expect that I can get to come home to see to it myself, and have a brush pile burnt in the pasture somewhere at a good place where the sun can shine on it, and sew the tobacco seeds on it and then have a brush fence put around it so the horses and things can't tramp on it. . . .

If your father did not get them hogs of mine yet, get him to look for them again, and if he can get them, have them five big boars killed and the white sow if she is fit to kill. Then if you get them have the rest of the bunch . . . put together. . . . Try and send a letter down to Double Bayou, that you will stand a better chance to get the salt, send the letter to James Jackson if you should get these hogs, weigh the bacon meat of all the hogs you kill. We have turned all of the beeves [cattle] loose and got short of them.

Take good care of my horse for I don't know how soon I will want him. I don't know when I will get off to come home. . . . I am glad that I have got my shirt and it fits me well. . . . So, goodbye at a distance, write often and plenty of it . . . Charles Wilborn.

On January 10, 1864, George Stengler wrote to Charles Wilborn, his brother-in-law, from the Stengler home in Liberty County, Texas. He and two of his brothers were back from Louisiana and somewhat surprisingly had been able to gain a leave of absence. "I arrived home Thursday evening late [January 7] and are going away on the 25th of this month again," he wrote. "Charley and Fritz will be in also today or tomorrow, and if you could get off any time between this and the 20th, you could see all of us."

A letter from Mina to her husband a week later, on January 17, 1864, covered a lot of topics. "Mother got a letter from John and he stated in his letter that . . . you was off somewhere . . . and that you had marching orders to go to Sabine Pass, and he didn't know whether you would get back in time enough to write or not. I should like very much to see you come home if possible as it has been a good while since you was at home."

Mina's letter included confirmation that news via the mail or the grapevine was often slow to arrive, even when it dealt with important family events.

Charly [Hankamer] came home last Monday [January 11] and found a big fat boy at home when he got there, which he wasn't aware of, though his name I can't tell you, for they haven't named him yet.

Charley, Fritz, and George are all at home and as bad as ever and [John] William was at home a few days between Christmas and New Year, but he is now in camp near Houston. Charley and Fritz will leave next Wednesday, they have to meet at Liberty, they are still on that beeves detail. George will leave tomorrow and he is going back to the command.

Her letter continued with more examples of the multitude of tasks facing wives while their husbands were away in the army.

Dear Husband, I had them three hogs killed which we had in the pen and they was fairly fat, I got about seven gallons of grease out of them. I thought it better to kill them than to keep them any longer for they was eating so much breadstuff. I hear Reuben Barrow wants to buy some potatoes and I think it better to sell some than to feed so much away, and I had a good chance to have them killed. I got Charley, Fritz, and George to kill them, Charley has killed his [hogs] too, and wants to kill one for William, too. The weather is a little bad and rainy today and if it ain't too bad tomorrow I want to get Fritz and George to take what forage we have to deliver up to Carter's Station, there will be a man there to receive it.

Mina also responded to her husband's comment in his previous letter that his arm was sore after he received a vaccination, probably for smallpox. She was clearly concerned about this relatively new medical procedure.

Dear Husband, I understood that some of the men in your company suffer right smart with their vaccination, and we also understood that one man had died from it, and I have been a little uneasy about you being it has served some of the balance so bad. I wish you would write as soon as possible and let me know how you are getting along, if you can't get off to come home. . . . I and the children send our love.

On January 26, 1864, Charles wrote from High Island, Texas, and mentioned both the price of corn and the uncertainty about getting any leave.

I can't say when I will be at home, maybe I will be at home in a week and then again it may be a month, try and get a hand from John White. If you can buy the . . . corn at the government price you had better do it, and the fodder at the government price, for corn is a dollar and three bits a bushel, the potatoes you can do as you please about them. I wish you would send me some tobacco by the first good chance for I am nearly out. . . . As for news, I don't [have] any. . . . I remain your true and loving Husband, Charles Wilborn.[10]

Comments in these letters about soldiers being home on leave in January 1864 are rather surprising given the urgent orders for Company F and other troops to hasten their return from Louisiana in December. When they finally reached Houston after that grueling trip in the bitter cold, those men fully expected to be sent to the Lower Brazos River area to help stem an expected Union advance from the southern Texas coast.

That Federal move toward Houston and Galveston failed to materialize, and ironically, one reason was the extreme cold that caused so much hardship for CSA troops during their return to Texas from Louisiana. Throughout history, the weather has proven to be a major factor affecting the outcomes of military campaigns, and the prolonged and unusually bitter cold during the winter of 1863–1864 caused misery for troops on both sides of the conflict.

On November 30, 1863, Union forces captured Fort Esperanza on the eastern shore of Matagorda Island, not far from Corpus Christi. Union General Washburn asked for additional troops, with which he would "go to Houston and take Galveston." Washburn also commented on the harsh conditions: "For the past two days my men have suffered greatly from the cold, and I shall expect much sickness growing out of the exposure on these islands."

The following day Washburn reluctantly acknowledged orders to hold his position for the time being, but noted, "the water here is bad, and no fuel. . . . As my men are without shelter, I was anxious to get into some place less inhospitable." Other accounts by Union soldiers on the South Texas coast described efforts to stay warm by wearing all the clothes they had and staying in bed, wrapped in as many blankets as they could find.[11]

One of those Union versions of the South Texas campaign was written after the war by Henry Shorey of the Fifteenth Maine Regiment. We would expect a resident of Maine to have considerable experience with winter weather, so his comments about the bitter cold on the Texas coast in late 1863 are especially instructive. "A 'Texas Norther' cannot be adequately described; it must be experienced to be fully appreciated," he wrote. "It may as well be said that these periodical gales are really a terror. Swooping down upon the bleak, unprotected coast . . . they are well-nigh unendurable. For genuine frigidity they completely throw our New England winter gales into the shade."[12]

Confederate troops in the area fared no better. One account by a Texas officer noted, "Our service on the coast during the latter part of the winter of 1863–4 was at times very hard owing to the severely cold weather. . . . We lost quite a number of our gallant young soldiers who were frozen to death in an attempt to make an attack upon a detachment of the enemy that had landed upon our coast."[13]

A second factor in military operations by both sides was the scarcity of even basic supplies for men and mounts. In late November, CSA Brigadier General Bee warned his superiors that the area around Corpus Christi was "barren and parched." He wrote, "This place is absolutely untenable for cavalry; there is neither water, grass, nor corn."[14]

Since no trees grew on the coastal islands and they were scarce on the nearby mainland, fuel for fires urgently needed for warmth and cooking was limited to pieces of driftwood found on the beach. Forage for livestock was so sparse that in mid-December, one Union commander in South Texas advised his headquarters not to send any more horses or mules; he reported eight to ten animals were dying of starvation each day on Matagorda Island. These conditions discouraged both Union and CSA commanders from large-scale troop movements in South Texas. What had begun as an impressive Federal invasion in the autumn of 1863 had stalled by the beginning of 1864.[15]

A third factor in the Union's failure to advance on Houston and Galveston was the cautious approach adopted by General Banks, the Federal commander in the area. He had already been seriously embarrassed by his defeat by a vastly inferior force only a few months earlier at Sabine Pass, and after his troops' initial success on the lower Texas Coast, he was reluctant to risk those gains by pushing ahead too quickly.

A combination of Magruder's bluster and Banks's caution slowed and then halted the Federal advance. An insider's look at the Confederates' strategy is provided by Frances Lubbock, a former governor of Texas who joined Magruder's staff in 1863. Lubbock later wrote that Magruder "had already, by proclamation, disclaimed any intention of abandoning the western country [Southwest Texas], and boasted of the strong works near San Antonio . . . and proposed to dispute every inch of ground with the invader. The enemy took Magruder at his word, and soon slowed up to a dead halt in his front."[16]

CSA troops and Texas residents who would have been threatened by a continued Union advance would be thankful that Magruder's bluster worked, because the Confederate general's words were a lot stronger than his military forces. On December 21, 1863, Magruder pleaded for the purchase of weapons desperately needed by the Texas troops tasked with halting the Union threat. Magruder's spokesman wrote, "The commanding general desires me to say in strict confidence . . . that all of that portion of our troops which are armed at all are badly armed, and fully one-fourth of his army are entirely without arms."

The needed firearms were not obtained. Former Governor Lubbock later wrote, "A few small arms were procured at intervals, but nothing like enough to supply our needs, and what we did have were of inferior quality. This irremediable condition ultimately proved fatal to our cause. The Yankees in our front were well supplied with arms and everything else necessary for campaigning, and outnumbered us more than two to one."[17]

Union General Banks's conservative approach may have saved Texas, but it was hardly welcomed by his commanders in the field. Major General Washburn, whose troops were suffering from the cold at Matagorda Bay, was anxious to get away from their exposed positions on the coast and advance inland. General Banks, however, had overestimated the Texans' capabilities, and ordered Washburn on December 5 to bide his time: "Understand that an advance of your forces will bring down upon you the concentrated forces of the enemy; and that you must be largely reinforced before such an advance is made."[18]

As the year drew to a close, reinforcements deemed adequate by Banks were not available, and the Union commander continued to be reluctant to risk another defeat. One Union account noted, "Our army unwittingly lapsed into a state of 'masterly inactivity.'" Perhaps General Banks's attitude was influenced by a personal communication he received from the White House on December 24, 1863. That message closed with the comment, "My thanks for your successful and valuable operations in Texas. Yours as ever, A. Lincoln." Having won the praise of the president for his gains along the Rio Grande, Banks saw no reason to risk a reversal in his fortunes by advancing farther into the state.[19]

Banks was also keenly aware that his superior officer in Washington,

Gen. Henry Halleck, continued to favor a different strategy for control of Texas—an invasion of the state through Louisiana, up the Red River via Shreveport. Halleck had already gained support for his plan from other Union officers, including Generals Grant and Sherman, and on January 23, 1864, Banks fell into line. The majority of his troops positioned along the southern Texas coast were ordered back to Louisiana via the Gulf of Mexico aboard Union ships to take part in the new Red River campaign.[20]

Once again Texas was spared the almost certain devastation that would accompany large-scale fighting in the state's towns and countryside. Freed from the imminent threat of Union invasion, CSA commanders shifted the men in Company F between a variety of tasks during the spring and summer of 1864. Charles Wilborn and the young soldier John H. Stengler also continued to serve in separate military units in Texas, but Charles saw a marked improvement in his assignment.

In mid-1864, military records show a Charles Wilborn was detailed to help the war effort in a seemingly very *un*military task—working as a miller in Chambers County. Cornmeal had become an increasingly vital staple for both troops and civilians as the war wore on, and mills powered by mules or oxen were the primary means of grinding corn in this very flat terrain.

Several documents for this detail included phonetic spellings of "C. Wilborn" and "C. Wilburn," an example of a common problem for historians. Mina Wilborn commented on this new assignment in a letter, indicating the "Wilborn" in this case was her husband. "You can readily imagine how happy I was when Charles was given his detail," she wrote. "I had been afraid he too would have to leave."[21]

Responsibility for running this mill offered a major benefit for Charles and his extended family; as long as this special detail lasted, he would remain close enough to home to make occasional visits. Those trips allowed Charles the chance to perform vital work on not only his farm but also on those of Mina Wilborn's brothers and parents. His help would become especially valuable in the coming months as the assignments for Company F became increasingly unpredictable.

29

UNCERTAINTY

We are happy... that you have returned from Louisiana.
I hope you will stay here. Charles tells me that you
have to leave again but that is not certain.
—JOHANETTE STENGLER, May 15, 1864

The American Civil War has been compared at times to a chess match, albeit one with enormous consequences. Commanders planned feints and movements of men and materiel based on their best calculations of the opposition's anticipated plans, strengths, and weaknesses. To the troops in Company F, however, a better analogy might be a game of checkers, with the unit jumping back and forth across parts of Texas and Louisiana. At times those changes occurred so rapidly that they may have literally expected to meet themselves coming and going.

The year 1864 began with mixed emotions for the troops in Company F and their families. By January 6, after its brutal winter march from Louisiana back to Texas, the unit finally arrived on the outskirts of Houston. The men were relieved to be closer to home but apprehensive about yet another threatened Union invasion of their state.[1]

Over the next several weeks those concerns subsided, at least temporarily. The Federal advance northward from the Rio Grande Valley appeared to stall, and most of the men even enjoyed some time off for visits home. Once back in camp near Houston, however, Company F found CSA superiors had some unwelcome changes in mind.

During their eight months in Louisiana, Company F had been detached from Spaight's Battalion and attached to Baylor's regiment, and in January 1864 CSA General Magruder decided to make this change a permanent one. That reassignment would allow them to remain a cavalry company, but they would lose their long-standing connection with Spaight's command and its close ties to Southeast Texas.

There was a chance their move could be reversed, but it would come at a significant cost—if they remained a part of Spaight's command, they would have to give up their horses and become infantry soldiers. Capt. William Duncan wrote to his wife about these changes on January 16, 1864.

> I think [the men] will dislike very much to give up their horses and go into the infantry service for [the rest of] the war. Walking would be too much like work to suit their notions. I have made up my mind to go with the majority. If they are in favor of being infantry and going to Spaight's, I will go with them; and if the majority is in favor of remaining with this Regiment [Baylor's], I will stay here.[2]

Given the uncertainty about the CSA's future military organization, it must have seemed a reasonable gamble for the troops to ask to stick with Spaight, and events would soon bear that out. By February 16, they learned they would retain their designation as Company F in Spaight's Battalion, but they also found themselves in an unexpected new role—they were going to help rebuild a railroad. Manning picks and shovels and hauling railroad ties may not sound very appealing, but there were advantages to the assignment. Work on the railroad between Beaumont and Sabine Pass would keep them fairly close to home, and they would also have easy access to the trains between Beaumont and Houston for both travel and a speedier source of mail and supplies.[3]

The Eastern Texas Railroad was supposed to run from Sabine Pass to Beaumont, but the last mile or two south of Beaumont had never been completed. Other parts of the line had suffered badly at the hands of both friend and foe. In October 1862, Union troops burned a vital bridge across Taylor's Bayou, and in the spring of 1863, CSA troops pulled up some of the rails to help construct Fort Griffin near the town of Sabine Pass. Now, in the spring of 1864, CSA commanders decided it was essential that the tracks between Beaumont and Sabine Pass be put into service. Railroads across the state were struggling to maintain both roadbeds and rolling stock, so a decision was made to assign some troops to the job of restoring the rails.[4]

By February 23, Company F was camped about a mile south of Beaumont and ready to go to work. The weather was reported to be "fine," and the land was "dry," a rare situation in often soggy Southeast Texas. Best of all, morning reports for the next six weeks recorded alternating six-day leaves of absence for visits home for all four brothers.[5]

Both troops and family members were enjoying the prospects of some time at home, and that was reflected in a more relaxed tone in some of their letters. On February 28, 1864, Mina Wilborn couldn't resist a little teasing of her younger—and unmarried—brother Fritz. "I saw all the girls at church last Sunday," Mina wrote. "Ellen was there, and Bette, Lucinda. . . . I cannot remember all the names. Martha Bingel came last Monday and brought a German girl along. She is a very pretty girl."

Her brother's new role working on the railroad also merited a comment. "I think it is good that they make you work, else you might forget how to work and that would be bad. Because when the war is ended you will have to work anyways. Of course, you will have to buy a farm first. I looked the girls at church over real good. Susanne was there too. I better close with this nonsense because you might get angry with me. Farewell till I see you."

Not all of Fritz's fellow soldiers may have agreed that the work was good for them, but progress on the railroad was being made at a steady pace, and within two weeks Company F moved their camp to a new site three miles farther south. The unit's detail continued through March, and on April 6 they received welcome news. Their recent move back to Spaight's Battalion did not mean a permanent change in status as foot soldiers after all; their new orders were to remount the company and assemble with their horses in Liberty.[6]

It was perhaps appropriate that their horses had not been ridden in quite a while, because a figurative wild ride in terms of rapidly changing orders was about to begin.

Before the men finished getting their horses and gear ready, the company was ordered once again to "dismount," leave their horses at home, and begin an eighty-mile march to Burr's Ferry, on the Sabine River north of Beaumont. They made it only as far as Beaumont, where they were told to pause and await further orders. During the next twelve days, they went back to Camp Lubbock near Houston; back to Beaumont; north to Niblett's Bluff; and back to Beaumont again. They were undoubtedly glad that at least some of their travel was by train.[7]

CHAPTER 29

Their commanders' uncertainty was the result of recent Union activity in Louisiana. CSA troops had stopped a major Federal thrust on April 8, barely two hundred miles to the north at Mansfield, Louisiana. Union General Banks had intended to invade East Texas via an advance up the Red River through Shreveport, but that effort failed. The Federal forces then began withdrawing to the southeast back down the Red River, but the chess match was underway again. Would the Union troops continue all the way back to New Orleans, or would they regroup and try again to enter Texas, this time via Burr's Ferry or Niblett's Bluff?[8]

Those questions were not yet resolved on May 5, and Company F was once again detached from the rest of Spaight's Battalion. This time they did not return to Houston but headed east to Lake Charles, Louisiana, a distance of about sixty miles. Their primary mission when they arrived was to guard CSA vessels and cotton at that location, and the company's morning report described their next three days with a terse entry: "Marching."[9]

While Company F was marching, the rest of Spaight's Battalion had become part of a contingent of three hundred men commanded by Col. W. H. Griffin. Their destination was Calcasieu Pass, located a short distance inland from the southwest Louisiana coast and about forty miles east of the Texas border. In late April, two Union Navy vessels, the USS *Wave* and the USS *Granite City*, moved into that area, and a report telegraphed to General Magruder predicted they planned to "proceed up Calcasieu Pass to Lake Charles, thence against Niblett's Bluff and flank Sabine Pass." Griffin was ordered to "disperse, defeat, or capture the expedition."[10]

Griffin's force made a stealthy move east from Sabine Pass, and as the sun rose on May 6, it launched a successful surprise attack on the two Union gunboats and accompanying infantry. The engagement lasted less than two hours and resulted in a CSA victory. Company F missed this action, but by May 10 was headed back to Texas, possibly helping haul a large quantity of captured supplies and weapons back to Texas.[11]

Shortly after its return to Texas, Company F began what may have been the least stressful period of the men's military service. On May 19, they moved their camp to Spindletop, four miles south of Beaumont. This area of relatively high ground was also known locally as the "Big Hill," and there was a reason for the distinctive terrain. Spindletop was located atop a large salt dome, and thirty-six years later, the discovery of the vast

FIGURE 18. This 1864 sketch, "Our Camp at Spindle Top," was drawn by H. Rosenbaum, a private in CSA Company F. Courtesy of Julia Duncan Welder Collection, Sam Houston Regional Library and Research Center, Texas State Library and Archives Commission.

quantity of oil it contained would help launch the modern American petroleum industry. In 1864 it was simply a convenient place for Company F to set up camp, and the rural location offered a nice bonus—the chance to supplement their diet with some local venison.[12]

The good hunting was suggested by a June 22, 1864, letter from Capt. William Duncan to his wife, in which he mentioned sending her a "a ham of fine venison" and described his men drying other venison for future use. Included with his letter was a sketch of their camp at Spindletop, drawn by a soldier in Company F and included here as figure 18. Duncan provided the following commentary about the scene in his letter.

> It is a perfect picture of our camp except it [does] not show all the trees. You will recognize my little [tent] by its shape—it stands between the large oak and the other [tree]. My wagon stands back and is only partly visible. The two forks with a pole across is where we hang our blankets out to sun. You will see two small forks to the right and in front of the large tent—that is our dried venison hanging out in the sun.[13]

Johanette Stengler was relieved to have her sons back close to home, and the matriarch of the family included a little levity in a letter to Fritz and George. "We are happy that . . . you have returned from Louisiana," she wrote. "I hope you will stay here. Charles tells me that you have to leave again but that is not certain. . . . Maybe you would like to go. . . . What will the Louisiana girls say when they see such handsome, clean young men from Texas?" To the relief of these young men, the Louisiana girls did not see any more of Company F, and the unit remained at Spindletop for the next five months. Other than occasional special assignments for individuals or small groups, the majority of daily entries on the morning report recorded men going to and from home on leave.[14]

Several of those short-term assignments confirmed the confidence their superior officers had in the Hankamer brothers. Between April and October, those duties included swearing in and drilling recruits, leading details to look for deserters, and serving as couriers and provost guards. Both John W. Hankamer and Charles Hankamer were serving as sergeants; in October 1864, Charles Hankamer was acting 1st sergeant and signed the company morning report for at least sixteen days.[15]

Even with the absence of hostilities in Texas, these were worrisome times for family members back home. The lack of the quick and easy communication that we take for granted today could cause both confusion and stress, as illustrated by a situation in late June 1864. John Stengler had gone to the Spindletop camp to talk with Charles Hankamer, but six days later he had not returned home. His wife, Johanette, sent an anxious letter to her sons on June 30, 1864.

> Last Wednesday, June 25 your father left here to go to you to talk to Carl about the mill. He has not returned up to now, Monday, June 30 which worries us very much. He said he would return immediately. We are afraid something may have happened to him as he has no passport.
>
> Or maybe you are all sick or maybe he himself is sick. If he did not come to you at all, then you have to make inquiries and search for him right away, because I have no one to send. If he has not returned by morning, then I will send John [Henry Stengler] to the station house with the letter. Answer right away or come. I am afraid you may be sick.

We're left to guess about any more details, but life was back to normal by the time of the next letter a month later. These relatively tranquil months offered considerable free time for the men, and it was here the brothers spent many hours fabricating their hats, "sleighs," and other items handmade from strips of palmetto and cane that were described in an earlier chapter.

There was, of course, the inevitable routine of drill and inspections, and on October 16 it was Company F's turn to man the coastal lookout and defensive positions at Sabine Pass. They were still dismounted, so they packed up their gear at Spindletop and boarded the steamboat *Uncle Ben* in Beaumont for the trip south. This vessel was the same venerable workhorse that had been outfitted as a cottonclad gunboat in the January 1863 battle against two Union blockading ships off the coast of Sabine Pass. The trip was a reunion of sorts with the *Ben* for John W. and Fritz Hankamer since they had been among the sharpshooters assigned to the vessel during that naval engagement.

Within barely a month, the men in Company F would have yet another change of duty station, and once again they were able to ride instead of walk. On November 25, 1864, they boarded another CSA steamboat at Sabine Pass, and the *Florilda* took them north to Beaumont. They arrived a little after dark, and the next morning boarded the train for Houston and Camp Lubbock. With six weeks still left in the year, they must have wondered if this would be their final stop in 1864.[16]

30

FINALE

*I hope that the good Lord shall give his blessing
so that all of you soon can be home in peace.*
—JOHN STENGLER, May 15, 1865

Camp Lubbock was not Company F's first choice for a place to spend Christmas of 1864, but it was certainly preferable to their previous postings at Sabine Pass. "Lubbock" may now seem an unlikely name for a rudimentary army post on the outskirts of Houston, but it was named for a Texas governor of the period; the modern city of the same name in the Texas Panhandle was founded a decade later.

Company F spent the next several months near Houston, and the troops' assignment was the direct result of their determination the previous year to remain part of Spaight's command. In November 1864, Spaight's Battalion was expanded by the addition of four companies from Griffin's Battalion and redesignated as Spaight's Regiment. With this larger unit, Ashley Spaight was promoted to full colonel and assumed command of all CSA forces at Houston. His regiment, including Company F, was then assembled there.[1]

A key reason the CSA maintained this rather large force near Houston was the continuing concern about a Union attack somewhere along the Texas coast. Railroad access from Houston eastward to Beaumont and southward to Galveston offered the potential to move Spaight's Regiment fairly quickly to either of those potential trouble spots. Due to the uncertain military situation, few if any troops had leaves of absence approved for Christmas.[2]

When it became apparent her sons would not be home for the holiday for the third year in a row, Johanette Stengler expressed her disappointment in a letter written on Christmas Day to her son Charles Hankamer.

Dear beloved son Charles, . . . I am happy to hear that all of you are in good health which is very good because all of you had another poor Christmas. I am very sorry about that. We did not have so much either, but better than you. We have potatoes and could have potato bread, which I am sure you would have enjoyed too. It is now three Christmases that you could not be at home. The good Lord knows where you will be next Christmas, let us hope at home.

Johanette also wrote to Fritz Hankamer on December 25 with similar sentiments: "Oh, dear Son, Christmas is past and neither of you could be here. You can't imagine how I felt, because even if I had everything I wanted, but knowing how little all of you had, it made me hurt all over. . . . Oh, when will this unfortunate war end? I am afraid I will not live to see it. It looks bad, but maybe the end is nearer than we think."

As the end of the year approached, Johanette tried to console her boys about being away from home with the promise of a "care package" containing multiple items. "We are sending you for New Year potato bread, eggs, sausage, beef for hash, and a piece of pork," she wrote on December 30. "When you come, you may have more."

In retrospect, it was a good thing the young men didn't make it home during the holidays. On December 30, Mina Wilborn commented in a letter to Fritz that she "received your dear letter of the fifteenth and see that you are well, except for the itch. I see in your letter to mother that you, Karl, and George would get out of the itch house on the same day. I hope when this letter reaches you that all of you again are well."

The "army itch" was a very painful skin condition that was epidemic at times in both Union and Confederate military camps. Like most other infirmities of the time, there was considerable debate among the medical profession about the cause and proper treatment, with likely culprits variously listed as scabies, lice, or fleas. "Army itch" was more than a nuisance, and it caused tens of thousands of soldiers to be hospitalized during the war.

One highly trained Union Army physician, George Sternberg, was certain the culprit was scabies. Caused by microscopic mites that burrow into the skin, where they live and lay their eggs, scabies can spread rapidly in crowded conditions such as an army camp. Dr. Sternberg noted that a mite "squats upon a new recruit with every prospect of a long life and a large family, and burrows away, undisturbed by soap and sulphur, until every square barley-corn of the poor soldier's skin is like a New York tenement-house—full inside and out."[3]

Mina's reference to her brother's confinement in the "itch house" suggests that one approach to cases at Camp Lubbock was a wise one—quarantine the unfortunate victims to try to contain the outbreak. The difficulty in treating the malady is confirmed by a newspaper story that recounted the experience of one soldier who came home on leave and "brought the army itch."

The "whole family took it," so a doctor was called. The doctor left some medicine and asked for a report about the results. They were not promising, according to the father of the household, who said, "We have used the medicine internally and externally, the disease still rages infernally, and it looks to me as though it would last eternally." There were no further references to the problem in subsequent letters from the Hankamer and Stengler brothers, so they seemed to have made a better recovery than the family in the newspaper story.[4]

While no one knew what events would eventually unfold during the coming year, there was no shortage of speculation and hope as 1864 neared an end. Johanette Stengler mentioned some of the rumors that had reached rural Crackersneck when she wrote to her son Fritz on December 3, 1864.

> We are happy that you are yet in Houston. We had heard that you were to go to Arkansas. How shocked I was to hear that you had to leave again. I had hoped that you could stay at Sabine Pass this winter. . . . I have heard that five of our states want to go back into the Union and that France thought Texas belonged to Mexico. I do not know whether that is so, but that is what I heard.

Based on their earlier comments about Sabine Pass, it seems unlikely her sons shared Johanette's hope they would be based at the small coastal port, but she was comparing that location to faraway Arkansas. Houston was even closer to their homes than Sabine Pass, and it offered many more advantages as a duty station. Reliability of train service was always a question, but it was possible to take the Texas and New Orleans cars straight from Houston to Carter's Station, which was then only about a dozen miles from the brothers' homes.

Finale

FIGURE 19. Houston's Main Street in 1858. Courtesy of Houston History Research Center, Houston Public Library, image MSS0157-2535.

The growing town of Houston also offered some of the best access in the state to shopping for scarce items, and the soldiers took advantage of those opportunities. John Stengler wrote to his son Fritz on January 8, 1865, and asked him to look for a hard-to-find item in the city before his next visit home. "When you come, I wish you would bring me 2 ounces of Spirits of Hartshorn," John said. "I want to make a liniment for your mother, she uses it all the time and I can't get it here." Spirits of Hartshorn were traditionally manufactured from the hooves and horns of red deer, and along with oil of Hartshorn had various uses in nineteenth-century medicine.

On February 26, 1865, John Stengler wrote to Fritz again and asked him to do a little comparison shopping. The elder Stengler managed to squeeze a lot of information into a single sentence.

> I wish that you would inquire about the price of an ounce of quinine, and of the price of domestic, also price of a coping glass, and write me by the end of this week, for I want to go to Baxters and see if he wants to take my hogs I have in the pen, to Galveston, like he said two weeks ago he would on his next trip, but have not heard from

him, and so I would like to hear from you regarding prices of those items in the event they are cheaper in Houston than in Galveston.

On April 25, 1865, Johanette confirmed that Fritz had been able to take advantage of "city" shopping opportunities.

> I thank you very much for the pretty coffee pot you sent me. I am happy to have it because the old one is not very useful anymore. You should not spend your money for me because I know you get very little. Thank you also for the sugar but you should have kept it for yourself because I think you have not enough for yourself. . . . Oh, I almost forgot. Thank you very much for the newspaper you sent. I had not read any in a long time.

Even though 1865 got off to a quiet start for military hostilities in Texas, the potential for conflict was still there, and CSA officers were concerned about sabotage by Union sympathizers. We've already read that young John Henry Stengler and other soldiers in a local militia outfit were charged with guarding the telegraph line between Liberty and Beaumont, and similar worries led to a cold and wet special assignment for Sgt. John W. Hankamer.

He was put in charge of nine other men from Company F, including John W.'s brother, Pvt. George Stengler. On January 20, 1865, the morning report noted they were "detached to Liberty Bridge," and for the next twenty-four days, their task was to guard the major bridge on the Texas and New Orleans Railroad across the Trinity River. Their biggest enemy would turn out to be not Union saboteurs, but the Texas weather.

Things went smoothly for two days, but on Sunday, January 22, one of the infamous Texas "northers" brought high winds and much colder temperatures. The next morning, John W. Hankamer's diary recorded "plenty of ice" on the river. The ice and cold continued for a week, and although the very cold temperatures relented, they were replaced by rain, and plenty of it.

On February 1, the "river commenced rising," and by the next day, Sergeant Hankamer reported his concerns to Colonel Spaight about both the high water and a large "drift" of logs in the river. These large tangles of dead trees posed a serious threat when they jammed up against the bridge pilings, creating a natural dam and exerting great pressure on any object in their path. These drifts were also a danger to a group of flatboats used for a ferry crossing in the area.

During the next nine days, the men managed to clear away a heavy drift that had pinned the flatboats against the banks, and they then sent the boats downstream to safety. By the eleventh day another drift had filled up the river, but the crisis passed without serious incident, and Hankamer and his men returned to Camp Lubbock on February 15, 1865.[5]

The remainder of the spring was a period of uneasy inactivity for the troops in Spaight's Battalion, and news from the East was not encouraging for the CSA. Other than the usual drill and inspections, there were few demands on their time, and as had been the case in the latter half of 1864, many of the men were able to make at least one visit home.

John W. Hankamer was able to obtain a fourteen-day leave beginning on March 1, 1865, and his diary indicates he made the most of this opportunity to catch up on chores at home. He spent at least parts of nine days working on fences, and on one day that was rainy and very cold, he "hooped some tubs." He did take the opportunity to visit with nearby relatives, spending the morning of Sunday, March 12, with his mother and the afternoon with the family of his sister, Mina. He was back to work on the last full day of his leave, when he "cleaned out my chimney in the morning, made a rope, ploughed my garden."

On the same day as John W.'s visit, Johanette Stengler wrote to her son Fritz, and her letter revealed that three years of uncertainty and worry were beginning to take a serious toll on the family matriarch. She was approaching her sixtieth birthday, and the resilience she had demonstrated for most of her life was wearing thin.

"Soon it is time for George and Wilhelm to leave again," she wrote. "How time moves on so fast when you are at home. If only all of you could be home again once more and that we would have peace. I doubt that I will see that time, it looks bad and also my health is bad. As the Lord will have it. He knows what is best and I bow to His will."

Johanette then reverted to her longtime role of looking after her family and farm, and her letter continued in a more familiar tone.

> You wrote that I should send you two shirts. I will send them with George and 6 candles. . . . [I] am afraid if it should turn cold again you will have no warm clothing. We had ice last week. I am afraid

we will not get any fruit because the trees were in bloom already. We have not done anything in our field yet. If the weather permits John shall put manure in the field tomorrow. We have planted our garden. George made a support for the grapevines. I think that is better. There were no more vines on the pickets."[6]

The following week, on April 18, 1865, Charles Hankamer was home on leave and wrote to his brother Fritz. After noting that their younger brother John H. Stengler was in the Reserve Corps and had to report for duty the following week, he offered a report on the situation at home. His letter is another reminder of how closely the family's lives were tied to the land. "Everybody is mighty behind with their work, there is but little corn planted yet around here, Daddy has some planted but has got to plant it over," he wrote.

Charles then included a little humor for his single brother. "News I have but little worth writing. I believe that the Girls are all as healthy as ever & I know that one, if not more, would like very well to see you, I recken you know who she is, maybe better than I can tell you. You better try to get off the first of next month, as I think there will be a big wedding here."

He then reverted to a lengthy and largely optimistic update on the family livestock, assuring Fritz that his "little white sow has got pigs; four very nice ones," and his cows "Star and little Browny are alive yet and all the yearlings, cattle are picking up very fast, we have get up [corralled] two cows [and] get pretty plenty of milk."

Charles's letter concluded with a reminder that even though the railroad passed only a few miles north of home, there was no guarantee that a trip back and forth to Camp Lubbock was an easy one. "I had a terrible trip when I come," he wrote. "We had to walk all the way from West Liberty and [wade] Belly deep."

Shortly after Charles Hankamer returned to duty, he was given what sounds like a very unusual assignment for a soldier in the CSA. According to the Company F morning report for April 6, 1865, Sgt. Charles Hankamer and Pvt. Lafayette Maxwell were "detailed to collect tithes for 30 days." As a result, their arrival at households throughout their assigned area was not a welcome sight.

The term "tithes" is often associated with religious contributions, but in this case, it had a strictly secular function. In 1863 the Confederacy began collecting a "tax-in-kind" by requiring farmers to turn over 10 percent of everything they raised to the government. Edible items, such as potatoes, beans, grain, and bacon, were collected in regional depots for distribution to the troops. Other products, such as cotton and wool, were sold to raise revenue. It was, understandably, an unpopular system throughout the countryside.[7]

Charles wasn't the only Hankamer performing unusual duties during April 1865, and these details are shown on the morning report for Company F. Beginning on April 6 and continuing every day through May 10, the space on the report for the required "signature of the First Sergeant" reads "J. W. Hankamer, A.O.S." John W. Hankamer was filling this role in an "acting" capacity since the regular first sergeant had been granted an extended leave of absence in early April.

The first sergeant was the senior noncommissioned officer in an army company, so the selection of John W. Hankamer to fill this key role was one more indication of the trust placed in him by his superiors and peers. The accuracy of the morning report was taken very seriously since the information recorded included special assignments, disciplinary actions, and changes in rank that could affect a soldier's pay.

The confidence shown in John W. Hankamer by his fellow soldiers was also shared by another of the Hankamer brothers. Charles Hankamer returned from his tithe-collecting detail on May 10, and the following day he assumed the job of signing those morning reports as the acting first sergeant for Company F's remaining time in the Confederate Army. That date, it turned out, wasn't too far in the future, and it would be influenced by events across both the Confederacy and the Union.[8]

April 21, 1865, marked the third anniversary of the original mustering into CSA service for Company F, so it was ironic that a momentous message reached Houston from the East on that particular day. John W. Hankamer noted in his diary that news "came in late in evening that Gen. Lee had surrendered himself and army."

Although Lee's surrender of his Army of Northern Virginia is often viewed today as the end of the Civil War, his decision had no authority over other commands in the Confederacy. On April 21, the same day that news of Lee's surrender reached Galveston, Gen. E. Kirby Smith issued an appeal from his headquarters in Shreveport, Louisiana. Smith, who commanded CSA troops in the Trans-Mississippi Department, held out hope for help from other nations sympathetic to their cause, and he called upon his troops to "stand by your colors—maintain your discipline."[9]

Amid these conflicting developments elsewhere, activities by CSA commanders in Texas continued as planned. One of those involved a change in duty station for Spaight's Regiment, and those troops were notified on April 26 to prepare to move to Galveston, where they would relieve the Twentieth Texas Infantry. Company F joined other men from Spaight's Regiment in Houston on May 2, and after marching through town, spent the night camped near the train depot. By nine o'clock the next morning, they were headed for Galveston, and the six-hour trip by train was surprisingly uneventful. By nightfall, they had arrived at their new quarters and were getting settled in.[10]

Despite the news from other parts of the Confederacy, John W. Hankamer's diary indicates their daily routine continued as it had for months. On May 4 he noted, "cleaned up our quarters . . . [and] had dress parade in evening." Since the weather was "fair but warm," he packed up his blankets and a pair of pants to send home the next morning. The Union Navy had certainly not abandoned its post just offshore, and John W. "counted 11 Blockading vessels."

Concerns about the Union Navy weren't the only worries for CSA officers in Galveston. The economy of Texas was in dire straits, troops were poorly fed and equipped, and payment for some of them was long overdue. As a result, there was growing unrest in the town, desertions were increasing, and groups of soldiers even attempted to take over and loot military supply depots. Some of the troops that remained on duty were assigned to guard key points in town, with the difficult task of protecting them against both disgruntled fellow soldiers and Union troops from the blockading vessels visible just offshore.

John W. Hankamer referred to these events in his May 5 diary entry, writing, "Had to post guard in town, one at Q.M. [Quartermaster Office], one at wagon yard; . . . put guard on beach for Pickett duty for the night." On the following day, he noted, "detailed a guard for Galveston and Houston R.R. bridges on Clear Creek & at Dickerson [Dickinson] Bayou."[11]

In his role as acting 1st sergeant, John W. worked on muster rolls and attended drills, dress parades, and inspections. Not everyone was convinced the cause was lost, and on May 10, the company received word that General Magruder was coming to Galveston from Houston the next day to review the troops. The general followed the review with a speech, which Capt. William Duncan described in a letter to his wife. "[General Magruder] said that he and General Smith had been called on by the yankees to surrender Texas, or they would invade the state," Duncan reported. "He said he never would surrender but would fight them and begged the men to be true to themselves and their country, and act like men and fight to the last, and he believed we would succeed." Captain Duncan later noted in his diary that the speech "revived my drooping spirits but seemed to have no effect upon the men."[12]

Company F's commanding officer may have been pleased with General Magruder's determination to fight on, but John Stengler left no doubt about his reaction when news of the speech reached rural Liberty County. On May 15, John wrote to Fritz Hankamer:

Dear son Fritz: . . . This is my prayer to the Lord, I hope that the Lord soon will make an end of the war. I was in Liberty last week just at the time as a man by the name of Adams was there on Wednesday, who arrived from the other side of the Mississippi. He is the man who now carries all letters to and from all the men from Texas who are on the other side of the Mississippi. He said that Lee and Johnson had surrendered and all our soldiers had laid down their arms and the war had ended. He also said that 4 commissioners from our side had gone to Washington and had returned before he (Adams) left, and reported that the North was giving us all our constitutional rights, except that the Negroes shall be free.

Oh, Dear Son, I saw in Carl's [Charles's] letter which he wrote to Johanne [Charles Hankamer's wife] that all of you soon would have to fight Northern soldiers. I can't see why old Gen. Magruder wants to fight. Looks to me like he would love to see many of our boys yet killed. I hope though that when he wants to fight that the soldiers will let him do it alone. It looks to me as if your officers will not be satisfied until everything yet in Texas has been destroyed. I think that it is so according to what Adams said. I hope that the soldiers in Galveston will have sense enough. I hope that the Dear Lord will postpone old Magruder's plan. . . .

I wish that all of you could have been home yesterday and last Saturday. We had two days of prayer here. Mr. MacDonald preached two times last Saturday. The school was packed like I never saw before. Yesterday he preached at B. Abshire's. The crowd could not all go into the house, many had to stand outside. They had singing from 9 to 11 and preaching from 11 to 1 o'clock. I hope that the good Lord shall give his blessings so that all of you soon can be home in peace.

A week later, on May 16, it appeared John Stengler's hopes would be realized. A report began to circulate around Galveston that Gen. Kirby Smith, who commanded all CSA troops west of the Mississippi River, had surrendered. That rumor soon proved to be untrue, but it caused William Duncan to accept the inevitable. "If that is not the case," he wrote to his wife on May 17, "no doubt it will be before long. I am satisfied now that the Southern Confederacy has played out for the present."[13]

Gen. Kirby Smith had, in fact, not yet surrendered. On May 13 he decided to relocate his headquarters from Shreveport to Houston and confirmed that decision in a general order issued on May 18. He headed to Texas, in hopes of rallying the remnants of his army, and left Gen. Simon B. Buckner in charge in Shreveport. Smith arrived in Houston in late May only to learn, "The army in Texas disbanded before my arrival here."

Faced with mass desertions of his troops, General Buckner had traveled from Shreveport to New Orleans. On May 26, acting under his authority as Smith's second-in-command, Buckner surrendered the CSA's Trans-Mississippi Department. It was a moot point, for by then most of Smith's army had evaporated. On June 2, 1865, Gen. Kirby Smith reluctantly bowed to the inevitable and added his signature to the surrender documents.[14]

For the men of Spaight's Battalion, their orders to disband were actually received before Smith's formal surrender. On May 22, 1865, Capt. William Duncan addressed a letter to his wife with the news that John Stengler and so many others had been waiting for. "The order this morning is to evacuate this island and the troops [are] to go home," Duncan wrote. "The work of getting everything off of the island is going on."

The final entry in the morning report for Company F was made on May 22, 1865, and included the notation, "orders to evacuate Galveston Island." It was signed by Charles Hankamer as acting 1st sergeant and Capt. William Duncan as commanding officer. Duncan noted in his diary that four companies of Spaight's Regiment left the island by train, with the remainder traveling by boat.

John W. Hankamer's diary entry for Monday, May 22, 1865, was made in his usual low-key fashion. He wrote, "Packed up all our things, cooked . . . received orders to be aboard the steamer *Orizaba* by 12 ½ o'clock . . . started on the steamer by 2 o'clock, arrived at Anahuac by a little before sundown, walked home, was disbanded."

It would be more than a year before the official end to this difficult chapter in the story of the United States was finalized. On August 20, 1866, President Andrew Johnson issued a proclamation announcing the end of the Civil War, stating that he did "hereby proclaim and declare that the insurrection which heretofore existed in the State of Texas is at an end . . . and that peace, order, tranquility, and civil authority now exist in and throughout the whole of the United States of America."[15]

Long before that document was finalized, the only actions that really mattered to the families in this story had already been completed.

A father, five sons, and a son by marriage all returned safely from the war to Liberty and Chambers counties by the end of May 1865. Five of the seven men were German-born, but all were now Texans—and would soon be Americans once again. Three Hankamers—Charles, John W., and Fritz; three Stenglers—John, George, and John Henry; and Charles Wilborn all counted themselves blessed. They were among those fortunate to return to being farmers and ranchers, fathers, husbands, and sons—back home again on the Saltgrass Prairie.

31

HOME AGAIN

*Got up my oxen in the morning, . . . made a hoe
handle & ploughed up some potato rows.*

—JOHN W. HANKAMER, May 23, 1865

The return to civilian life was certainly faster for these men than for many of their fellow soldiers when the war ended for their respective units. Less than twenty-four hours after his commanding officer received the order "to evacuate this island and the troops [are] to go home," John W. Hankamer was back at home, already at work.

"Got up my oxen in the morning," he noted in his diary on May 23, 1865. "Charlie went down after our things with them." When John W. Hankamer and his brothers departed Galveston the previous day on the steamer *Orizaba*, they were leaving the army for good and brought all of their personal belongings from their final duty station. When they disembarked from the boat at Anahuac just before sundown, they had no means of carrying all those items home—and they were in a hurry to get there.[1]

The overland trip from Anahuac to the Crackersneck area in those days covered about twelve miles, and the walk in the dark wasn't an easy one, so they probably left most of their belongings near the boat landing and headed inland. The use of John W. Hankamer's oxen to retrieve their "things" the next morning is an example of the common use of those animals in nineteenth-century Texas.[2]

By late May the farming season was already far advanced along the Texas coast, and returning soldiers had much catching up to do. Once the baggage run was underway, John W. Hankamer's diary noted a return to familiar tasks; he "made a hoe handle & ploughed up some potato rows."

FIGURE 20. John William Hankamer. Courtesy of Chambers County Museum at Wallisville, Wallisville, Texas.

The following day was Wednesday, May 24, 1865, and it included the final entry in his journal. The weather was "pleasant," the wind "high," and he "ploughed corn all day."

John W. Hankamer returned home at the age of twenty-nine to plenty of family responsibilities, and he would soon add more. He and his wife, Lurenda, owned 321 acres in the far northern edge of Chambers County, northwest of the little community of Crackersneck. The couple had one son, who had just turned three, and during the next seven years, they would add five sons and two daughters to their household.

By 1876, John W. was also serving as a justice of the peace for Precinct Two in Chambers County, and his position occasionally came in handy for both family and neighbors. On September 14, 1876, serving in his role as "Justice Peace and Ex Officio Notary Public," he verified a deed recording the sale of land by his stepfather and mother, John and Johanette Stengler, to the couple's youngest son, John H. Stengler. The parties to that transaction lived within two or three miles of John W.'s farm, which made his "notary service" much more convenient than a lengthy round trip ride to the courthouse.[3]

Before the war interrupted their lives, a second Hankamer son, Charles, had also moved a short distance to the south of his parents' place. He married Joanah Higginbotham in 1859, and the following year they purchased fifty-two acres "with improvements" on the east side of Turtle Bayou. Their property, about two miles northwest of Crackersneck, was just inside the northern boundary of Chambers County, so Charles and his brother John W. were neighbors, at least in rural Texas terms.

Charles lived just far enough from his younger (and single) brothers Fritz Hankamer and George Stengler that it was easier to write them a letter than take time away from the pressing demands at his farm to go talk to them in person. Charles and Joanah were either adding onto or building new "improvements," and they were looking for some strong backs and willing hands from his siblings. On September 27, 1865, Charles addressed the same letter to both Fritz and George.

> Dear Brothers, you requested me to let you know as soon as I got my timber out so that we could go to work; well, I have not got it all quite yet, but expect to get done by next Monday; that is all but the joists and gallery dies. I wish one of you to help me get them. So, I intend to go to hauling at Monday, if one of you, or both can get off now to help me; from now on, I would be very glad, as I will have no help till one or both of you comes. For William [John W. Hankamer] is behind with his work; a sore hand and bad weather has set him back; and it is getting late in the season. So, I will look for one of you next week.

Charles's letter also illustrates one of the reasons that land near Turtle Bayou or similar waterways was a popular choice for settlers. The Saltgrass Prairie was a fine place to raise livestock, but houses and barns required trees large enough for building purposes. Timber from cypress, oak, and even pine was a prized commodity, and it was found primarily along the area's bayous and rivers. The oxen like those used to fetch the returning soldiers' baggage back home in May were even more valuable when it was time for Charles Hankamer to "go to hauling" his logs.[4]

John W. and Charles Hankamer returned from the war to their wives and children, but despite the best matchmaking efforts of their sister, Mina, the youngest Hankamer brother, Fritz, came back home a bachelor at age twenty-seven. He rejoined his parents' household in southern Liberty County, and references in family letters confirm that John and Johanette Stengler had for many years encouraged both Fritz and George Stengler to raise their own crops and livestock on the family farm.

That was a good situation for a young single man, but Fritz wanted to try his hand at something new after his army years. Perhaps his brief stint on the cottonclad gunboat *Uncle Ben* in January 1864 stirred some interest in working on the water, but whatever his motivation, the 1870 US Census listed Fritz's occupation as "sailor."

We don't know if his new job involved time on a riverboat, on vessels on Trinity or Galveston Bay, or aboard larger ships farther afield. By 1871 Fritz had satisfied his wanderlust, and he returned home and married a local girl named Annie Chism. Before their marriage, Annie had taught in a school for girls in the Crackersneck area. Fritz was thirty-three and she was twenty-nine when they were wed. The couple had one child, a daughter, who lived to adulthood, and probably two sons, both of whom died at a very young age.[5]

The year after their marriage, Fritz and Annie Hankamer settled down near the northern edge of Chambers County, and he spent the rest of his life there. His parcel of 253 acres, just south of the boundary with Liberty County, might seem large enough to keep many men busy, but Fritz ended up with the use of and responsibility for a much larger piece of property.

When Fritz and Annie acquired their land in 1872, one side of their property shared a common boundary with a larger piece belonging to other family members. Four years earlier, Charles Wilborn purchased an 1,122-acre parcel but never lived on it, and in 1874 the Wilborns entered into a mutually beneficial arrangement with Fritz. In March 1916, Fritz Hankamer filed an affidavit that included a good summary of his long-term connection with this sizeable piece of property.

In the year 1874, [Charles Wilborn] made a verbal lease with me for all of his 1122-acre tract. Under [this] lease I was to look after this tract, protect it from trespassers, and was to pay one dollar per year for the use of the land, and was to have the . . . right to take off timber and wood therefrom, and to cultivate as much of the land as I could use.

Cattle rustlers, timber poachers, squatters, and other unwelcome sorts were a potential problem in those years, especially for absentee landlords. Having someone you trusted to keep an eye on a large piece of rural real estate was a wise idea, so the terms of that lease were a good bargain for both men. This verbal arrangement continued for Charles Wilborn's lifetime and was then formalized in a written agreement with other family members. This large tract "adjoins the place on which I live and have lived since the year 1872," Fritz wrote in 1916, so he was able to make practical use of the property.

"Beginning with the year 1874," Fritz continued, "I have had the possession of this 1122-acre tract, selling wood or timber off same to charcoal burners, and cutting and selling timber therefrom." Around 1875, he fenced about eight acres out of this tract and put it into cultivation, and he later fenced an additional fifteen acres to use as a pasture. The location and the arrangements must have satisfied Fritz Hankamer because he continued to live there for forty-four years.[6]

Like his older brother Fritz Hankamer, George Stengler was a bachelor when he returned home from the war in May 1865, but family letters indicate he already had his mind and heart firmly set on a future with Caroline Higginbotham. They were married within a year; he was twenty-four, and she was a year younger. He must have liked his brothers' location, because George was soon eyeing some property of his own along Turtle Bayou.

Whatever holiday celebrations were being held on July 4, 1870, they didn't interfere with real estate transactions, and George and Caroline Stengler completed a purchase of 319¼ acres along the east side of Turtle Bayou on that date. They paid $300 for the property, and the deed describes a tract that included both prairie and timber plus stream frontage, so at a little under a dollar an acre, it was a good investment.[7]

During the next fifteen years, George and Caroline added five daughters

FIGURE 21. Frederick "Fritz" Hankamer. Courtesy of Chambers County Museum at Wallisville, Wallisville, Texas.

and one son to their family, and the couple would spend all their married lives in this same area. Like their siblings, they were involved in both farming and the cattle business, and some aspects of that life didn't change much during the decades before and after the Civil War.

The legal description for a piece of property purchased by John H. Stengler in 1876 notes it was bounded "on the east by public land." A decade after the end of the war, the era of the open range in Liberty and Chambers counties was not yet over, and livestock continued to wander and graze across wide areas. From a practical standpoint, this meant ranchers had only a general idea about both the number and location of their stock until it was time for one of the periodic roundups.[8]

FIGURE 22. George and Caroline Stengler. Courtesy of Chambers County Museum at Wallisville, Wallisville, Texas.

A good example of that informal system of ranching is seen in a transaction between George and Caroline Stengler and their nephew James P. Wilborn. In a document recorded in May 1875 in the Chambers County Clerk's Office, the Stenglers sold to James for $110 the rights "to all our wild cattle (gentle being retained) now running in Chambers County and adjoining counties and branded thus [sketch included] and earmarked such [described.]" The four-county area where those wild cattle were potentially "running" was larger than the entire state of Delaware, so this portion of Southeast Texas was still far from tamed in 1875.[9]

The youngest member of the Stengler family was, not surprisingly, the last to marry. John Henry Stengler served in a local militia unit, otherwise known as Texas State Troops, so he did not spend the last month of the war alongside his brothers in Galveston. A standard military discharge and "Parole of Honor" form dated June 30, 1865, was signed by John Stengler, noting he served in Company B, Texas State Troops. Because of the similarity of their names, it's not possible to determine if that record referred to the younger John Henry Stengler or his father, John Stengler.

When his relatives came home from the war in May 1865, John Henry was about to celebrate his eighteenth birthday. Seven years later, in 1872, he married Lurenda Smith, a granddaughter of Silas Smith Sr., thus reinforcing the ties between two families that dated back to the Stenglers' earliest days in Texas. John Henry and Lurenda Stengler soon gave their parents additional grandchildren; a son and three daughters were born in the first four years of their marriage. In August 1876, the young couple bought from his parents 470 acres along Turtle Bayou. This transaction also revealed close family ties, even in the world of real estate.

The elder Stenglers had purchased this property in 1873 from their son-in-law and daughter, Charles and Mina Wilborn. The large parcel included "the homestead known as the Charles Wilborn place," and came with "all the houses and improvements thereon." The Wilborns were relocating, but they kept their first home in the family by selling it to her parents. This 470-acre tract adjoined land John and Johanette Stengler had lived on since 1855, and that established farm would continue to be the Stenglers' home for many years. With the benefit of hindsight, we know the parents weren't interested in expanding their personal holdings—they were simply holding onto this piece of property until their youngest son was ready to buy it.

That opportunity arrived three years later in 1876, and the delay may have been necessary to allow the young married couple time to save their money. John and Johanette sold this land for the same price they had paid for it, but it was not a giveaway to their son. The purchase price was $1,000, although it must be remembered it had been in use by the Wilborns for perhaps twenty-five years and thus included a house and other improvements. Acquiring a functioning farm versus raw real estate gave the young Stenglers a big head start for their entry into farming and ranching.[10]

This purchase of adjoining parcels also made the two generations of Stenglers close neighbors. John Henry and Lurenda Stengler would spend fifty years of marriage in this area and have a total of seven daughters

FIGURE 23. John Henry and Lurenda Stengler. Courtesy of Chambers County Museum at Wallisville, Wallisville, Texas.

and four sons. Sadly, as was not uncommon in those years, only six of their eleven children lived to adulthood.

It must have been satisfying for John and Johanette Stengler to see all their children settle in the local area. Perhaps because they were older, the elder Stenglers did not acquire as much real estate and livestock as their offspring. Letters cited in earlier chapters confirm that John Stengler did get into the farming and livestock business as a matter of economic necessity, but that would not be his only occupation.

His role in helping his neighbors as "Doctor Stengler" during the 1860s may have helped establish German-born John Stengler as a trusted citizen of the area, and he became active in county government. In a July 29,

FIGURE 24. John and Johanette Stengler. Courtesy of Chambers County Museum at Wallisville, Wallisville, Texas.

1864, letter to his son Fritz, John mentioned he was running for justice of the peace, but we aren't sure if he won that election. In August 1867, he signed a certificate as the "Register of Names and Residence of qualified electors of Liberty County," and he served as a justice of the peace in 1868. In his most visible role, he signed the Liberty County tax rolls as the tax assessor and collector between 1865 and 1870. John Stengler's neat script rivaled the work of professional calligraphers, making his tax records a bonus for later generations of historians.[11]

The final member of the family to return home from the war was Charles Wilborn, and at age forty-two, he and his wife, Mina, were already well-established on their farm. That was a good thing, since they had plenty of mouths to feed with four sons (ages twelve, seven, four, and nearly two) and a ten-year-old daughter. Another son was born in 1865, two months after the army disbanded, and one more daughter arrived in 1869.

We've already learned that Charles and Mina accumulated well over one thousand additional acres in the early 1870s, and they later sold some of their property to various family members. We may wonder how the couple managed to acquire so much land within three years of his return from the war, and the answer is likely found in the financial situation in Texas at the time. While Texas largely escaped the physical devastation resulting from the war in other parts of the South, the state's economy was still in poor shape. Confederate currency, which had been in use during the CSA years, was now worthless, but Texans who had been able to obtain even relatively small amounts of cash in other forms had some excellent opportunities.[12]

Deed records show the Wilborns purchased their 1,122-acre tract in 1868 via a tax sale for only $9.88. The Wilborns could hardly be considered wealthy in the post-war years, but the purchase showed they were prudent in setting aside what money they could during difficult times. Despite her ongoing health problems, letters confirm that Mina Wilborn took advantage of opportunities during the war to raise and ship farm goods such as chickens and eggs to eager buyers in Galveston. During a period when "no sort of chick could be had for less than a dollar," and eggs sold for four dollars a dozen, perhaps Mina's large flock of hens helped ensure the family's financial future.[13]

The family's decision in 1846 to settle in the southeastern part of the state also worked to their advantage, especially when times were hard. Although the weather in Liberty County was sultry in the summer, the coastal climate provided a longer growing season and more reliable rainfall than inland regions of the state. The Saltgrass Prairie was suitable for growing both livestock and a variety of crops, and there was sufficient timber along rivers and bayous to provide wood for building and fuel for cooking and heating. There were potential buyers for animals and crops in nearby Galveston and Houston, and transportation was available via both water and the railroad.

By contrast, many other parts of the state were primarily prairie or brush country, and the lack of dependable water sources made some of those regions more suitable for livestock than other types of agriculture. Potential markets for animals and crops were also farther away, and transportation options were limited. As a result, rural families in such locations were less likely to be self-sufficient even if they were landowners.[14]

By the mid-1870s, the entire extended family seemed to be well settled along or near Turtle Bayou and on both sides of the line dividing Liberty and Chambers counties. We don't know what prompted the move, but in 1873 the Wilborns sold their homestead along Turtle Bayou to Mina's parents. As discussed above, the elder Stenglers then sold this same 470-acre parcel to their son John Henry Stengler in 1876, so perhaps a proviso in the deal was the Wilborns' continued use of the land until they had located a new place of their own.

That second sale occurred in early 1876, and the Wilborns pulled up stakes and moved about eighteen miles to the southern part of Chambers County. Their new property included 552 acres on the south fork of a major stream known as Double Bayou. A small community in the area, which included a post office, took its name from that waterway. The Wilborns' new ranch was about four miles southeast of that settlement, and they were off to a very promising start, with five hundred head of cattle listed on the tax rolls during their first year.[15]

Their new home offered several potential advantages over their previous location in the Turtle Bayou area. Double Bayou was usually navigable for several miles inland from Trinity Bay and thus provided direct access by boat to Galveston. That reduced the time and costs required for obtaining supplies and shipping their products to market.

The Wilborns may also have been looking for slightly drier footing. Several letters from the family's years along Turtle Bayou mentioned the difficulty in getting to both Liberty and Anahuac from their farms after heavy rains. Such travel woes were part of life in these coastal lowlands, but perhaps the Wilborns decided getting around the Double Bayou area would be a little easier. There isn't much variation in the terrain anywhere in Chambers County, but the spot the Wilborns selected for their new home has proven over ensuing years to be just high enough to offer some protection from the flooding that accompanies coastal storms.[16]

Barely a year into the Wilborns' move to the Double Bayou area, they found themselves in the midst of a much different kind of storm, one that would quickly become the biggest crisis the Stengler family had faced since its arrival in Texas over thirty years earlier. Ironically, this threat arrived via one of those boats that offered easier access to Galveston and the rest of the world. According to local sources, a "Captain Turner from New Orleans" arrived in the Double Bayou area in December 1876, probably unaware that he was harboring a deadly virus when he arrived in Chambers County.[17]

Fevers were common at that time and were associated with many maladies endemic along the Gulf Coast. As discussed in previous chapters, many individuals experienced recurring bouts of chills from malaria and other diseases, and thus a fever was not in itself undue cause for alarm. In this case, however, a fever signaled the point at which a person could actively transmit a stealthy but potentially fatal scourge—smallpox. This disease was especially insidious because, until the onset of a fever, the patient did not usually feel ill during the incubation period of seven to nineteen days. Even once the fever began, there could be a delay of several days before the telltale rash began, and that rash could be mistaken in its early stages for chicken pox, another common illness.

The result was a perfect scenario for calamity. Victims could unknowingly spread the disease before they realized they were infected with a contagious and deadly illness, and anyone in close contact with a carrier for as long as a month after the onset of the fever was at serious risk of infection. Although there was no shortage of folk remedies, there was no effective treatment for smallpox, and as many as a third of those who became ill died.[18]

One additional factor may have contributed to the seriousness of this outbreak. The first recorded death occurred on January 2, 1877, and the length of the incubation period means the virus had arrived in the area by Christmas. The traditional holiday visits with family and friends probably helped spread the still-undiscovered disease more rapidly and widely than usual.

According to several sources, a neighbor of the Wilborns named James Jackson sent to Galveston for vaccine once the nature of the crisis was known. He had his family and ranch workers inoculated, and then rode from home to home in the area, offering to administer the preventative measure to his neighbors. In some cases, the well-intentioned effort was too late, and in others, people who were suspicious of the vaccine declined his help.

Perhaps the inoculations given to some CSA soldiers and civilians during the war helped reduce the number of cases. Several of those men in the area contracted the illness but had relatively mild cases; others apparently escaped infection completely, even though members of their households died. Only one member of the Stengler family who had been in the army, Charles Wilborn, is known to have lost his life to the disease. The toll was especially heavy among that family's wives, perhaps because they assumed the brunt of nursing duties.

Before the epidemic had run its course in March 1877, the Wilborn and Hankamer families would be especially hard hit. The first recorded victim in Chambers County was Charles Wilborn, whose death on January 2 at the age of fifty-four was followed within a few days by the losses of his sons James P. (age twenty) and Andrew (eighteen).[19]

The Stengler family household with the largest toll was that of John W. Hankamer, who lost not only his wife, Lurenda, but also three sons. A fourth son died in April 1877, after the outbreak was believed to have ended, and his cause of death is not documented. The terrible strain on everyone during this epidemic—and the heroic measures attempted by some—are described in a letter from John W. Hankamer to his sister, Mina Wilborn, on January 26, 1877.

> Dear Sister: Grief has stricken us too. . . . I expect every day to see some of my children stricken down with that dreadful plague, and I am here alone with them, shunned by all persons, not one except John and Fritz [his brothers John Henry Stengler and Fritz Hankamer] have been about the place. Johan was the only woman with courage enough to venture into my house when death was in it, but dear Sister, I do not blame them, yet it looks so hard. I too have the complaint, but in such light form that I have not been confined to bed one hour with it, but have to keep indoors on account of pain I am subject to when I expose myself. I feel very well now, except worried and tired.

"Johan" probably referred either to his sister-in-law Joanah Hankamer, the wife of his brother Charles Hankamer, or to John W.'s mother,

Johanette Stengler. Joanah Hankamer died twelve days after this letter was written. The family's matriarch, Johanette Stengler, died of smallpox at the age of seventy-one on February 21, 1877. One other family household lost both a spouse and mother to smallpox—Fritz Hankamer's wife, Annie, died on February 11, 1877. Local records list at least sixteen families in Liberty and Chambers counties who lost members due to this outbreak.

Mina Wilborn, whose family had moved south to the Double Bayou area within the previous year, suddenly found herself widowed, but she was not left alone. Her daughters Martha and Johanette were twenty-one and seven, and her sons George F. and Charles J. were fifteen and thirteen. The close family ties remained intact, and her brother John W. Hankamer wrote to her on January 26. He offered some encouragement amid the loss of his own wife and three children, writing, "You and the children must keep your courage. . . . We have yet duties to perform on this earth, and with Christian resignation let us perform them." He assured Mina he would help settle her financial affairs, noting, "I think we can fix up everything so you will have no debts, get you a place, and save enough for your living."[20]

The following chapter, "Legacy," summarizes the family's final decades in the nineteenth century and into the twentieth century and highlights a few of the significant impacts made by their children and grandchildren on life in their county, state, and nation.

32

LEGACY

I am now ready to meet my God in peace.
—JOHN STENGLER, February 10, 1910

It is ironic that a family who came to Texas from Germany in 1845 and successfully overcame numerous obstacles during the next twenty-five years was suddenly at risk of being defeated by a smallpox pandemic that originated in Europe in 1870 and 1871 and spread to the United States over the next several years by the crews and passengers of ships. One of them may have been a ship's captain who traveled from New Orleans to Double Bayou in December 1877. Once again, the Stengler, Hankamer, and Wilborn families persevered in the face of adversity, and events in the years following this tragic episode confirmed that the values demonstrated by John and Johanette Stengler had been both learned and applied.[1]

Amid his own formidable set of challenges, John W. Hankamer kept his word to his sister, Mina Wilborn, and helped settle her husband's estate. She was able to remain on the ranch the Wilborns had purchased only the year before the epidemic, spending the remaining eleven years of her life there. Mina apparently took an active role in helping her sons George and Charles manage the family ranching enterprise, which she referred to in her will as, "My present Homestead on Double Bayou, Chambers County, Texas." The names of Mina and both of her sons are all shown individually on the official register of cattle brands in the county.[2]

Mina, the eldest of the seven children in the family who came to Texas from Germany in 1845, died in November 1888 at the age of fifty-seven. George Wilborn continued to operate and expand the ranch started by his parents for the remainder of his life, and his obituary in 1932 described a respected member of the area. "The community has lost a true and worthy citizen," it read. "He was a friend to all, always hearing the call of those in need, always ready to go when sickness called him. He stood high in his church and community, as a man of highest honor and integrity."[3]

George Wilborn's sons, Elwood and Carroll, continued the family tradition as successful and innovative ranchers in the Double Bayou area, and Elwood was also active in government and civic roles. His contributions included serving as justice of the peace, county commissioner, and a member of the Board of Directors of the Baptist Hospital in Beaumont, Texas.[4]

The "Double Bayou Homestead" that Charles and Mina Wilborn acquired in 1876 is still in the family, and the house where later generations of Wilborns raised their children remains in use. Carroll Wilborn Jr., the great-grandson of Charles and Mina Wilborn, devoted a forty-one-year career to public service in Chambers County, including nearly thirty years as a highly respected district judge.

The Hankamer branch of the family also weathered the difficult year of 1877 to leave its mark on Southeast Texas, and three of the brothers were elected to public office in Chambers County. John W. Hankamer served two terms as a county commissioner and two as a justice of the peace; Charles Hankamer served as a county commissioner; Frederick ("Fritz") Hankamer served a term as justice of the peace and two terms as constable.

Following the death of his wife Annie in 1877, Fritz Hankamer remarried, and he and his second wife, Minerva, continued to live on the same 253-acre farm near the Liberty-Chambers county line for nearly all of their lives. He lived to be seventy-nine, passing in the year 1917.

Charles Hankamer also lost his wife, Joanah, in the smallpox epidemic of 1877, leaving him with six children, ages sixteen down to only four months. Three of those children were under the age of six, so it's not surprising he remarried only seven months later. Charles outlived his second wife, Katherine Icet, by thirty-one years, and her death in 1895 once again left him as a single father.

One of Charles Hankamer's sons, Earl C. Hankamer, was three years old when his mother died in 1895. Later in life, Earl related the following account of his younger years in his father's household, which was published in the *Baylor Business Review*. It provides a glimpse of their daily life near the end of the nineteenth century.

> We typically got up about 5:00 in the morning. In those days, we parched and ground our own coffee, and when we were quite small, probably eight years old, we started drinking coffee. When we heard the coffee grinder, that was the alarm clock for all of us to get up, and by the time we were dressed and in the kitchen, Dad would have coffee ready for us. We had breakfast and by that time it was daylight, so we could go out and milk the cows and begin whatever farming needed to be done. Of course, that was in the summer. In the wintertime we went to school.

Earl Hankamer recalled his father raising his children "with kindness but firmness. Each one of us was provided with a horse," he said. "Dad gave me a horse when I was eight, and it was my responsibility to care for the horse." He left home at age thirteen to work in his married brother Roy's dry-goods store in Sour Lake, Texas, and lived with Roy and his wife, Rosa. As a youngster, he also sold and delivered newspapers morning and evening, eventually saving enough money to help pay his way to Baylor University.

The values instilled by John and Johanette Stengler in their children were certainly passed along to their grandson Earl Hankamer Sr. His reputation as an honest and astute businessman allowed him to gradually become successful in the growing Texas oil industry, and he created an outstanding legacy of philanthropy. He had an active role in the establishment of the Texas Medical Center in Houston, which has impacted the lives of countless thousands of people around the world. Earl Hankamer Sr. served as chairman of the board of the Baylor College of Medicine, and the Hankamer School of Business at Baylor University is named for him.[5]

Several of Charles Hankamer's other children and grandchildren were also successful in the business world and civic affairs, and their contributions reflected his character as well. An article in a local newspaper on Charles's ninetieth birthday in 1926 said he attributed his health to "a simple life and plenty of work with an optimism that overcomes all obstacles." That writer summed up his reputation in the community by noting "the love and esteem in which he is held by the many who know him."[6]

The final branch of this family, the Stenglers, had two of the three children born to John and Johanette Stengler live into the twentieth century.

FIGURE 25. Charles Hankamer on his ninetieth birthday in 1926. Courtesy of Ray Hankamer Jr.

Like their Hankamer and Wilborn relatives, members of the Stengler branch of the family made their own contributions to their communities.

John Henry Stengler was the youngest son and the only member of his generation in the family to be a native-born Texan. John Henry and Lurenda were married for fifty years and spent their entire lives within a few miles of their childhood homes. John Henry lived until 1923, to the age of seventy-three, and Lurenda until 1939, to the age of eighty-eight.

Like several other family members, George Stengler Sr. put down deep roots near Turtle Bayou. He served as a trustee on the school board in the Hankamer area, and the 1920 US Census showed George and his wife, Caroline, still living independently, with his occupation at the age of

FIGURE 26. The George Stengler family in front of the family home, 1899. Courtesy of Chambers County Museum at Wallisville, Wallisville, Texas.

seventy-eight listed as "Farmer." An article in an area newspaper recognized his eighty-fifth birthday in 1927 and noted his excellent reputation in the local area: "An outstanding attribute of his life, which might truly be classed great and it is so recorded in the hearts of many, is his wonderful, sympathetic nature, which has caused him for more than half a century to administer as counselor, doctor, and friend to the needs of those of the little town of Hankamer."[7]

George and Caroline Stengler celebrated fifty-six years of marriage together, with Caroline living to the age of seventy-nine and George to eighty-seven. His death on March 7, 1929, marked the passing of the last member of the Krantz-Hankamer-Stengler extended family that had come to Texas from Germany in 1845.

Two years after his wife Johanette died in 1877, the patriarch of this family, John Stengler, married a widow, Margaret Ness Sherman. They spent the remainder of their lives not far from Turtle Bayou. On February 10, 1910, at the age of ninety-one, John Stengler penned a brief autobiography that was published in a local newspaper, the *Anahuac Progress*. These words, written nine months before his passing, provided an excellent summary of the family's story and the values that shaped their lives.

> I was born in the city of Runkel, Nassau, Germany on January the 19th, 1819; married Mrs. Johanette Hankamer on the 12th day of September 1840, who was living in the City of Dietz, Germany, the mother of six children, one girl, four boys living, and one dead.
>
> In 1845 I immigrated to Texas for Fisher and Millers Colony, arrived in Galveston December 31, 1845. We heard of the suffering of the people who had gone to said colony and I stayed in Galveston till June 1846, when I moved to Anahuac. . . . Galveston, at that time was not as large as Anahuac is now, and this entire country was full of all manner of game, and wild beasts. People lived far apart in those days.
>
> There were so few settlers in the country and none of my family understanding English, we were rather in a bad condition to get information, as there were but few Germans in these parts at that time, but in the Autumn of 1846, I moved up to what is now Hankamer in the house formerly owned and occupied by Andrew Weaver. . . .
>
> While living at the Andrew Weaver place, one Dr. Whiteman, living at Goose Creek, came over to see if I would not move over to his place and cultivate his farm, but not knowing the man or place, I wouldn't go over on Goose Creek, but moved to Double Bayou in 1848, where I lived for about two years, when I moved up to what was then known as Cracker's Neck, near my daughter, and son-in-law Charles Wilborn, and lived there during the civil war, and until my wife died with the smallpox February 14, 1877, at the age of 71 years. . . . During the civil war I had three stepsons in the regular service, for more than three years, my youngest son and myself were in the service the later part of the war, yet for services rendered by myself or any of my children, there is not one drawing a pension, although I now need it.
>
> After the civil war I was assessor and collector during the sixties, for Liberty County, Texas, and was appointed U.S. Revenue assessor in which capacity I served for several years seizing distilleries in my district, which composed a large territory.

But now I am old, shut up and things of the past are by-gone, yet I cannot help but reflect on by-gone days, departed friends, newcomers moving in our neighborhood, improvements in so many ways, so many people living here where wild beasts roamed in my young days. Yet with all these changes, there is one unchangeable Being before whom we all have to appear at the day of judgment, and as I am now ready to meet my God in peace, oh, let me ask of you all who may read this as my last opportunity, to prepare yourselves to meet the Judge of the quick and the dead in peace, and clothed with his righteousness and not found wanting. John Stengler[8]

This story began with what may have seemed unlikely prospects for success on the Texas frontier in 1845—a couple and seven children from a small German village. Their circumstances in the Lahn River Valley in Europe offered only limited prospects, but the young inspector of chimneys and fireplaces and his determined bride shared big dreams, willing hands, and strong faith. Together they embraced opportunities, faced challenges, and overcame adversities in a strange and distant land called Texas to leave a legacy on the Saltgrass Prairie that, by any worthy measure, has not been found wanting.

LIST OF KEY CHARACTERS

Johanette (Schuster) **Stengler** (born 1805 in Germany)

- First marriage to Gottfried Krantz in 1828 in Germany; he died in 1831

    CHILDREN

    Unnamed son (1829–1831)

    Wilhelmina (Mina) Krantz (born 1831 in Germany); married **Charles Wilborn**

- Second marriage to Johannes Hankamer in 1833 in Germany; he died in 1839

    CHILDREN

    John William Hankamer (born 1834 in Germany); married Lurenda Smith (born 1835)

    Charles Hankamer (born 1836 in Germany); married Joanah Higginbotham

    Frederick ("Fritz") Hankamer (born 1837 in Germany); married Annie Chism

    Karl Hankamer (born 1839 in Germany; died in Texas in 1849)

- Third marriage to **John Stengler** in 1841 in Germany; they emigrated to Texas in 1845

    CHILDREN

    George Stengler (born 1842 in Germany); married Caroline Higginbotham

    Rudolph Stengler (born 1844 in Germany; died in Texas in 1846)

    John Henry Stengler (born 1847 in Texas); married Lurenda Smith (born 1851)

Related to Johanette Stengler by Marriage

　Charles Wilborn (born 1822), husband of Mina (Krantz) Wilborn

　Joanah (Higginbotham) **Hankamer**, (born 1841), wife of Charles Hankamer

　Lurenda (Smith) **Hankamer** (born 1835), wife of John William Hankamer

　Lurenda (Smith) **Stengler** (born 1851), wife of John Henry Stengler

　Silas Smith Sr. (born 1785), stepfather of Charles Wilborn

ABBREVIATIONS

The following abbreviations are used for sources cited
in the following Notes and Bibliography.

AUTH   Family documents in the author's personal collection.

BCAH   The Dolph Briscoe Center for American History, University of Texas at Austin.

CCCO   Chambers County Clerk's Office, Anahuac, Texas.

CCMW   Chambers County Museum at Wallisville, Wallisville, Texas.

CMLA   Cushing Memorial Library and Archives, Texas A&M University, College Station, Texas.

GTHC   Galveston and Texas History Center, Rosenberg Library, Galveston, Texas.

HAAS   Oscar and Clara Haas translations and transcriptions of Stengler-Hankamer-Wilborn family letters; copies at BCAH and CCMW.

HHRC   The Houston History Research Center, Houston Public Library, Houston, Texas.

JDWC   Julia Duncan Welder Collection, Sam Houston Regional Library and Research. Center, Texas State Library and Archives Commission, Liberty, Texas.

LCCO   Liberty County Clerk's Office, Liberty, Texas.

OR   United States War Department, *The War of the Rebellion: A Compilation of the Official Records of the Union and Confederate Armies*. All references from this source are from volumes in Series 1 unless otherwise noted.

ORN	United States Naval War Records Office, *Official Records of the Union and Confederate Navies in the War of the Rebellion.* All references from this source are from volumes in Series 1 unless otherwise noted.
SHRL	Sam Houston Regional Library and Research Center, Texas State Library and Archives Commission, Liberty, Texas.
SOPH	Sophienburg Museum and Archives, New Braunfels, Texas.
TPTH	University of North Texas Libraries, The Portal to Texas History.
TSLA	Texas State Library and Archives, Austin, Texas.
UNCL	University of North Carolina at Chapel Hill, Louis Round Wilson Special Collections Library.

NOTES

To avoid redundancy, citations are not provided in the notes for letters and diary entries when the author and full date of the items are clear in the text. This applies to sources from the Stengler-Hankamer-Wilborn family and from the William Duncan letters and diary.

CHAPTER 1

1. The current spelling of this town is usually "Diez," but "Dietz" was common in the nineteenth century and is used in historical documents directly related to this narrative. "Dietz" is also easier phonetically in the English language, so that version will be used in this book.

2. Murray, *Handbook for Travellers*, 507.

3. Dunt, *Journey to Texas*, 6–8; Biesele, *German Settlements*, 83–4.

4. Tiling, *History of the German Element*, 54; Benjamin, "Germans in Texas," 17–9.

5. The names "Johannes" and "Johann" are two common forms of the same name in German, and both appear in various documents for this individual. The "Johann" form will be used hereinafter unless it is a direct quote from a historical document. Shortly after reaching Texas, he anglicized his name to "John." Sources in note 7 for this chapter have more family details.

6. Translation of an "Extract of the Building-Tax Register of Diez for the Widow of Johannes Hankamer" includes information about the family's history and Johanette Hankamer's financial situation before her marriage to Johann Stengler. The family name was usually spelled "Kranz" in the original German, but it is often anglicized to "Krantz." Copy in author's files, hereinafter AUTH; Murray, *Handbook for Travelers*, 507.

7. Extract of the Building-Tax Register of Diez, Microfilm 1995480, record 4, pg. 94, Family History Library, Salt Lake City, Utah. Stengler, Wilborn, and Hankamer family files, Chambers County Museum, Wallisville, Texas, hereinafter shown as CCMW.

8. Struve, *Germans and Texas*, 46; Biesele, *German Settlements*, 66, 69.

9. Biggers, *German Pioneers*, 16; Geue, *A New Land*, 2; Struve, *Germans and Texans*, 45.

10. Benjamin, "Germans in Texas," 30.

11. Cook, "The Audacious Launch of the City of Houston," 139–41.

12. Benjamin, "Germans in Texas," 37–8; Biesele, *German Settlements*, 84-85; Jordan, *German Seed*, 43.

13. Benjamin, "Germans in Texas," 37-38; Jordan, *German Seed*, 43.

14. Johann Stengler, letter to the society, October 3, 1845, BCAH.

15. Johann Stengler, letter to the society, mid-October 1845, BCAH.
16. Johann Stengler, "Story of the Voyage from Dietz," CCMW.

CHAPTER 2

1. Stengler, "Story of the Voyage." His use of a local German dialect posed challenges for translation into English, resulting in slightly different versions of the translation found in several libraries. These quotations are from a translation by Mr. Gerhard Hankammer of Hamburg, Germany. CCMW.
2. The Bible is in the author's personal collection, hereinafter shown as AUTH.
3. Stengler, "Immigration Agreement," SOPH.
4. *The Civilian and Galveston (Tx) Gazette*, 8, ed.1, Saturday, February 21, 1846, 1, University of North Texas Libraries, The Portal to Texas History, crediting The Dolph Briscoe Center for American History, hereinafter TPTH, https://texashistory.unt.edu/ark:/67531/metapth80287/.
5. Qualls, "Passenger List for the Barque *Harriet*"; Geue, *New Land*, 145, 159.
6. Stengler, "Story of the Voyage."
7. Vogel letter to family members in Germany, SOPH.
8. Houstoun, *Texas and the Gulf of Mexico* 1: 188–90, 192, 149–150; Roemer, *Texas*, 44; Fiske, *Visit to Texas*, 112.
9. Vogel letter to family, SOPH.
10. Roemer, *Texas*, 48.
11. Friend, "Contemporary Newspaper Accounts," 267.

CHAPTER 3

1. Vogel to family, SOPH.
2. Roemer, *Texas*, 39–40; Houstoun, *Texas and the Gulf of Mexico* 1: 257–58
3. Roemer, *Texas*, 49.
4. *The Civilian and Galveston Gazette* (Galveston, Tex.), 7, ed. 1, December 17, 1845, TPTH.
5. Geue, *New Land*, 6.
6. Roemer, *Texas*, 46.
7. Tiling, *History of German Element*, 90; Vogel to family, SOPH.
8. Roemer, *Texas*, 149, 155, 158; Geue, *New Land*, 7, 12.
9. Biggers, *German Pioneers*, 31; Roemer, *Texas*, 71; Geue, *New Land*, 12.
10. Tiling, *History of German Element*, 86–7; Biggers, *German Pioneers*, 31–2.
11. Benjamin, *Germans in Texas*, 48–51; Biggers, *German Pioneers*, 32–6; Tiling, *History of German Element*, 80–7; Roemer, *Texas*, 21–3, 159; Nixon, *Medical Story*, 414-15.
12. Struve, *Germans and Texans*, 50; Jordan, *German Seed*, 53; Roemer, *Texas*, 46.
13. *The Civilian and Galveston Gazette*, December 17, 1845, 7, TPTH.
14. Fiske, *Visit to Texas*,180.
15. *The Civilian and Galveston Gazette* (Galveston), vol. 8, ed. 1, February 21, 1846; Smith, *The War with Mexico*, 149–50; "South Texas Loses Pioneer," June 1926, newspaper obituary, copy in Hankamer family file, CCMW.
16. John Stengler autobiography, CCMW.

CHAPTER 4

1. Fiske, *Visit to Texas*, 138; Roemer, *Texas*, 149.
2. Gallaway, "Past Human Role"; Winningham, *Traveling the Shore of the Spanish Sea*, 27; Olmsted, *Journey through Texas*, 364–65, 375.
3. Parker, *Trip to the West*, 175–76.
4. Fiske, *Visit to Texas*, 91–2.
5. David H. Burr, *New Map of the State of Texas 1845* (New York: R. S. Fisher, 1845), accessed September 18, 2024, https://exhibits.stanford.edu/ruderman/catalog/xk898dc4455; State of Delaware, "Delaware Facts and Symbols," accessed September 18, 2024, https://delaware.gov/guides/facts/. US Census, Liberty County, 1850; A common criterion for a "frontier" area is a population below two people per square mile. US Census Bureau, "Following the Frontier Line, 1790-1890," accessed September 19, 2024, https://www.census.gov/dataviz/visualizations/001/.
6. Sibley, *Travelers in Texas*, 24.
7. John Stengler autobiography, CCMW.
8. National Archives, *Seventh Census, 1850*, Liberty County, Texas.
9. "South Texas Loses Pioneer," *The Progress* (Anahuac, Texas), June 18, 1926, Hankamer Family files, CCMW; John Stengler autobiography.
10. Ladd, "The Andrew and Julia Weaver Family"; Frederick Hankamer Affidavit 6306, March 31, 1916, Deed Records 6: 404–05, CCCO.
11. "Births" page in Hankamer family Bible, CCMW.
12. "School Report" for Wilhelmina Krantz, signed April 8, 1845, Diez, AUTH; Unnamed newspaper clipping dated January 24, 1926, "Charles Hankamer, 90, of Sour Lake, Has Lived 84 years in South Texas," in Hankamer family files, CCMW.
13. John Stengler autobiography, CCMW.
14. National Archives, *Seventh Census, 1850*, Liberty County, Texas.
15. Parker, *Trip to the West*, 181.
16. Hankamer family Bible, Hankamer Family Files, CCMW.

CHAPTER 5

1. Texas General Land Office, *Map of Liberty County, Texas, 1879*. This map shows the Silas Smith tract and the Andrew Weaver tract adjoining each other near the southern county line; both families are shown on the 1850 US census for Liberty County; John Stengler autobiography.
2. Marriage record no. 31, Lafayette Parish, Louisiana, September 11, 1827, for Silas Smith and "Lurinda Willborn, widow of Elijah Willborn," Wilborn family files, CCMW. Texas General Land Office (GLO) records show Silas Smith immigrated to Liberty County in 1830. That information is on line 65 of a document showing land grants in Liberty County. It is available at https://cdn.glo.texas.gov/ncu/SCANDOCS/archives_webfiles/arcmaps/webfiles/landgrants/PDFs/1/0/6/1/1061908.pdf. There are additional details about his land in this GLO document: https://cdn.glo.texas.gov/ncu/SCANDOCS/archives_webfiles/arcmaps/webfiles/landgrants/PDFs/2/4/8/248978.pdf. His family is listed in an 1834 census of Southeast Texas in Jean Epperson, "1834 Census: Anahuac Precinct,

Atascosito District," *The Southwestern Historical Quarterly* 92, no. 3 (1989): 444, http://www.jstor.org/stable /30240096. An 1842 land grant is shown in Liberty County Deed Book 83, pages 138–40, LCCO; Frederick Hankamer Affidavit no. 6306, March 31, 1916, Deed Records 6: 404–05, CCCO.

3. National Archives and Records Service, "Non-Population Schedule (Agriculture) of The Seventh Census of The United States, 1850," Texas, Liberty County, Roll 2, pg. 523. "Texas, County Tax Rolls, 1837–1910, Liberty County, 1850," microfilm, reel 114601, image 12 of 21, Texas State Library and Archives Commission, SHRL.

4. Author's analysis of 1850 US census data for Liberty County, Texas.

5. Frederick Hankamer Affidavit no. 6306, March 31, 1916, Deed Records 6: 404–05, CCCO; Maria F. Wilborn, affidavit, Chambers County, Texas, March 5, 1936, CCCO; Charles Wilborn and his wife Mina are shown in the 1850 US census for Liberty County, sheet 352A, as part of the household of his stepfather, Silas Smith, on September 20, 1850.

6. Liberty County, Texas, tax records for 1851 are found on tax rolls from the office of the Liberty County tax assessor-collector, microfilm reel 114601, SHRL, https://www.tsl.texas.gov/arc/local/liberty.html; Liberty County Deed Book D, page 445–46, includes the "homestead" reference and describes a combination of wooded areas along the bayou and open prairie nearby, LCCO.

7. John Stengler autobiography.

8. "Hankamer Home Recognized as Historic House by CCHC," *The Progress* (Anahuac, Texas), July 26, 2006, page 4A; Harry, *A History of Chambers County*, 75.

9. Liberty County Deed Book C, 145; Letter from Mina Wilborn to her brother Fritz on November 27, 1863, confirmed the proximity of the two households, HAAS.

10. Chambers County Deed Book Z, 197–8; marriage dates from Hankamer family Bible, Hankamer family files, CCMW.

11. Chambers County Deed Book B, 278–79, 282. The name of Charles Hankamer's wife appears in various documents as "Joanna" and "Joahanna," but the most consistent use, including on her tombstone, is "Joanah." Affidavit by Earl C. Hankamer, April 18, 1945, Affidavit no. 1013, Deed Records, vol. 99: 171, CCCO.

12. Charles Hankamer to "Fritz" Hankamer, March 25, 1858, HAAS.

13. Mina Wilborn to Fritz Hankamer, April 30, 1858, HAAS.

14. At least eleven letters between family members between 1858 and 1865 include the use of the term "howdy" as a greeting, HAAS.

CHAPTER 6

1. Rommel, "American Breeds of Beef Cattle," 7.

2. Morison, *Life and Voyages of Christopher Columbus*, 210–17; Wishart, *Encyclopedia of the Great Plains*, 365; Dobie, "First Cattle," 171–75; Texas Historical Commission, "The Pass of the North," *Texas Historic Sites Atlas*, marker no. 5395, https://atlas.thc.state.tx.us.

3. Cox, *Historical and Biographical Record*, 195–96; Bancroft, *History of the*

North Mexican States, 610, 663; Dobie, "First Cattle," 175–77; Holden, *Alkali Trails*, 22.

4. Harry, *History of Chambers County*, 31–2; Winningham, *Traveling the Shore*, 27.

5. Nance and Eve, "Letter Book of Joseph Eve," 488; Fiske, *Visit to Texas*, 91; Dobie, "First Cattle," 191.

6. Dary, *Cowboy Culture*, 71–2; Cox, *Historical Record*, 196.

7. Holden, *Alkali Trails*, 21–2; "Texas Cattle Raising," *Harper's Weekly*, October 19, 1867, 665; Dary, *Cowboy Culture*, 126.

8. Dobie, "First Cattle," 189–91; Cox, *Historical Record*, 196.

9. Olmsted, *Journey*, 369–70.

10. Block, "The Opelousas Trail"; Jackson, *They Pointed Them East*, xi, 1, 9; Kemp, "Atascosito Road." Some historians say the section of this route west of the Trinity River was called the Atascosito Road, while the eastern extension was known as the Opelousas Road.

11. Weddle, *Changing Tides*, 156; Fiske, *Visit to Texas*, 91–2; Parker, *Trip to the West*, 186; Woodman, *Guide to Texas Emigrants*, 62–3; Switzler, *Report on the Internal Commerce*, 517; Gibson, "Population of the 100 Largest Urban Places: 1860."

12. Hardee, "Reminiscences of Texas as a Republic," June 10, 1897, SHRL; XIT Ranch, "XIT Ranch History," accessed September 23, 2024, https://xitranch.com/xit-history/; The King Ranch, "The King Ranch Legacy," accessed September 23, 2024, https://king-ranch.com/; Block, "The Opelousas Trail."

13. US Bureau of Topographic Engineers, "Map of Texas and Part of New Mexico," HHRC; Report of Commander Hunter, January 11, 1862, *ORN* 17: 158.

14. National Archives, *Seventh Census, 1850*, Liberty County, Texas.

15. National Archives, *Eighth Census, 1860*, Liberty County and Chambers County, Texas.

16. Rollins, *The Cowboy*, 218–19; Love, "History of the Cattle Industry," no. 1: 3; Cox, *Historical Record*, 417, 592, 654.

17. Charles Hankamer to Frederick ("Fritz") Hankamer, June 2, 1858, HAAS.

18. Similar prices are found in Hardee, "Reminiscences of Texas," July 8, 1897.

19. "City Population History from 1850–2000."

20. Olmsted, *Journey*, 374, said prairie land was selling for "about fifty cents an acre" in the mid-1850s; Land prices from Liberty County, Texas, Deed Book C, 145–46, Deed Book Z, 197–198, Deed Book D, 469, Deed Book D, 472–73, LCCO; tax assessments for Liberty County, Texas, 1850–1860, are found on tax rolls from the office of the Liberty County tax assessor-collector, microfilm reel 114601, SHRL, https://www.tsl.texas.gov/arc/local/liberty.html.

21. The family land and livestock holdings are shown on the tax assessor records and deed files for Liberty and Chambers counties, cited above in note 20 for chapter 6; 1860 US Census, "Non-Population Schedule (Agriculture) for Liberty and Chambers County, Texas."

22. Jordan, *German Seed*, 35–8.

CHAPTER 7

1. De Bow, "City of Galveston," 348–49.
2. Olmsted, *Journey*, 60–1; Houstoun, *Texas and the Gulf of Mexico*, 2: 187.
3. Olmsted, *Journey*, 374.
4. Family letters on June 22, 1862; July 5, 1862; August 13, 1862; August 18, 1862; December 26, 1862; September 15, 1863; May 15, 1864; December 25, 1864; December 30, 1864; March 12, 1865, HAAS.
5. Charles Hankamer to Fritz Hankamer, March 25, 1858, and June 2, 1858, HAAS; George Stengler to Mina Wilborn, March 6, 1863, AUTH.
6. Fritz Hankamer to Mina Wilborn, May 2, 1863, AUTH.
7. Mina Wilborn to her brothers Fritz, George, and Karl, June 8, 1862, HAAS.
8. Mina Wilborn to Fritz Hankamer August 13, 1862; Fritz to Mina, August 30, 1862, HAAS.
9. Mina Wilborn to Fritz Hankamer and George Stengler, June 22, 1862, HAAS.
10. Johanette Stengler to Fritz Hankamer, July 5, 1862, HAAS.
11. Johanette Stengler to Fritz Hankamer, March 12, 1865, HAAS; John Stengler to Fritz Hankamer, April 20, 1865, HAAS.
12. Celima Duncan to her unnamed sister, May 19, 1863, JDWC.
13. Johanette Stengler to Fritz Hankamer, September 19, 1864, HAAS.
14. John Stengler to Fritz Hankamer, February 13, 1865, HAAS.
15. Animal fat from cattle or sheep is called "tallow"; fat from swine is called "lard." Although lard can be used to make soap or candles, it was more frequently used for cooking, and lard was generally considered inferior to tallow for candles or soap.
16. Mina Wilborn to Fritz Hankamer, December 26, 1862, HAAS; Johanette Stengler to Fritz Hankamer, September 15, 1863, HAAS; Hart, "History of Pioneer Days," 143; Jackson, *Home on the Double Bayou*, 21; Jacobs, "Drug Conditions," 184.
17. John W. Hankamer Diary, October 2, 5, 14, 1864, CCMW; "Chinkapin Oak," Trees of Texas, Texas A&M Forest Service, http://texastreeid.tamu.edu/content/pdf/Chinkapin_Oak.pdf.
18. John W. Hankamer Diary, October 25 and 29, 1864, and May 10, 1865, CCMW; Olmsted, *Journey*, 374; "Dwarf Palmetto," US Department of Agriculture, accessed September 24, 2024, https://plants.usda.gov/DocumentLibrary/plantguide/pdf/cs_sami8.pdf.
19. Ellis, *Official Descriptive and Illustrated Catalogue*, 577–78. This catalog for a world's fair in 1851 mentions plaited hats, including some made from palmetto; Revels, *Grander in Her Daughters*, 62; John W. Hankamer diary, August 11, 12, 13, 15, 16 and September 2, 3, 5, 6, 7, 1864, CCMW; John Stengler to Fritz Hankamer, February 1, 1865, HAAS.
20. Bronson, *Early American Weaving and Dyeing*, ix; Knight, *American Mechanical Dictionary*, 1903, 2203, 2207.

CHAPTER 8

1. Charles Hankamer to Fritz Hankamer, May 14, 1858, HAAS.
2. Olmsted, *Journey*, 365.
3. Olmsted, *Journey*, 90; Seale, "River People," 47; Gard, "Trinity River Navigation."
4. Fitzsimons, *150 Years of North American Railroads*, 18; Texas State Library and Archives Commission, "The Railroads Come to Texas," 2, April 3, 2024, https://www.tsl.texas.gov/exhibits /railroad/beginnings/page2.html; Partlow, *Liberty County*, 202; Werner, "Railroads."
5. Muir, "Railroads Come to Houston," 48–53; Briscoe, "The First Texas Railroad," 283; Werner, "Railroads."
6. Lane, *I Married a Soldier*, 81.
7. Fremantle, *Three Months*, 64.
8. *The Tri-Weekly Telegraph* (Houston, Texas) 28, no. 38, June 13, 1862: 3, c. 1, TPTH; Briscoe, "First Texas Railroad," 285.
9. *The Weekly Telegraph* (Houston, Texas), 26, no. 50, February 12, 1861: 1, c. 8, TPTH.
10. Pickett, *Historic Liberty County*, 114–15; Williams, "Texas and New Orleans Railroad."
11. Julius Pratt to Commander Hunter, CS Navy, *ORN* 16: 829; W. W. Morris to Capt. T. Herman, October 27, 1863, file "NA, T&NO 10/27/1863" and E. L. Herriot to Capt. E. P. Turner, file "NA, RRB 9/29A/1863," in Bright, "Confederate Railroads," accessed September 24, 2024, https://www.csa-railroads.com.
12. A. M. Gentry to Geo. W. Randolph, secretary of war, May 1, 1862, *OR* series 4, vol. 1, section 2: 1109; E. H. Cushing, editorial in the *Houston Telegraph*, November 27, 1861, File "NP, HT 11/27/1861," in Bright, "Confederate Railroads," accessed September 24, 2024, https://www.csa-railroads.com.
13. *Tri-Weekly Telegraph* (Houston, Texas), 28, no. 35, June 6, 1862: 4, TPTH.
14. Ripley, *From Flag to Flag*, 72.
15. Johanette Stengler to Fritz Hankamer, October 15, 1862, HAAS.
16. John W. Hankamer Diary, July 18, 1864, CCMW.
17. John W. Hankamer Diary, November 16, 1864, CCMW.
18. "Capt. Bose Letter Tells Trials of Company on Trip to Houston," *New Braunfels (Texas) Herald*, May 8, 1962, 2B, reprint of the original story from December 4, 1863, CCMW.
19. Muir, "Railroads Come to Houston, 1857-61," 50–1.
20. A. M. Gentry to General Hebert, CSA, December 16, 1861, *OR* 4:158; V. Sulakowski to Major Kellersberg, CSA, October 5, 1863, *OR* 26, part 2: 299; Werner, "Railroads"; Company F morning report, February 22, 1863.

CHAPTER 9

1. National Archives, *Eighth Census, 1860*. Eighty-eight percent were born in states that joined the CSA, 6 percent were born in Union states, and 6 percent were born outside the United States; Stephens, *Texas: A Historical Atlas*, 170–71.

2. John W. Hankamer to Mina Wilborn April 12, 1863. AUTH.

3. Grear, *Why Texans Fought*, 41–2; Wooster, "A People at War," 5–6; Wagner, Gallagher, and Finkelman, *Civil War Desk Reference*, 372.

4. "J.O.L.O. Observatory Record Book," entries for July 2, 1861, 83. The meaning of the acronym "J.O.L.O" for the lookout's post on top of the Hendley Building is unknown; Report of Commander Alden, USN, July 8, 1861, *ORN* 16: 576.

5. Texas Historical Commission, Texas Historic Sites Atlas, Atlas Number 5507017600, historical marker for "Fort Sabine," accessed September 24, 2024, https://atlas.thc.state.tx.us/; Block, "Swamp Angels," 44–46.

6. Spaight, "Muster Roll"; Simpson and Wright, *Texas in the War*, 108–09.

7. "General Orders No. 30, CSA," *OR*, series 4, vol. 1, section 2: 1094–96; Matthews, *Public Laws:* 30, 61–2, 211.

8. Oates, *Confederate Cavalry*, 47; Fremantle, *Three Months*, 75.

9. General N. P. West to General William Byrd, July 22, 1861, Brigade Correspondence, Texas State Troops records, TSLA.

10. Ashley Spaight to Col. J. Y. Dashiell, March 10, 1862, TSLA.

11. Ashley Spaight to J. Y. Dashiell, April 17, 1862. TSLA. There is potential confusion due to the almost identical names for two leaders of CSA units from Texas, both of which are pronounced "spate"—J. W. Speight from Central Texas and Ashley W. Spaight from Southeast Texas.

12. Civil War military service summaries for the Hankamer and Stengler brothers are in "National Archives and Records Service, Compiled Service Records of Confederate Soldiers Who Served in Organizations from the State of Texas, reels 411–412, Twenty-first Infantry (Spaight's Regiment)," 1960. These records are available online from multiple sources; "Descriptive Roll of Company F," JDWC; Spaight, "Muster Roll," BCAH.

CHAPTER 10

1. Details about the muster location are included with a note for a letter dated December 22, 1862, JDWC.

2. Payments described in *OR*, series 4, vol. 1, sec. 1: 126–27; Lester and Bromwell, A *Digest of the Military and Naval Laws*, 43–4. An example is on the death certificate for Silas Smith, Jr. May 14, 1863, JDWC.

3. Wm. Austin, adjutant, CSA, May 7, 1861, *OR* 1: 634

4. Johnston, *Narrative of Military Operations*, 427–29.

5. General Johnston, CSA, September 22, 1861, to Governor Pettus of Mississippi, *OR* 4: 422.

6. For payments for personal firearms see *OR*, series 4, vol. 1, section 2: 1096; Lester and Bromwell, *Digest of Laws*, 62.

7. Brig. Gen. N. P. West to adjutant general, State of Texas, January 9, 1862, TSLA; Wooster, *Texas and Texans in the Civil War*, 29–30.

8. Steuart, "Gun Manufacturing During the Civil War"; "Small Arms of the Civil War," American Battlefield Trust website, January 9, 2024, https://www.battlefields.org/learn/articles/small-arms-civil-war.

9. William Duncan to Celima Duncan, October 7, 1862, JDWC.

10. These documents are part of the Julia Duncan Welder Collection, SHRL.

11. Details about the four brothers are in the "Descriptive Roll" for Company F, JDWC.

12. "Descriptive Roll," JDWC.

13. William Duncan to Celima Duncan on May 12, 1862, and May 14, 1862, JDWC.

14. William B. Duncan's diary entries for May 13–June 3, 1862. This and subsequent quotations from this diary are from a transcription made by the San Jacinto Museum of History in 1940, and now available as part of the Julia Duncan Welder Collection (JDWC) at the Sam Houston Regional Library and Research Center (SHRL). It is shown hereinafter as "Wm. Duncan diary." Receipts for drum and bugles in October 1862 and April 1863, JDWC. "List of Members of Co. F, 1864," JDWC; Noel, *Campaign from Santa Fe to the Mississippi*, 7–8; Blessington, *Campaigns of Walker's Texas Division*, 20–21; Davis, *The Fighting Men of the Civil War*, 42.

15. Fornell, "Island City," 25.

16. Captain Eagle, USN, to Brigadier General Hebert, CSA, May 17, 1862, *OR* 9: 710.

17. Brigadier General Hebert, CSA, to Colonel Cook, May 19, 1862, *OR* 9: 712; Eagle to Hebert, *OR* 9: 711.

18. Raines, *Six Decades in Texas*, 387. An 1862 reference to football may come as a surprise to us today, although the term dates back several centuries and referred to a much different game than the current version.

CHAPTER 11

1. Kingsley, "Sabine Pass Lighthouse."

2. "City of Sabine and Sabine Pass," Texas Historical Commission, Texas Historic Sites Atlas Number 5245010500, accessed September 24, 2024, https://atlas.thc.state.tx.us/; Wooster, "Sabine Pass, TX."

3. A. M. Gentry to CSA General Hebert, *OR* 4: 158; Muir, "Railroads," 51–2; Kemp, "Atascosito Road."

4. Report of Commander Hunter, CSN, July 8, 1861, *ORN* 16: 831–32; Charles Hankamer to Mina Wilborn, January 11, 1863, AUTH.

5. Charles Hankamer to Charles and Mina Wilborn, June 12, 1862, AUTH; William Duncan to Celima Duncan, June 3, 1862, JDWC; Wm. Duncan diary, June 6-8, 1863, JDWC; The location of Grigsby's Bluff is described in *OR* 15, 834.

6. Spaight, "History of Spaight's Regiment"; Ragan, "Diary of Captain George W. O'Brien," 30–31; Block, "Swamp Angels," 46; Summary of Company F history on Compiled Military Service Records for the Hankamer and Stengler brothers, TSLA.

7. CSA General Orders No. 30, *OR*, series 4, vol. 1, section 2: 1096; Charles Hankamer to Mina Wilborn, June 1862, AUTH.

8. Caudill, *Moss Bluff Rebel*, 15–21; Jackson, *They Pointed Them East*, xiv, 1; Traylor, "Liberty and Slavery," 116–17.

9. Charles Hankamer to Mina and Charles Wilborn, June 1862, AUTH.

10. William Duncan to Celima Duncan, June 25, 1862, JDWC.

11. Charles Hankamer, June 1862, AUTH.

12. "Rations for Company F, May 1, 1862, to June 1, 1862," JDWC.

13. Charles Hankamer, June 1862, AUTH.

CHAPTER 12

1. Major Kellersberg, CSA, to Colonel Debray, July 30, 1862, *OR* 9: 729; Report of Colonel Debray, CSA, September 25, 1862, *OR* 15: 143.

2. Keith, "Military Operations," 66; Keith, "Memoirs," 57.

3. Keith, "Memoirs," 57–58; Bell, "Trans-Mississippi Miasmas," 3–4; "The Epidemic at Sabine Pass," The *Tri-Weekly Telegraph* (Houston) 28, no. 76, September 10, 1862: 2, col. 3, TPTH. Dr. George Holland, who was experienced in treating yellow fever, visited the area in early September 1862 and concluded that the first victim in the current outbreak "was taken sick on the 10th of July."

4. Wiggins, "Combating Yellow Fever in Galveston," 240; Boyce, *Yellow Fever*, 42; Hayes, *History of the Island*, 342–44.

5. Keith, "Military Operations," 66; *Galveston (Texas) Weekly News*, September 3, 1862: 1.

6. *Galveston (Texas) Weekly News*, September 17, 1862: 1, c. 1.

7. Humphreys, *Yellow Fever and the South*, 2–4, 8–9.

8. US Sanitary Commission, *Report . . . on Yellow Fever*, 9, 22; Bell, *Mosquito Soldiers*, 33–4; Chambers, *Oxford Companion to American Military History*, 231.

9. Hildreth, "The Howard Association," 34; Augustin, *History of Yellow Fever*, 871, 1011; Patterson, "Yellow fever epidemics," 855–65.

10. Ralph J. Smith, *Reminiscences of the Civil War, and Other Sketches* (Waco, Texas: W. M. Morrison, 1911), 18.

11. Bell, *Mosquito Soldiers*, 1–2; Alfred Jay Bollet, "The Major Infectious Epidemic Diseases of Civil War Soldiers," *Infectious Disease Clinics of North America* 18, no. 2 (June 2004): 293–309; J. S. Sartin, "Infectious Diseases During the Civil War: The Triumph of the 'Third Army,'" *Clinical Infectious Diseases* 16, no. 4 (April 1993): 580–4.

12. Reilly, "Medical and Surgical Care During the American Civil War," 138–142; Bell, *Mosquito Soldiers*, 24–25.

13. US Sanitary Commission, *Report . . . on the Nature and Treatment of Yellow Fever*, 8; Jo Ann Carrigan, "The Saffron Scourge: A History of Yellow Fever in Louisiana, 1796–1905," PhD diss., Louisiana State University, 1966, 131, 367; Hildreth, "The Howard Association of Galveston," 34; Reilly, "Medical and Surgical Care," 138–42.

14. George Stengler to Mina Wilborn, March 6, 1863, AUTH.

15. Lieutenant N. H. Smith, CSA, to Major General Howe, August 26, 1863, BCAH.

16. "About Malaria," Centers for Disease Control and Prevention, September 6, 2024, http://www.cdc.gov/malaria/about/faqs.html; Bell, "Trans-Mississippi Miasmas," 11.

17. Barnes, *Medical and Surgical History*, 67, 92, 233.

18. Hasegawa, "Quinine Substitutes," 650–5; John Stengler to Fritz Hankamer, February 26, 1865, HAAS.

19. John Stengler to his sons Fritz and George, January 28, 1863, HAAS; John W. Hankamer to Mina Wilborn, March 1, 1863, AUTH; Wm. Duncan diary, March 8, 1863, JDWC.

CHAPTER 13

1. Davis, "Unregulated Potions," 19; Jacobs, "Drug Conditions," 167–68; Brown, "Medical Education"; Bryan, "'Whip them like the Mischief,'" 70.
2. Reilly, "Medical and Surgical Care," 138–42; Texas Medical Board, "Texas Medical Board History"; Nixon, *The Medical Story of Early Texas*, 396–97; Bollet, *Civil War Medicine*, 64.
3. Mastin, "The Medical Profession in the Civil War," 479.
4. Jacobs, "Drug Conditions," 166–67.
5. Author's analysis of the 1860 federal census data for Liberty and Chambers Counties, Texas.
6. John Stengler to his sons, July 1862, HAAS.
7. F. Hankamer to General Magruder, July 23, 1863, AUTH.
8. William Duncan to Celima Duncan, November 4, 1863, JDWC.

CHAPTER 14

1. Family letters dated June 12 and August 2, 5, 18, 21, and 30, 1862, confirm Company F was based at Grigsby's Bluff; Wm. Duncan diary, June 6–8, 1862, and August 26, 1862, JDWC.
2. "The Epidemic at Sabine Pass," The *Tri-Weekly Telegraph* (Houston) 28, no. 76, September 10, 1862: 2, col. 3, TPTH.
3. Wm. Duncan diary, September 8–10 and 15, 1862, JDWC.
4. Keith, "Memoirs," 58.
5. Report of Master Hooper, USN, October 5, 1862, *ORN* 19: 219–20; Report of Lieutenant Colonel Spaight, CSA, September 26, 1862, *OR* 15: 144.
6. Wm. Duncan diary, September 25, 1862, JDWC.
7. Report of Colonel Debray, CSA, September 25, 1862, *OR* 15: 143.
8. Report of Master Hooper, USN, *ORN* 19, 220.
9. Report of Lieutenant Colonel Spaight, September 26, 1862, *ORN* 19: 232.
10. Colonel Debray, CSA to Captain Mason, September 26, 1862, *OR* 15: 813.

CHAPTER 15

1. Duncan diary, September 26, 1862, JDWC; Report of Lieutenant Colonel Spaight, September 26, 1862, *ORN* 19: 233.
2. Report of Colonel Debray, CSA, September 28, 1862, *OR* 15: 814–15.
3. Wm. Duncan diary, September 28–29, 1862, JDWC; Report of Lieutenant Colonel Spaight, September 29, 1862, *ORN* 19: 234; William Duncan to Celima Duncan, October 16, 1862, JDWC.
4. Wm. Duncan diary, September 30, 1862, JDWC.
5. Report of Lieutenant Colonel Spaight, October 2, 1862, *ORN* 19: 235; Wm. Duncan diary, October 2, 1862, JDWC.
6. Report of Lieutenant Colonel Spaight, September 29, 1862, *ORN* 19: 234.
7. John W. Hankamer to his brothers, October 3, 1862, HAAS; Ladd, *Chambers County*, 252.
8. Report of Colonel Debray, CSA, October 5, 1862, *ORN* 19: 261; Report of

Brigadier General Hebert, CSA, *ORN* 19: 790; Report of Commander Renshaw, USN, *ORN* 19: 255–60; Report of Colonel Cook, CSA, *ORN* 19: 262–63.

9. Renshaw, *ORN* 19: 257–58; "Galveston Taken Possession of," *Galveston Weekly News*, October 15, 1862: 1, c.1 and 2, c. 2.

10. William Duncan to Celima Duncan, October 7, 1862, JDWC; Wm. Duncan diary, October 5, 1862, JDWC.

11. Debray, *OR* 15, 814.

CHAPTER 16

1. Wooster, "Aurora, TX"; "Minutes of the Board of Directors of the Eastern Texas Railroad, June 7, 1861," file UT, ET 6/7/1861, in Bright, "Confederate Railroads, accessed September 24, 2024, www.csa-railroads.com. The original settlement called Aurora was about eight miles by railroad from the southern end of the line, which terminated north of the town of Sabine Pass. The modern city of Port Arthur now occupies the former site of Aurora.

2. John W. Hankamer to Mina Wilborn, November 15, 1862, AUTH. There are nearly a dozen references in family letters to the brothers serving as pickets for Company F; Wagner, Gallagher, and Finkelman, *Civil War Desk Reference*, 476–77; Hess, *Civil War Infantry*, 99.

3. For a description of the bridge over Taylor's Bayou see "Minutes of the Board of Directors of the Eastern Texas Railroad, June 7, 1861," file UT, ET 6/7/1861, and "E. S. Pitts, Special Engineer, to the Board of School Commissioners," June 7, 1861, file TX, ET 6/11/1861 in Bright, "Confederate Railroads," accessed September 24, 2024, https://www.csa-railroads.com.

4. Report of Lieutenant Colonel Spaight, CSA, October 2, 1862, *ORN* 19: 235.

5. Wm. Duncan diary, October 15, 1862, JDWC.

6. In their correspondence during the war, William B. Duncan and some others quoted in the following chapters occasionally showed their disdain for their adversaries by declining to capitalize the word "yankees." I have preserved their original spelling where this occurs for the sake of historical accuracy.

7. William Duncan to Celima Duncan, October 16, 1862, JDWC.

8. John W. Hankamer to Mina Wilborn, October 19, 1862, AUTH.

9. William Duncan to Celima Duncan, October 16, 1862, JDWC.

10. Acting Master Crocker, USN, October 24, 1862, *ORN* 19: 227–28.

11. Crocker, *ORN* 19: 227–28; William Duncan to Celima Duncan, October 16, 1862, JDWC.

12. John Stengler to one of his sons, October 20, 1862, HAAS.

CHAPTER 17

1. John W. Hankamer to Mina Wilborn, October 19, 1862, AUTH; Wm. Duncan diary, October 26, 1862, JDWC.

2. John W. Hankamer to Mina Wilborn, December 3, 1862, AUTH.

3. "Make Your Own Cloth," *Galveston (Texas) Weekly News*, September 24, 1862: 2 c. 1.

Notes to Pages 106–119 271

4. CSA General Orders No. 100, *OR*, series 4, vol. 2: 229-230.
5. Clothing Record for Company F, Spaight's Battalion, JDWC.
6. Johanette Stengler to Fritz Hankamer, July 5, 1862, HAAS.
7. Wiley, *Life of Johnny Reb*, 111.
8. Jacobs, "Drug Conditions," 180; Harry, *History of Chambers County*, 51.
9. Johanette Stengler to George Stengler and Fritz Hankamer, November 4, 1862, HAAS.
10. John and Johanette Stengler to Fritz Hankamer, March 14, 1864, HAAS.
11. John Stengler to Fritz Hankamer, January 24, 1863, HAAS; Mina Wilborn to her husband Charles, October 29, 1863, AUTH; CSA pay in *OR*, series 4, vol. 1, section 1, 130.
12. Mina Wilborn to Fritz Hankamer, October 30, 1864, and April 19, 1865, HAAS.
13. Johann Stengler, letters to the Society for the Protection of German Immigrants, October 1845, BCAH, and on November 6 and November 30, 1862, HAAS; Charles Hankamer to Mina and Charles Wilborn, June 19, 1862, AUTH.
14. Reid, "Confederate Shoemakers," 35-9.
15. John Stengler to Fritz Hankamer, January 24, 1863, HAAS.
16. Reid, "Confederate Shoemakers," 38.
17. Charles Hankamer to Mina and Charles Wilborn, April 29, 1863, AUTH; William Duncan to Celima Duncan, January 9, 1864, JDWC.
18. Spaulding, *Civil War Recipes*, 25; Ford, "Alkalies in Bread," 44.
19. Mina Wilborn to her brothers at Grigsby's Bluff, December 21, 1862, HAAS.
20. John W. Hankamer to Mina Wilborn, December 21, 1862, AUTH.
21. Celima Duncan to William Duncan, June 17, 1862, JDWC.
22. Johanette Stengler to Fritz Hankamer, September 19, 1864, HAAS; Mina Wilborn to Fritz Hankamer, September 18, 1864, HAAS.
23. John Stengler to Fritz Hankamer, February 13, 1865, HAAS.
24. *Galveston Weekly News*, January 14, 1862: 2.
25. Fremantle, *Three Months*, 79.
26. Wooster, *Texas and Texans in the Civil War*, 122-23; Jacobs, "Drug Conditions,"180; Dary, *Cowboy Culture*, 130.

CHAPTER 18

1. Mina Wilborn to Fritz Hankamer, October 25, 1862, HAAS.
2. References to overnight picket duty by the brothers are in letters dated November 15, December 3, 1862, December 13, 1863, AUTH, and December 18, 1862, HAAS.
3. Acting Master Crocker, USN, to Farragut, *ORN* 19, 225.
4. *Galveston (Texas) Weekly News*, October 15, 1862: 1, c. 4.
5. Acting Master Hooper, USN, December 5, 1862, *ORN* 19, 392; Lieutenant Commander Law, USN, to Commander Renshaw, December 7, 1862, *ORN* 19, 394-95.
6. Matthews, *Public Laws of the Confederate States of America*, 61-2.
7. Mina Wilborn to Fritz Hankamer, December 21, 1862, HAAS.
8. Charles Hankamer to Mina Wilborn, December 28, 1862, AUTH.

9. A. W. Spaight to W. B. Duncan, December 24, 1862, JDWC.

10. Wm. Duncan diary, December 24-25, 1862, JDWC.

11. Handwritten draft notice for Charles Wilborn, copy in Wilborn Family File, CCMW.

CHAPTER 19

1. Detailed report of Major General Magruder, CSA, February 26, 1863, *ORN* 19, 470; Barr, "Texas Coastal Defense," 14; Franklin, *Battle of Galveston*, 4.

2. Rear Admiral Farragut, USN, to Commander Renshaw, October 14, 1862, *ORN* 19, 260.

3. Thompson and Wainwright, *Correspondence of Gustavus Vasa Fox*, 321.

4. Butler and Marshall, *Correspondence of Gen. Benjamin F. Butler*, 465-6.

5. Butler and Marshall, *Correspondence of Gen. Benjamin F. Butler*, 470-1.

6. Butler and Marshall, *Correspondence of Gen. Benjamin F. Butler*, 525.

7. C. Forshey, consulting engineer, CSA, to Colonel Debray, December 25, 1862, *OR* 15: 908; "Naval Engagement at Galveston," *ORN* 19: 468-469; Barr, "Texas Coastal Defense," 14; Wagner, Gallagher, and Finkelman, *Civil War Desk Reference*, 504; Williams, "Spirited Account," 207; Magruder, *ORN* 19: 472.

8. Magruder, *ORN* 19: 472-3.

9. Moore, *Rebellion Record* 6: 339; "Proceedings of court of enquiry," January 12, 1863, ORN 19: 447; *Report of the Secretary of the Navy*, 310, 314.

10. Williams, "Spirited Account," 206-7; Frazier, *Cottonclads!*, 38.

11. Report of Assistant Engineer Long, USA, January 10, 1863, *ORN* 19: 459.

12. Magruder, *ORN* 19: 471.

13. Rear Admiral Farragut, USN, to Secretary of Navy Welles, *ORN* 19: 431; Magruder, *ORN* 19: 471; Butler and Marshall, *Correspondence of Gen. Benjamin F. Butler*, 565-66.

14. Franklin, *Battle of Galveston*, 6; "Naval Engagement at Galveston," *ORN* 19: 469.

15. Long, *ORN* 19: 460; Magruder, *ORN* 19: 473.

16. Major Burt, USA, to Major General Banks, January 1, 1863, *ORN* 19: 455; Report of Lieutenant Commander Wilson, USN, January 6, 1863, *ORN* 19: 439; *Report of the Secretary of the Navy*, 312-13.

17. Long, *ORN* 19: 459-61; Burt, *ORN* 19: 455-57; Magruder, *ORN* 19: 473; Moore, *Rebellion Record* 6: 337.

18. Noel, *Campaign from Santa Fe*, 42.

19. John W. Hankamer to Mina Wilborn, January 4, 1863, AUTH.

20. Federal Writers' Project, "Jacob Branch," 140-41.

21. Fremantle, *Three Months*, 71.

22. Wm. Duncan diary, January 1-2, 1863, JDWC.

23. Magruder, *ORN* 19: 472; Williams, "Spirited Account," 207.

24. "Proceedings of court of enquiry," January 12, 1863, *ORN* 19: 447-49; Williams, "Spirited Account," 207-13; Magruder, *ORN* 19: 474; "Naval Engagement at Galveston," *ORN* 19: 469; Franklin, *Battle of Galveston*, 7-8.

25. Williams, "Spirited Account," 208; Burt, *ORN* 19: 455.

26. "Court of Enquiry," *ORN* 19: 449; Magruder, *ORN* 19: 475–76; Report of Lieutenant Davis, USA, January 10, 1863, *ORN* 19: 457–59; Statement of Colonel Burrell, USA, January 23, 1863.

27. Report of Commander Hunter, CSN, January 7, 1863, *ORN* 19: 466; Magruder, *ORN* 19: 475; "Court of enquiry," *ORN* 19: 450; Reports of Rear Admiral Farragut, USN, no. 46, February 12, 1863, and no. 56, February 26, 1863, *ORN* 19: 452–53.

28. Burt, *ORN* 19, 455–57; Hunter, *ORN* 19: 466.

29. "Naval Engagement at Galveston," *ORN* 19: 469–70; Court of Enquiry, *ORN* 19: 448–50; "Destruction of the U. S. Flagship *Westfield* and Capture of the *Harriet Lane*," *Frank Leslie's Illustrated Newspaper*, vol. 15 (New York), January 24, 1863: 279, c. 3.

30. Thompson and Wainwright, *Confidential Correspondence*, 324.

31. Banks to Secretary of War Stanton, April 6, 1865, *OR* 26, part 1: 7.

32. Wm. Duncan diary, January 1-2, 1863, JDWC.

33. John W. Hankamer to Mina Wilborn, January 4, 1863, AUTH.

34. Farragut to Welles, *ORN* 19: 431; Major General Banks, USA, to Major General Halleck, January 7, 1863, *ORN* 19: 454–55; Lewis Bach, Steamer *Cambria*, to Major General Banks USA, *OR* 15:205–06.

35. Banks, *OR* 26, part 1: 5-7.

36. Rear Admiral Farragut, USN, to Commodore Bell, January 3, 1863, *ORN* 19: 479; Bell to Farragut, January 11, 1863, ORN 19: 504.

37. Bell to Farragut, *ORN* 19: 504.

38. Frederick Thompson from the USS *New London*, January 15, 1863, *ORN* 19: 504–05.

39. *Report of the Secretary of the Navy*, January 12, 1863, 319–24.

40. Report of Commander Semmes, CSN, May 12, 1863, *ORN* 2: 683-684; Semmes, *Memoirs*, 520, 540–42.

41. Commodore Bell, USN, to Rear Admiral Farragut, January 12, 1862, *ORN* 19: 510.

42. Rear Admiral Farragut, USN, to Secretary of Navy, January 15, 1863, *ORN* 19: 506.

43. Commodore Bell, USN, to Rear Admiral Farragut, January 24, 1863, *ORN* 19: 554.

44. Rear Admiral Farragut, USN, to Secretary of Navy, January 21, 1863, *ORN* 19: 552-553.

CHAPTER 20

1. Evans, *Confederate Military History*, 99–100; Keith, "Memoirs," 60; Block, "Requiem for a Confederate Gunboat."

2. Chas. Hankamer to Mina Wilborn, January 11, 1863, AUTH; Report of Major Watkins, CSA, January 23, 1863, *ORN* 19: 565; "Naval Fight off Sabine," January 21, 1863, *ORN* 19: 572.

3. Wm. Duncan diary, January 5, 1863, JDWC; Chas. Hankamer to Mina Wilborn, January 11, 1863, AUTH.

4. "Naval fight off Sabine," *ORN* 19: 570; Lieutenant Commander Law, USN, to Commander. Renshaw, *ORN* 19, 394-395.

5. Commodore Bell to Rear Admiral Farragut, January 18, 1863, *ORN* 19: 538; Block, "Swamp Angels," 49; "Velocity I (Sch)" and "Morning Light (8-gun ship)," US Naval History and Heritage Command website, October 21, 2015, https://www.history.navy.mil/research/histories/ship-histories/danfs.html.

6. "Naval Fight off Sabine," *ORN* 19: 570-571; Evans, *Confederate Military History*, 101.

7. Assistant Surgeon Sherfy, April 12, 1864, *ORN* 19: 558-560; Frazier, *Cottonclads!* 103; Keith, "Memoirs," 61-62.

8. Wm. Duncan diary, January 21, 1863, JDWC.

9. Farragut to Wells, *ORN* 19: 553; Farragut to Commander Alden, January 27, 1863, *ORN* 19: 584.

10. Report of Lieutenant Commander Read, January 26, 1863, *ORN* 19: 555; Block, "Swamp Angels," 50.

11. John Stengler to Fritz Hankamer, January 24, 1863, HAAS.

CHAPTER 21

1. John W. Hankamer to Mina Wilborn, January 4, 1863, AUTH.
2. Charles Hankamer to Mina Wilborn, January 11, 1863, AUTH.
3. John Stengler to Fritz Hankamer, January 24, 1863, HAAS.
4. Fremantle, *Three Months*, 82.
5. *OR*, series 4, vol. 1, section 2: 975; Matthews, *Public Laws*, 31.
6. Moore, *Conscription and Conflict*, 27-30; Van Zant, "Confederate Conscription," 56.
7. Mina Wilborn to Fritz Hankamer, February 23, 1863, HAAS.
8. Frederick Hankamer to Mina Wilborn, March 5, 1863, AUTH.
9. Descriptive Roll for Company F, Spaight's Battalion, JDWC.
10. Moore, *Conscription and Conflict*, 44-50; Van Zant, "Confederate Conscription," 65; Matthews, *Public Laws*, 172; *OR*, Series 4, vol. 3, section 1, 11-12.
11. Frederick Hankamer to General Magruder, July 23, 1863, AUTH.
12. Moulis and Martin-Blondel, "Scrofula," 1061; Civil War Muster Roll Index Card for C. Wilborn shows he enlisted in Company B, 2nd Brigade, Texas State Troops on August 10, 1863, TSLA.

CHAPTER 22

1. George Stengler to Mina Wilborn, March 6, 1863, AUTH; Wm. Duncan diary, February 27, 1863, JDWC.
2. Wm. Duncan diary, March 23, 1863, JDWC; *Houston Tri-Weekly*, 2, col. 4, January 4, 1863.
3. William Duncan to Celima Duncan, April 8 and April 10, 1863, JDWC; Ragan, "Diary of Captain George W. O'Brien," 45; Gallaway, "Past Human Role."
4. Wm. Duncan diary, April 14, 1863, JDWC.
5. Johanette Stengler to Fritz Hankamer, April 26, 1863, HAAS.
6. William Duncan to Celima Duncan, April 10, 1863, JDWC; Wm. Duncan diary, April 9, 13, 14, 15, 1863, JDWC.

7. Company F morning reports, April 1863.
8. Charles Hankamer to Mina and Charles Wilborn, April 29, 1863, AUTH.
9. Wiley, *Life of Johnny Reb*, 106; A letter from Charles Hankamer to Mina Wilborn, June 12, 1862, said eight or nine men shared one "oven," perhaps referring to a heavy iron pot called a Dutch oven, or a heavy iron skillet. AUTH.
10. Charles Hankamer to Mina Wilborn, June 12, 1862, AUTH.
11. G. M. Scales to Capt. William Duncan, January 14, 1863, JDWC.
12. William Duncan to Celima Duncan, April 21, 1863, JDWC.
13. Mina Wilborn to Fritz Hankamer, undated but from context probably in 1864, HAAS.
14. "Mutiny at Galveston, Tex. August 10-13, 1863," *OR* 26, part 1: 241-48.
15. Winsor, *Texas in the Confederacy*, 51.
16. Charles Hankamer to Mina and Charles Wilborn, April 29, 1863, AUTH.
17. Fritz Hankamer to Mina Wilborn, May 2, 1863, AUTH.
18. Company F morning report, May 1863; Wm. Duncan diary, May 8, 9, 1863, JDWC.
19. Company F morning reports, April and May 1863; Charles Hankamer to Mina and Charles Wilborn, April 29, 1863, AUTH; CSA Death Certificate for Silas Smith Jr., May 12, 1863, JDWC.
20. Company F morning reports, May 1863.
21. Wm. Duncan diary, May 10-11, 1863, JDWC.
22. Fremantle, *Three Months*, 74-75.

CHAPTER 23

1. Winters, *Civil War in Louisiana*, 284; Beecher, *Record of the 114th Regiment*, 137-38.
2. Company F morning reports, May 1863; Wm. Duncan diary, May 7-14, 1863, JDWC.
3. Company F morning reports, May 1863; Ragan, "Diary of Captain George W. O'Brien," 45; Martin, "Niblett's Bluff."
4. Company F morning reports, May 1863; Block, "Swamp Angels," 51; Ragan, "Diary of Captain George W. O'Brien, 1863," 31.
5. "Details for Opelousas Trail," Texas Historic Sites Atlas, Texas Historical Commission, historical marker no. 10549, accessed September 25, 2024, http://atlas.thc.state.tx.us.
6. Ragan, "The Diary of Captain George W. O'Brien, 1863," 45; Company F morning reports, May and June 1863, JDWC; John W. Hankamer, June 4, 1863, HAAS.
7. "The Louisiana Jayhawkers," *Tri-Weekly Telegraph* (Houston) 29, no. 70, August 31, 1863: 1, c. 1, TPTH; Winters, *Civil War in Louisiana*, 307.
8. Edmund P. Turner to W. R. Scurry, *OR* 26, part 2: 125-26.
9. This widespread looting is also described in Beecher, *Record of the 114th Regiment*, 148-53.
10. Wm. Duncan diary, July 19-21, 1863, JDWC.
11. Fritz Hankamer to Mina Wilborn, May 2, 1863, AUTH.

CHAPTER 24

1. Company F morning reports, June–August 1863. During this time, about one-third of the unit, an average of twenty-five men per day, were either gone on sick leave or sick in camp.
2. Company F morning reports, August and September 1863; CSA pay in *OR*, series 4, vol. 1, section 1: 130.
3. Charles, "American Civil War vs. Postage Due."
4. Williams, *Rebel Brothers*, 164.
5. Mina Wilborn to Fritz Hankamer, May 29, 1862, HAAS.
6. John Stengler to Fritz Hankamer, February 26, 1865, HAAS.
7. William Duncan to Celima Duncan, August 28, 1863, JDWC.
8. William Duncan to Celima Duncan, August 20, 1863, JDWC.
9. Ragan, "The Diary of Captain George W. O'Brien, 1863," 38; "Sabine Pass Battleground History," Texas Historical Commission, accessed September 25, 2024, https://thc.texas.gov/state-historic-sites/sabine-pass-battleground/sabine-pass-battleground-history.

CHAPTER 25

1. Raines, *Six Decades*, 510–15; Crook, "Benjamin Théron," 432–54; Confederate States Commission to CSA Secretary of State, November 7, 1862, *ORN*, series 2, vol. 3: 600–04; John Andrew, governor of Massachusetts, to G. V. Fox, assistant secretary of Navy, November 27, 1861, *OR* 15: 412; Abbott and Brush, "Business Travel," 259–271; Abraham Lincoln to Major General Grant, August 9, 1863, *OR* 24, part 3: 584; Dupree, *Planting the Union Flag*, 2–6.
2. Major General Banks, USA, "The Texas Expedition," April 6, 1865, *OR* 26, part 1: 18–21.
3. Banks, *OR* 26, part 1: 18; Major General Banks to Major General Franklin, August 31, 1863, *OR* 26, pt. 1: 287; Winters, *Civil War in Louisiana*, 294.
4. Banks to Franklin, *OR* 26, part 1: 287; Banks to President Lincoln, October 22, 1863, *OR* 26, part 1: 290; Banks to Major General Halleck, October 16, 1863, *OR* 26, part 1: 767–68.
5. Banks, *OR* 26, part 1: 18–19.
6. Banks to Lincoln, *OR* 26, part 1: 291.
7. Banks to Lincoln, *OR* 26, part 1: 292.
8. Pellet, *History of the 114th Regiment*, 150; Banks to Halleck, *OR* 26, part 1: 285–87.
9. Kellersberger, "Memoirs," 30; Major Julius Kellersberger used the European spelling of his surname in his "Memoirs." The anglicized version "Kellersberg" is found in his correspondence and reports cited in this book and it is used on these pages for consistency with those sources; Thatcher to Canby, *OR* 48, part 2: 692; Tolbert, *Dick Dowling*, 82–4; Report of Major General Franklin, USA, September 11, 1863, *ORN* 20: 528.
10. Kellersberger, "Memoirs," 30; Wagner, Gallagher, and Finkelman, *Civil War Desk Reference*, 504.

11. Kellersberger, "Memoirs," 30; Cotham, *Sabine Pass*, 79–81.

12. Cotham, *Sabine Pass*, 81; "Details for Site of Fort Griffin," *Texas Historical Sites Atlas,* Texas Historical Commission, accessed September 25, 2024, htttp://atlas.thc.state.tx.us/Details/5245010525.

13. Kellersberger, "Memoirs"; Barr, *Texas Coastal Defense*, 24; Tolbert, *Dick Dowling*, 86-7.

14. Commodore Bell, USN, to secretary of the Navy, September 4, 1863, *ORN* 20: 515; Report of Captain Roe, USA, February 2, 1864, *OR* 26, part 1: 293–94.

15. Commodore Bell, USN, to Lieutenant Commander Madigan, September 2, 1863, *ORN* 20: 515; Pellet, *History of the 114th Regiment*, 150.

CHAPTER 26

1. Pellet, *History of the 114th Regiment*, 150.

2. "The Texas Expedition," *OR* 26, part 1: 19.

3. Second report of Lieutenant Crocker, USN, April 21, 1865, *ORN* 20: 544; Report of Major General Franklin, USA, September 11, 1863, *ORN* 20: 527.

4. Crocker, *ORN* 20: 544

5. Crocker, *ORN* 20: 544-45.

6. Report of Lieutenant Commander Madigan, USN, September 13, 1863, *ORN* 20: 524–25.

7. Moore, *Rebellion Record 7*, 426; Report of Brigadier General Weitzel, USA, September 11, 1863, *OR* 26, part 1: 298-299.

8. Franklin, *ORN* 20: 527–28; Cotham, *Sabine Pass*, 109; Crocker, *ORN* 20: 544–45.

9. Crocker, *ORN* 20: 545.

10. Crocker, ORN 20: 545; Browning, *Lincoln's Trident*, 374; Report of Lieutenant Commander Dana, USN, *ORN* 20: 522; Report of Lieutenant Dowling, CSA, September 9, 1863, *OR* 26, part 1: 311.

11. Franklin, *ORN* 20: 528; Crocker, *ORN* 20: 545–46; Weitzel, *OR* 26, part 1: 299.

12. Commodore Bell, USN, to Welles, in *Report of the Secretary of the Navy*, Appendix, 391; Bell to Welles, September 11, 1863, *ORN* 20: 519; Crocker, *ORN* 20: 545–46.

13. Report of Acting Master Lamson, USN, September 10, 1863, *ORN* 20: 523; Dowling, *ORN* 20: 559; Moore, *Rebellion Record* 7: 425.

14. "Dick Dowling Won," *The Galveston Daily News*, 52, no. 313, January 30, 1894: 2, c. 6, TPTH, Abilene Library Consortium.

15. Report of Lieutenant Crocker, USN, September 12, 1863, *ORN* 20: 540–41; "Dick Dowling Won."

16. Crocker, *ORN* 20: 539–41; Report of Lieutenant Dowling, CSA, September 9, 1863, *OR* 26, part 1: 311; Report of Assistant Surgeon Nestell, USN, *ORN* 20: 549.

17. Drummond, "Battle of Sabine Pass," 364–65; "Dick Dowling Won."

18. Major General Magruder, CSA to General Cooper, September 27, 1863, *OR* 26, part 1: 305; Confederate States of America, *Compilation of The Messages and Papers* 1: 425–26; Davis, *Rise and Fall of The Confederate Government* 2: 239.

19. *Frank Leslie's Illustrated Newspaper* (New York), October 10, 1863, vol. 17, 39, c. 3.
20. Moore, *The Rebellion Record* 7: 426.
21. Johanette Stengler to Fritz Hankamer, September 15, 1863, HAAS.

CHAPTER 27

1. Major General Banks, USA, "The Texas Expedition," *OR* 26, part 1: 19; Lowe, *Texas Overland Expedition*, 27–31; General Halleck, USA, to Major General Banks, August 6, 1863, *OR* 26, part 1: 672; Townsend, "The Rio Grande Expedition," 21.
2. Lowe, *Texas Overland Expedition*, 25, 34–36; Banks, *OR* 26, part 1:19.
3. Company F morning reports, October 1863; Report of Major General Taylor, CSA, October 6, 1863, *OR* 26, part 1: 386.
4. Major General Franklin, USA, October 14 and 17, 1863, *OR* 26, part 1: 338–39.
5. Franklin, October 24 and November 1, 1863, *OR* 26, part 1, 340–41.
6. Edmonds, in "Surrender on the Bourbeux," noted that this battle is referred to in various sources as the Battle of Bayou Bourbeau, Bourbeux, or Bourbeaux and the Battle of Grand Coteau, Carrion Crow, or Carencro Bayou.
7. Report of Brigadier General Green, CSA, November 4, 1863, *OR* 26, part 1: 393–94; Lowe, *Texas Overland Expedition*, 73; Report of Colonel Guppey, USA, January 9, 1864, *OR* 26, part 1: 364; Edmonds, "Surrender on the Bourbeux," 63.
8. "Battle of Bourbeaux—Interesting Personal Narrative," Wisconsin Historical Society, November 9, 1863, https://www.wisconsinhistory.org/Records/Newspaper/BA14825; Guppey, *OR* 26, part 1: 364; For CSA feints the day before the battle, see Report of Brigadier General Burbridge, USA, *OR* 26, part 1: 359–60; Lowe, *Texas Overland Expedition*, 74–82.
9. Wisconsin Historical Society, "Battle of Bourbeaux."
10. Blessington, *Campaigns of Walker's Texas Division*, 138–45; Noel, *Campaign from Santa Fe*, 69; Walker, "Spaight's Battalion," 25; Washburn, *OR* 26, part 1: 357.
11. Union casualty figures in *OR* 26, part 1: 359; CSA casualty figures in *OR* 26, part 1: 395; Major General Washburn, USA, November 7, 1863, *OR* 26, part 1: 359; Major General Taylor, CSA, to Major General Magruder, November 4, 1863, OR 26, part 1: 391.
12. Brigadier General Green, CSA, to Major General Magruder, December 4, 1863, *OR* 26, part 2: 477; Company F morning report for November 9, 1863.
13. William Duncan to Celima Duncan, November 19, 1863, JDWC.
14. Report of Major General Banks, USA, November 7, 1863, *OR* 26, part 1: 396–97.
15. Major General Banks, USA, to Brigadier General Meigs, November 3, 1863, *OR* 26, part 1: 785; Major General Washburn, USA, to Banks, *OR* 26, part 1: 417; Banks to Major General Halleck, December 12, 1863, *OR* 26, part 1: 847.
16. Major General Magruder, CSA, to Lieutenant General Smith, November 27, 1863, *OR* 26, part 2: 448-449.
17. Green to Magruder, *OR* 26, part 2: 477.

18. Lieutenant Cunningham, CSA, to Major General Magruder, December 2, 1863, *OR* 26, part 2: 468.
19. Wm. Duncan diary, November 29-30, JDWC.
20. Wm. Duncan diary, November 30, December 2, 5, 7, 8, 12-13, 1863, JDWC.
21. Wm. Duncan diary, December 17, 1863, JDWC. Bayou Plaquemine Brulé is in southwest Louisiana, west of Lafayette.
22. Brigadier General Green, CSA, to Major General Magruder, December 17, 1863, *OR* 26, part 2: 512; Beecher, *Record of the 114th Regiment*, 280-84.
23. Wm. Duncan diary, December 17-21, 1863, JDWC.
24. Major General Magruder, CSA, to Brigadier General Green, December 15, 1863, *OR* 26, part 2: 508-09.
25. Wm. Duncan diary, December 21-31, 1863, JDWC.
26. Fort, *A Feast of Reason*, 141.
27. William Duncan to Celima Duncan, January 7, 1864, JDWC; Captain Turner, CSA, to Brigadier General Major, December 23, 1863, *OR* 26, part 2: 527.
28. Noel, *Campaign from Santa Fe*, 74.

CHAPTER 28

1. Civil War Muster Roll Index Cards and Compiled Military Service Records, TSLA. Charles Wilborn enlisted as a private in Company B, 2nd Brigade, Texas State Troops, on August 10, 1863, then served in a CSA unit. One source shows him in Company K, 21st Texas Infantry (Spaight's Regiment); Ladd, *Chambers County*, 140, 156.
2. Mina Wilborn to Fritz Hankamer, September 20, 1863, HAAS.
3. CSA Circular, December 3, 1863, *OR* 26, part 2: 474.
4. For CSA monthly pay see *OR*, series 4, vol. 1, section 1: 130; Johanette Stengler to Fritz Hankamer, September 20, 1863, HAAS.
5. Charles Wilborn to Mina Wilborn, from context appears to be mid-October 1863, AUTH.
6. Mina Wilborn to Fritz Hankamer, November 27, 1863, HAAS.
7. Edmund Turner, CSA, to Major Cave, December 3, 1863, *OR* 26, part 2: 472; Edmund Turner to Brigadier General Slaughter, December 3, 1863, *OR* 26, part 2: 474.
8. Major General Banks, USA, to Major General Halleck, December 12, 1863, *OR* 26, part 1: 847.
9. Mina Wilborn to Fritz Hankamer, December 18, 1863, HAAS.
10. Charles Wilborn to Mina Wilborn, January 26, 1864, AUTH.
11. Reports of Major General Washburn, USA, November 30-December 1, 1863, *OR* 26, part 1: 416-18; Arnold, "Fort Esperanza"; "The War in Texas, The Capture of Fort Esperanza," *New York Times*, December 27, 1863; Townsend, *Yankee Invasion of Texas*, 68-69.
12. Shorey, *Story of the Maine Fifteenth*, 62.
13. Raines, *Six Decades in Texas*, 532.
14. Brigadier General Bee, CSA, to Turner, November 21, 1863, *OR* 26, part 1: 437.
15. Washburn to Banks, *OR* 26, part 1: 418; Major General Washburn, USA, to

Brigadier General Stone, December 13, 1863, *OR* 26, part 1: 849; Townsend, "Rio Grande Expedition," 68–69.

16. Raines, *Six Decades in Texas*, 529–30.

17. Captain E. Turner, CSA, to Lieutenant Colonel Hutchins, December 20, 1863, *OR* 26, part 2: 517–18; Raines, *Six Decades*, 530–31.

18. Brigadier General Stone, USA, to Washburn, *OR* 26, part 1, 420; Banks to Halleck, *OR* 26, part 1: 847.

19. President Lincoln to Major General Banks, USA, December 24, 1863, Abraham Lincoln papers: Series 1. General Correspondence. Manuscript/Mixed Material. Library of Congress, https://www.loc.gov/item/mal2888000/; Shorey, *Story of the Maine Fifteenth*, 70.

20. Major General Banks, USA, to Secretary of War Stanton, April 6, 1865, *OR* 34, part 1: 194–96.

21. CSA Service Record for Charles Wilborn, TSLA; Undated letter from Mina Wilborn to one of her brothers. The context indicates it was written in mid-1864, HAAS.

CHAPTER 29

1. William Duncan to Celima Duncan, January 7, 1864, JDWC.

2. William Duncan to Celima Duncan, January 16, 1864, JDWC.

3. Company F morning report, February 1864; William Duncan to Celima Duncan, February 16, 1864, JDWC.

4. "Consolidated inspection report of the Trans-Mississippi Dept.," *OR* 22, part 2: 1132; "Eastern Texas Railroad [#1]," *Handbook of Texas*; Werner, "Railroads"; Chief Engineer Sulakowski, CSA, to J. Kellersberg, *OR* 26, part 2: 299.

5. Company F morning reports, February–April 1864; William Duncan to Celima Duncan, February 24, 1864, JDWC.

6. Company F morning report, April 6, 1864.

7. Company F morning report, April 10–13 and 20–30 and May 2, 1864.

8. Leatherwood, "Red River Campaign."

9. Company F morning reports, May 1864; Block, "Swamp Angels," 53.

10. Telegram to Magruder and Order of General Hebert to Colonel Griffin, *OR* 21: 895.

11. Company F morning reports, May 1864; Report of Colonel Griffin, CSA, May 11, 1864, *OR* 34, part 1: 912–14; Report of Rear Admiral Farragut, USN, May 18, 1864, *OR* 21: 247–64; Caudill, *Moss Bluff Rebel*, 107; Block, "Swamp Angels," 53.

12. Company F morning reports, May 1864; Lamar University, "Spindletop History."

13. William Duncan to Celima Duncan, June 22, 1864, JDWC.

14. Johanette Stengler to her sons, May 15, 1864, HAAS.

15. Company F Morning reports, April through November 1864.

16. Company F Morning reports, November 1864; John W. Hankamer diary, entries for November 1864, CCMW.

CHAPTER 30

1. Spaight, "History of Spaight's Regiment"; CSA organization in Texas, November 1864, *OR* 41, part 4: 1085; Camp Lubbock is described as "near Houston" in multiple issues of the *Houston Tri-Weekly Telegraph*, including July 17, 1863, May 11, 1863, and June 22, 1863, HHRC.

2. Johanette Stengler to Charles Hankamer and Fritz Hankamer, December 25, 1864, HAAS.

3. Cropley, "The 'Army Itch,'" 302–8; Sternberg, "Scabies—'Army Itch,'" 298; Bollet, *Civil War Medicine*, 324–25.

4. This account, "Larkin Mason's Report," was published in the *Saline [Michigan] Observer*, March 22, 1906, 2, c. 5, https://digmichnews.cmich.edu.

5. John W. Hankamer, January 20–February 15, 1865, CCMW.

6. Johanette Stengler to Fritz Hankamer, March 12, 1865, HAAS.

7. Company F morning reports for April 1865; Gentry, "Confederates and Cotton," 25–26; Smith, Mullins, and Medford, "Diary of H. C. Medford," 120; "Confederate Currency and Taxes," Texas State Library and Archives Commission, May 20, 2016, https://www.tsl.texas.gov/lobbyexhibits/civil-war-money.

8. Company F morning reports, April and May 1865.

9. General Smith to "Soldiers of the Trans-Mississippi Army," April 21, 1865, *OR* 48, part 2: 1284.

10. Special Orders No. 116, April 26, 1865, *OR* 48, part 2: 1287; John W. Hankamer diary, May 2, 1864, CCMW.

11. Major General Magruder to General Smith, CSA, May 16, 1865, *OR* 48, part 2: 1308.

12. William Duncan to Celima Duncan, May 11, 1865, JDWC; Wm. Duncan diary, May 11, 1865, JDWC.

13. William Duncan to Celima Duncan, May 17, 1865, JDWC; Wm. Duncan diary, May 16, 1865, JDWC.

14. CSA General Orders 48, May 18, 1865, *OR* 48, part 2: 1312; Gen. K. Smith, CSA, May 30, 1865, *OR* 48, pt. 1, sect. 1: 193; Surrender terms and approval, May 26, 1865, and June 2, 1865, *OR* 48, part 2: 600–01.

15. "Presidential Proclamation 157 of August 20, 1866," President Andrew Johnson. This proclamation concluded the Civil War. Library of Congress, accessed September 25, 2024, https://www.loc.gov/resource/rbpe.23600100/?sp=2&st=text.

CHAPTER 31

1. John W. Hankamer diary, May 23—24, 1865, CCMW.

2. Oxen are mentioned in six family letters, a diary entry for John W. Hankamer, and in the list of livestock owned by family members in the 1860 census. For the use of oxen in Texas during the mid-nineteenth century, see: Lanning, *Texas Cowboys*, 23, 105, and Roemer, *Texas*, 70–71.

3. Hankamer family files, CCMW; Chambers County, Texas, Deed Book Z, 197, CCCO; Liberty County, Texas, Deed Book D, 447, LCCO.

4. Hankamer family files, CCMW; Chambers County, Texas, Deed Book B, 278–80, CCCO; Olmsted, *Journey through Texas*, 375. "Witness trees" used to describe property corners in early deeds confirm there was timber on family land along Turtle Bayou, including oak, hickory, gum, and pine. For an example see Liberty County, Texas, Deed Book C, 145–46, LCCO.

5. Henson and Ladd, *Chambers County: A Pictorial History*, 71.

6. Frederick Hankamer Affidavit no. 6306, March 31, 1916, Deed Records 6: 404–05, CCCO.

7. Chambers County, Texas, Deed Record C: 194, CCCO.

8. Liberty County Deed Book D, 445–46, LCCO, shows this sale of 470 acres in southern Liberty County by John Stengler to his son John H. Stengler on August 25, 1876. The deed notes the tract was "bounded on the east by public land." Texas is still, to some extent, an "open range" state. See, "A summary of Texas Livestock Laws compiled by the Texas and Southwestern Cattle Ranchers Association," accessed September 24, 2024, http://tscra.org/what-we-do/theft-and-law/livestock-laws/; "Texas Stock Laws by County," Matthiesen, Wickert & Lehrer, S. C. website, January 13, 2022, https://www.mwl-law.com/wp-content/uploads/2020/01/TEXAS-STOCK-LAWS-BY-COUNTY.pdf; Gallaway, "Past Human Role," 25.

9. Chambers County, Texas, Deed Record A, 34, May 12, 1875, CCCO.

10. Liberty County, Texas, Deed Book C, 145, 40.83 acres, February 27, 1855; Charles Wilborn to John Stengler, 470 acres, Liberty County Deed Book D, 444, January 3, 1873; John Stengler to John H. Stengler, Liberty County Deed Book D, 445, August 25, 1876, LCCO.

11. John Stengler to Fritz Hankamer, July 29, 1864, HAAS; *Texas Almanac* for 1867 (Galveston: W. Richardson & Co., December 1866), 239; *Texas Almanac* for 1868, 215; *Texas Almanac* for 1869, 198; https://texasalmanac.com/archive. His signature on August 9, 1867, as "Register of Names and Residence of qualified electors of Liberty County," SHRL; "Texas County Tax Rolls, 1837–1910, Liberty County, image from Texas State Archives, Austin, Texas, https://familysearch.org/ark:/61903/3:1:939J-HMS7-YQ?wc=M63X-FP8%3A161654201%2C161397601&cc=1827575.

12. Chambers County, Texas, Deed Book A, 31, CCCO; Smith, *US Army and the Texas Frontier Economy*, 4; Moneyhon, *Texas After the Civil War*, 32; Dary, *Cowboy Culture*, 136.

13. Mina Wilborn to Fritz Hankamer, undated but from context appears to be in 1864, HAAS; Mina Wilborn to Fritz Hankamer, April 30, 1858, HAAS; William Duncan to Celima Duncan, April 21, 1863, JDWC.

14. Dary, *Cowboy Culture*, 129, 136–140.

15. Chambers County, Texas, Deed Book A, 127, CCCO. The property and livestock appear on the 1876 tax roll for Chambers County. Copies are in the Wilborn family files, CCMW.

16. Carroll Wilborn Jr. in interview with the author, January 2015, Anahuac, Texas.

17. Henson and Ladd, *Chambers County*, 75.

18. Centers for Disease Control, "Smallpox."
19. Henson and Ladd, *Chambers County*, 217.
20. John W. Hankamer, January 26, 1877, to his sister Mina Wilborn, AUTH.

CHAPTER 32

1. United States CDC, "Smallpox."
2. Handwritten will by Wilhelmina Wilborn dated December 1, 1887, CCCO; Liberty County, Texas, transcribed brand book 1, pages 7 and 8, SHRL.
3. George F. Wilborn obituary from area newspaper, 1932, copy in Wilborn family file, CCMW.
4. Harry, *History of Chambers County*, 199 and 201; "Family Honors Mr., Mrs. Wilborn on Their Anniversary," *Anahuac (Texas) Progress*, September 16, 1965; "Elwood A. Wilborn," *The Historical Encyclopedia of Texas*, Texas Historical Society, (year unknown), pg. 1127, copy in Wilborn family files, CCMW.
5. Elmore, "Sharing the Wealth"; Lesley Williams Brunet, "Alan Gregg and the Early Years of the Texas Medical Center," *The Houston Review* 12, no. 2 (1990): 96–112.
6. Newspaper clipping dated January 24, 1926, titled "Charles Hankamer, 90, of Sour Lake, Has Lived 84 years in South Texas," in the Hankamer family files, CCMW.
7. "Has Lived Eighty-Two Years in Texas," newspaper article published in "Anahuac, Chambers County (Texas)" in 1927, copy of clipping in Stengler family files, CCMW.
8. John Stengler autobiography, CCMW.

BIBLIOGRAPHY

Abbott, Peyton O. and S. B. Brush. "Business Travel Out of Texas During the Civil War: The Travel Diary of S. B. Brush, Pioneer Austin Merchant." *The Southwestern Historical Quarterly* 96, no. 2 (October 1992): 259–71.

Arnold, J. Barto. "Fort Esperanza." In *Handbook of Texas Online* (Texas State Historical Association). Updated January 1, 1995. https://www.tshaonline.org/handbook/entries/fort-esperanza.

Augustin, George. *History of Yellow Fever*. New Orleans: Searcy & Pfaff, 1909.

Bancroft, Hubert Howe. *History of The North Mexican States and Texas, 1531–1800*, vol. 1. San Francisco: A. L. Bancroft, 1884, 610.

Barnes, Joseph K. *The Medical and Surgical History of The War of The Rebellion*, part 1, vol. 1. Washington: Government Printing Office, 1870.

Barr, Alwyn. "Texas Coastal Defense, 1861–1865." *The Southwestern Historical Quarterly* 65, no. 1 (July 1961): 1–31.

Beecher, Harris H. *Record of the 114th Regiment*. Norwich, New York: J.F. Hubbard, 1866.

Bell, Andrew M. *Mosquito Soldiers: Malaria, Yellow Fever, and the Course of the American Civil War*. Baton Rouge: LSU Press, 2010.

Bell, Andrew M. "Trans-Mississippi Miasmas: Malaria & Yellow Fever Shaped the Course of the Civil War in the Confederacy's Western Theater." *East Texas Historical Journal* 47, no. 2, Article 6 (2009): 3–12, https://scholarworks.sfasu.edu/ethj/.

Benjamin, Gilbert G. "The Germans in Texas: A Study in Immigration 1909." Edited by Marion D. Learned. *American Germanica*, New Series, vol. 11. New York: D. Appleton, 1909.

Biesele, Rudolph Leopold. *The History of the German Settlements in Texas, 1831–1861*. Austin: Von Boeckmann-Jones, 1930.

Biggers, Don H. *German Pioneers in Texas: A Brief History of Their Hardships, Struggles and Achievements*. Fredericksburg, Texas: Fredericksburg Publishing Company, 1925.

Blessington, Joseph P. *The Campaigns of Walker's Texas Division . . . By a Private Soldier*. New York: Lange, Little & Co., 1875.

Block, W. T. "The Cottonclad Gunboat 'Uncle Ben': Cotton-Carrying Workhouse of the Sabine." W. T. Block Jr. website. October 24, 1974. http://www.wtblock.com/wtblockjr/uncleben.htm.

Block, W. T. "The Opelousas Trail: Bellowing Cows Marked First Trail to New Orleans." W. T. Block Jr. website. 1975. http://www.wtblock.com/wtblockjr/opelousa.htm.

Block, W. T. "Requiem for a Confederate Gunboat: The CSS Josiah H. Bell." W. T. Block Jr. website. April 1, 2003. http://www.wtblock.com/wtblockjr/josiah_h_bell.htm.

Block, W. T. "The Swamp Angels: A History of Spaight's 11th Battalion, Texas Volunteers, Confederate States Army." *East Texas Historical Journal* 30, no. 1, Article 10 (1992): 44–57, https://scholarworks.sfasu.edu/ethj/.

Bollet, Alfred Jay, MD. *Civil War Medicine*. Tucson, Arizona: Galen Press, 2002.

Bollet, Alfred Jay, MD. "The Major Infectious Epidemic Diseases of Civil War Soldiers." *Infectious Disease Clinics of North America* 18, no. 2 (June 2004): 293–309.

Boyce, Sir Rubert William. *Yellow Fever and Its Prevention: A Manual for Medical Students and Practitioners*. New York: E. P. Dutton, 1911.

Bright, David L. "Confederate Railroads." https://www.csa-railroads.com.

Briscoe, P. "The First Texas Railroad." *Southwestern Historical Quarterly* 7 (April 1904): 279–85.

Bronson, J. and R. Bronson. *Early American Weaving and Dyeing: The Domestic Manufacturer's Assistant and Family Directory in the Arts of Weaving and Dyeing*. New York: Dover Publications, 1977.

Brown, D. Clayton. "Medical Education." In *Handbook of Texas Online* (Texas State Historical Association). May 1, 1995. https://www.tshaonline.org/handbook/entries/medical-education.

Browning, Robert M. Jr. *Lincoln's Trident: The West Gulf Blockading Squadron During the Civil War*. Tuscaloosa: University of Alabama Press, 2015.

Bryan, Jimmy L. Jr. "'Whip them like the Mischief:' The Civil War Letters of Frank and Mintie Price." *East Texas Historical Journal* 36, no. 2 (1998): 68–84, https://scholarworks.sfasu.edu/ethj/.

Butler, Benjamin F. and Jessie Ames Marshall. *Private and Official Correspondence of Gen. Benjamin F. Butler, during the Period of the Civil War*, vol. 2. Norwood, MA: Plimpton Press, 1917.

Carrigan, Jo Ann. "The Saffron Scourge: A History of Yellow Fever in Louisiana, 1796–1905." PhD diss., Louisiana State University, 1961.

Caudill, Philip R. *Moss Bluff Rebel: A Texas Pioneer in the Civil War*. College Station: Texas A&M University Press, 2009.

Chambers, John Whiteclay. *The Oxford Companion to American Military History*. New York: Oxford University Press, 1999.

Charles, Harry K. Jr. "American Civil War Postage Due: North and South." Paper presented at the Postal History Symposium, Bellefonte, PA, November 2012. https://stamps.org/Portals/0/Symposium/CharlesSlides.pdf.

"City Population History from 1850–2000." *Texas Almanac*. Accessed September 26, 2024. https://texasalmanac.com/sites/default/files/images/CityPopHist%20web.pdf.

Company F, Spaight's Battalion, Morning Reports, Descriptive Rosters and Clothing Records, 1862–1865. Julia Duncan Welder Collection, Sam Houston Regional Library and Research Center, Texas State Library and Archives Commission, Liberty, TX.

Cook, Stephen C. "The Audacious Launch of the City of Houston: Capital of the Republic of Texas." *Southwestern Historical Quarterly* 121, no. 2, (October 2017): 139–41.

Cotham, Edward T. Jr. *Sabine Pass: The Confederacy's Thermopylae*. Austin: University of Texas Press, 2004.

Cox, James. *Historical and Biographical Record of the Cattle Industry and the Cattlemen of Texas and Adjacent Territory*. St. Louis: Woodward and Tiernan, 1895.

Crook, Carland Elaine. "Benjamin Théron and French Designs in Texas during the Civil War." *The Southwestern Historical Quarterly* 68, no. 4 (1965): 432–54.

Cropley, "The 'Army Itch:' a Dermatological Mystery of the American Civil War," *Journal of the American Academy of Dermatology* 55, no. 2 (August 2006): 302–8.

Dary, David. *Cowboy Culture: A Saga of Five Centuries*. New York: Alfred Knopf, 1981.

Davis, Jefferson. *The Rise and Fall of the Confederate Government*, vol. 2. New York: D. Appleton, 1881.

Davis, Larry E. "Unregulated Potions Still Cause Mercury Poisoning." *Western Journal of Medicine* 173, no. 1 (2000): 19.

Davis, William C. *The Fighting Men of the Civil War*. London: Salamander Books, 1999.

Day, James M. "Leon Smith: Confederate Mariner." *East Texas Historical Journal* 3, no. 1 (1965): 34–59.

De Bow, J. D. B., ed. "The City of Galveston." *The Commercial Review of the South and West* 3, no. 4 (April 1847): 348–349.

"Descriptive Roll of Company F, Spaight's Battalion, Texas Mounted Volunteers," JDWC.

"Dick Dowling Won," *The Galveston Daily News*, 52, no. 313, January 30, 1894. TPTH, Abilene Library Consortium.

Dobie, J. Frank. "The First Cattle in Texas and the Southwest Progenitors of the Longhorns." *The Southwestern Historical Quarterly* 42, no. 3 (January 1939): 171–97.

Dowell, Greensville. *Yellow Fever and Malarial Diseases Embracing A History Of The Epidemics Of Yellow Fever In Texas*. Philadelphia: Medical Publication Office, 1876.

Drummond, John A. "The Battle of Sabine Pass." *Confederate Veteran* 25, no. 8 (August 1917): 364–65.

Duncan, William B. Civil War diaries, 1862–1865, original and transcribed copies. JDWC.

Duncan, William B. Original letters to and from his wife Celima, 1862–1865. JDWC.

Dunt, Detlef. *Journey to Texas, 1833*. Edited by James C. Kearney and Geir Bentzen. Translated by Anders Saustrup. Austin: University of Texas Press, 2015.

Dupree, Stephen. *Planting the Union Flag in Texas: The Campaigns of Major General Nathaniel P. Banks in the West*. College Station: Texas A&M University Press, 2008.

"Eastern Texas Railroad [#1]." In *Handbook of Texas Online* (Texas State Historical Association). Updated August 1, 1995. https://www.tshaonline.org/handbook/entries/eastern-texas-railroad-1.

Edmonds, David C. "Surrender on the Bourbeux: Honorable Defeat or Incompetency under Fire." *Louisiana History: The Journal of the Louisiana Historical Association* 18, no. 1 (Winter 1977): 63–85.

Elmore, Barbara. "Sharing the Wealth: The Story of Oilman Earl Hankamer." *Baylor Business Review* 26, Issue 2 (Spring 2008): 32–37. https://www.proquest.com/docview/201181473.

Ellis, Robert, ed. *Official and Descriptive Catalogue of the Great Exhibition of the Works of Industry of all Nations,* vol. 2. London: Spicer Brothers, 1851.

Evans, Clement Anselm, ed. *Confederate Military History: A Library of Confederate States History*, vol. 11. Atlanta: Confederate Publishing Company, 1899.

Federal Writers' Project. "Jacob Branch." *Slave Narrative Project*, vol. 16, *Texas*, part 1. Washington, DC: Library of Congress, 1941, https://www.loc.gov/item/mesn161/.

Fiske, William Hooker. *A Visit to Texas: Being the Journal of a Traveller Through Those Parts Most Interesting to American Settlers*. New York: Goodrich and Wiley, 1834.

Fitzsimons, Bernard. *150 Years of North American Railroads*. Secaucus, New Jersey: Chartwell Books, 1982.

Ford, James, MD. "Alkalies in Bread." *The Cincinnati Lancet and Observer* 19 (1876): 44.

Fornell, Earl Wesley. "Island City: The Story of Galveston on the Eve of Secession, 1850–1860." PhD diss., Rice University, 1955.

Fort, Karen. *A Feast of Reason: The Civil War Journal of James Madison Hall*. Abilene, Texas: State House Press, 2017.

Franklin, Robert M. *Battle of Galveston, January 1st, 1863*. Galveston: The Galveston News, 1911.

Frazier, Donald S. *Cottonclads! The Battle of Galveston and the Defense of the Texas Coast*. Fort Worth: Ryan Place Publishers, 1996.

Fremantle, Lt. Col. *Three Months in The Southern States: April–June, 1863*. New York: John Bradburn, 1864.

Friend, Llerena. "Contemporary Newspaper Accounts of the Annexation of Texas." *The Southwestern Historical Quarterly* 49, no. 2 (October 1945): 267–81.

Gallaway, Alecya. "Past Human Role." In *The State of the Bay: A Characterization of the Galveston Bay Ecosystem,* 4th edition. Houston: Texas Commission on Environmental Quality, 2020. https://www.stateofgalvbay.org/overview/past-human-role#sec3-2.

Gard, Wayne. "Trinity River Navigation Projects." In *Handbook of Texas Online* (Texas State Historical Association). August 1, 1995. https://www.tshaonline.org/handbook/entries/trinity-river-navigation-projects.

Gen. N. P. West, 2nd Brigade, Texas Militia, to the Adjutant General, State of

Texas, January 9, 1862. Texas State Troops records, Civil War records, Texas Adjutant General's Department, Brigade Correspondence, 1861–1865, Box 401-825, TSLA.

Gen. N. P. West, 2nd Brigade, Texas Militia, to Gen. William Byrd, adjutant general, State of Texas, July 22, 1861. Texas State Troops records, Civil War records, Texas Adjutant General's Department, Brigade correspondence, 1861–1865. TSLA.

Gentry, Judy. "Confederates and Cotton in East Texas." *East Texas Historical Journal* 48, no. 1 (2010): 25–26, https://scholarworks.sfasu.edu/ethj/.

"German Emigration to Texas." *The Civilian and Galveston Gazette*. February 21, 1846, 8.

Geue, Chester, and Ethel. *A New Land Beckoned: German Immigration to Texas, 1844–1847*. Baltimore: Genealogical Publishing Company, 1982.

Gibson, Campbell. "Population of the 100 Largest Cities and Other Urban Places in The United States: 1790 to 1990." US Census Bureau, 1998. https://www.census.gov/library/working-papers/1998/demo/POP-twps0027.html.

Grear, Charles David. *Why Texans Fought in the Civil War*. College Station: Texas A&M University Press, 2012.

Hankamer, John William. Civil War Diary, transcribed pages and photocopy of original, CCMW.

Hankamer, Stengler, and Wilborn family papers, 1845–1877. Copies or translations of letters and other family documents are available at BCAH and CCMW.

Hardee, David Carlton. "Reminiscences of Texas as a Republic." *The Patron and Gleaner* (Rich Square, Northampton County, North Carolina), June 10, 1897, and July 8, 1897. SHRL.

Harry, Jewel H. *A History of Chambers County*. Dallas: Taylor Publishing Company, 1981.

Hart, John A. "History of Pioneer Days in Texas and Oklahoma." In *Pioneer Days in the Southwest from 1850 to 1879*, 143–44. Guthrie, Oklahoma: The State Capital Company, 1909.

Hasegawa, Guy R. "Quinine Substitutes in the Confederate Army." *Military Medicine* 172, no. 6 (June 2007): 650–5.

Hayes, Charles W. *History of the Island and the City of Galveston*. Austin: Jenkins Garrett Press, 1974.

Henson, Margaret, and Kevin Ladd. *Chambers County: A Pictorial History*. Norfolk, VA: Donning Company, 1988.

Hess, Earl J. *Civil War Infantry Tactics: Training, Combat, and Small-Unit Effectiveness*. Baton Rouge: LSU Press, 2015.

Hildreth, Peggy. "The Howard Association of Galveston: The 1850s, Their Peak Years." *East Texas Historical Journal* 17, no. 2 (1979): 33–44.

Holden, William Curry. *Alkali Trails, or, Social and Economic Movements of the Texas Frontier, 1846–1900*. Lubbock: Texas Tech University Press, 1998.

Houstoun, Matilda C. *Texas and the Gulf of Mexico, Yachting in the New World*, 2 vols. London: John Murray, 1844.

Humphreys, Margaret. *Yellow Fever and the South*. Baltimore: The Johns Hopkins University Press, 1999.

Jackson, Jim Bob. *They Pointed Them East First*. Houston: Kemp, 2008.

Jackson, Ralph Semmes. *Home on the Double Bayou: Memories of an East Texas Ranch*. Austin: University of Texas Press, 2013.

Jacobs, Joseph. "Some of the Drug Conditions During the War Between the States, 1861–5." *Southern Historical Society Papers* 33 (January-December 1905): 161–87.

Johnston, Joseph E. *Narrative of Military Operations: Directed, During the Late War Between the States by Joseph E. Johnston, General, CSA*. New York: D. Appleton, 1874.

J.O.L.O. Observatory Record Book, 1861, MSS-27–0701, Rosenberg Library, Galveston, Texas.

Jordan, Terry G. *German Seed in Texas Soil: Immigrant Farmers in Nineteenth-Century Texas*. Austin: University of Texas Press, 1966.

Keith, Captain K. D. "Military Operations, Sabine Pass." In *Burke's Texas Almanac and Immigrant's Guide for 1883*, 66–69. Houston: J. Burke, 1883.

Keith, K. D. "The Memoirs of Captain Kosciuszko D. Keith." *The Texas Gulf Historical and Biographical Record* 10, no. 1 (November 1974): 41–64.

Kellersberger, Getulius. "Memoirs of an Engineer in the Confederate Army in Texas." Translated by Helen S. Sundstrom. Undated typed copy at Briscoe Center for American History, University of Texas at Austin, call number T973.782/K286.Ts.

Kemp, L. W. "Atascosito Road." In *Handbook of Texas Online* (Texas State Historical Association). Updated April 18, 2017. https://www.tshaonline.org/handbook/entries/atascosito-road.

Kingsley, Karen. "Sabine Pass Lighthouse." In *SAH Archipedia*, edited by Gabrielle Esperdy and Karen Kingsley. https://sah-archipedia.org/buildings/LA-01-CM2.

Knight, Edward H. *American Mechanical Dictionary: A Description of Tools, Instruments, Machines, Processes, and Engineering*, vol. 3. Boston: Houghton, Mifflin and Company, 1884.

Ladd, Kevin, "The Andrew and Julia Weaver Family." August 2013. Center for Regional Heritage Research, Stephen F. Austin University. http://www.sfasu.edu/heritagecenter/7917.asp.

Ladd, Kevin. *Chambers County, Texas, in the War Between the States*. Baltimore: Gateway Press, 1994.

Lamar University. "Spindletop History." April 17, 2024. https://www.lamar.edu/spindletop-boomtown-museum/spindletop-history/index.html.

Lane, Lydia Spencer. *I Married a Soldier; or, Old Days in the Old Army*. Philadelphia: J. B. Lippincott, 1893.

Lanning, James, and Judy Lanning. *Texas Cowboys: Memories of the Early Days*. College Station: Texas A&M University Press, 1995.

Leatherwood, Art. "Red River Campaign." In *Handbook of Texas Online* (Texas State Historical Association). March 29, 2018. https://www.tshaonline.org/handbook/entries/red-river-campaign.

Lester, W. W., and William J. Bromwell. *A Digest of the Military and Naval Laws of the Confederate States.* Columbia, S.C.: Evans and Cogswell, 1864.

"Life of a Texas Woman During the War." *The Confederate Veteran Magazine* 14, no. 9 (September 1906): 422.

Love, Clara M. "History of the Cattle Industry in the Southwest, II." *The Southwestern Historical Quarterly* 20, no. 1 (July 1916): 1–18.

Lowe, Richard. *The Texas Overland Expedition of 1863.* Fort Worth, Texas: Ryan Place Publishers, 1996.

Martin, Madeleine. "Niblett's Bluff." In *Handbook of Texas Online* (Texas State Historical Association). Updated March 23, 2019. https://www.tshaonline.org/handbook/entries/nibletts-bluff.

Mastin, Claudius H., M. D. "The Medical Profession in the Civil War." *Southern Historical Society Papers* 13 (January-December 1885): 476–80.

Matthews, James M., ed. *Public Laws of the Confederate States of America, First Congress, 1862–1864.* Richmond, VA: R. M. Smith, Printer, 1864.

Moneyhon, Carl H. *Texas After the Civil War: The Struggle of Reconstruction.* College Station: Texas A&M University Press, 2004.

Moore, Albert Burton. *Conscription and Conflict in the Confederacy.* New York: The Macmillan Company, 1924.

Moore, Frank, ed. *The Rebellion Record: A Diary of American Events* 6. New York: G. P. Putnam, 1863.

Moore, Frank, ed. *The Rebellion Record: A Diary of American Events* 7. New York: D. Van Nostrand, 1864.

Morison, Samuel Eliot, ed. *Journals and Other Documents on the Life and Voyages of Christopher Columbus.* New York: Heritage Press, 1963.

Moulis, G., and G. Martin-Blondel. "Scrofula, the King's Evil." *CMAJ: Canadian Medical Association Journal* 184, no. 9 (2012): 1061.

Muir, Andrew Forest. "Railroads Come to Houston, 1857–61." *The Southwestern Historical Quarterly* 64 (July 1960–April 1961): 48–63.

Murray, J. *A Handbook for Travellers on the Continent: Being a Guide Through Holland, Belgium, Prussia, and Northern Germany.* 5th ed. London: John Murray, 1845.

Nance, Joseph Milton, and Joseph Eve. "A Letter Book of Joseph Eve, United States Chargé d' Affaires to Texas, Part III." *The Southwestern Historical Quarterly* 43, no. 4 (April 1940): 486–510.

National Archives and Records Service. *Population Schedules of The Seventh Census of The United States, 1850, roll M432-912, Texas, Liberty County.*

National Archives and Records Service. *Population Schedules of The Eighth Census of The United States, 1860, roll M653-1291, Texas, vol. 3, Chambers County.*

National Archives and Records Service. *Population Schedules of The Eighth Census of The United States, 1860, roll M-653-1300, Texas, vol. 7, Liberty County.*

Nixon, Pat Ireland, M. D. *The Medical Story of Early Texas, 1528–1853.* Lancaster, Pennsylvania: Mollie Bennett Lupe Memorial Fund, 1946.

Noel, Theo. *A Campaign from Santa Fe to the Mississippi: Being a History of the Old Sibley Brigade from Its First Organization to the Present Time.* Shreveport, LA: Shreveport News Printing, 1865.

Oates, Stephen B. *Confederate Cavalry West of the River*. Austin: University of Texas Press, 1961.

Olmsted, Frederick Law. *Journey Through Texas, or, A Saddle-trip on the Southwestern Frontier: With a Statistical Appendix*. New York: Dix, Edwards & Co., 1857.

Parker, A. A. *Trip to the West and Texas: Comprising a Journey of Eight Thousand Miles, Through New-York, Michigan, Illinois, Missouri, Louisiana, and Texas*. 2nd ed. Concord, NH: W. White, 1836.

Partlow, Miriam. *Liberty, Liberty County, and the Atascosito District*. Austin: The Pemberton Press, 1974.

Patterson, K. D. "Yellow fever epidemics and mortality in the United States, 1693-1905." *Social Science and Medicine* 34, no. 8 (April 1992): 855-65.

Pellet, Elias Porter. *History of the 114th Regiment, New York State Volunteers*. Norwich, NY: Telegraph and Chronicle Power Press Printing, 1866.

Pickett, Arlene. *Historic Liberty County*. Dallas: Tardy Publishing Co. 1936.

Qualls, Wanda. "Passenger List for the Barque *Harriet*." Gillespie County Historical Society. Accessed September 24, 2024. http://www.rootsweb.ancestry.com/~txgilles/s-harr.html.

Ragan, Cooper K. "The Diary of Captain George W. O'Brien, 1863." *The Southwestern Historical Quarterly* 67, no. 1 (July 1963): 28-54.

Raines, C. W., ed. *Six Decades in Texas, or Memoirs of Francis Richard Lubbock*. Austin: Ben C. Jones & Company, 1900.

Reid, Thomas R. "The Confederate Shoemakers of Town Bluff, Texas." *East Texas Historical Journal* 44, no. 1 (2006): 35-39, https://scholarworks.sfasu.edu/ethj/.

Reilly, Robert F, M. D. "Medical and Surgical Care During the American Civil War, 1861-1865." *Baylor University Medical Center Proceedings* 29, no. 2 (April 2016): 138-42.

Report of the Secretary of the Navy with an Appendix Containing Reports from Officers. Washington: Government Printing Office, December 1863.

Revels, Tracy J. *Grander in Her Daughters: Florida's Women During the Civil War*. Columbia, SC: The University of South Carolina Press, 2004.

Richardson, James D., comp., *A Compilation of the Messages and Papers of The Confederacy: Including the Diplomatic Correspondence, 1861-1865*, vol. 1. Nashville: United States Publishing Company, 1905.

Ripley, Eliza McHatton. *From Flag to Flag: A Woman's Adventures and Experiences in the South During the War, in Mexico, and in Cuba*. New York: D. Appleton and Company, 1889.

Roemer, Ferdinand Dr. *Texas, With Particular Reference to German Immigration and the Physical Appearance of the Country: Described Through Personal Observation*. Bonn: 1849. Translated by Oswald Mueller. San Antonio: Standard Printing Company, 1935.

Rollins, Ashton. *The Cowboy: An Unconventional History of Civilization on the Old-time Cattle Range*. Norman: University of Oklahoma Press, 1997.

Rommel, George M. "American Breeds of Beef Cattle," *United States Bureau of Animal Industry Bulletin* no. 34. Washington: Government Printing Office, 1902.

Rosenberg, William von. "*Kritik*: A History of the Society for the Protection of German Immigrants to Texas." Translated by Louis E. Brister. *Southwestern Historical Quarterly* 85, no. 2 (October 1981): 162.

Sartin, J. S. "Infectious Diseases During the Civil War: The Triumph of the 'Third Army.'" *Clinical Infectious Diseases* 16, no. 4 (April 1993): 580–4.

Seale, William. "River People," *East Texas Historical Journal* 5, no. 1 (1967): 47.

Semmes, Raphael. *Memoirs of Service Afloat During the War Between the States*. Baltimore: Kelly, Piet, and Co., 1869.

Shorey, Henry A. *The Story of the Maine Fifteenth: Being a Brief Narrative of the More Important Events in the History of the Fifteenth Maine Regiment*. Bridgton, ME.: Press of the Bridgton News, 1890.

Sibley, Marilyn M. *Travelers in Texas: 1761–1860*. Austin: University of Texas Press, 1967.

Simpson, Harold B., and Marcus J. Wright. *Texas in the War: 1861–1865*. Hillsboro, Texas: Hill Junior College Press, 1965.

Smith, Justin Harvey. *The War with Mexico*, vol. 1. New York: Macmillan, 1919.

Smith N. H. to M. G. Howe, August 26, 1863, in the Milton G. Howe Papers, Box 2E, 256, BCAH.

Smith, Ralph J. *Reminiscences of the Civil War*. Waco, Texas: W. M. Morrison, 1911.

Smith, Rebecca W., Marion Mullins, and H. C. Medford. "The Diary of H. C. Medford, Confederate Soldier, 1864." *The Southwestern Historical Quarterly* 34, no. 2 (October 1930): 106–40.

Smith, Thomas T. *The US Army and the Texas Frontier Economy: 1845–1900*. College Station: Texas A&M University Press, 1999.

Soper, Fred L. M.D. "The Newer Epidemiology of Yellow Fever," *American Journal of Public Health* 27, no. 1 (January 1937): 1.

Spaight, Ashley to Col. J. Y. Dashiell, adjutant general of Texas, March 10, 1862, and April 17, 1862. Brigade Correspondence, Texas State Troops records, Civil War records, Texas Adjutant General's Department, 1861–1865, Texas State Library and Archives, Austin, Texas.

Spaight, Ashley W. "History of Spaight's Regiment, Texas Volunteer Infantry," March 4, 1865. Ashley Wood Spaight Papers, urn:taro:utexas.cah.02381, BCAH.

Spaight, Ashley W. "Muster Roll of Captain Spaight's Cavalry Company (Moss Bluff Rebels)." Ashley Wood Spaight papers, urn:taro:utexas.cah.02381, BCAH.

Spaulding, Lily May, and John Spaulding. *Civil War Recipes: Receipts from the Pages of Godey's Lady's Book*. Lexington: University Press of Kentucky, 2013.

Stengler, Hankamer and Wilborn family papers, 1845–1877. Copies or translations of letters and other family documents are available at BCAH and CCMW.

Stengler, Johann. Immigration Agreement with the Society for the Protection of German Immigrants in Texas, October 30, 1845, copy of translation from the German, SOPH.

Stengler, Johann. "Story of the Voyage from Dietz, Prussia, to Texas in 1845," in a journal translation in Stengler family files, CCMW.

Stengler, Johann. Letters to the Society for the Protection of German Immigrants in Texas at Mainz, October 3, 1845, and mid-October 1845. Johann Stengler Papers, camh-arc-004979, BCAH.

Stengler, John. "Autobiography." In *Anahuac (Texas) Progress*, February 10, 1910.

Stephens, A. Ray. *Texas: A Historical Atlas*. Norman: University of Oklahoma Press, 2014.

Sternberg, G. "Scabies—"Army Itch." *The Medical and Surgical Reporter (Philadelphia)* vol. 14 (April 14,1866): 298. https://archive.org/details/medicalsurgical r1866phil.

Steuart, Richard D. "Gun Manufacturing During the Civil War." In *Handbook of Texas Online* (Texas State Historical Association). Updated January 23, 2020. https://www.tshaonline.org/handbook/entries/gun-manufacturing-during-the-civil-war.

Struve, Walter. *Germans and Texans*. Austin: University of Texas Press, 1996.

Switzler, Wm. F. *Report on the Internal Commerce of the United States*. Washington, DC: US Government Printing Office, 1886.

"Texas Cattle Raising." *Harper's Weekly*, October 19, 1867: 665.

Texas General Land Office. "Buffalo Bayou, Brazos, and Colorado—the First Railroad in Texas." 2016. https://medium.com/save-texas-history/buffalo-bayou-brazos-and-colorado-the-first-railroad-in-texas-a1ff662f72b.

Texas General Land Office. "History of Texas Public Lands." 2018. https://www.glo.texas.gov/history/archives/forms/files/history-of-texas-public-lands.pdf.

Texas General Land Office. *Map of Liberty County, Texas, 1879*. St. Louis: August Gast & Co, 1879. https://www.loc.gov/item/2012590031/.

Texas Medical Board. "Texas Medical Board History." Accessed September 24, 2024. http://www.tmb.state.tx.us/page/medical-board-history.

Texas State Library and Archives Commission. "The Railroads Come to Texas," 1–3. April 3, 2024. https://www.tsl.texas.gov/exhibits/railroad/index.html.

Thompson, Robert Means, and Richard Wainwright, eds. *Confidential Correspondence of Gustavus Vasa Fox, Assistant Secretary of the Navy, 1861–1865*. New York: De Vinne Press, 1918.

Tiling, Moritz. *History of The German Element in Texas from 1820–1850*. Houston: Moritz Tiling, 1913.

Tolbert, Frank X. *Dick Dowling at Sabine Pass*. New York: McGraw-Hill Book Company, 1962.

Townsend, Stephen A. "The Rio Grande Expedition 1863–1865." PhD diss., University of North Texas, 2001.

Townsend, Stephen A. *The Yankee Invasion of Texas*. College Station: Texas A&M University Press, 2006.

Traylor, Ronald D. "Liberty and Slavery: The Peculiar Institution in Liberty (and Chambers) County, Texas." *East Texas Historical Journal* 49, no. 1 (2011): 109–34.

United States Bureau of Topographic Engineers. "Map of Texas and Part of New Mexico, compiled chiefly for military purposes." New York: H. F. Walling, 1857. HHRC.

United States Centers for Disease Control and Prevention. "Smallpox." 2017. https://www.cdc.gov/smallpox/index.html

United States Naval History and Heritage Command. "USS *Morning Light*." August 11, 2015. https://www.history.navy.mil/research/histories/ship-histories/danfs/m/morning-light-8-gun-ship.html.

United States Naval History and Heritage Command. "USS *Velocity*." Accessed September 27, 2024. https://www.history.navy.mil/content/history/nhhc/research/histories/ship-histories/confederate_ships/velocity.html.

United States Naval War Records Office. *Official Records of the Union and Confederate Navies in the War of the Rebellion*, 30 vols. Washington, DC: Government Printing Office, 1894–1922. All references from this source are from volumes in Series 1 unless otherwise noted.

United States Postal Service. "Mail Service and the Civil War."Accessed September 27, 2024. https://about.usps.com/news/national-releases/2/pr12_civil-war-mail-history.pdf.

United States Sanitary Commission. *Report of a Committee of the Associate Members of The Sanitary Commission, on the Subject of the Nature and Treatment of Yellow Fever*. New York: Wm. C. Bryant, 1862.

United States War Department. *The War of the Rebellion: A Compilation of the Official Records of the Union and Confederate Armies*. 128 vols. Washington: Government Printing Office, 1880–1901. All references from this source are from volumes in Series 1 unless otherwise noted.

Van Zant, Jennifer. "Confederate Conscription and the North Carolina Supreme Court." *The North Carolina Historical Review* 72, no. 1 (1995): 54–75.

Vogel, Christian. Letter to family members in Germany, February 18, 1846, typed transcription in Solms-Braunfels archives, vol. 5:41–45, SOPH.

Volanto, Keith J., and Gene B. Preuss. "When was the Republic of Texas No More? Revisiting the Annexation of Texas." *Southwestern Historical Quarterly* 123, no. 1 (July 2019): 32–59.

Wagner, Margaret E., Gary W. Gallagher, and Paul Finkelman, eds. *The Library of Congress Civil War Desk Reference*. New York: Simon and Schuster, 2002.

Walker, Charles R. "Spaight's Battalion, CSA." *Texas Gulf Historical and Biographical Record* 8, no. 1 (November 1972): 25.

Weddle, Robert S. *Changing Tides: Twilight and Dawn in the Spanish Sea, 1763–1803*. College Station: Texas A&M University Press, 1995.

Werner, George C. "Railroads." In *Handbook of Texas Online* (Texas State Historical Association). Updated October 27, 2017. https://www.tshaonline.org/handbook/entries/railroads.

Whitehead, John. "How Have American Historians Viewed the Frontier?" Presented at the Meeting of Frontiers Conference, Fairbanks, Alaska, May 2001. https://www.loc.gov/rr/european/mofc/whitehead.html.

Wiggins, Melanie. "Combating Yellow Fever in Galveston, 1839–1905." *Southwestern Historical Quarterly* 119, no. 3 (January 2016): 236–52.

Wilborn, Stengler, and Hankamer family papers, 1845–1877. Copies or translations of letters and other family documents are available at BCAH and CCMW.

Wiley, Bell Irvin. *The Life of Johnny Reb: The Common Soldier of the Confederacy.* New York: Bobbs-Merrill Company, 1943.

Williams, Edward B., ed. *Rebel Brothers: The Civil War Letters of the Truehearts.* College Station: Texas A&M University Press, 1995.

Williams, Edward B. "A 'Spirited Account' of the Battle of Galveston, January 1, 1863." *The Southwestern Historical Quarterly* 99, no. 2 (October 1995): 200–15.

Williams, Howard C. "Texas and New Orleans Railroad." In *Handbook of Texas Online* (Texas State Historical Association). Updated May 14, 2020. https://www.tshaonline.org/handbook/entries/texas-and-new-orleans-railroad.

Winningham, Geoff. *Traveling the Shore of the Spanish Sea: The Gulf Coast of Texas and Mexico.* College Station: Texas A&M University Press, 2010.

Winsor, Bill. *Texas in the Confederacy: Military Installations, Economy and People.* Hillsboro, Texas: Hill Jr. College Press, 1978.

Winters, John D. *The Civil War in Louisiana.* Baton Rouge: LSU Press, 1991.

Wishart, David J. *Encyclopedia of the Great Plains.* Lincoln: University of Nebraska Press, 2004.

Woodman, David Jr. *Guide to Texas Emigrants.* Boston: M. Hawes, 1835.

Wooster, Ralph A. *Texas and Texans in the Civil War.* Austin, Texas: Eakin Press, 1995.

Wooster, Ralph A., and Robert Wooster. "A People at War: East Texans during the Civil War." *East Texas Historical Journal* 28, no. 1 (1990): 3–16, https://scholarworks.sfasu.edu/ethj/.

Wooster, Robert. "Aurora, TX (Jefferson County)." In *Handbook of Texas Online* (Texas State Historical Association). Updated November 1, 1994. https://www.tshaonline.org/handbook/entries/aurora-tx-jefferson-county.

Wooster, Robert. "Sabine Pass, TX." In *Handbook of Texas Online* (Texas State Historical Association). Updated February 5, 2019. https://www.tshaonline.org/handbook/entries/sabine-pass-tx.

INDEX

Abshier, Benjamin, 87
Abshire, B., 230
Abshire, Mrs., 108
Alabama, CSS, 135–36, 180
Anahuac, 24, 26, 52, 231
Anahuac Progress, 252–53
annexation of Texas, 16, 23
Antwerp, Belgium, 10, 11, 12–13
Arizona, USS, 181, 183, 185
Arkansas, 222
army itch, 221–22
Atascosito Road/Trail, 73, 263n10
Atchafalaya River, 164, 165
Aurora (Sparks), 99, 270n1 (ch 16)

Banks, Nathaniel P. (Louisiana successes), 160
Banks, Nathaniel P. (Texas invasion plans): advancement caution, 210–12; Brownsville occupation, 192; Galveston Island occupation, 204–205; on lack of reinforcements, 133; on loss of Galveston, 133; Louisiana land campaign, 188. *See also* Sabine Pass, Union retaking plan
Barrow, Elizabeth, 28
barter system, 112
Baton Rouge, 160
Baxter, C., 111–12, 156
Baylor, George W., 161
Baylor Business Review, 248–49
Baylor University, 249
Bayou Bourbeau, 188–90, 278n6
Bayou City, 125, 130
Bayou Serpent, 197
Bayou Teche, 160, 188
Beaumont (the town): rail service, 55, 56–57, 58, 73, 174, 214–15; sick soldiers, 161; yellow fever, 91, 94
Bee, General, 210
beeves. *See* cattle operations
Bell, CSS, 138, 139, 140–41
Bell, H. H., 133–34, 135–36, 140
Berwick Bay, 191
Berwick's Bay, 164
Bingel, C., 87
Bingel, Carl, 9–10
Bingle, Christian, 64, 69, 266n12
biscuit-making, 47
blockade runners, 78, 97, 123, 152
Bolivar Point, 43
Branch, Jacob, 129
Brashear City, 164, 165, 188
Brazos Island, 192
Brazos River, 54, 73, 199
bricks, Galveston, 17, 22
Brooklyn, USS, 133–34
Brownsville, 192, 205
Buckner, Simon, 230
Buffalo Bayou, 8, 127
Buffalo Bayou, Brazos, and Colorado Railway, 54
Bureau of Topographic Engineers, 40–41
Burr's Ferry, 215
Butler, B. F., 124–25
butter prices, 157

Calcasieu Pass, 216
Calcasieu River, 197
Camp Lubbock, 82, 215, 219–20, 225
Camp Texas, 161, 163
candle making, 49, 110–11, 225, 264n15
cane for weaving, 50–51

carpentry work, 36
Carrion Crow Bayou, 189
Carter's Station, 57, 58, 198, 205, 222
cattle operations: during Civil War, 166–67, 208; drives to markets, 39–40, *42, 43, 75*; on Hankamer/Stengler farms, 226; military-oriented surveys, 40–41; role of wild cattle, 37–39, 98, 238; roundups, 39, 42–43; Spanish activity, 37; taxation system, 38–39, 41; Texas heritage, 1
Cavallo, USS, 131
Cayuga, USS, 182
Cedar Bayou, 57
census records: birth origins, 28, 60, 265n1 (ch 9); livestock statistics, 32, 44; occupations, 30, 41, 235, 250–51; unmarried women, 32. *See also* population statistics
Chambers County: creation of, 33; Hankamer properties, 233, 234; occupations, 85; secession votes, 60; smallpox epidemic, 244–45; Wilborn property, 34, 243
chickens and eggs, 35, 46, 48, 120, 156, 221, 242
Chinquapin Oak, 50
Chisholm Trail, 40
Chism, Annie (later Hankamer), 235, 246
Christmas, 119–21, 126, 197, 220–21, 244
The Civilian and Galveston Gazette, 13, 19, 22–23
Clear Creek, railroad bridge, 228
Clifton, USS, 126, 134, 136, 181, 182, 183, 185
cloth/clothing: care packages, 170, 193, 225; issued at enlistment, 106; from reeds, 50–51; requests for, 106
coffee, 76, 112, 157, 203, 205, 249
Columbia, Texas, 198–99
Company A, 95, 152, 154, 161
Company B, 91, 132, 138, 279n1
Company E, 90

Company F: advantages of Texas assignments, 170; Christmas, 119–20; Eagle Grove camp, 152–59; Galveston assignment, 151–52; illness and disease, 160–61, 167, 221–22, 276n1 (ch 24); members characterized, 68–69; news from Galveston battle, 132–33; official designation, 75; railroad bridge defense, 95, 99–103; Sabine Pass assignments, 69–70, 73, 94, 95–96; substitute hiring, 148; temporary disbandment, 91–94. *See also* Grigsby's Bluff; Hankamer *entries;* Moss Bluff Rebels
Company F, Louisiana assignments: absent soldier problem, 158; Bayou Bourbeau battle, 188–90; cattle operations, 166–67, 203; mail problem, 168, 171–72; map, *162;* renegades problem, 163; report on countryside devastation, 164, 175; return to Texas, 195–98; rumors about, 157, 193, 194–95; skirmish strategy, 188–90; travel to, 158–61, 163; and Union battle successes, 164–65
Company F, after return to Texas: disbanding after surrender news, 230–31; Galveston assignment, 227–29; Lake Charles assignment, 216; order changes, 213–14, 215, 219; railroad work, 214–15; Sabine Pass guarding, 219; Spindletop camp, 216–19; tithe collection duty, 226–27
Concord, 144
conscription, Confederate States, 62, 115–16, 117, 145
conscripts/renegades, 163
corn crops: in barter system, 112; in coffee substitutes, 112; Confederate shortages, 76, 152, 163, 197; in Duncan's care package, 120; Hankamer farms, 36, 111, 117, 233; Saltgrass Prairie suitability, 26; Stengler farm, 46, 48, 111, 226; Union

shortages, 210; Wilborn farm, 35, 47, 111, 148, 208–209
cornmeal, 47, 76, 156, 212
Corpus Christi, 192, 205, 210
cotton-clad gunboats, 125, 130–31, 137–38, 140
cotton shipments, 70, 114
cows, on Hankamer/Stengler farms, 226
Crackersneck, 33, 57
Criswell, A. J., 69
Crocker, Frederick, 92, 102, 114, 178, 180, 181–83
Crossed W brand, 38

Dan, USS, 102
Dane, Henry C., 184–85, 186
Dashiell, J. Y., 63
Davis, Jefferson, 186–87
Davis Guards, Fort Griffin, 185
Dawson, Berta Mary Wilborn, ix–x
death rates, German emigrants, 21. *See also* disease
Debray, X. B., 92, 93, 94, 96, 97, 98
desertions, 191–92, 228, 230
Dickinson Bayou, railroad bridge, 228
diets, 45–46, 154, 155, 167, 217
Dietz, Germany, 5, 11, 259n1
disease: among stranded emigrants, 21; lowland vulnerabilities, 30; post-Civil War, 243, 244–46; soldiers, 76–77, 80–81, 154–55, 157–58, 206, 221–22; Wilborn household, 149
diseases, specific: malaria, 81, 82; measles, 154–55, 157; scabies, 221–22; smallpox, 88–89, 244–46; yellow fever, 78–82, 89–91, 268n3
Double Bayou, 29, 32, 129, 243–44
Dowling, Dick, 177, 182, 185, 186
Duncan, Celima, 89, 169, 171
Duncan, George C., 75, 95
Duncan, William B.: background, 40, 75; on Christmas, 120, 197; courier service, 193, 194; election as captain, 75; envelope making, 169; furlough for illness, 167; on oyster aftermath, 154; on return travel conditions, 196, 197, 198; Sabine Pass news, 92; troop relocation order, 98; on weather conditions, 105, 194
Duncan, William B. (correspondence topics): care package appreciation, 171; chicken farming suggestion, 156; Company F's performance, 70; Louisiana *vs.* Texas assignments, 192; Magruder's Galveston speech, 229; mail delivery plan, 171–72; reassignment potential, 214; return plans, 195, 198; Spindletop camp, 217; surrender news, 230; Taylor's Bayou bridge, 100, 101; vaccination program, 89; weapons request, 68
dyes for cloth, 50, 106–107

Eagle, Henry, 70–71
Eagle Grove camp, 152–57
Eastern Texas Railroad, 59, 73, 214–15
eggs and chickens, 35, 46, 120, 156, 221, 242
Elias Pike, USS, 131
11th (Spaight's Battalion), designation of, 75. *See also* Company F *entries;* Spaight's *entries*
eye problems, Wilborn household, 149

farming: Saltgrass Prairie suitability, 25–26; weather challenges, 47, 109, 208, 225–26. *See also* cattle operations; corn crops; livestock; potato crops
Farragut, D. G., 114, 124, 133, 136, 142
fiddle request, F. Hankamer's, 105
Fifteenth Main Regiment, 209–10
figs, 46, 47
Fisher and Millers Colony, 24
fishing and hunting, 26, 46–47
1st Texas Cavalry (U.S.), 124–25
fleas, 154
Florilda, CSS, 219
flour prices, 155–56, 157

42nd Massachusetts Volunteer Regiment, 126
football reference, Galveston evacuation, 71, 267n18
Fort Esperanza, 209
Fort Griffin, 175–76, 182–83, 214
Fort Hudson surrender, 164–65
Fort Point raid, 97
Fort Sabine evacuation, 91–92, 176. *See also* Sabine Pass *entries*
Fort Sumter, 60
Fourth Texas Cavalry, 198–99
Fox, Gustavus V., 124, 132
France, 173, 222
Frank Leslie's Illustrated Newspaper, 131, 187
Franklin, William B., 178, 181, 183, 188-89
Fremantle, Arthur, 54, 62, 159

Galveston, before Civil War: as cattle market, 43; cotton shipments, 70; descriptions of, 17–19; F. Hankamer's move to, 34–36; rail service, 55, 58–59, 73; Stengler family arrival, 14–17, 21; supply importance, 45, 70
Galveston, Confederate retaking: battle aftermath, 129, 134, 136; impact on Union commander, 132; Magruder's troop review, 228–29; plan and attack, 125–32; reports about, 132–33, 142; timing significance, 127, 133; troop reinforcement, 151–52, 204
Galveston, shoe prices during Civil War, 109–10, 153
Galveston, Union arrival: blockade action, 61, 97, 105, 123–24; Confederate expectations, 61; correspondence about, 119; evacuation of, 71, 113, 123; land-based troops, 123–25, 126–27; strategic value for Union, 132; surrender demands, 70–71, 97, 114; yellow fever's impact, 97. *See also* Sabine Pass *entries*
Galveston, Union retaking effort, 133–36
Galveston, Houston, and Henderson Railroad Company, 58–59
Galveston Drug Store, 19
Galveston Island, 59, 204–205
Galveston Weekly News, 79, 105, 112, 115
General Banks, USS, 183, 186
German immigrants, generally: appeal of Texas, 1–2, 5–6, 7–8, 12–13; statistics, 13, 20, 21. *See also* Verein zum Schutze . . . in Texas
Goose Creek, 29
Gottshuz, George, 13
Granite City, USS, 180, 181, 183, 186, 216
Grant, Ulysses S., 212
Green, Thomas, 190, 191–93, 195, 196
Griffin, W. H., 216
Griffin's Battalion, 220
Grigsby's Bluff, 73, 90, 94, 95, 98, 99,
Gulf of Mexico, 14, 115, 135–36, 175

Haas, Clara, ix–x
Haas, Oscar, ix–x
Halleck, Henry, 212
Hankamer, Annie (earlier Chism), 235, 246
Hankamer, Charles: anglicization of name, 22; correspondence with brother, 34–36, 43; education, 29; farm life, 28; land purchase, 34; marriage, 34; on Mexican War threat, 24; physical description, 68; work with Wilborn, 42–43
Hankamer, Charles (Civil War service): cattle herding duty, 203; clothing issue, 106; correspondence from mother, 220–21; correspondence to unnamed recipients, 82, 109, 157; correspondence with brothers, 96, 226; illness, 111, 160–61; leadership positions, 69, 218, 227; leaves/furloughs, 208, 226; military sign up, 64–65; Sabine Pass camp, 73;

Index

tithe collection duty, 226–27; during yellow fever outbreak, 91

Hankamer, Charles (correspondence to sister): camp conditions, 76, 155; cattle herding assignment, 166–67; conscription of C. Wilborn, 117–18, 144; election of captain, 75; farm assistance of C. Wilborn, 116–17, 148; Galveston status, 119; illness in camp, 86, 154–55; lack of mail, 167–68, 170; Louisiana assignment, 166–67; paper shortage, 168; Sabine Pass status, 73, 119, 138–39; shoe prices, 153; wartime expectations, 76–77. *See also* Wilborn, Mina (correspondence to brothers)

Hankamer, Charles (post-Civil War): civic service, 248; correspondence with brothers, 234; farm activity, 234; household routine, 248–49; photo of, *250*; remarriage, 248; timber activity, 234–35

Hankamer, Earl C., 248–49

Hankamer, Ellen, 68

Hankamer, Frederick Adolph, 12, 22. *See* Hankamer, Fritz *entries*

Hankamer, Fritz (before Civil War): in family cattle operations, 43; hatmaking, 50; move to Galveston, 34–36; physical description, 68. *See also* Stengler family, emigration journey

Hankamer, Fritz (Civil War service): correspondence from brother, 96, 163, 226; correspondence to parents, 104, 119; correspondence to sister, 46–47, 157–58, 165; exemption request for C. Wilborn, 148–49; illness, 64–65, 82, 87, 157, 160; leaves/furloughs, 64–65, 87, 208; military sign up, 64–65; Sabine Pass retaking plan, 138. *See also* Stengler, Johanette (correspondence to sons); Stengler, John (correspondence to sons); Wilborn, Mina (correspondence to brothers)

Hankamer, Fritz (post-Civil War): assistance request from brother, 234; civic service, 248; death, 248; farm activity, 234, 236; land responsibilities, 234–35; marriages and children, 235, 248; photo of, *237*; smallpox epidemic, 245, 246

Hankamer, I. A., 33

Hankamer, Joanah (earlier Higginbotham), 34, 42, 68, 116, 148, 234, 245–46, 255

Hankamer, Johannes, 7, 22, 255

Hankamer, Johann Wilhelm. *See* Hankamer, John W. *entries*

Hankamer, John W.: anglicization of name, 22; marriage, 34; Turtle Bayou land, 34;

Hankamer, John W. (Civil War service): bridge defense duty, 224–25; clothing issue, 106; correspondence to brothers, 96, 113; deserter hunt duty, 191; Eagle Grove camp, 152–53; Galveston departure, 231; Galveston duties, 228–29; leadership positions, 69, 95, 96, 167, 218, 227; military sign-up, 64–65, 68; physical description, 68; railroad bridge raids, 100, 103; Sabine Pass retaking plan, 138; on train travel, 57; during yellow fever outbreak, 91

Hankamer, John W. (correspondence to sister during Civil War): candle selling, 111; Christmas, 119; drafting of C. Wilborn, 144; Eagle Grove camp, 152–53; Galveston battle, 133; illness in camp, 157; mail delivery, 170; military service motives, 60–61; railroad bridge actions, 101; war's devastation, 164, 175; weather conditions, 105; yellow fever outbreak, 90. *See also* Wilborn, Mina (correspondence to brothers)

Hankamer, John W. (post-Civil War): children of, 233; civic activity, 233–34, 248; correspondence with sister, 246; farm activity, 232–33; photo of, *233*;

Hankamer, John W. (*continued*)
during sister's widowhood, 246; smallpox epidemic, 245
Hankamer, Karl Christian, 12, 22 *See* Hankamer, Charles *entries*
Hankamer, Karl Ludwig, 12, 30.
Hankamer, Katherine (earlier Icet), 248
Hankamer, Lurenda (earlier Smith), 34, 42, 44, 68, 233, 245, 255
Hankamer, Minerva, 248
Hankamer, Roy, 249
Hankamer (the town), 33. *See also* Crackersneck
Harriet (European ship), 13–15
Harriet Lane, USS, 126, 130-131, 133–34
Harrisburg, rail service, 54
hats, 50, 219
Hatteras, USS, 134–35
hay crops, 111
Hebert, Paul, 63, 71
Hendley Building, Galveston, 61
Henry James, USS, 91–92
Higginbotham, Caroline (later Stengler), 108, 236, 238, 250–51, 255
Higginbotham, Joanah (later Hankamer), 34, 42, 68, 116, 148, 234, 245–46, 255
hogs: on Hankamer/Stengler farms, 42, 44, 111–12, 206, 223, 226; Saltgrass Prairie suitability, 25–26; on Wilborn farm, 207, 208
Holland, George, 79, 91, 268n3
home remedies, 50, 85–86, 223
honey crops, 46, 48
Hooper, Quincy, 115
horses: for Company F, 66, 76, 152, 197; Hankamer household, 249; Wilborn farm, 33, 49, 206, 207
hostilities in U.S.-Mexico conflict, threats to emigrants, 20, 23–24
Houston: Company F's arrivals, 158–59, 198; rail service, 54, 55, 56–57, 58–59, 73, 153, 155–56, 214–15; in romanticized publication, 8; Spaight's Regiment, 220; supply advantages, 223–24; Union occupation plan, 174–75
Houston Telegraph, 71, 140
Houston Tri-Weekly, 152
Houstoun, Matilda, 8, 15, 17–18
Hunter, William W., 73
hunting and fishing, 36, 46–47, 217

Icet, Katherine (later Hankamer), 248
"Immigration Agreement," 12–13
Indianola, 19–20
insects, 81–82, 95, 154, 161
invasion of Texas, Union plans: advancement failure factors, 209–11; Banks' strategy, 175, 177–78; Fort Griffin defenses, 175–77; Louisiana overland expedition, 188–91, 192; navigation problem, 179–81; Red River campaign, 212, 216; southern coastal area, 192; troop landing challenges, 183–84; weather impact, 209–10. *See also* Galveston *entries;* Sabine Pass, Union retaking plan

Jackson, James, 207, 244
Jayhawkers, 163
Jefferson County, 33
John F. Carr, CSS, 125
Josiah H. Bell, CSS, 138-41

Keith, K. D., 78, 79, 91, 132, 138
Kellersberg, Julius, 78, 176–77, 276n9 (ch 25)
Kensington, USS, 91
King's Evil disease, 149
Koblenz, Germany, 11
Krantz, Gottfried, 7, 22, 255, 259n6
Krantz, Wilhelmina (Mina): anglicization of name, 22, 259n6; departure from Europe, 12; education, 29; marriage, 32, 262n5. *See also* Wilborn, Mina *entries*

Index

Kuhn's Wharf, Galveston, 126, 128, 131

Lahn River, Germany, 5
Lake Charles, 197, 216
land promises, Verein's, 8–9, 12–13
Law, Commander, 139
leaves/furloughs, Company F: from Camp Lubbock, 225, 227; for farm work, 206; from Grigsby's Bluff, 119; at Louisiana return, 197, 207; during railroad duty, 215; from Spindletop camp, 218
Lee, Robert E., 227, 229
Liberty Bridge, 224–25
Liberty County: overview, 24–27, 29–30, 41, 43, 242; secession votes, 60
Liberty (the town), 53, 55, 107–108
lighthouse, Sabine Pass, 72, 186
Lincoln, Abraham, 174, 211
livestock: census records, 32, 44; in Charles-Fritz correspondence, 34–35, 226; evacuation from Galveston, 71; Saltgrass Prairie suitability, 25–26, 242–43; Smith operations, 32; tax assessments, 38–39. *See also* cattle operations; chickens and eggs; hogs; horses
looting, 164, 175, 228

Magruder, John B.: appeal for troops, 192–93, 195, 201–202; defense bluster impact, 210–11; exemption request for C. Wilborn, 149; Galveston reinforcement, 151–52; Galveston troop review, 228–29; reassignment of Company F, 213–14; reports about troop return, 196; return orders to Taylor, 196; Sabine Pass retaking plan, 137–40; on Second Battle of Sabine Pass, 186; weapons plea, 211. *See also* Galveston, Confederate retaking
Major, James P., 161, 192, 195-96
malaria, 4, 30, 81, 82

Marsh, Captain, 95, 98, 152, 154, 194
Matagorda Bay, 19, 209, 211
Matagorda Island, 209, 210, 211
measles, 81, 154–55, 157
medical care, state of, 84–86. *See also* disease *entries;* home remedies
Mexico, 3, 5, 20, 23–24, 66, 173, 222
Morning Light, USS, 140–42, 177
mosquitoes, 81–82, 95, 161
Moss Bluff Rebels, 62–68, 75. *See also* Company F; Spaight *entries*
mumps, 81-2
music, 105

naval blockades. *See* Galveston, Union arrival; supply shortages; Union boats
Neches River, 37, 72-3, 90, 175–76
Neptune, 125, 130
New Braunfels, 2, 20
New Iberia, Louisiana, 166-67, 189
New London, USS, 134
New Orleans, 40, 73, 80, 131, 136, 160, 164, 230
New Year's Day, 119, 127–29
Niblett's Bluff, 161, 163, 193, 197, 215
northers. *See* weather conditions

O'Brien, Captain, 95
occupations: Chambers County, 85; Company F, 69, 70; Liberty County, 30, 41, 85; post-Civil War, 235
ocean voyage, 8, 13–14
Olmsted, Frederick Law, 25, 39, 46, 52–53
114th Regiment, New York Volunteers, 179
Opelousas, 190
Opelousas Trail/Road, 40, 73, 263n10
Orange (the town), 55, 138–39, 161
overland transportation, Verein's plan, 19–21
Owasco, USS, 126, 130, 180–81
oxen, 204, 212, 232, 235, 281n2 (31)

oyster reef, 176, 184-5
oysters, 154-55

palmettos, 50–51, 219
pay, soldier, 107, 146, 157, 161, 167, 169, 202
peach crops, 46-47
Pellet, Elias Porter, 179
picket duty: Company F, 99, 100, 114, 167, 270n2; Union troops in Galveston, 126, 128
Pine Island camp, 94, 96
population statistics: Galveston, 17, 43; German emigrants, 20, 28; Liberty County, 26, 32; New Orleans, 40
postage stamps, in barter system, 112
postal system, Confederate, 168-71
potash, 49, 110
potato crops, 35, 36, 47, 148, 208, 209, 232
prices: candles, 111; chickens, 242; clothing, 109–10, 202; conscription substitute, 146; corn, 208–209; fabric, 107; food, 155–56, 157, 242; land transactions, 43, 236, 242; livestock, 43, 242; paper, 168-9; private mail delivery, 171-172

quinine, 82, 85, 88, 223

Rachel Seaman, USS, 91–92, 139, 140
railroad bridges: in Magruder's Galveston plan, 125–26; renewed defense, 152–53; Taylor's Bayou skirmish, 99–102; Union burnings of, 95, 103, 214
railroads: Company F assignment, 214–15; construction of, 53–54, 56; cotton shipments, 70; network of, 73; Sabine Pass importance, 114; Stengler family uses, 57; travel difficulties, 54–58; troop travel, 95, 99, 160, 198, 220; Union control plan, 174; war damages, 214; yellow fever impact, 80

Red River campaign, 212, 216
renegades/conscripts, 163
Renshaw, William B., 97, 124, 126, 130–31
Rhine River, 8, 11, 12
road conditions, 23, 25, 52, 127, 189, 195, 197 *See also* weather conditions

Sabine and Galveston Bay Railroad, 55
Sabine Lake, 72, 95, 102, 114, 139, 176
Sabine Pass: commerce importance, 73; Company F assignments, 69–70, 73, 94, 95–96; location and terrain description, 72–73; rail service, 59, 73, 214; strategic value, 73, 76; yellow fever outbreaks, 78–80, 90–91, 92, 98, 268n3
Sabine Pass, Confederate control: abandonment of fort, 92–93; defense success, 140–42; early protective measures, 61–62; Magruder's plan for, 137–40
Sabine Pass, Union control: Confederate defense success, 140–42; demand for town's surrender, 92; resources for, 139–40; stalemate status, 114–15; strategic value, 114; warships arrival, 91–92
Sabine Pass, Union retaking plan: battle outcome, 185–87; defense preparations, 175–77, 185–86; gunboat movements, 180–83, 184–85; map about, *184*; planning for, 173–74, 175, 179–80, 183–84, 185–86; reconnaissance activity, 182–83
Sabine Pass Guard, 61–62
Sabine River, 72, 161, 175–76, 197, 215
Sachem, USS, 126, 181, 183, 184–85, 186
Saleratus, 110
salt, 76, 167, 203, 207
Saltgrass Prairie, description, 25–26, 49, 242–43
sandbars, 15, 53, 72, 91, 176, 183
scabies, 221–22
Sciota, USS, 134

scrofula, Wilborn household, 149
secession votes, 60
Semmes, Raphael, 135
2nd Brigade, Texas Militia, 62
sewing skills, 106–107, 109
sharpshooters: in Confederate retaking plans, 125, 130, 137, 138, 140–41; in Union invasion plan, 178, 183
Sherman, General, 212
Sherman, Margaret Ness (later Stengler), 251
shoes, 101–102, 106, 108–10, 193, 196, 202
Shorey, Henry, 209–10
shortages. *See* supply shortages
Shreveport, Louisiana, 212, 217, 230
Slaughter, General, 204
slaves, 89, 129, 144, 229
sleighs, 50–51, 219
smallpox, 88–89, 208, 244–48, 252
Smith, Kirby, 192–93, 227, 229-30
Smith, Lurenda (daughter of Silas, later Hankamer), 34, 44, 68, 233, 245, 255
Smith, Lurenda (granddaughter of Silas, later Stengler), 34, 239–40, 245, 250, 255
Smith, Lurinda (earlier Wilborn), 261n2 (ch 5)
Smith, Silas (and family), 31–32, 42, 255, 261nn1–2 (ch5), 262n5
Smith, Silas Jr., 64, 154, 158
soap making, 49, 264n15
The Society for the Protection . . . in Texas, 7, 9-10, 12–13, 17, 19–20
soda shortage, 110
Sour Lake Station, 58
South Carolina, USS, 61
Spaight, Ashley: promotions, 75, 220; yellow fever precautions, 90, 91. *See also* Company F; Moss Bluff Rebels
Spaight's Battalion, designation of, 75
Spaight's Regiment, disbanding after surrender news, 230–31
Sparks (Aurora), 99, 100, 270n1 (ch 16)

Speight, J. W., 266n11
Spindletop camp, 82, 216–19
Stafford, rail service, 54
stake planting, Fort Griffin, 177, 185
stamps, Confederate, 112, 168, *169*. *See also* postal system, Confederate
Stanton, Edwin, 124–25
steamer travel, 11–12, 53, 232
Stengler, Caroline (earlier Higginbotham), 108, 236–37, 238, 250–51, 255
Stengler, George (before Civil War): anglicization of name, 22; broken leg, 35, 36; cattle operations, 43. *See also* Stengler family, emigration journey
Stengler, George (Civil War service): bridge defense duty, 224–25; camp cook duties, 155; cattle herding duty, 167, 203; correspondence from brother, 96, 163; correspondence from father, 139, 142, 146; correspondence from mother, 106, 107, 114; correspondence to sister, 81, 146–47, 151, 164, 168; correspondence with C. Wilborn, 207; farm work during leave, 226; holiday leave potential, 119; illness, 82, 87, 157, 160–61, 221; military sign up, 64–65; physical description, 68
Stengler, George (post-Civil War): assistance request from brother, 234; cattle transaction, 238; civic activity, 250; death, 251; land purchase, 236; marriage and children, 236–37; photo of, *238*; reputation in community, 250–51
Stengler, Johanette: background in Europe, 6–7; children of, 12, 29, 255; death, 251; health problems, 116; land sale, 234, 239, 282n8; Liberty supply trip, 108; post-Civil War photo, *241*; smallpox epidemic, 245–46. *See also* Stengler family, emigration journey

Stengler, Johanette (correspondence to sons): care package contents, 46, 57, 104, 106, 193, 196, 221, 225; Christmas disappointment, 220–21; cloth prices, 107; coffee pot/sugar thank you, 224; Eagle Grove Camp advantages, 153; farm challenges, 47–48, 225–26; Houston posting, 222; husband's Spindletop visit, 218; Louisiana girls, 218; supplies requests, 106, 109, 153; war concerns, 114, 116, 187, 193–94, 221, 222, 225; Wilborn household difficulties, 202–203; young John's enlistment, 200–201

Stengler, Johann. *See* Stengler, John *entries;* Stengler family, emigration journey

Stengler, John (before and after Civil War): anglicization of name, 22; autobiography, 251–53; civic activity, 29, 240–41; land transactions, 33–34, 234, 239, 282n8; livestock operations, 43; marriages, 5, 251; photo of, *241*. *See also* Stengler family, emigration journey

Stengler, John (Civil War period): conscription vulnerability, 115–16; medical services, 86–88; militia enrollment, 201; shoemaking skills, 108; Spindletop visit, 218; on weather problems, 48

Stengler, John (correspondence to sons): birthday wishes, 139; care package contents, 86; clothing production, 107; drafting of C. Wilborn, 121–22, 143, 145; farm challenges, 143, 145; Galveston battle, 142; hog sales, 111–12; medical bill collection, 87–88; militia duty, 116; money delivery, 170; paper prices, 168–69; Sabine Pass retaking, 139, 142; supply requests, 82, 223–24; surrender news and resistance, 229–30; war worries, 103, 139; weather

conditions, 109; yellow fever precautions, 91

Stengler, John Henry (son of John Stengler): birth, 22, 29; children of, 239–40; Civil War service, 58, 204, 238–39; correspondence with brothers, 205; death, 250; farm work, 111, 143; land purchase, 234, 237, 239, 282n8; marriage and children, 34, 239, 250; militia enrollment, 200; photo of, *240*; shoes, 109; smallpox epidemic, 245; in Stengler cattle operations, 43

Stengler, Karl Georg. *See* Stengler, George *entries;* Stengler family, emigration journey

Stengler, Lurenda (earlier Smith), 34, 239–40, 245, 250

Stengler, Margaret Ness (earlier Sherman), 251

Stengler, Rudolph, 12, 21

Stengler family, emigration journey: anglicization of names, 22; arrival in Galveston, 14–17; boat travel from Galveston, 24, 26; departure from Europe, 11–13; farm tenancies, 28–30, 31; German background, 5, 6–7; land purchase, 33–34; ocean voyage, 8, 13–14; overland travel challenges, 19–21, 22–24; planning for, 7–10, 108. *See also* Hankamer *entries;* Stengler *entries;* Wilborn, Mina *entries*

Stengler family, history overview, 2–4, 252–54, 255. *See also* Hankamer *entries;* Stengler *entries;* Wilborn, Mina *entries*

Stephenson, Elisha, 129

"Story of the Voyage" (Stengler), 11, 12, 14

straw hats, 50

substitute hiring system, 145–48

sugar, 19, 76, 86, 112, 224

Sulakowski, Valery, 176

Sunflower, CSS, 120, 132

supply shortages: among stranded emigrants, 21; at Christmas season, 120; clothing for soldiers, 105; dyes, 153; fabric, 104–105, 107–108; food for soldiers, 76, 155–56; horse feed, 76, 152, 210; leather, 108–109; medications, 82, 84–85; and Union invasion plans, 205; Union troops, 189, 204; writing materials, 168–69
surrender news/resistance, 227–30
sweet potatoes, 35, 45, 112

tallow, 49, 264n15
tax systems, 38–39, 226–27, 241
Taylor, James Gilbert, 96–97
Taylor, Richard, 160, 161, 188, 189, 191
Taylor's Bayou, 95, 96, 98, 99–102, 214
telegraph line, during Civil War, 58, 129, 201, 204, 205, 216, 224
Texas and New Orleans Railroad, 55–56, 59, 73, 138, 222, 224–25
Texas State Troops, 116, 200–201, 239, 279n1
Third Texas Infantry, food shortages, 156
tithe collection duty, 226–27
tobacco, 50, 193, 202, 203, 207, 209
tree islands, 49–51, 234–35, 236, 282n4
Trinity River, 53, 224–25
Turtle Bayou, 32, 234, 239, 282n4
Twentieth Texas Infantry, 228

Uncle Ben, 138, 139, 177, 219
Union boats: in Banks' invasion plan, 175, 177–83; at Calcasieu Pass, 216; Fort Point raid, 97; in Mina-Fritz correspondence, 113; railroad bridge raids, 95, 100–103; railroad depot raid, 96; sympathizer guide, 97; weapons advantages, 92, 93, 102; withdrawal from Sabine waterway, 115; yellow fever fears, 92, 94, 97, 115
Union sympathizers, 96–97, 115, 125, 201, 224

vaccination programs, 88–89, 206, 208, 244–45
Velocity, USS, 140–41
Verein zum Schutze . . . in Texas, 7–10, 12–13, 19–21, 22–24
Vermilion Bayou, 189, 194, 196
Vermilionville, Louisiana, 160, 161, 163–64, 204
Vicksburg surrender, 164–65
Victoria (British ship), 78
Virginia Point, 59, 124, 152, 154
Vogel, Christian, 14, 15, 17
Vosburg, Sarah, 79

wages, soldier, 107, 146, 157, 161, 167, 169, 202
Wainwright, W. M., 124
Washburn, C. C., 190, 209, 211
watermelons, 46, 47
water transportation, 26, 34, 52, 53, 120, 243
weapons: Confederate shortages, 66–68, 100, 137, 159, 176, 211; with enlistment, 121, 200–201; Fort Griffin, 176–77; in Magruder's Galveston plan, 125–26; in Magruder's Sabine Pass plan, 137, 138; removal from Fort Sabine, 92; renegades, 163; Union warships, 92, 93, 126, 140
weather conditions: during emigration travel, 14, 15, 16; farm activity, 47, 109, 208, 225–26, 233; during Liberty Bridge defense, 224–25; Louisiana assignment, 194–96, 197, 204; near Columbia, 198–99; Niblett's Bluff, 161; Sabine Pass camps, 70, 104, 151; travel challenges, 52–53, 243; and Union advances, 209–10, 211; Wilborn farm advantages, 242–43
Weaver, Andrew, 28–29, 261n1 (ch5)
weaver's reed, 50–51
Weitzel, General, 181, 183
Welles, Gideon, 136, 142
Westfield, USS, 126, 131
White, James Taylor, 37–38, 40

White, John, 36, 206
whooping cough, 89
Wilborn, Andrew, 88, 204, 245
Wilborn, Carrol, 248
Wilborn, Carrol Jr., 248
Wilborn, Charles: cattle ranching, 42–43, 243; children of, 86, 88, 242; death, 245; descendants, 247–48; hand injury, 111; land transactions, 33–34, 235–36, 239, 242, 243; marriage, 32, 262n5; multiple farm responsibilities, 116–17, 143–44, 148, 206, 212; in Smith household, 31; Stengler medical testimony, 87; Turtle Bayou land, 32–33, 262n6
Wilborn, Charles (Civil War service): company enrollments, 201, 279n1; conscription substitute, 145–46; conscription vulnerability, 115–18, 121, 142; correspondence with wife, 88–89, 107, 202–203, 206–209; exemption request, 148–49; impact on household, 143–44, 202–3, 206–7; milling duty, 212; return to military duty, 149–50
Wilborn, Charles J., 246, 247
Wilborn, Ellen, 88
Wilborn, Elwood, 248
Wilborn, George F., 246, 247–48
Wilborn, James, 111, 238, 245
Wilborn, Johanette, 246
Wilborn, Martha, 85–86, 88, 202, 246
Wilborn, Mina: chicken flock, 242; children of, 88; correspondence with husband, 88–89, 107, 202–203, 206–209; on daughter's eye problem, 85–86; death, 247; descendants, 247–48; health problems, 108, 144, 149, 204; on husband's milling duty, 212; land transactions, 243; smallpox epidemic, 245; widowhood, 246–47
Wilborn, Mina (correspondence to brothers): biscuit making, 47; C. Wilborn's home visit, 206; C. Wilborn's substitute loan, 146–47; camp conditions, 81, 121, 151; candles, 110–11; captain election, 75; care package contents, 170–71; cattle herding duty, 166–67; chickens and eggs, 156; Christmas, 119, 120–21; cold weather worries, 194; disease and illness, 88, 90; Eagle Grove camp, 152–53, 154–55; Fort Hudson surrender, 164–65; during Fritz's Galveston venture, 35; Galveston battle, 133; Galveston status, 113; girls at church, 215; home remedy advice, 85–86; husband's military service, 117, 144–45, 146–47, 149–50, 201, 204; lack of mail, 167–68, 170; medicinal remedies, 85, 86; paper shortage suggestion, 169; return of husband from military duty, 148; Sabine Pass retaking plan, 138–39; Saleratus, 110; soap making, 49; soldier training, 75; supply shortages, 107–108, 110, 168, 169; Taylor's Bayou bridge raid, 101; vaccination program, 88–89; Vicksburg surrender, 164–65; weather worries, 194; young John's militia duty, 201
Wilborn/Willborn, Elijah, 261n2 (ch 5)
Wilborn/Willborn, Lurinda (later Smith), 261n2 (ch 5)
wild cattle. *See* cattle operations
wildlife, Saltgrass Prairie, 26, 36, 46
wine-making, 111
witness trees, 282n4
woodlands, products from, 49–51, 82, 85, 242
Wooten, Captain, 204

yellow fever (yellow jack), 78–82, 89–91, 94-95, 97-98, 115, 268n3
yellow jaundice, 154, 158